12/99

Shakespeare's histories

CONTENTS

Editor

Gary Carey, M.A.
University of Colorado

Consulting Editor

James L. Roberts, Ph.D.
Department of English
University of Nebraska

ISBN 0-8220-0040-7

Henry VI, Parts 1, 2, and 3 Notes © Copyright 1985; Richard III Notes ©
Copyright 1966; King John Notes © Copyright 1983; Henry IV, Part 1 Notes
© Copyright 1971; Henry IV, Part 2 Notes © Copyright 1963; Henry V
Notes © Copyright 1981; Henry VIII Notes © Copyright 1984; by Cliffs
Notes, Inc. All Rights Reserved. Printed in U.S.A.

1999 Printing.

ACKNOWLEDGMENT

Authors of the following Notes on Shakespeare's histories are: *Henry
VI, Parts 1, 2, and 3*, W. John Campbell, Ph.D.; *Richard III*, James K.
Lowers, Ph.D.; *King John*, Evelyn McLellan, Ph.D.; *Richard II*, Denis
Calandra, Ph.D.; *Henry IV, Part 1*, James K. Lowers, Ph.D.; *Henry IV,
Part 2*, James K. Lowers, Ph.D.; *Henry V*, Jeffrey Fisher, M.F.A.; *Henry
VIII*, W. John Campbell, Ph.D.

Cliffs Notes, Inc.   Lincoln, Nebraska

shakespeare's life and background

many books have assembled facts, reasonable suppositions, traditions, and speculations concerning the life and career of William Shakespeare. Taken as a whole, these materials give a rather comprehensive picture of England's foremost dramatic poet. Tradition and sober supposition are not necessarily false because they lack proved bases for their existence. It is important, however, that persons interested in Shakespeare should distinguish between *facts* and *beliefs* about his life.

From one point of view, modern scholars are fortunate to know as much as they do about a man of middle-class origin who left a small country town and embarked on a professional career in sixteenth-century London. From another point of view, they know surprisingly little about the writer who has continued to influence the English language and its drama and poetry for more than three hundred years. Sparse and scattered as these facts of his life are, they are sufficient to prove that a man from Stratford by the name of William Shakespeare wrote the major portion of the thirty-seven plays which scholars ascribe to him. The concise review which follows will concern itself with some of these records.

No one knows the exact date of William Shakespeare's birth. His baptism occurred on Wednesday, April 26, 1564. His father was John Shakespeare, tanner, glover, dealer in grain, and town official of Stratford; his mother, Mary, was the daughter of Robert Arden, a prosperous gentleman-farmer. The Shakespeares lived on Henley Street.

Under a bond dated November 28, 1582, William Shakespeare and Anne Hathaway entered into a marriage contract. The baptism of their eldest child, Susanna, took place in Stratford in May 1583. One year and nine months later, their twins, Hamnet and Judith, were christened in the same church. The parents named them for two of the poet's friends, Hamnet and Judith Sadler.

Early in 1596, William Shakespeare, in his father's name, applied to the College of Heralds for a coat of arms. Although positive proof is lacking, there is reason to believe that the Heralds granted this request, for in 1599, Shakespeare again made application for the right to quarter his coat of arms with that of his mother.

Entitled to her father's coat of arms, Mary had lost this privilege when she married John Shakespeare before he held the official status of gentleman.

In May 1597, Shakespeare purchased New Place, the outstanding residential property in Stratford at that time. Since John Shakespeare had suffered financial reverses prior to this date, William must have achieved success for himself.

Court records show that in 1601–02, William Shakespeare began rooming in the household of Christopher Mountjoy in London. Subsequent disputes over the wedding settlement and agreement between Mountjoy and his son-in-law, Stephen Belott, led to a series of legal actions, and in 1612, the court scribe recorded Shakespeare's deposition of testimony relating to the case.

In July 1605, William Shakespeare paid four hundred and forty pounds for the lease of a large portion of the tithes on certain real estate in and near Stratford. This was an arrangement whereby Shakespeare purchased half the annual tithes, or taxes, on certain agricultural products from parcels of land in and near Stratford. In addition to receiving approximately ten percent income on his investment, he almost doubled his capital. This was possibly the most important and successful investment of his lifetime, and it paid a steady income for many years.

Shakespeare is next mentioned when John Combe, a resident of Stratford, died on July 12, 1614. To his friend, Combe bequeathed the sum of five pounds. These records and similar ones are important, not because of their economic significance but because they prove the existence of a William Shakespeare in Stratford and in London during this period.

On March 25, 1616, William Shakespeare revised his last will and testament. He died on April 23 of the same year. His body lies within the chancel and before the altar of the Stratford church. A rather wry inscription is carved upon his tombstone:

> Good Friend, For Jesus' sake, forbear
> To dig the dust enclosed here;
> Blest be the man that spares these stones,
> And curst be he who moves my bones.

The last direct descendant of William Shakespeare was his granddaughter, Elizabeth Hall, who died in 1670.

These are the most outstanding facts about Shakespeare the man, as apart from those about the dramatist and poet. Such pieces of information, scattered from 1564 through 1616, declare the existence of such a person, not as a writer or actor, but as a private citizen. It is illogical to think that anyone would or could have fabricated these details for the purpose of deceiving later generations.

In similar fashion, the evidence establishing William Shakespeare as the foremost playwright of his day is positive and persuasive. Robert Greene's *Groatsworth of Wit*, in which he attacked Shakespeare, a mere actor, for presuming to write plays in competition with Greene and his fellow playwrights, was entered in the Stationers' Register on September 20, 1592. In 1594, Shakespeare acted before Queen Elizabeth, and in 1594 and 1595, his name appeared as one of the shareholders of the Lord Chamberlain's Company. Francis Meres, in his *Palladis Tamia* (1598), called Shakespeare "mellifluous and hony-tongued" and compared his comedies and tragedies with those of Plautus and Seneca in excellence.

Shakespeare's name appears as one of the owners of the Globe in 1599. On May 19, 1603, he and his fellow actors received a patent from James I designating them as the King's Men and making them Grooms of the Chamber. Late in 1608 or early in 1609, Shakespeare and his colleagues purchased the Blackfriars Theatre and began using it as their winter location when weather made production at the Globe inconvenient.

Other specific allusions to Shakespeare, to his acting and his writing, occur in numerous places. Put together, they form irrefutable testimony that William Shakespeare of Stratford and London was the leader among Elizabethan playwrights.

One of the most impressive of all proofs of Shakespeare's authorship of his plays is the First Folio of 1623, with the dedicatory verse which appeared in it. John Heminge and Henry Condell, members of Shakespeare's own company, stated that they collected and issued the plays as a memorial to their fellow actor. Many contemporary poets contributed eulogies to Shakespeare; one of the best known of these poems is by Ben Jonson, a fellow actor and, later, a friendly rival. Jonson also criticized Shakespeare's dramatic work in *Timber: or, Discoveries* (1641).

Certainly there are many things about Shakespeare's genius and career which the most diligent scholars do not know and cannot explain, but the facts which do exist are sufficient to establish Shakespeare's identity as a man and his authorship of the thirty-seven plays which reputable critics acknowledge to be his. Someone obviously wrote these dramatic masterpieces, and Shakespeare remains the only candidate worthy of serious consideration.

the plays

1590-92

henry vi
parts 1, 2, and 3

HENRY VI, PARTS 1, 2, AND 3

LIST OF MAJOR CHARACTERS

Henry VI

Son of Henry V and the grandson of Henry IV, Henry VI is the infant king at the beginning of Part 1. He belongs to the House of Lancaster, the "red roses," and is killed at the end of Part 3.

John, Duke of Bedford

Uncle of Henry VI and younger brother of Henry V.

Humphrey, Duke of Gloucester

Uncle of Henry VI and younger brother of Henry V; Lord Protector of England while Henry is an infant; he is arrested for treason and murdered in Part 2.

Henry, Duke of Exeter

Great-uncle of Henry VI.

Bishop of Winchester (Cardinal Beaufort)

Great-uncle of Henry VI; very ambitious, he becomes Cardinal Beaufort, using religion to suit his own purposes; a lifelong enemy of Gloucester, he conspires in the Lord Protector's death and dies unrepentant.

Richard Plantagenet

Son of the late Richard, Earl of Cambridge, he becomes Duke of York and claims to be the rightful heir to the throne occupied by Henry VI. He is killed in Part 3, after which his sons Edward and Richard become kings and restore the Yorkists to the throne.

John Beaufort

Earl of Somerset, later Duke of Somerset; he supports Henry VI.

Earl of Salisbury

Military leader of the English armies in France alongside Lord Talbot; killed in Part 1.

Earl of Warwick

Named Richard Neville, he is a son of the Earl of Salisbury; this "king maker" supports the Duke of York's attempts to capture the throne.

Lord Talbot

A central figure in Part 1, he is general of the English armies in France and opposes Charles, the Dauphin of France, and Joan of Arc; killed in Part 1.

Edmund Mortimer

Earl of March and uncle of Richard Plantagenet; he spends most of his adult life in jail after his supporters try to place him on the throne as the rightful heir; the Duke of York will pledge to carry out Mortimer's request that the Yorkists have the throne restored to them.

Sir John Fastolfe

A cowardly soldier who deserts Talbot's army in France; the early editions of *Henry VI* call him Sir John Falstaff, but he should *not* be confused with the Falstaff of *Henry IV* and *The Merry Wives of Windsor*.

Charles, the Dauphin

Dauphin of France, made king during Part 1; initially skeptical about Joan of Arc's visionary powers, he eventually welcomes her but fails to save her from being burned to death.

Lewis XI

King of France in Part 3.

Reignier

Duke of Anjou and titular King of Naples; father of Queen Margaret, who marries Henry VI.

Joan la Pucelle

Joan of Arc; French peasant whose vision inspires her to protect France from the English; she is burned at the stake by the English in Part 1.

Margaret

Daughter of Reignier, Duke of Anjou; marries Henry VI.

Eleanor

Duchess of Gloucester; condemned as a witch.

Margery Jordan

A witch.

Lady Grey

Queen of Edward IV; afterward, mother of Elizabeth (*not* Elizabeth I).

Earl of Suffolk

He arranges for Henry VI's marriage to Margaret of Anjou; he becomes the king's favorite and in Part 2 is elevated to the rank of duke.

Lord Clifford

A supporter of Henry VI and Queen Margaret; killed by the Yorkists in Part 2.

Young Clifford

Son of Lord Clifford, he becomes Queen Margaret's favorite in Part 3; he is determined to avenge the death of his father.

SUMMARIES AND COMMENTARIES

HENRY VI, PART 1

ACT I

The play opens in Westminster Abbey at the funeral of Henry V, once the shining Prince Hal, "this star of England." Henry V leaves behind him the boy Henry VI, who is too young to reign. Several of the principal characters of this trilogy are present at the funeral, including Humphrey (the good Duke of Gloucester), who is an uncle of Henry VI and has been designated to reign in Henry VI's place as Lord Protector until Henry is old enough to assume an active role. Also present are another of Henry VI's uncles, the Duke of Bedford, who is Regent of France, and Warwick, who (as an earl) has significant influence in the kingdom and is known as "the king maker." In addition, there is a great-uncle of Henry VI, Henry Beaufort (who will soon become the Cardinal of Winchester).

The Duke of Bedford and the Duke of Gloucester bemoan the passing of their late king: "England ne'er lost a king of so much worth." As early as the first speech of the play, then, Shakespeare sets the tone for trouble: A beloved king has died, and there is no one to take his place. Henry V was virtuous, was an excellent soldier, and was a fearless competitor: "He ne'er lift up his hand but conquered." Now the throne risks being conquered by outsiders. The Duke of Exeter (another great-uncle) suggests that some wicked French "sorcerers" conspired to bring about Henry V's end; this suggestion prepares us for the eventual role played by Joan la Pucelle (more commonly known as Joan of Arc, or the Maid). Winchester states that part of Henry's glory was due to the Church, which aided Henry's victories because Henry always fought "the battles of the Lord." Gloucester, however, retorts that the Church had *nothing* to do with Henry's glorious reign. Rather, the churchmen did not pray sufficiently—if at all—for the king; they wanted a monarch who was an "effeminate prince," one whom they could dominate. Shakespeare establishes Gloucester as being the defender of the throne, of the royal family, and of the country: Gloucester will become the prime obstacle for several ambitious nobles, and this struggle will unravel dramatically in Part 2 of the trilogy. Gloucester represents a set of beliefs contrary to those held by such people as Winchester.

Whereas Gloucester is the Lord Protector of England and has the country's best interests at heart, many of his peers seek to aggrandize themselves at the expense of the monarchy. They wish to have influence at the royal court and see their personal, ambitious desires brought to fruition. A major conflict, then, is drawn in this first scene: There will be a struggle between opposing factions for the monarchy. The old order will be called upon to defend itself from those who see themselves as legitimate heirs, those who feel that they should be on the throne.

Bedford finally puts an end to the arguing and calls upon the ghost of Henry V to keep the realm from "civil broils"—or else "our isle be made a nourish of salt tears." A messenger enters then with news from France: The English have suffered enormous losses and have been defeated at Rheims, Orleans, Champagne, and other French towns in their quest for the French throne. The English losses, he says, were due to a lack of manpower and money—not because of any French "sorcery"; moreover, the English soldiers are aware of various divisive factions at work back in England. They realize that there is confusion in the court and that the English generals do not have the necessary support at court in order to make victory possible. The messenger warns the nobles to resolve their petty arguments and realize that many human lives are at stake abroad: "Let not sloth dim your honours new-begot." He says that "England's coat one half is cut away." Bedford proclaims his patriotism and states his intention to fight for "the cause"; he says that he intends to conquer France for England ("Wounds will I lend the French").

Another messenger enters and announces that Charles, the Dauphin of France, has been crowned king in Rheims and that the Bastard of Orleans is with him, as well as the Duke of Anjou. The nobles are seemingly unanimous in their desire to fight France, but Gloucester and Bedford exchange sharp words about Bedford's true dedication to the cause. The seeds of dissent are present, then, even in an otherwise "unified" cause.

A third messenger enters with the news that Lord Talbot, general of the English armies, has been overthrown: He was surrounded by a French army of 23,000 men, almost four times the size of the English army (6,000 soldiers). Talbot fought valiantly for three hours and would have won, but Sir John Fastolfe "played the coward" and fled the battle scene, damaging morale and bringing about a general massacre. Talbot was wounded (a spear in his back) and taken prisoner, but his life was spared; most of his men, however, were slaughtered. Bedford vows to revenge the act by wrenching the Dauphin's crown: He will take ten thousand soldiers with him to France and aid the weak forces of the Earl of Salisbury. Exeter recalls the oath that they all took to the late King Henry: "To quell the Dauphin utterly / Or bring him in obedience to your yoke." Gloucester hastens to the Tower so that he can examine the artillery available, stating that he will proclaim young Henry the new King of England. Exeter says that he plans to go to Eltham, where Henry VI is, so that he can prepare for the king's safety. When Exeter is gone, Winchester is left alone. He reveals his plan to steal the young king and "sit at [the] chiefest stern of public weal." In other words, he wishes to have power over everyone.

The scene shifts to Orleans, France, where the Dauphin (Charles) is in conversation with the Duke of Alencon and Reignier (Duke of Anjou). Charles is pleased that fate is on the side of the French and that they have defeated the English. Spontaneously, he and Reignier decide that there is no point in waiting to attack the English again: "Let's raise the siege; why live we idly here?" Talbot has been captured and only the "mad-brained Salisbury" remains. Thus, they sound the alarum, but, later, they are surprised to find themselves driven back by the English. Charles concludes that his men are cowards; they abandoned him amidst the enemy. They discuss the English courage and audacity.

Just as they are about to leave the English behind them, the Bastard of Orleans enters with news: He has brought with him a "holy maid," Joan la Pucelle, or Joan of Arc, who has been allegedly ordained by heaven to raise the siege against the English and drive them out of France. Seemingly, the maid is gifted with prophecy exceeding even that of the "nine sibyls of old Rome." Charles consents to speak with her, but he first decides to test her skill: He asks Reignier to stand in his place as Dauphin. When Joan enters, however, she identifies the trick immediately: "Reignier, is't thou that thinkest to beguile me?" She then insists on speaking privately with the Dauphin.

Joan tells Charles how she was seated in the field one day and was greeted with a vision from "God's mother." Mary instructed Joan to leave her "base vocation" and save her country from calamity. Charles agrees to take Joan to battle with him; if she is successful, he will place all his confidence in her word. But first, he challenges her to a duel; if, in single combat, she "vanquishes" Charles, he will know that her words are "true." They spar with swords, and Joan bests him. Charles is impressed: "Thou art an Amazon . . . that must help me. . . . Let me thy servant and not sovereign be." Joan argues that France must fight till the end and never surrender. She predicts that England's glory is at an end because Henry V is dead. Reignier urges haste; she must drive the English from Orleans "and be immortaliz'd."

The scene moves once again to London; as is typical of the *Henry VI* plays, Shakespeare jumps back and forth from country to country. In London, Gloucester arrives to survey the Tower of London but is told by the guards that he is unable to enter: Winchester (Henry Beaufort) has forbidden it; Gloucester and his people have been blacklisted by Winchester. This action is the first unmistakable proof that we have that Winchester intends to seize control of the kingdom—despite *any* possible consequences. Winchester enters then and gloats in the presence of Gloucester, who boldly calls Winchester a "manifest conspirator" and states that Winchester sought to murder Henry V. Gloucester insists on being allowed in the Tower or else he vows to drive Winchester back.

A skirmish breaks out between their men, and the mayor arrives, demanding that everyone return home. His officer commands them to put away their weapons—or be executed. Winchester warns Gloucester to be careful, and Gloucester warns Winchester that he will stamp Winchester's hat (his religious symbol) beneath his feet. The conflict between the two men is drawn: Winchester, as a representative of the Church, desires power, and he will try to impose himself through the authority of the Church—even if his intentions have nothing to do with religion or God. Gloucester, on the other hand, is the rightful Protector of England, and he is prepared to bring force to bear whenever necessary in his attempts to protect both Henry VI and the English people. Thus, it is clear that religion, law, and politics all disappear into the background as personal ambition and a drive for power consume Winchester. Even the mayor himself exclaims that Winchester is "more haughty than the devil."

At Orleans, in France, Salisbury welcomes Talbot back to the action, asking him questions about his treatment while he was a

French prisoner (Talbot was released from jail through an arrange-ment with the Duke of Bedford, who exchanged another prisoner for Talbot). Talbot says that he was publicly humiliated by the French, exposed in the market place, and mocked as the "terror of the French, / The scarecrow that affrights our children."

As the two men are talking, Salisbury is shot from somewhere in the town; one of his eyes is destroyed and he dies. Then a messen-ger announces that the Dauphin has joined forces with Joan la Pucelle and that the French are gathering strength.

Talbot drives back the Dauphin, but then Joan enters and drives back some Englishmen. Joan and Talbot duel; Talbot curses her, claiming that she is a witch and that he will send her back to "him thou serv'st." They exchange more sharp words, and she taunts him to action. Then she announces that she will rescue Orleans. She dares Talbot to follow her and attempt to overtake her army. Her confidence is unfailing: She believes that divine strength is on her side. Talbot is confused by her; he believes that her "witch powers" are responsible for defeating the English. He bemoans the fact that the English soldiers lack courage and that Joan will reclaim Orleans—despite his efforts to hold her back. In the next scene, Charles confirms that Joan has indeed recovered Orleans.

Act I, then, sets up the major conflict of the play—a struggle for power on a number of levels: personal ambition (Gloucester versus Winchester); monarchic ambition (Gloucester's attempts to protect the young king's interests); and international ambition (England at war with France). Chaos and disorder reign in the place of a stable monarchy, an idea that will be further developed as the drama unfolds.

ACT II

This act opens outside Orleans, with a French sergeant instruct-ing his sentinels (guards) to alert him if there are any signs of the English. Talbot enters with Bedford and Burgundy; the Duke of Bur-gundy's father has been murdered by the Dauphin, which has caused Burgundy to become an ally of the British. The three men discuss the French army's brazen attitude of celebration, and Talbot suggests that they enter the city, where the French lie asleep.

The French sentinel sounds the alarum, and the French soldiers are clearly caught off-guard. Charles scolds Joan for deceitful planning; he claims that she flattered the French with minor gains but set them up for major losses. She replies that her powers cannot work *all* of the time, that they are unable to prevail when she is *sleeping*. She blames the attack on unreliable watchmen.

The next day, Talbot orders that the body of Salisbury is to be brought to the marketplace so that the French can see *why* Talbot revenged Salisbury (". . . hereafter ages may behold / What ruin happened in revenge of him"). The English armies, we learn, having fought all night, successfully revenged themselves on their enemies. And it seems that Joan and the Dauphin fled the scene when they realized how serious a threat the English actually were.

But there is a French plan afoot to recapture Talbot: The Countess of Auvergne invites him to visit her castle, and Talbot accepts. Burgundy and Bedford fear chicanery on the part of the countess, but Talbot decides to see her anyway. Before going, he whispers something in his captain's ear.

Once inside the castle, Talbot becomes the countess' prisoner: She wishes to prevent him from causing any more damage to the French. Talbot does not take her seriously. Through a refined manipulation of irony, he dodges her insults and succeeds in alerting his men. She quickly acquiesces and apologizes for her abuse of him. The sudden strength of Talbot and his men makes her realize with whom she is dealing.

Back in London, Richard Plantagenet (who will become the Duke of York) meets with Warwick ("the king maker"), the Duke of Somerset, the Earl of Suffolk, and others in the Temple-garden. An argument has taken place inside the Temple-hall between Richard and Somerset, and the group has withdrawn into the garden where things are more private. Somerset calls upon Warwick to decide who is right in the argument, but both Warwick and Suffolk decline to pass judgment since they feel unequipped to assess the subtle points of the dispute. Their argument concerns the throne of England, which will eventually be the cause of the Wars of the Roses: Richard Plantagenet and his followers choose a white rose as their symbol; Somerset and his group opt for a red rose. Warwick dons a white rose and sides with Plantagenet. Suffolk takes a red one. Already, in this initial discussion, there is a clear suggestion of the bloodshed and sorrow ahead. Somerset warns, "Prick not your finger as you pluck it off, / Lest bleeding you do paint the white rose red." The Yorks, on the side of Richard Plantagenet, are set against the Lancasters, supported by Somerset. The young King Henry VI is conspicuously absent from this colloquy; this absence shows to what extent the future of the English monarchy is being decided by factions that do not involve the king directly. Henry will be brought into the conflict only because of his bloodline, and it is not significant that he appear at this point in the play. Rather, it is the *crown* of England that is of importance, not the *person* of the young king. But Henry's ultimate weakness as a ruler is already foreshadowed in his absence from this serious debate.

A lawyer present at the discussion claims that Somerset is wrong in his belief that the "red roses" are the legitimate heirs to the throne of England. He sides with Plantagenet and the white roses. Warwick interrupts and informs Somerset that he is in error about Plantagenet: The latter's grandfather was Lionel, Duke of Clarence, third son to Edward III, King of England. This royal link surely justifies Richard's claim to the throne. Shakespeare, however, errs in the genealogy of Richard since there are actually four generations between Plantagenet and Lionel. But the lineage *is* genuine, and Richard does have a legitimate claim to the crown. Somerset argues that Richard's father was executed for treason, but the young Plantagenet counters, "Condemn'd to die for treason, but no traitor. / . . . / I'll note you in my book of memory / To scourge you for this apprehension." The scene ends with Warwick declaring his allegiance to the white rose faction.

Richard meets then with his aging uncle, Edmund Mortimer, Earl of March, in the Tower of London, and Mortimer relates his story to Richard in a weak, dying voice: Henry IV, grandfather to the present king, deposed his nephew Richard, Edward's son, who was also the first-born son and the lawful heir to the throne. The Percies of the North found this usurpation unjust and attempted to advance Mortimer to the throne, reasoning that he was the legitimate heir to the throne since Richard II had no children.

Mortimer reasons that he was, by birth, derived from Lionel, Duke of Clarence, the *third* son of King Edward III, whereas Henry IV was the son of John of Gaunt, the *fourth* son of Edward III. But when Henry V came to the throne, Mortimer was thrown in jail. Thus, Mortimer now pronounces his nephew Richard Plantagenet to be his heir but warns him to be careful in his attempt for the monarchy: "Be thou politic. / Strong-fixed is the house of Lancaster / And like a mountain, not to be remov'd." Mortimer dies, and Richard vows to revenge his lineage.

Act II advances the plot by explaining in detail the reasons behind Richard Plantagenet's rebellion: He believes himself to be the rightful heir to the throne and shall proceed to confront the Lancasters with this fact.

ACT III

The act opens at the Parliament House in London during an open conflict between Gloucester and Winchester about a bill, which Gloucester attempts to submit and which Winchester rips apart. Gloucester accuses Winchester of having designs on the king: "If thy thoughts were sifted, / The King, thy sovereign, is not quite exempt / From envious malice of thy swelling heart." Winchester retorts that his uncle, Gloucester, seeks to be the only one in the kingdom with power over Henry VI. Then Warwick speaks up in favor of Gloucester: "Is not his Grace Protector to the King?"

At this point, Henry enters and attempts to reconcile the two men in a speech that depicts him as a precocious young man (in point of actual fact, Henry would be only five years old). Henry pleads for family unity and peace, and he hints that this kind of internal struggle augurs badly for the country: "Believe me, lords, my tender years can tell / Civil dissension is a viperous worm / That gnaws the bowels of the commonwealth."

The mayor enters and a skirmish follows: The supporters of Gloucester and Winchester have begun stoning one another and have wrought havoc in the town. Significantly, Henry calls upon Gloucester, *not* Winchester, to quell the strife: It is as if he has greater trust and faith in his Lord Protector.

Henry's first speeches portray him as a weak and fearful king, and although he is young, he is of royal blood and is expected to emulate the greatness of his ancestors. But from the very beginning, he shows no signs of strength or power; he defers to others and laments his sorrowful plight: "O, how this discord doth afflict my soul!" It should be remembered that the conflict in the streets between Gloucester's and Winchester's men has nothing to do with the Wars of the Roses, yet eventually, both conflicts will combine into a rising torrent of terror and bloodshed.

Winchester and Gloucester strike a begrudging agreement, and the skirmish is called off. When the two factions leave, Henry is offered a scroll by Warwick, and he reestablishes Richard Plantagenet to his royal bloodline, thereby making Richard Duke of York. Richard pledges an ironic allegiance to the young king: "Thy humble servant vows obedience / And humble service till the point of death." In other words, Richard will remain faithful until Henry's death—at which point he intends to assume the throne himself.

Gloucester suggests that Henry leave for France in order to be crowned king, and Henry reveals his dependence on his uncle: "When Gloucester says the word, King Henry goes." Exeter, in a monologue, predicts that the feigned love of the peers for one another will break out into vicious dissension: "Till bones and flesh and sinews fall away, / So will this base and envious discord breed." He predicts that an old prophecy uttered in the time of Henry V will come true—namely, that Henry V would *win* all and that Henry VI would *lose* all. This prophecy is another indication that the reign of Henry VI promises to be less than glorious.

Back in Rouen, France, Joan is in disguise; she plans to enter the city with four soldiers dressed like peasants. Her plan succeeds, and once inside the gates, she reasons that it will be possible to give notice to the French troops and that Charles will be able to launch an attack. This capture of Rouen has no basis in historical fact: The city actually remained under English control until 1449, eighteen years after Joan of Arc had been burned there.

Once inside the city, Joan sets a torch ablaze and flashes it for Charles to see. She is elated at the possibility of conquering the English inside the town and of restoring French rule to Rouen: "Behold, this is the happy wedding torch / That joineth Rouen unto her countrymen, / But burning fatal to the Talbotites!" Charles and his men storm the city, and Talbot flees, promising revenge and blaming the French treachery on Joan, "that witch, that damned sorceress."

Talbot invites the Frenchmen to fight the battle on the field, but Alençon refuses. Talbot then beseeches Burgundy to help restore the town to the English. Burgundy replies, "My vows are equal partners with thy vows," but this vow will soon prove to be devoid of meaning since Burgundy will betray the English and commit himself to supporting his native Frenchmen. Bedford, who is dying, resolves to remain close to the front so as to inspire courage in his soldiers. Talbot and Burgundy leave to gather their forces in preparation for a renewed attack on the French. Once again, Fastolfe flees camp in order to save his life. Left alone, Bedford dies.

Talbot and Burgundy re-enter with the news that Rouen has been taken from the French: "Now will we take some order in the town." It seems that Joan, Charles, and the Bastard had all fallen asleep.

The scene shifts to Joan and the two men, somewhere between Rouen and Paris; they are discussing the fall of Rouen to the English. Joan says that they should not be worried about it: "Let frantic Talbot triumph for a while / And like a peacock sweep along his tail. / We'll pull his plumes and take away his train, / If Dauphin and the rest will be but rul'd." She recommends order and discipline, and Charles agrees to support her. She vows furthermore to sway the allegiance of the Duke of Burgundy; Talbot, she says, would be weakened by such a desertion.

In an impassioned, persuasive speech to Burgundy, Joan argues the virtues of her homeland under threat by a foreign invader: "See, see the pining malady of France! / Behold the wounds, the most unnatural wounds, / Which thou thyself hast given her woeful breast." She convinces Burgundy to support the French effort against the English. As with the recapturing of Rouen, this episode did *not* take place as such in reality: Burgundy's abandonment of the English did not take place until several years after Joan's death. But in the play, Joan uses patriotism as a leverage to lure Burgundy back into the French camp: "When Talbot hath set footing once in France / And fashion'd thee that instrument of ill, / Who then but English Henry will be lord / And thou be thrust out like a fugitive?" Burgundy is portrayed as a man entranced by the language of persuasion; he does not appear as one who is invincible in his convictions or whose allegiance to a group of people is unbending. Whatever suits his needs of the moment is what determines Burgundy's affiliation. Shakespeare weaves a touch of irony into Joan's response to Burgundy's conversion: "Done like a Frenchman; turn, and turn again!"

At the palace in Paris, Talbot takes a break during his war activities and presents himself to the king. He says that he is the epitome of loyalty through and through; he is proud to recite the sites of his conquests in France: fifty fortresses, twelve cities, and seven walled towns of great strength. Henry has grown older than the last time we saw him, but he is still a young king; Shakespeare does his best to hurry the aging process so that we are not dealing with an irresponsible youth. Instead, we are dealing with a vulnerable young adult. Henry lauds Talbot for his many years of devotion to the country; in recognition of Talbot's faithfulness to the royal family, Henry elevates him to the rank of Earl of Shrewsbury. The act ends with a minor skirmish between Vernon and Basset—the former is a supporter of Richard Plantagenet, the latter is faithful to Somerset. The skirmish serves to remind us, symbolically, that the Wars of the Roses are imminent and that the York-Lancaster conflict is nowhere near to being settled.

ACT IV

As the act opens, Henry is being crowned by Winchester in Paris. Fastolfe enters with the news that Burgundy has betrayed the English, and Talbot, in turn, rails at Fastolfe for having deserted the English forces at the battle of Patay. Henry banishes Fastolfe, on pain of death, and Fastolfe scurries from the room.

The letter from Burgundy, which Fastolfe brought with him, discloses Burgundy's new allegiance to Charles, "the rightful King of France." Henry, in his naiveté, orders Talbot to confer with Burgundy about the desertion and to chastise him for his conduct—another sign that the young king has little understanding of the politics of power.

York (Richard Plantagenet) and Somerset bring their quarrel to the king, who addresses them as "good cousins both." Henry commands a peace between them. He claims that there is no room for argument among the English, particularly as they are in France and must present a facade of unity. In an attempt to reconcile the two factions, Henry plucks a red rose and puts it on his uniform, claiming that "Both are my kinsmen, and I love them both." Then he sends the Duke of York (Richard Plantagenet) off to be a regent in France and instructs Somerset to provide auxiliary support to York's forces.

Outside the gates of Bordeaux, Talbot announces that the French should give themselves up to the English and proclaim Henry their king. Talbot is then met head-on by a general who asserts that the town is well fortified and prepared for a fight. Talbot discovers that the general means business: An enormous troop of Frenchmen descend on the meager English forces. Motivated by his feud with York, Somerset has refused to send the horses that Talbot requires.

Sir William Lucy blames the English slaughter at Bordeaux on the discord between York and Somerset: "Whiles they each other cross, / Lives, honours, lands, and all hurry to loss." He rages at Somerset for withholding necessary support from Talbot: "The fraud of England, not the force of France, / Hath now entrapp'd the noble-minded Talbot." Somerset dispatches the horsemen, but it is too late: The English are losing the battle and nothing will help.

In an emotional scene between Talbot and his son John, Talbot orders the young boy to flee the battlefield lest he be killed. The son refuses to abandon his father, so the two remain together in their fight for England's victory. After a number of skirmishes, the two of them are slain, and the English suffer tremendous losses. In a mocking, naturalistic style, Joan permits Sir Lucy to remove the corpses of the two Talbots: "For God's sake, let him have [them]. / To keep them here, / They would but stink, and putrefy the air." Sir Lucy proclaims that their ashes shall become a phoenix that shall cause holy terror.

ACT V

In London, Gloucester tells the king of the pope's message—that peace must be achieved between England and France so that the bloodshed can end. As a means to this end, Gloucester informs the king that the Earl of Armagnac, a man of great authority in France, has offered his only daughter to Henry as his future wife. Henry summons the royal ambassadors and promises to go along with their advice on the matter.

Winchester enters, dressed as a cardinal, and Exeter remarks that Henry V's prophecy is about to be fulfilled: "Henry the Fifth did sometime prophesy / If once he come to be a cardinal, / He'll make his cap co-equal with the crown." In other words, Winchester has advanced one step further in his quest for absolute power.

Henry informs the group of ambassadors that he shall indeed marry the Earl of Armagnac's daughter. He sends as a symbol of agreement a jewel for the French woman. In a brief aside, Winchester establishes his contention to be inferior to none, especially to

Gloucester: "I'll either make thee stoop and bend thy knee, / Or sack this country with a mutiny."

On the plains of Anjou, a scout announces to Charles (the Dauphin) and Joan that the English armies are headed in their direction and shall presently launch an attack on the French. Joan requests help from the spiritual bodies on whom she has depended, but when they appear before her, she finds them unwilling to cooperate with her. This inaction means trouble for France, and Joan prepares for defeat: "See, they forsake me! Now the time is come / That France must vail her lofty-plumed crest / And let her head fall into England's lap." Burgundy and York (Plantagenet) fight hand to hand, and the French soldiers flee the scene, leaving Joan in York's power. They exit, and Suffolk and Margaret enter. Suffolk, who is married, admires Margaret of Anjou's beauty. She is a daughter of the King of Naples, and Suffolk decides to win her for Henry. The only problem is that her father is poor, but Suffolk wagers that the youthful Henry will nonetheless be drawn to her beauty. Her father agrees to the proposition provided he be allowed to enjoy peace and quiet in the territories of Anjou and Maine.

At Anjou, York orders that Joan be brought forth. He heaps insults on her, and she denies her earthly lineage. In fact, she denies *all* blood relationship with her shepherd father. Her forefathers, she says, were "kings; / Virtuous and holy; chosen from above . . . / To work exceeding miracles on earth." She denies that she ever had anything to do with "wicked spirits." She tells York and the others that they—not she—are "polluted . . . and stained . . . and corrupt." She has been "chaste and immaculate" since infancy. And when the English will not listen to her defense, Joan announces that she is pregnant and defies them to murder not only her but "the fruit within [her] womb." The English scoff, but Joan is adamant. The child's father, she says, is Reignier (who will soon become the father-in-law of Henry). York tells Joan that her "words condemn thy brat and thee." Joan is led away but not before she utters a curse upon England: "May never glorious sun reflex his beams / Upon the country where you make abode."

Winchester (Henry's great-uncle) announces that a peace treaty has been struck between England and France. York, outraged at the idea of surrendering everything which England has fought for, foresees with grief the loss of France. Charles (the Dauphin) is insulted at Henry's suggestion that he be named viceroy to the King of England and that he become a liege to the English crown. Alençon, however, advises Charles to accept the truce in order to bring peace to an otherwise torn-apart country, adding that Charles can always break the truce when it serves his purposes. So Charles accepts the proposal.

At the palace in London, Suffolk spares no effort to persuade Henry to marry Margaret. Gloucester reminds Henry that he is already engaged to someone else, a lady of esteem and a daughter of a man whom England cannot afford to offend—the influential Earl of Armagnac. Exeter argues that Armagnac is wealthy whereas Margaret's father is poor; surely it would be more advantageous to marry a woman of wealth. But Suffolk prevails, and Henry decides in Margaret's favor. He asks Suffolk to sail for France and bring her back to be his queen. Part 2 of the trilogy will begin with the arrival of Margaret in England.

Suffolk, left alone at the end of Part 1, acknowledges to himself that he has won an important victory with the king. He realizes that he now has power in the royal circle and can set himself up as someone to be reckoned with: "Margaret shall now be Queen, and rule the King; / But I will rule both her, the King, and realm." Alongside the other nobles in pursuit of this influence (Gloucester, Winchester, and Plantagenet, the rebellious Duke of York), Suffolk completes the tableau of a vicious, bitter struggle in the making.

HENRY VI, PART 2

ACT I

Part 1 of *Henry VI* is centered largely around the conflict for power in England and Joan la Pucelle's role in the defense of France against the English; Part 2 is devoted to an examination of the mounting conspiracy against the extremely unselfish and noble Gloucester and the resultant chaos that ensues after his murder.

The play opens in a stateroom at the palace in London. Suffolk has arrived back in England with the new queen-to-be, Margaret of Anjou, who will not only come to despise Henry but will actually take matters in her own hands and rule the kingdom as she pleases. At this point in the drama, however, Margaret meets Henry for the first time, and he is instantly infatuated with her "beauteous face."

As a part of the marriage contract, a peace treaty with France is announced, one that calls for an eighteen-month period of peace. Moreover, England will relinquish to Margaret's father, the King of Naples, the duchy of Anjou and the county of Maine, and Henry agrees to marry Margaret despite the fact that she has no dowry. These terms of marriage are *extremely* unsatisfactory to Gloucester, Henry's uncle, who is so stunned that he drops the marriage contract on the floor while he is reading it in disbelief. But King Henry is quite happy with his new bride; as a gesture of appreciation, he elevates Suffolk to the rank of duke. At the same time, the Duke of York (Richard Plantagenet) is relieved of his title as Regent of France until the eighteen-month period of truce is over.

In particular, Gloucester resents the fact that his own brothers, King Henry V and the Duke of Bedford, worked so hard to conquer France for England only to have their efforts now tossed aside by an inexperienced youth smitten with love:

> O peers of England, shameful is this league,
> Fatal this marriage, cancelling your fame,
> Blotting your names from books of memory,
> Razing the characters of your renown,
> Defacing monuments of conquer'd France,
> Undoing all, as all had never been!
>
> (I. i. 98–103)

The nobles then discuss amongst themselves the pros and cons of their king's marriage: Cardinal Beaufort (formerly Winchester), a great-uncle of Henry's, is critical of Gloucester's opposition to the king; Warwick reminds them of his personal efforts on the battlefield, which helped to win Anjou and Maine for England, and he is clearly infuriated that Henry has frivolously given them over to the King of Naples. York has no sympathy for France and holds Suffolk in disdain: "For Suffolk's duke, may he be suffocate, / That dims the honour of this warlike isle!" The situation, then, is this: Henry has opted for a marriage based solely on physical attraction; his marriage has no monetary or political advantages, and Henry's nobles (with the exception of Suffolk, who sees personal gain in the marriage, and Cardinal Beaufort, whose attitudes always fall on the opposite side of the coin from Gloucester's) are dissatisfied with the conjugal union. Gloucester prophesies that England will lose France entirely before long.

Beaufort attempts to persuade the other nobles that they should not trust Gloucester because of his "smoothing words" and his "flattering gloss"; obviously, he has designs on the throne. Accordingly, Buckingham suggests that they get rid of Gloucester, and Beaufort leaves immediately to put matters in motion. Somerset, however, warns the nobles that Cardinal Beaufort is not to be trusted either: "His insolence is more intolerable / Than all the princes in the land beside." Basically, the situation develops because of a conflict between pride and ambition; none of the nobles is exempt from these emotions, and survival will depend on a combination of integrity and strength.

The Earl of Salisbury then appeals to Warwick and to the Duke of York, asking them to put the public good before personal gain and to stamp out the ambitions of Somerset, Buckingham, Suffolk, and Cardinal Beaufort: They should respect and "cherish Duke Humphrey's [Gloucester's] deeds / While they do tend the profit of the land." So there are now two opposing factions, even if only tenuous: Beaufort, Suffolk, Somerset, and Buckingham, who oppose Gloucester and support Henry's marriage, versus Salisbury, Warwick, and York, who support Gloucester. York supports Gloucester because it is convenient to do so: Were he to support Beaufort, Suffolk, or anyone else, he would have more obstacles in *his* way to the crown. As it is, Gloucester is a known commodity and is more easily handled than a completely new "regime." This knowledge is what prompts York to say in a monologue,

> A day will come when York shall claim his own;
> And therefore I will take the Nevils' [Warwick's
>   and Salisbury's] parts
> And make a show of love to proud Duke
>   Humphrey;
> And when I spy advantage claim the crown,
> For that's the golden mark I seek to hit.
>
> (I. i. 239–43)

Note that York has no love for Henry, whom he calls "proud Lancaster," and who, York says, holds the sceptre "in his childish fist."

For the first time, we meet Gloucester's wife, Eleanor, a woman who will cause a great deal of trouble for both her husband and the country. She is an ambitious woman, anxious to be queen, and she intends to push Gloucester closer and closer to the throne:

What seest thou there? King Henry's diadem
[crown],
Enchas'd with all the honours of the world?
If so, gaze on, and grovel on thy face,
Until thy head be circled with the same.

(I. ii. 7–10)

As Duchess of Gloucester, Eleanor provides a parallel to the ambitious Margaret: Her husband becomes an instrument of her own desires, and, as a human being, he counts for little—in her estimation. Gloucester is aware of this trait in his wife, and he beseeches her to dispense with it: "O Nell, sweet Nell, if thou dost love thy lord, / Banish the canker of ambitious thoughts!" The fact that she will do precisely the opposite of what her husband wishes should tell us something of her love for him. He is no more than a means to an end, and this fact reinforces the tragedy of Gloucester's position: Gloucester does *not* wish to be king, yet he wishes to prevent others from obtaining the crown. He tells Eleanor of a dream he had in which "on the pieces of the broken wand / Were plac'd the heads of Edmund Duke of Somerset, / And William de la Pole, first Duke of Suffolk." Eleanor interprets her husband's dream as meaning that whoever attempts to harm Gloucester will have his head cut off. Eleanor then relates a dream wherein Henry and Margaret kneeled before her and placed the crown on *her* head. Gloucester scolds her openly for such presumptuousness.

Gloucester is called away to Saint Albans, and in his absence, Eleanor receives Sir John Hume, a priest, whom she will entrust with her secret desire to use witches and spirits in her quest for the throne. Hume is a flatterer and does not hesitate to accept Eleanor's money for his "services"; however, unbeknownst to her, Hume has *already* been hired by Suffolk and Cardinal Beaufort to work *against* her. Eleanor, meanwhile, asks Hume whether he has conferred with Margery Jordan, a "cunning witch," and Roger Bolingbroke, a "conjurer." Hume replies that they have promised to bring Eleanor in contact with "a spirit" who will answer her questions.

Inside the palace, Queen Margaret and Suffolk encounter a group of petitioners, one of whom incorrectly assumes that Margaret is accompanied by Gloucester—not by Suffolk. He wishes to present complaints to Gloucester, their Lord Protector, about certain goings-on in the township. They are surprised and somewhat fearful when Suffolk glances at the names of the men charged with the complaints: One of the complaints is directed against Suffolk himself for "enclosing the commons of Melford"; another is directed against Thomas Horner for claiming that the Duke of York is the rightful heir to the throne. The queen rips up the supplications and chastises the petitioners for wanting to be "protected" by Gloucester. It is clear that *she* is among those who would do away with the Lord Protector.

In a speech to Suffolk, Margaret questions the English system of monarchy whereby Henry must still defer to a Protector; in particular, she dislikes the fact that she herself is "subject to a duke." She is also critical of Henry's religious devotion and of the fact that he is not more courageous and more manly. She delineates the other nobles whom she holds in disdain (Beaufort, Somerset, Buckingham, and York), but none of them bothers her as much as does Eleanor, Gloucester's wife: "Shall I not live to be aveng'd on her?" Suffolk tells Margaret that he has laid a snare for Eleanor and that, though they dislike Beaufort, they must join forces with him and the other nobles in bringing about the downfall of Gloucester; "So, one by one, we'll weed them all at last, / And you yourself shall steer the happy helm."

The king enters, surrounded by his nobles, and an argument develops immediately over who should be appointed to the regency of France—York or Somerset. Gloucester states that it should be the king's decision and no one else's. Immediately, several of the nobles and Margaret, as well, heap insults on Gloucester. Margaret drops her fan, and when Eleanor refuses to pick it up, Margaret boxes her on the ear. A few nasty quips are tossed back and forth between the women before the king interrupts them. Suffolk then introduces Horner, a man whose apprentice (Peter) has stated that Horner said that York felt he was the rightful heir to the throne. York denies such a claim and asks for Peter's execution. Gloucester says that he believes that Peter's charge casts some doubt on York's reputation; York, therefore, should *not* be chosen Regent of France. The king thus chooses Somerset in his place. A combat is then scheduled between Thomas Horner and his apprentice, Peter, the two who are involved in the alleged claims made by York.

Meanwhile, in Gloucester's garden, the witch Margery Jordan meets with the two priests, Hume and Southwell, as well as with

Roger Bolingbroke, a scholar and a conjurer. Eleanor is seated in her chair, and a spirit is conjured up, one who welcomes their questions. First, they ask what shall become of the king, and they are told that the king will outlive a certain duke who would depose him and that this duke will die a violent death. The spirit reports further that Suffolk will die "by water" and that Somerset should "shun castles," that he will be safer on sandy plains. The spirit vanishes as York and the Duke of Buckingham arrive on the scene. Eleanor and the others are arrested, and York congratulates Buckingham on being so efficient.

ACT II

At St. Albans, an argument breaks out amongst the various political factions: Gloucester versus his uncle Beaufort (Winchester), Margaret versus Gloucester, and so on. This scene makes for exceedingly poor drama since there is neither poetic stamina to the verse nor any suspense about plot development. In fact, it is often annoying and tedious. These nobles are grown men who have been fighting since the beginning of Part 1, and it seems highly unlikely that their feud would continue for so long without some form of violence or royal ultimatum. In short, there is nothing new on any front—simply more of the same. In fact, Henry sums up the situation quite nicely: "How irksome is this music to my heart!"

Buckingham arrives to report that Eleanor (Gloucester's wife) has conspired with witches against the state and has been arrested. Gloucester is dismayed and hurt, and he states that if his wife is guilty, he will banish her from his household. Henry decides that he will return to London in the morning and look into the matter more carefully.

In London, York (Plantagenet) relates his claim to the throne in a conversation with Salisbury and Warwick. The scene is best read with a family genealogy on hand; it resembles those sections of the Old Testament that flow with "he begat so and so" and another person "begat so and so." Warwick, known as "the king maker," sees York's point of view: "Till Lionel's issue fails, his [John of Gaunt's] should not reign. / It fails not yet, but flourishes in thee [that is, York]." When he is finished, York tells Salisbury and Warwick to tolerate Suffolk and Winchester and the others until they have "snared" Gloucester; then, as they meet the king's wrath, York will seize the throne. Warwick says that he will make York king, and he proclaims his fidelity to the rightful king: "Long live our sovereign Richard, England's king!" Richard Plantagenet, Duke of York, promises to reward Warwick well.

In a hall of justice in London, Henry assembles various members of state, including his queen, York, Salisbury, and Gloucester, for the purpose of banishing Gloucester's wife, Eleanor, from England. Margery Jordan, Hume, Southwell, and Bolingbroke are also brought in. Eleanor is banished to the Isle of Man, and the four others are sentenced to be executed. Eleanor's banishment is a major blow to Gloucester, who is now torn between his loyalty to his wife and his loyalty to his kingdom. He recognizes his wife's wrong-doings, and he believes that the hardship of his remaining Protector to the king would be too stressful, given the circumstances. So he resigns his position, with the ready encouragement of Margaret, and Henry gives him permission to go with Eleanor to the Isle of Man. Henry then states that he will be his own "Protector" and that God will be his "hope and guide."

York, meanwhile, is eager to have the combat begin between Thomas Horner and his apprentice, Peter Thump. It is a scene of mild comedy because Horner and his neighbors arrive drunk. Peter slays his master, but just before he falls dead, Horner utters: "I confess, I confess treason." This confession reflects badly on York since suspicions are now even more strongly aroused concerning Peter's testimony that York has ambitions for the throne.

In a street scene, Gloucester watches as Eleanor is escorted to the place where she must do three days' penance before beginning her term of exile. Eleanor, barefoot in a white sheet, scorns her husband for allowing her to be treated so basely. She warns him about his death, which she says is imminent, and she relates the names of all those who have "lim'd bushes to betray thy wings." In a moment of surprising naiveté, Gloucester answers that he is safe. He says that he is absolutely guiltless, and he would have to do something truly vile before anyone would attempt to kill him: "All these [men] could not procure me any scathe / So long as I am loyal, true, and crimeless." He advises his wife to remain quiet and to expiate her sins through patience. Eleanor is led away by Stanley, and she proudly tells him to lead the way: "I long to see my prison."

ACT III

Act III is the beginning of Gloucester's final downfall. It opens at the Abbey at Bury St. Edmund's with the king and his entourage at Parliament. The king notes that Gloucester is not present, an unusual characteristic of the former Protector. Margaret attempts to sour Henry on Gloucester: "Will ye not observe . . . / How insolent of late he is become, / How proud, how peremptory, and unlike himself?" Suffolk claims that Gloucester instigated Eleanor's treasonous acts and that he desires the downfall of the king. Beaufort and York each voice complaints about Gloucester. Henry, however, will have nothing to do with their gossip. He remains faithful to Gloucester.

Somerset arrives with the news that all is lost in France. Gloucester enters, and Suffolk arrests him for treason. This is an unsteady scene with little dramatic development; there was no "scene of decision" to arrest Gloucester before his arrival, and Suffolk's dramatic action to do so comes as a complete surprise. Gloucester defends himself systematically against their charges and, in doing so, gains much sympathy from us. He shows no signs of moral or ethical weakness, nor is there any evidence in the play to support the accusations levied against him. Suffolk pronounces that Gloucester shall be put under the control of his old nemesis, his uncle, Cardinal Beaufort (Winchester). During this scene, Henry's spinelessness comes through very clearly: He makes absolutely *no* attempt to defend his former Lord Protector, nor does he substantiate his earlier claims that Gloucester is "virtuous, mild, and too well given / To dream on evil." Henry is clearly an impotent pawn whose usefulness as a king is limited by his inexperience and his lack of courage.

In a long and searing speech, Gloucester exposes the motivation of his enemies, pointing the finger at each of them for their vicious plotting: "Beaufort's red sparkling eyes blab his heart's malice, / And Suffolk's cloudy brow his stormy hate." Gloucester shows himself to be astute of judgment and wise in the ways of human psychology. He knows that Henry will never survive in their midst, but he is prepared to die in order to defend the principle of truth: "For, good King Henry, thy decay I fear."

When Gloucester is taken away, Henry hastens to give the nobles total liberty for taking action against Gloucester: "My lords, what to your wisdoms seemeth best, / Do or undo, as if ourself were here." He is, to the end, a grief-stricken wimp. He knows that Gloucester's enemies are about to do him wrong, yet he cannot muster sufficient courage to act against them. After he leaves, his wife, Margaret, assesses her husband's abilities as a king: "Henry my lord is cold in great affairs, / Too full of foolish pity." The problem of Gloucester, in effect, can be understood from both sides: On the one hand, Gloucester has been a strong protector of Henry and the country, so it is clear why Henry feels so close to his uncle; on the other hand, Gloucester has been an obstacle to the nobles in their quest for greater authority, and from their point of view, no advances are possible until he is out of the way. Henry is guilty of weakness and of a lack of insight; the nobles are guilty of devising various plans for bloody violence.

A messenger arrives from Ireland to report that rebels are killing the Englishmen in that country and that help is badly needed. Cardinal Beaufort (Winchester), who quickly assumes the power that Gloucester once possessed, nominates York (Plantagenet) to serve as the nation's leader against the rebels. Suffolk confirms Beaufort's recommendation, adding that they represent the will of the king: "Why, our authority is his consent, / And what we do establish he confirms." The nobles exit, leaving York behind. In a long monologue, York vows to carry out his *own* plan. The men whom he has been given to conquer the Irish rebels are *precisely* the forces needed to seize the English throne: "Twas men I lack'd and you will give them me." While he is in Ireland, he says, he intends to stir up a "black storm" in England that will not cease to rage until "the golden circuit" sits on his head. He has chosen John Cade of Ashford as the one to incite a rebellion in England. Cade is a headstrong Kentishman who will act for York under the name of John Mortimer, whom he resembles. York plans to use Cade to fire York's popularity with the commoners. If Cade is caught, it is highly unlikely that he will confess to the nature of York's plan. Thus, with Gloucester dead, only Henry VI will stand between York and the throne.

In the next scene, the murderers of Gloucester run through a room in the palace, reporting to Suffolk that the deed is done. When the king enters, ignorant of Gloucester's death, he orders that Gloucester be summoned and that a fair trial to judge his treason be held. Suffolk returns, pale and trembling, with the news that Gloucester has been found "dead in his bed." Henry faints, and

Margaret shouts: "Help, lords! the king is dead." When Henry is revived, he pierces Suffolk with accusations that the latter is a vicious, evil man: "Hide not thy poison with such sug'red words. / Lay not thy hands on me; forbear, I say! / Their touch affrights me as a serpent's sting." The first prophecy of the sorcerers, then, is fulfilled—that is, a king (Henry) *did* outlive a duke (Gloucester), who died a violent death.

In a long and hypocritical speech, Margaret bemoans the death of Gloucester, claiming that she will now be looked upon as an accomplice in his murder. She tries to win Henry's faithfulness to her, but she gets nowhere with him. She concludes, "Ay me, I can no more! Die, Margaret! / For Henry weeps that thou dost live so long."

Warwick enters to report that Gloucester was murdered by Suffolk and Beaufort (Winchester). The citizens have formed a mob and are lusting for revenge, regardless of their object. Henry asks Warwick to examine Gloucester's corpse in an effort to determine *how* he was killed. Warwick then wheels the deathbed into the king's room for all to behold. What they witness is a ghastly, sordid sight that proves that the duke was indeed murdered:

> His face is black and full of blood,
> His eyeballs further out than when he liv'd,
> Staring full ghastly like a strangled man;
> His hair uprear'd, his nostrils stretch'd with
>   struggling.
>
> (III. ii. 168–71)

Warwick exchanges harsh words with Suffolk, accusing him of involvement in the murder and promising to "cope" with him. Salisbury enters to report that the crowd outside demands the death of Suffolk. Henry replies that his thoughts have centered more and more on Suffolk as the murderer. Suffolk is thus banished from the country. This action is the first time that Henry asserts himself powerfully as king; it demonstrates the depth of his love for Gloucester and, in an indirect way, shows that he is capable of enforcing his will when moved to anger. Left alone, Margaret and Suffolk declare their love for one another and bid each other painful farewells.

Vaux, a gentleman of the court, arrives to report that Cardinal Beaufort (Winchester) is on the point of death: "For suddenly a grievous sickness took him, / That makes him gasp and stare and catch the air, / Blaspheming God and cursing men on earth." In

Beaufort's bedchamber, the Cardinal confesses to having conspired toward the murder of Gloucester, but when the king invites him to make a signal of hope concerning life after death, Beaufort makes no sign. He dies unrepentant.

ACT IV

By the end of Act III, Shakespeare has gotten rid of Gloucester, Eleanor, Suffolk, and Beaufort—four pivotal characters surrounding the king. Now we are left with York (Plantagenet) and his supporters, and the king and his entourage. The conflict of personal ambition gives way to that of a more sustained struggle for the throne. It is at this point that the Wars of the Roses occupy the forefront of the action, with the white roses of the house of York in opposition to the red roses of the house of Lancaster.

Suffolk, who was banished in Act III, disguised himself in rags and left the country onboard a ship. Pirates at sea captured the ship and beheaded him for his evil doings, thus fulfilling another aspect of the sorcerers' prophecy. A gentleman close to Suffolk returns with his remains to England, where the queen or Suffolk's friends, he assumes, may revenge his death.

The beginning of the York protests (the faction of the white roses) takes place in Scene 2, at Blackheath, with various supporters of Jack Cade: George Bevis, John Holland, Dick the Butcher, and Smith the Weaver, along with Cade himself. Cade announces that his father was a Mortimer and his wife a Plantagenet; therefore he is heir to the throne of England. And as he declaims about how he will rule the kingdom when he becomes king, Sir Humphrey Stafford enters and instructs Cade and his followers to drop their plans. The king will be merciful, he claims, and Cade will not suffer if he gives up his plan to revolt. Cade has been speaking to his men as if he were Sir John Mortimer, but Stafford knows his true identity and scoffs at his intentions: "Villain, thy father was a plasterer, / And thou thyself a shearman." Stafford and his brother realize that they cannot stop Cade from proceeding, so they order that the king's army be brought in to overcome the rebel and his supporters. Cade is not worried: He stands for liberty, and he will not be deterred. In the fight that ensues, both Staffords are slain, auguring well for the rebellion. Cade dresses himself in one of the Staffords' armor, and he and Dick the Butcher and their followers leave for London to free all the prisoners.

At the palace in London, the queen is caressing Suffolk's severed head just as the king walks in with a supplication from the rebels. Henry decides to talk directly with Jack Cade instead of having the rebel's supporters put to death. A messenger enters and announces that Cade's men are savagely destroying anything in their path, that they have captured London Bridge, and that Cade intends to crown himself in Westminster. Moreover, the fickle mob has joined forces with Cade, and "they jointly swear / To spoil the city and your royal court." Henry and Margaret flee to Killingworth Castle until an army can be raised to defend them.

The Cade rebellion is in full force, with its men running all over London. The rebels capture the Tower of London, and Cade, disguised as Mortimer, claims that he is "lord of the city." Absolute chaos is the result, with men being murdered for any reason whatsoever. Cade orders that both London Bridge and the Tower of London be set on fire; he orders the burning "of all the records of the realm." The melee resembles a proletariat revolution, where everything is "by and for the people." As Cade says, "Henceforward all things shall be in common."

As a representative of Henry, Buckingham proclaims a royal pardon to the populace; if they will abandon Cade and his rebellion, Henry will *not* punish them. The mob then shouts out in favor of the king, showing their fundamental fickleness. After Cade makes a speech to them, however, they swing back to his side. This back-and-forth wavering continues for a while, and then Cade flees, disgusted with them all. Buckingham offers a thousand crowns to anyone who brings him Cade's head.

At Killingworth Castle, Henry regrets aloud that he is a king and *not* a subject. Buckingham enters with a repentant mob, and Henry "redeems" Cade's followers and praises them for having decided to support the monarchy.

It is learned that York is back from Ireland with a force of heavily armed Irish soldiers. Their intention, supposedly, is *not* to overthrow the king but to get rid of Somerset, whom they believe to be a traitor. Henry asks Buckingham to meet with York and "ask him what's the reason of these arms." He instructs Buckingham to tell York that Somerset has been sent to the Tower and that he will release Somerset once York's troops have disbanded.

Cade finds himself in a country garden in Kent after having

been in hiding for five days. The proprietor of the garden, Alexander Iden, comes upon him, and, after a brief discussion, they begin to fight. Iden slays Cade and drags him to a dunghill, "which shall be thy grave." He cuts off Cade's head and prepares to show it triumphantly to the king, leaving Cade's body "for crows to feed upon."

ACT V

The act opens in some fields between Dartford and Blackheath. York and his army of Irishmen plan to "pluck the crown from feeble Henry's head." Buckingham arrives and asks York why he has assembled such a great army in a time of peace and in a location so close to the court. York is outraged, but he quells his anger and replies that his purpose is to get rid of Somerset, whom he considers to be seditious and a threat to Henry. Buckingham reports that Somerset is already in the Tower as a prisoner, so York abruptly and surprisingly dismisses his army. The two men are then greeted by the king, who is scarcely able to say a word before Iden enters with Cade's head. Iden is knighted for his efforts.

At this point, the queen enters with Somerset. York discovers the ruse and is furious with Henry for being so dishonest: "False king! why has thou broken faith with me, / Knowing how hardly I can brook abuse? / King did I call thee? No, thou are not King, / Not fit to govern and rule multitudes." This instance is the first time that York has openly declared his hostility to Henry: "Thy hand is made to grasp a palmer's staff / And not to grace an awful princely sceptre." He informs Henry that, by heaven, Henry shall rule no longer over him who is the rightful heir. Somerset makes a move to arrest York for treason, but York demands that his sons be present; they will bail him out of his present situation. His sons, Edward and Richard, arrive and vow to defend their father. York asserts openly to all present that *he* is king, and he requests that Warwick and Salisbury be brought to him.

Warwick enters, but he does not bow before the king, and Henry realizes that the Nevilles do *not* support him. Salisbury states his belief that York is the rightful heir to the throne. Henry calls for Buckingham and requests that he arm himself. This action leads directly to the Battle of Saint Alban's.

At Saint Alban's, Warwick challenges Clifford of Cumberland to fight with him. York also wishes to slay Clifford, which he does in short order. Clifford's son sees what has happened and swears that he will spare "no York" in battle (young Clifford will reappear in Part 3 of the trilogy).

Richard (York's son) and Somerset begin fighting, and Somerset is killed. Margaret and Henry arrive on the scene, with Margaret urging that they flee. Henry seems indecisive and unable to decide whether to fight or flee. Ultimately, Henry opts for flight, a suitable option for a hopeless fighter.

The play ends when Salisbury arrives on the scene from the battle. Despite his age, he has fought valiantly and is a fitting model for younger soldiers in the camp. Young Richard Plantagenet helped him three times during the battle, and Salisbury pays tribute to him. But he cautions that they have not won *yet*, and York adds that the Lancasters should be pursued before the writs go forth. The spirit of battle is re-ignited by Warwick:

> Saint Alban's battle won by famous York
> Shall be eterniz'd in all age to come.
> Sound drums and trumpets, and to London all;
> And more such days as these to us befall!
>
> (V. iii. 30–33)

The play ends on this note of optimism for the Yorks: They are the legitimate heirs to the throne, and they intend to make this a reality.

HENRY VI, PART 3

ACT I

Part 3 of this trilogy might aptly be subtitled: "Crown, crown, who's got the crown?" The English crown is taken and won several times throughout the drama, and it is sometimes difficult to remember precisely *who* is on *which* side of the struggle.

The play begins as the Duke of York, his sons (Edward and Richard), and Warwick have returned to Parliament in London. Warwick wonders how Henry escaped from the Yorkists after the Battle of Saint Alban's. York explains that Henry slyly stole away during the battle and deserted his men, who were soon slaughtered.

York's sons then recount their triumphs in battle, and each brags about whom he killed; Richard proudly displays Somerset's head. This bragging emphasizes how Part 3 is not the most theatrically satisfying of the three dramas; it is a panorama of egos, challenges, and bloody fights-to-the-death that often makes for tiresome, difficult scene changes.

Young Richard has gained the approval of his father by beheading Somerset, York's longtime enemy, and Warwick vows that he will kill Henry unless Henry renounces his crown in favor of York and his heirs. Warwick then escorts York to the throne just before the entrance of the king, Clifford (Margaret's favorite), Northumberland, Westmoreland, Exeter, and others. Henry immediately realizes that York, backed by Warwick, means to have the throne, and when Northumberland and Clifford impulsively vow to avenge their fathers' deaths at the hands of York, Henry stops them, reminding them that the people of London support the rebels. For his part, Henry says that he refuses to fight in the "parliament-house" (another sign of weakness in this appeasing, peace-seeking young king). Instead of using weapons, Henry says, "frowns, words, and threats / Shall be the war that Henry means to use." Then he states that his right to the throne comes from his father, King Henry V, who seized France. He asserts that York is merely the son of a duke and the grandson of an earl. Warwick, in turn, accuses Henry of having lost France, but Henry retorts that it was the Lord Protector (Gloucester) who lost it—not Henry—because Henry was but an infant of nine months when that happened.

York's sons urge their father to "tear the crown" from Henry's head; they are willing to fight. Henry grows impatient; he threatens a war that will "unpeople" his realm before he allows his crown to be taken from him, arguing that *he* is the true heir to the throne. York, in turn, argues that Henry IV rebelled against Richard II and got the throne "by conquest." Henry admits that this is true, but he does so *only* in an aside. Openly, he maintains that Henry IV was Richard II's *heir*. Thus, what might otherwise have seemed like a very straightforward matter is converted into an impossible imbroglio, resolvable only on the battlefield.

At this point, Exeter, who had been on the king's side earlier, decides that York is the "lawful king." Clifford, however, refuses to kneel to York, the man who killed his father. Warwick demands that Henry resign; in order to appear more threatening, Warwick stamps his foot and soldiers appear, ready to take away the prisoners. Henry, seeing that he is outnumbered, begs Warwick to allow him to remain king for at least the rest of his life. York agrees to this idea but *only* on the condition that Henry name him and his sons as direct heirs. He does so, and Westmoreland, Northumberland, and Clifford chastise the king for disinheriting his only son (calling him a "faint-hearted and degenerate king"), and then they depart to inform Queen Margaret. Henry regrets his decision to compromise, but he is more concerned with the present than the future. He wants to take an oath to cease the civil war. Again he repeats his wish to be treated as king and sovereign by York and his followers, and so York pledges his loyalty and returns to his castle. Warwick, however, stays behind in London with his soldiers to guard the city. Seemingly, the houses of York and Lancaster are reconciled.

Exeter and Henry are ready to depart when they see Margaret and young Prince Edward approaching. She rails against Henry for what she considers to be an extremely foolish concession on his part. And Edward, of course, questions Henry's decision; as Henry's son, he has just lost his claim to the throne. Henry replies that he had no choice: He was forced by circumstances to act as he did. Margaret warns him that he has forfeited his safety and honor, and she refuses to see him again until their son is restored as Henry's heir to the throne. She announces plans to enlist the aid of the northern lords in the fight against the Yorkists, and although Henry begs them to stay, young Edward vows not to see his father until such time as he, Edward, returns victorious from the battlefield. Henry can do nothing but let them fight while he tries to regain the favor of Westmoreland, Northumberland, and Clifford.

On a plain before Sandal Castle near Wakefield, York enters to hear his sons arguing. Edward urges him to seize the crown now, and young Richard explains that the oath that their father took has no meaning since it did not take place before a magistrate. His argument with his brother, he says, arose over who should plead the case to York; both believe that their father is the rightful heir, and both wish to see him disregard his oath *not* to claim the throne during Henry's lifetime. York is convinced of the truth of his sons' arguments, and so he dispatches them to gather support for an uprising. He is interrupted, however, by a messenger who warns him that Margaret and all the northern earls and lords plan to lay siege to the York castle. Moreover, Margaret and Edward have 20,000 men with them, so they present a very real threat to the Yorkist position. York decides to keep his sons with him and sends his brother Montague to London to warn the nobles of the upcoming events. York's uncles, Sir John and Sir Hugh Mortimer, arrive and set off to meet the queen in the field. They have only 5,000 men in contrast to Margaret's 20,000, but Richard is nonetheless confident of success ("A woman is general; what should we fear?").

An alarum sounds, and York's young son Rutland enters with his tutor, looking for a means of escape. Instead, they are captured by Clifford, and the tutor is taken away by soldiers. Rutland begs for his life, but he is cruelly slaughtered by Clifford as an act of revenge for York's having murdered Clifford's father. This only serves to intensify York's eventual wrath, of course.

York enters, tired and faint, mourning the death of both his uncles and the success of Margaret's army. Unable to escape or fight, the exhausted York is taken prisoner by Northumberland and Clifford, but he vows that success will ultimately come from his death. As Clifford, the queen's favorite, prepares to execute York, Margaret stops him in order to insult York with one final humiliation. She has him led to a molehill and taunts him about his desire to rule England, and she mocks his "mess of sons" who are incapable of helping him now. Then she offers him a handkerchief soaked in Rutland's blood, puts a paper crown on York's head, and says, "Off with the crown; and, with the crown, his head." Before Margaret and Clifford stab him, York tears off the crown and curses her. Then he is beheaded, and his head is set on the gates of the castle so that it "may overlook the town of York."

ACT II

Several days later, York's sons, Edward and Richard, march onto a plain in Herefordshire, fearful of their father's fate, which is as yet unknown to them. A messenger dashes in with the story of York's humiliation and his murder, and Edward dissolves into grief. Richard, however, is fired with anger and calls for revenge. Then Edward rallies and claims the title of Duke of York. But Richard encourages his brother to demand more—demand Henry's *throne*.

Warwick and his men enter and are told of York's death. Warwick, however, has already heard about it and says that he gathered together an army in London and marched to Saint Alban's for the purpose of intercepting Queen Margaret. He had been told that she intended "to dash" the pledge given by York concerning Henry's right to reign during York's lifetime. Since Margaret intends to nullify York's oath in favor of her own son's succession, Warwick committed himself to defending the oaths taken by Henry and York. But when his soldiers were assembled, Warwick discovered that they were not really interested in fighting, even with the promise of higher pay. He guesses several reasons for their refusal: the king's gentleness, rumors of Margaret's fierceness, and the fear of Clifford.

Richard derides Warwick for retreating but explains to Warwick that it is only out of frustration that he is critical of Warwick ("But in this troublous time what's to be done?"). Warwick tells the young men that the queen, Clifford, and Northumberland have gone to London to defy the king's oath to deliver his throne, eventually, to Richard's heirs. Thirty thousand soldiers have gone in support of them, and Warwick urges York's sons to try to assemble at least 25,000 men in an attempt to counterattack Margaret and claim the throne. Richard and Edward promise to help; Edward is assured by Warwick that in every borough they pass through on their way to London, he will be named king. Those who do not support him will forfeit their heads.

Margaret and Henry arrive at York Castle with the Prince of Wales (Edward, their son), Northumberland, and Clifford. Margaret delights in showing York's impaled head to Henry, but Henry pleads to God that this bloody deed was not his fault. Clifford reminds the king that York made him disinherit Edward, his son, but Henry argues that perhaps the crown is not his to give because it was "illgot." Margaret then urges Henry to steel his "soft courage" and give Edward his promised knighthood immediately. Henry obeys her.

A messenger enters to warn of the enormous Yorkist march and of the Yorkists' gaining men as they progress toward London. Clifford and Margaret urge Henry to withdraw from the battlefield because of his indifference to war, but the Yorkists enter, and York's son Edward immediately challenges Henry to surrender the crown. Henry tries to speak, but he is shouted down by an exchange of insults. Both sides part ways and group their troops for battle.

Edward, Warwick, and George (another of York's sons) withdraw from the battlefield in Yorkshire since the ranks of their soldiers are broken and "Edward's sun is clouded." Richard (York's son) enters to report the death of Warwick's brother at the hands of Clifford, which sufficiently angers Warwick, Edward, and George to return to the battle. Revenge *must* be sought.

Henry enters alone, having been forced by Margaret and Clifford to leave the battle; they told him that they were more successful in battle if he was absent. Henry sits down and reflects on his condition, as he has done in other parts of this trilogy; he wishes that he were a "homely swain" rather than a king. As he sits alone, a young man enters, one who has just killed his father by mistake in battle; and moments later, a father enters who has mistakenly killed his son. Henry cries out in anguish, and he sympathizes with them deeply, but his horror of this kind of slaughter is impotent, suggesting Henry's fundamental inadequacy throughout the battle. Despite his desire to help bring peace to England, there is not much he can do to influence matters. Margaret, Edward, and Exeter urge Henry to escape with them since the battle has turned against them. Henry, indifferent to his safety, does as he is told.

A wounded Clifford enters, sensing a Lancastrian defeat, and faints. The Yorkists arrive and hear a groan from Clifford as he dies. Warwick has the Duke of York's head removed from the castle gate and has it replaced with Clifford's. He announces that they will proceed to London for Edward's coronation, and then he will depart for France, where he will ask the king for the hand of Lady Bona, sister of the French queen, for Edward. This action will assure French support for the Yorkist efforts. Edward then names Richard as the Duke of Gloucester and George as the Duke of Clarence.

ACT III

This act opens in a forest in the northern part of England, where two gamekeepers are hiding themselves under a thick bush; they are stalking a deer. A disguised Henry enters, carrying a prayer book and counting his sorrows. One of the keepers recognizes the king and makes a move to capture Henry, but he is stopped by the other so that they may hear more of the king's story, which Henry relates aloud to himself. He confesses that Margaret and his son have gone to France for aid, but he fears that they will be unsuccessful. The keepers corner him and lead him away to the authorities. They state that their loyalties lie with King Edward.

Lady Grey appears before King Edward in order to win back the lands of her husband, who was slain in battle at Saint Alban's in the cause of the Yorkists. Edward's brothers comment upon the exchange between their brother the king and Lady Grey, in which he attempts to woo her as his queen in exchange for the lands. Edward is pressing his suit to marry her when he is interrupted by a messenger, who announces that Henry VI has been taken prisoner. Edward orders that Henry be taken to the Tower while he and his brothers question the man who arrested him. Richard stays behind and, in a long soliloquy, reflects on his desire that Edward should produce no heirs if he marries Lady Grey; not having heirs would make it easier for Richard to claim the throne after Edward's death. He bemoans his unsightly, hunchbacked appearance and vows to do whatever is necessary in order for him to become king.

In France, Margaret secures an audience before King Lewis. He listens to her eloquent plea for help against the Yorkists, then he asks her to be patient. Warwick enters suddenly with his request that Lewis' sister-in-law, Lady Bona, be allowed to marry Edward, the new King of England. Lewis asks Margaret to leave him alone with Warwick, who immediately assures King Lewis that Edward is honorable in his love and is the rightful King of England. Lady Bona, who is present, agrees to the marriage proposal, and so Lewis informs Margaret of his change of heart: He has opted to help a strong monarch (Edward) instead of a weak one (Henry). He will not be able to do anything political for her.

A messenger enters with letters for Margaret, Lewis, and Warwick that contain news of King Edward's sudden marriage to Lady Grey. An enraged Warwick renounces King Edward and returns to Henry VI's side. He tells Margaret that he is her "true servitor," and he vows to "replant Henry in his former state."

At this point, the machinations of the plot resemble the melodramatics of a soap opera. Warwick volunteers to land French soldiers on England's coast in an effort to unseat King Edward. Thus, the messenger is sent back to England to announce the imminent arrival of French forces. Lewis vows to send 5,000 soldiers with Warwick and a fresh supply with Henry's son, Edward, the Prince of Wales. Warwick, to further prove his loyalty, gives his eldest daughter in marriage to Henry's son, ending the act on a firm note that he and King Lewis seek revenge on Edward, who would mock England's throne and renounce a proposed marriage to a lady of the

French court. Furthermore, Edward's fickle choice of wife has made Warwick look ridiculous.

ACT IV

In London, Gloucester (Richard, the hunchbacked son of Plantagenet) and Clarence (George, Richard's brother) argue over their brother Edward's marriage to Lady Grey. Clarence confronts Edward, who has just entered, with the fact that France and Warwick will not willingly submit to such humiliation as Edward has dealt them. Gloucester warns Edward that a "hasty marriage seldom proveth well," but he says that he does not ultimately oppose his brother's marriage to Lady Grey. Montague (Warwick's brother) and Lord Hastings warn Edward that England *must* be prepared to fight. In addition, both Clarence and Gloucester are jealous of the wives whom Edward has bestowed on his new wife's brother and son. Discontent reigns in the house of York. Clarence even announces his decision to leave the court and find a wife for himself. The queen (Lady Grey) tries to intervene and make peace among the brothers, and Edward warns them that they *must* bend to his will—or experience his wrath.

The messenger from France enters with the message from Lewis, Margaret, and Warwick regarding the imminent arrival of French troops on English soil. Edward is not unduly upset; he states that he will meet them in war. Clarence then decides to marry Warwick's younger daughter (thereby joining Warwick's camp), and he challenges his supporters to go with him. Somerset follows him. Gloucester (Richard) remains behind, not for love of Edward but for love of the crown. Edward announces that preparations for war are to begin immediately.

Warwick welcomes Clarence and Somerset into his camp and vows that Clarence shall marry his younger daughter. He then informs them that King Edward's camp may be easily taken. Only three watchmen guard the king, who has vowed not to sleep until either he or Warwick is killed. He has chosen to stay in the field with only a small guard ("carelessly encamp'd") since "'Tis the more honour, because more dangerous."

Warwick, Clarence, Oxford, Somerset, and several French soldiers enter, and Edward's watchmen, followed by Richard and Hastings, flee when they realize they are outnumbered. Edward is brought out of his tent, and Warwick announces that Edward is not the Duke of York and seizes the crown from him. He orders that Edward be conveyed to Warwick's brother, the Archbishop of York, and that the rest of them shall march to London to seat Henry once again on his rightful throne.

Queen Elizabeth (the former Lady Grey) has heard that Edward was taken prisoner, and she tells this news to Rivers, her brother, revealing that she must be strong since she carries Edward's heir. She asks Rivers to help her escape in order to save the unborn child.

Gloucester (Richard) meets with Hastings and Sir William Stanley in a park in Yorkshire, where he hopes to rescue Edward, his brother. Edward is encountered along with his huntsman, and he is told that he is to go to Flanders for his own safety; his huntsman is to accompany him. Warwick, Clarence, Somerset, Oxford, Montague, and young Henry (Earl of Richmond) free Henry from the Tower, and since Warwick made it all possible, he announces that he will be in charge of the government even though Henry shall remain king. Warwick chooses Clarence as Protector and says that he and Clarence will govern jointly so that Henry can, as he wishes, lead a quiet, private life.

Warwick then proclaims that Edward is a traitor, and he orders that all of Edward's lands and goods be confiscated. Henry requests that Margaret and their son, Prince Edward, be sent for so that his joy may be complete. Then he notices the young Earl of Richmond, Henry, and says that he is England's hope for the future: "His head by nature [is] fram'd to wear a crown." A messenger suddenly announces that Edward (York) has escaped, and Warwick blames the Archbishop of York for the carelessness. He withdraws to plan strategy with the others while Somerset and Oxford remain with the young Earl of Richmond. They decide that he must be sent to Brittany for safety's sake, "till storms be past of civil enmity."

Edward (York), his brother Gloucester (Richard), and Hastings approach the gates of York with soldiers from Burgundy only to find the gates locked. The mayor appears on the walls and explains that he and his colleagues are loyal to Henry. Hastings claims that *they* are Henry's friends, and Edward says that he is still Duke of York. Therefore, the mayor (deceived) lets them enter, and Edward "vows" to defend the town.

Sir John Montgomery marches up with soldiers and offers to

help Edward regain the crown. Edward tells Gloucester that he will not stake his claim until he is stronger, and the latter replies that he will proclaim Edward as king, which will bring many supporters to the cause. Edward is therefore proclaimed king, and Montgomery throws down his gauntlet as a challenge to anyone who usurps the position.

In London, at the palace, Warwick announces that Edward is marching toward London with many supporters and that troops must be gathered in order to oppose him. King Henry, meantime, will remain in London. Later, Henry and Exeter discuss the reasons why people chose Edward over him and also discuss their chances. Suddenly, Edward, Gloucester, and soldiers break in and seize Henry and order him to the Tower. Then they begin their march toward Coventry to meet Warwick.

ACT V

In Coventry, Warwick receives reports from messengers about the location of his commanders. He hears a flourish, which heralds the arrival of Edward, Gloucester (Richard), and their men, and, unaware that they were so close by, Warwick is taken by surprise and has no defense plan in motion. Within minutes, Oxford, Montague, and Somerset arrive with reinforcements. Clarence also arrives, but he takes the red rose of Lancaster from his hat and pledges his allegiance to the side of his brother Edward, who orders Warwick and his troops to prepare for battle. Warwick shouts that he will not defend Coventry but that he will meet Edward at Barnet, and the latter responds by leading the way.

On a field near Barnet, King Edward (Plantagenet) enters, dragging a wounded Warwick. He exits to find Montague since he intends to kill him too. Somerset and Oxford enter to inform Warwick of the queen's arrival from France with reinforcements. Just before Warwick dies, they tell him that Montague has also been killed.

King Edward celebrates his victory, but he knows that Margaret must yet be defeated. Margaret tells Oxford and Somerset that they will replace Warwick and Montague as the anchors of the quest to get Henry back on the throne. Edward arrives, and the battle begins.

Shortly afterward, Margaret, Somerset, and Oxford are taken prisoners by King Edward and Gloucester (Richard). Oxford is sent as a prisoner to Hames Castle, and Somerset is beheaded. The captured Prince Edward is brought in, resolute in his demands that King Edward must yield up the throne. King Edward, Gloucester, and Clarence all stab the young prince. Margaret faints, and Gloucester tells Clarence that he is off to London "on a serious matter" in the Tower. Margaret is led away to prison. Edward asks for Gloucester, and Clarence tells him that he has gone "to make a bloody supper in the Tower." Thus, Edward makes plans to return to London also.

At the Tower, Gloucester and Henry walk along the walls, talking. Henry suspects that his death is at hand. As Gloucester stabs him, Henry warns him that more slaughter will follow. Evil omens, he says, were abroad when Richard, the "indigested and deformed lump," was born. Gloucester stabs him one more time in order to send him to hell, and then, talking to himself, he plots a scheme to poison Edward's mind against Clarence: "Clarence, beware! Thou keep'st me from the light, / But I will sort a pitchy day for thee; / For I will buzz abroad such prophecies / That Edward shall be fearful of his life, / And then, to purge his fear, I'll be thy death." Gloucester, of course, hopes to be the future Richard III, and he will stop at nothing to obtain the crown for himself.

In London, Edward recounts a list of men who have died because they desired the throne. Then he calls forth his queen with their son, for whose sake he fought the war. He asks Gloucester (Richard) and Clarence to kiss the child, but as Gloucester does so, he mutters in an aside that his kiss is a "Judas kiss" that will bring harm to the child. Edward then orders that Margaret be sent back to France, desiring that the time now be spent "with stately triumphs, mirthful comic shows, / Such as befits the pleasure of the court."

When we recall that *Henry VI* was written early in Shakespeare's career, we realize that the drama's shortcomings are often compensated for by the hint of what is to come in future works. In conjunction with *Richard III*, this trilogy constitutes the first series of history plays that Shakespeare wrote, and it is a genre that he will develop considerably as he matures. The three parts of *Henry VI* can be read separately or as parts of a whole, but it must be remembered that the dramas are *not* an accurate presentation of history. Shakespeare contorts and bends historical reality to suit his dramatic purposes, which often causes confusion if one attempts to follow their plots along strictly historical lines. The historical chroniclers of that era, especially Holinshed and Halle, document an ongoing series of battles and feuds that run through the fifteenth century. Shakespeare, in turn, chooses events that interest him most and uses them as a backbone for his human drama—one of overpowering ambition, courage, and energy.

Henry VI, whose reign spanned the period from 1422 to 1471, was a weak and disastrous king. He was ill-equipped to control the turbulent forces at work in his own country, and he was in no way prepared to lead a defense against the invasion of foreigners. As England sinks deeper and deeper into trouble, Henry's reign unravels as a desperate, insecure tenure. Gloucester represents the old spirit of England, one of faith and courage, of determination and honor. But even Gloucester is unable to stand undaunted by the disintegration of the monarchy, and he is killed in Part 2, the turning point in the trilogy. Without Gloucester, Henry is exposed for what he is: immature, unschooled, and doomed. The chaos of the mob is the most obvious sign of this confusion and represents the low point from which the kingdom must build itself anew. The murder of Gloucester signals the end of an epoch and the beginning of a period that will lead to the relatively more stable reign of the Tudors. Gloucester is one of the few characters for whom we have sympathy and deep feeling; most of the other characters are cold, steel-like caricatures of politically hungry vultures, or else they are one-dimensional, singularly ambitious beings. It causes us no real pain to witness Suffolk's murder. To be sure, it is a tragedy of sorts, but in the overview of the country's situation, this seems like a necessary, inevitable event.

The trilogy presents constant problems of character identification, family lineage, and so on. But when one grasps the notion that there is a handful of central, key figures, one ceases to worry unduly about the occasional minor characters who float in and out of the dramas. Insofar as the characterization is concerned, Shakespeare has obviously done better work. But there are glimmerings of interesting people and of conflicts that stimulate good drama, and the *Henry VI* plays may be considered as essential groundwork for the study of Shakespearean psychology.

It is the pursuit of the crown that primarily intrigues Shakespeare in these dramas, and within this context, his trilogy makes for many gripping moments. The individual characters may suffer at the expense of the general effect, but when one remembers that this trilogy was one of Shakespeare's initial attempts at professional drama, it can be seen as a fortunate event in the history of theater.

1593

RICHARD III

RICHARD III

LIST OF MAIN CHARACTERS

Richard, Duke of Gloucester, afterward Richard III

Richard was the youngest son of the third Duke of York, who was killed at Wakefield in 1460. In *Henry IV, Part 2*, and more particularly in *Henry VI, Part 3*, he first appeared as a vigorous Yorkist and warrior. But then he emerged in the latter play as "hard-favored Richard," "a ragged fatal rock," and "an undigested lump"—each phrase suggesting that his deformity was the reflection of his profoundly evil character. He identified himself as one who would outdo Machiavelli—that is, as a super-Machiavelli—in his efforts to win the crown of England. The basic characteristics of the stage Machiavelli of Elizabethan drama are indeed his: boundless ambition, egotistical action, masterly dissembling, defiance of God, great but misguided intellectuality.

King Edward IV

Edward IV, the eldest son of the Duke of York, ruled England from 1461 to 1483. Anything but a weak ruler, he nevertheless had his difficulties. First, his marriage to Elizabeth Woodville, which had led to the disaffection of the Earl of Warwick, the chief support of the Yorkists, was a continuing source of trouble, for he tended to favor her relatives at the expense of the Nevilles and other families, the members of which had favored the Yorkist cause. Second, his reputation as a loose gallant, and particularly his relationship with the beautiful Jane Shore, daughter of a London goldsmith, made possible charges that his mistress adversely influenced his conduct of public affairs. Finally, a well-known clergyman, one Dr. Ralph Shaw, referred to in Act III, Scene 5, publicly charged that, in the words of the chronicler Robert Fabyan (*The Concordance of Histories*, 1516), "the children of King Edward IV were not legitimate, nor rightful heirs of the crown." This charge was based upon the widely circulated story that Edward had been secretly married before his union to Lady Elizabeth Grey and that his first wife was still alive. Richard of Gloucester of the play capitalized upon all three of these sources of difficulty. Edward appears in *Richard III* as the ailing ruler, one actually on his deathbed. His great concern is to quiet dissension and to insure the orderly succession of the crown.

George, Duke of Clarence

The third son of the Duke of York and brother to Edward IV and Richard of Gloucester first appeared in *Henry VI, Part 3*. In that play, he is described as a "quicksand of deceit" and for good reason. Clarence had been elevated to a dukedom by his newly crowned brother after the defeat of Queen Margaret's forces near Towton. But he joined the disgruntled Warwick and was betrothed to the earl's second daughter. It was to Clarence as well as to Warwick that the liberated Henry VI resigned his government, while Edward IV was forced to find haven on the Continent. But once more Clarence changed loyalties, removing the red rose from his helmet and proclaiming himself to be the "mortal foe" of Warwick, who denounced him as "perjur'd and unjust." In *Henry VI, Part 3*, Clarence also is made to join Edward and Richard in stabbing Prince Edward, son of Henry VI and Margaret of Anjou. History records that he was constantly involved in quarrels with his older brother.

Henry, Duke of Buckingham

Buckingham inherited his title from Humphrey Stafford, one of the commanders of the royal forces at the first Battle of St. Alban's. Understandably Queen Margaret first praises him as blameless. Holinshed described him as "easie to handle," and for a time so the Richard of this play found him to be. To Richard he was the "deep-revolving, witty Buckingham" who functioned as the villain-hero's Warwick, or king-maker. But unlike Warwick, Buckingham is depicted as, to use another of Richard's phrases, one "of many simple gulls," susceptible to gross flattery and convinced that his fortunes will be advanced if he serves the ambitious Richard. Too late he learns that he has judged falsely.

Henry Tudor, Earl of Richmond, afterward King Henry VII

Richmond was the nearest male representative of the Lancastrians. He was the son of Owen Tudor and Katherine, the widow of Henry V. He was also the lineal descendant, by Katherine Swynford, of John of Gaunt. Henry thus inherited the Lancastrian line, although he was debarred by Parliament from the throne. Nevertheless, he had many English supporters, and when he escaped to France after the Battle of Tewkesbury, he bided his time for a while and then issued a manifesto calling upon Englishmen to join him in crushing Richard, "the unnatural tyrant who bore rule over them." Thanks to his marriage to Elizabeth, daughter of Edward IV, he was able to unite the dynastic claims of both parties. Shakespeare followed his sources in depicting Henry as the God-sent savior of England.

Queen Margaret, Widow of Henry VI

She appeared with increasing prominence in each of the *Henry VI* plays. Daughter of the Duke of Anjou, titular King of Naples, and niece of Charles VII, she was a determined, strong-minded woman who offered a complete contrast to her pious, well-meaning, weak husband. When the Duke of Somerset was slain in the first Battle of St. Alban's (1455), Margaret came forward as head of the royal party prosecuting the civil war against the Yorkists. After her defeat at Tewkesbury, she was imprisoned, but she was then released on payment of a ransom by France. Actually she died in 1482 but survived in Shakespeare's play, where she functions as a terrifying chorus, a symbolic figure standing for the doom of the house of York.

Elizabeth, Queen to Edward IV

Elizabeth was the widowed daughter of Sir Richard Woodville and patron of the Woodville faction, who were of Lancastrian connection. In the play, this faction is represented by her brother, Earl Rivers, and her two sons by her first husband, the Marquis of Dorset and Lord Grey. In *Richard III,* she appears to yield to Richard's blandishments, but since she survived to see her daughter become Queen of England, it may be questioned whether she was the "relenting fool and shallow changing woman" described by Richard.

Lady Anne

The widow of Edward, Prince of Wales, son of Henry VI, was the daughter of the Earl of Warwick and thus a Neville. The fact that she possessed much property is not the sole reason why Richard of Gloucester should have turned ardent wooer. The Neville connection fitted in with his ambitions to gain the crown.

The Duchess of York

The mother of King Edward IV, Clarence, and Richard was the daughter of Ralph Neville, first Earl of Northumberland. Since her husband first made his bid for the crown, she had endured "accursed and wrangling days," surviving not only the Duke of York's death but also the deaths of her sons. She also endured the agonizing realization that Richard was one who was "damned," one who had come "on earth to make [her] earth a hell" and who deserved his mother's "most grievous curse."

William, Lord Hastings

Hastings, an adherent to the Yorkist cause, was described as "a noble man" by Holinshed. He served as lord chamberlain to Edward IV but was opposed by Queen Elizabeth because the king favored him. Like Buckingham, then, he was at odds with the Woodvilles. Holinshed links him with Buckingham as one whom Richard first considered as "easie to handle." It is difficult to avoid the conclusion that Hastings was obtuse. When Richard arrested members of the queen's faction, he decided that the action was necessary for the safety of the realm, and he was confident that his own position was secure. Obtuse or not, he emerged as one representing loyal nobility, faithful to the throne rather than to one faction or another. Inevitably, Richard denounced him as a traitor and saw to it that he was put to death without a trial, as Shakespeare's sources reported.

SUMMARIES AND COMMENTARIES

ACT I

Summary

Appearing on a London street, Richard, Duke of Gloucester, soliloquizes, providing much exposition and revealing a great deal about himself. The long years of the Lancastrian supremacy are over, and the house of York, like the rising sun, is now in the ascendant. Those who have distinguished themselves in the grim arts of war are relaxing in the pleasure of love. Richard refers particularly to his brother Edward IV.

The thought of his handsome brother reminds Richard of his own deformity. He has one withered arm and a hunched back and so concludes that he is unfit for love. Therefore he will play the villain. The first of his wicked plots is already under way: He has told Edward about a prophecy that says that someone with a name beginning with "G" will murder Edward's heirs. The king has taken this to mean his other brother, George, Duke of Clarence.

Richard's thoughts are interrupted by the entrance of Clarence, who is guarded by Brackenbury, Lieutenant of the Tower, much to the apparent surprise and concern of Richard. Clarence explains that he is being sent to the Tower because Edward has listened to the prophecy about the letter "G." Richard is quick to attribute the king's action to the fact that he is ruled by his wife, Elizabeth Woodville, who with her brother had had Lord Hastings imprisoned. He declares that the king's blood relatives and supporters are no longer safe.

Richard and Clarence then talk disparagingly of the queen and of the king's mistress, Jane Shore, whom they accuse of ruling the kingdom by gossip. Brackenbury intervenes, not wishing to overhear such dangerous talk. Insisting that there is no question of treasonable discourse, Richard then demonstrates his wit and sense of irony as he slyly speaks of the "noble Queen" and catalogues the attractions of Jane Shore. With resignation, Clarence agrees to accompany Brackenbury, and his brother assures him that he will either deliver him from prison or take his place as a prisoner. Alone, however, Richard restates his determination to have his brother's soul sent to heaven.

Hastings, newly released from prison, enters. He vows that he will avenge himself upon those responsible for his imprisonment and brings news that the king is ill. Richard blames this illness on Edward's self-indulgence and promises to follow Hastings to his bedside. The scene ends with another soliloquy in which Richard elaborates his evil plans. Clarence must be disposed of at once, before King Edward's death. Then Richard will marry Warwick's daughter Anne, though he had killed her husband, Edward, Prince of Wales, and her father-in-law, Henry VI. He explains that the marriage will further his ends. Aware that his plans are barely started, he goes off to take definite action.

Lady Anne, second daughter of the Earl of Warwick, appears onstage, following the funeral cortege of the slain Henry VI, whom she identifies as her father-in-law. She is escorting the body of this "holy King," last great member of the house of Lancaster, to Chertsey in Surrey for burial. Making reference also to herself as the wife of Edward, the "slaughtered son" of the dead ruler, she calls upon the ghost of Henry to hear her lamentations. Heaping curses on the murderer, she implores God to punish him: Let any child of his be born prematurely and prove to be monstrous; if he marry, let his wife endure the misery of his death, even as Anne herself now suffers.

At this point, Richard enters and violently stops the procession in order to speak to Anne. She denounces him vehemently and utters the prophetic cry, "For thou hast made the happy earth thy hell." She points out that King Henry's wounds have started to bleed again as a result of Richard's presence. Gloucester appeals to her charity. In a dialogue of quick and studied repartee, she heaps more curses upon him, while he parries with flattering words and begs for the chance to explain himself. Though she scorns him and even spits upon him, he is not to be deterred. He presses his suit, declaring that if he was guilty of Henry's and Edward's deaths, he had been motivated solely by his desire to possess her beauty. When she denounces him as a "foul toad" that infects her eyes, Richard insists that the beauty of her eyes makes him weep—he, who remained dry-eyed when his brother Rutland and his father had been slain. This recital merely excites her scorn; so he bares his bosom, gives her his sword, and—admitting that he indeed killed Henry and Prince Edward—invites her to kill him. When Anne refuses to be his executioner, he urges her to tell him to kill himself, but to do so not in rage. At last Anne is in some doubt and says: "I would I knew thy heart." Richard is quick to press his advantage and prevails on her to accept a ring. When she takes it, she states that she promises nothing in return. Nevertheless, when he asks her to repair to Crosby Place, his London residence, and there to wait for him while he buries King Henry with his "repentant tears," she promptly agrees to do so.

Alone, Richard gloats over this conquest of Lady Anne made when the odds were so great against him—the fact that she changed from a mood of venemous hate to one of ready acquiescence and found him "to be a marvelous proper man," particularly in contrast to her dead husband, whom he had killed at Tewkesbury some three months earlier. He reveals his plan to "have her, but . . . not keep her long." In view of his success so far, he finds that his deformity pleases him.

At the palace, Queen Elizabeth is discussing with Lord Rivers, her brother, and Lord Grey, her son, the king's illness. Elizabeth is especially concerned with what her fate will be if her husband should die. As she points out to Lord Grey, her young son, the Prince of Wales, is "put unto the trust of Richard Gloucester," whom she knows to be her enemy and that of all the Woodville faction. The Duke of Buckingham and the Earl of Derby (also called Lord Stanley) enter and courteously greet the queen. To Derby she remarks that the Countess Richmond, his wife, would not say amen to his prayer for her happiness, for she is a woman of "proud arrogance" who does not cherish the queen. Derby insists that his wife is the victim of "false accusers"—either that or her attitude toward Elizabeth stems from perverse sickness, not malice. In response to a question, Buckingham reports that King Edward seems to have improved in health: He "speaks cheerfully" and is especially desirous of ending the quarrel between the queen's brothers and the offended Buckingham and Hastings. Elizabeth can only voice her fervent wish that all were well and express the fear that her fortunes will not improve.

Richard, Hastings, and Lord Dorset (son to Elizabeth by her first marriage) enter. "They do me wrong and I will not endure it." These are the first words of Richard, who presents himself as injured innocence, enraged because the queen's relatives have misrepresented him to the king. He offers himself as a simple, plain man, wronged by the insinuations of sly flatterers whom he cannot match because deception is no part of his character. When Rivers protests, Richard accuses him and all his family for troubling the king with vulgar complaints against him. Elizabeth explains that the king, seeing the hatred of the two families, merely wishes to find the cause of their ill will by having them meet with each other. Richard retorts that he can no longer understand matters now that the world is upside down, with every common fellow made a gentleman and every gentleman rudely treated like a common fellow.

The queen brings the quarrel into the open, saying that Gloucester envies the advancement of her family. Richard counters with the charge that the queen is responsible for Clarence's imprisonment. She protests. When Lord Rivers breaks in to defend her, Richard taunts her with having married a "handsome bachelor stripling," implying that she, an older widow, was not fit for one so young. The queen is stung by this and threatens to tell the king of all the insults she has borne from Richard.

Old Queen Margaret, widow of Henry VI, enters and stands apart, listening to the wrangling of her enemies and now and then interjecting scathing comments on the words of successive speakers. To her it is a source of satisfaction that Elizabeth has small happiness in being Queen of England. Richard continues to speak to Elizabeth in his defense. Margaret interrupts him, calling him a devil and blaming him for the death of her husband and her son. Richard continues to address Elizabeth, ignoring the withering remarks of the aged Margaret. He states that, while Elizabeth and members of her family were on the side of the Lancastrians, he was the loyal Yorkist who helped Edward to the throne. Clarence, he continues, forsook his father-in-law Warwick, committing perjury in order to fight on Edward's side; for this offense he is now imprisoned. Interspersed between each of his statements are Margaret's denunciations, but Richard continues to ignore her. Lord Rivers argues that he and members of his family have been loyal always to their lawful king, as they would be to Richard were he the ruler. Richard is quick to protest that he would rather be a beggar: "Far be it from my heart, the thought thereof!" When this causes Elizabeth to bemoan her joyless lot once more, Margaret insists on being heard.

"Hear me, you wrangling pirates," she exclaims, and describes them as rebels who now are quarreling over that which they took from her. All who hear her join in reviling her for the indignity done to the Duke of York, whose severed head was fitted with a mock crown, and for the murder of his son Rutland. Margaret retaliates by asking whether all her sorrows and wrongs are not enough to justify that act of hers. Edward IV, Elizabeth, Rivers, Dorset, Hastings—all are the recipients of her curses as she calls upon God to punish her adversaries. Especially she curses Gloucester: may the "worm of conscience" afflict him; may only "deep traitors" be his friends; may he be deprived of restful sleep. She concludes by making much of his deformity as a sign that hell and the evil forces of nature have marked him for their own. Richard tries to turn the curses back on her. And when Elizabeth states that Margaret has indeed cursed herself, this "Poor painted [imitation] queen," as she bitterly calls herself, concentrates her attack upon her royal successor and the Woodville faction in general, whom she identifies as upstarts. Ironically, Gloucester interposes an endorsement of her denunciation of Dorset and boasts that his own exalted status will prevent his fall. When Buckingham tries to restrain Margaret, she voices words of praise for him: Since he had not fought against the Lancastrians, her curses do not apply to him. But Buckingham rejects her offer of "league and amity." It is then that Margaret warns him to beware of Richard, upon whom "Sin, death, and hell have set their marks." Finally she leaves.

Gloucester now sanctimoniously voices sympathy for Margaret and expresses regret for his part in having opposed her. When Elizabeth says that she is blameless, he points out that she has benefited by Margaret's downfall, whereas Richard himself had merely sought to help others. Again he makes reference to his brother Clarence, saying that Clarence suffers for the same reason and asking God to pardon those who are responsible for his brother's imprisonment. Lord Rivers sarcastically remarks on this "virtuous and Christianlike conclusion," but Richard remains unperturbed. His aside, however, makes it clear that, in praying for the forgiveness of any responsible for Clarence's fate, he avoided cursing himself.

Catesby enters and summons the group to the king's chambers. All except Richard leave, and in the final soliloquy he gloats over his villainy. He has furthered his ends by fooling Hastings, Derby, and Buckingham into believing that the queen's family is behind Clarence's ruin. When they try to persuade him to seek revenge, he puts on a saintly air and talks of returning good for evil. A fitting conclusion to this villainous speech is the entry of the two murderers whom he has hired to get rid of Clarence. They have come for the warrant that will provide for their admission to the Tower. He instructs them to feel no pity and not to be swayed by Clarence's eloquence. The first murderer assures Richard that they are doers, not talkers, and will carry out his instructions. They are instructed to go to Richard's home at Crosby Place after the deed is done.

The action now takes place in the Tower of London, toward

which the murderers repair. The imprisoned Clarence tells Brakenbury, the Lieutenant of the Tower and therefore his jailer, about the
miserable night he has endured. He explains that he thought that he
was on a ship bound for Burgundy when his brother Gloucester
induced him to come and walk the deck. As they talked of their
adventures during the recent wars, Richard stumbled, and when
Clarence tried to help him, Clarence himself was struck by his
brother and fell overboard. The royal prisoner then gives a most
vivid description of his dream of drowning, which was continued to
the point where his soul was being ferried over the "melancholy
flood" of the River Styx by the ferryman Charon. There he met Warwick, whom he had betrayed, followed by the ghost of Prince
Edward, whom he had stabbed at Tewkesbury. Clarence hears himself described as "false, fleeting, perjured Clarence." Convinced that
he was in hell, Clarence remembers all the deeds that might have
sent him there. He prays God to punish him if He must but to spare
his wife and children.

As Clarence sleeps, Brakenbury, moved by the recital, reflects
on the sorrow of princes who, despite their high rank, often feel "a
world of restless care," as do lesser folk. He is interrupted by the two
murderers. They show their warrants and are left in charge of the
sleeping prince while the lieutenant goes back to the king to resign
his commission.

The murderers discuss killing Clarence while he sleeps, but the
mention of "judgment" arouses the conscience of the second murderer. It is the fear that he will face damnation despite the warrant
to perform the deed received from Richard. In contrast, the first
murderer is obviously one who will dare damnation to earn the
promised monetary reward. At the mention of that reward, the
second murderer finds that his conscience no longer is an impedi-
ment. As the two are talking about the inconveniences of conscience and holding a kind of dialogue between conscience and the
devil, they finally decide to strike Clarence over the head and then
drop him into a butt of malmsey wine. Clarence awakes and calls for
a cup of wine. Grimly ironical, the first murderer replies: "You shall
have wine enough, my lord, anon"—that is, immediately.

In the colloquy that follows, Clarence learns that these are his
executioners and is first led to believe that they have been sent on
the orders of King Edward to put to death one guilty of treason. He

is eloquent in his own defense and attempts to dissuade the murderers, but they remain adamant. They remind him of his heinous crimes of perjury and murder, for (we now learn) he had joined his brother Richard in killing Prince Edward. Clarence declares that he had acted solely on behalf of his brother Edward, who therefore is quite as deep in sin as is Clarence himself. In this exchange, the royal prisoner refers repeatedly to his brother, meaning Edward, but soon learns, to his utter dismay, that the determined first murderer uses the term to refer to Gloucester. Again Clarence invokes God's name, urging his adversaries to relent. And again the second murderer wavers, even warning Clarence that the first murderer is about to strike him. But it is too late. Clarence is stabbed several times, and his murderer leaves with the duke's body, which he will throw into the "malmsey-butt within." Now the second murderer is indeed conscience-stricken. The act ends with the actual murderer accusing the accessory of cowardice and threatening to denounce him to Richard.

Commentary

In having the titular hero appear first onstage and soliloquize at length, Shakespeare was following a convention that he later outgrew. In the more mature plays, the way is prepared by means of expository dialogue before the tragic hero's entrance. The opening soliloquy in Scene 1 accomplishes all that a prologue would, and subtlety is the last thing to look for here. Gloucester paints himself as an unnatural monster. He is lame, ugly, "rudely stamped." A common belief of the time was that the warped moral being of the individual was often reflected in his physical appearance.

In the first two lines is found a typical Shakespearean play upon a word—the word *sun* in this instance. Edward IV was the son of the Duke of York and bore a sun on his armorial crest. Metaphorically, he was the bright sun of the Yorkist party, now in the ascendant. And, of course, the sun is a well-known symbol of royalty. Notice how skillfully Shakespeare sustains the sun metaphor:

> Why, I, in this weak piping time of peace,
> Have no delight to pass away the time,
> Unless to see my shadow in the sun
> And descant on mine own deformity.

(24–27)

As a dedicated Machiavellian, he takes pride in his deviousness and treachery and emerges as one filled with envy (a Deadly Sin) and motivated by criminal ambition. The adjective "piping" and the verb "descant" relate to the shepherd's life, the shepherd being a familiar symbol of the tranquility that Richard scorns.

Already the action has begun to rise. We know about Gloucester's ambition; we know what is the first step he has taken to realize that ambition. When he protests to Clarence, "Alack, my lord, that fault is none of yours," we witness the first display of Machiavellian dissembling. His exchange with the apprehensive Brackenbury provides a good example of his wit and gift for irony. These two qualities are further illustrated by his use of "abjects" for "subjects" and by his expression of deep concern for his brother: "Meantime, this deep disgrace in brotherhood / Touches me deeper than you can imagine" (111–12). "Disgrace in brotherhood" has three levels of meaning: the unnatural action of a brother (Edward IV); Richard's own underhanded behavior; and disgrace to a brother (Clarence). Similarly, the word "lie" in the final words to Clarence means, on the surface, that Gloucester will take Clarence's place in prison; but it also means that the villain-hero will tell more lies about his brother.

With the arrival of Lord Hastings, two circumstances that may work to Richard's advantage are revealed. First, Hastings is determined to avenge himself upon those who were responsible for his imprisonment; therefore, Richard may find him a useful ally. Second, King Edward is "sickly, weak, and melancholy." The reader will not miss the irony of Gloucester's voiced reaction: "Now, by Saint John, that news is bad indeed." He will make use of such sacred oaths frequently and thus provide further evidence of his hypocrisy. Despite his outward show of loyalty and fraternal love, he does not fail to indict Edward as one whose "evil diet" has "overmuch consumed his royal person." What with the Woodville faction alienating powerful nobles like Hastings, and with the ruler incapacitated as the supposed result of a dissolute life, a way may be found for Richard to seize power. His plan to marry Lady Anne, if carried out successfully, will work to his advantage. But immediately all depends upon what happens to Clarence and to Edward.

A recapitulation of what has been accomplished in Scene 1 should be useful. Richard is presented as by far the most important character in the play. The present situation in the kingdom is made clear: Edward IV, the ailing ruler, appears to be dominated by his wife, and the older nobles are resentful. The relation between the three sons of the Duke of York is set forth: Edward is a dying king; Clarence a traitor and perjurer; Richard the destroyer of his brothers. The scene also provides the motives for Richard's villainy and shows that by his lying words he will be able to stir up more dissension. Finally, the scene prepares for the courtship of Lady Anne.

There has been some dispute as regards the question of whether or not Lady Anne Neville actually had been married to Prince Edward, although there is no question as to the betrothal of the two. Margaret of Anjou did object at first to the proposed marriage of her son to Warwick's second daughter; but, perhaps under pressure of Louis XI, she finally gave her consent. Edward and Anne were married on December 13, 1470, by the Grand Vicar of Bayeux. The queen, however, left herself as free as possible to disavow or annul the marriage later. It is doubtful that the young couple ever lived together as man and wife.

In Scene 2, when the dramatist has Anne point out that the wounds of the dead King Henry have started to bleed again, he makes effective use of the popular belief that the wounds of a murdered man bleed in the presence of the murderer.

Anne repeatedly addresses Richard as "thou" and "thee," whereas the villain-hero addresses her as "you." Anne shifts to the latter form when she tacitly indicates her willingness to favor Richard's suit: "Well, well, put up your sword." The familiar "thou" and "thee" are a way in which Anne makes clear how she looks down on Gloucester with contempt. Thus, in *Othello* (I. i. 118-19), Brabantio, aroused in the night to be told that his daughter has eloped, denounces Iago in these words: "Thou art a villain." Iago replies, "You are—a Senator."

In this contrived scene, Richard's heartless cruelty and extreme egotism receive sufficient emphasis early and late. It is not stoicism primarily that explains his failure to shed a tear when Rutland and the Duke of York were slain, for he was already dedicated solely to the advancement of his own fortunes to the exclusion of any concern even for blood relatives. Near the end of the scene, he callously refers to the corpse of Henry VI: "But first I'll turn yon fellow in his grave"—that is, he will toss or tip the body of his royal victim into the grave. He then tells the sun to shine so that he may see his shadow as it passes. Richard is saying that his physical deformity, symbol of his evil nature, is most pleasing to him since it makes possible his advancement.

If the stress were placed solely upon Richard's monstrosity, upon the extreme violence of his actions, the villain-hero would not be the fascinating character that he is. Playing the role of a lover with consummate skill, he exhibits the daring, the superior wit, the profound sense of irony, the sheer intellectuality which mark him as one who indeed can outdo Machiavelli. He is apparently unperturbed when Anne denounces him as a "dreadful minister of hell" and as a "foul devil"; he seems to turn the other cheek and addresses her as a "sweet saint" and gently reproves her for knowing "no rules of charity." Would even a ferocious beast know "some touch of pity" as Anne declares? Then, concludes the villain, he is not a beast! Once having conceded that he did kill Henry VI, Richard claims a kind of credit: He has helped the king to reach heaven. Essaying the role of the Petrarchan lover, that swain whose avowals of undying love for his lady were recorded in the sonnet cycles already so popular in Shakespeare's England, Richard uses a typical conceit, or fanciful metaphor: He has been wounded to the quick by a glance of Anne's beautiful eyes.

But, like most of Shakespeare's villains, Richard can be completely honest with himself, as we learn from his soliloquies. That Anne, whose murdered husband is represented as having been a paragon of physical attractiveness and virtue, should have permitted this misshapen villain to win her so easily is, to Richard, most comically ironical. One other point, not to be ignored, is the irony in Anne's words when she exclaims: "I'll rest betide the chamber where thou liest" (112). In view of what we learn later, after Anne has been married to Richard for some time, this line is prophetic.

Finally, Scene 2 reveals Richard's boundless energy. He has wasted no time in arranging the match with Lady Anne, as, at the end of the previous scene, we learned he planned to do.

In Scene 1, reference was made to the bitter quarrel between the members of the Woodville faction, headed by Queen Elizabeth, and high-ranking Yorkists, as well as such aristocrats as Lord Hastings, lord chamberlain to King Edward IV. In Scene 3, the quarrel itself is dramatized, recrimination following recrimination. The extent of the dissension is indicated by the fact that the Countess

Richmond, wife of Lord Stanley, Earl of Derby, detests Elizabeth as an upstart. It may be noted here that the countess is the mother of the Earl of Richmond, who will prove to be Richard's nemesis. But it is the Duke of Buckingham, in a sense an outsider as regards this quarrel, who clearly leans toward Gloucester despite Queen Margaret's ominous warning. We may expect Richard to make the most of this turn of events.

A kind of suspense is achieved when Buckingham reports that the king's health seems to have improved and that Edward has moved to establish peace within his realm. Nothing is farther from Richard's wishes, to be sure; and he is relentless in his attack upon those who stand in his way. As the accomplished dissembler, he is no less effective than he was in the previous scene. Now he presents himself as the loyal, selfless subject of Edward IV opposed to those who are criminally ambitious—those whom he describes as "wrens" (the smallest of English birds) who "make prey where eagles dare not perch." The eagle, of course, is a symbol of royalty. Richard thus makes tacit reference to himself; he confidently states that he is not one headed for catastrophe since he was "born so high" (in contrast to the others present in this scene). Were not the Yorkists descended from Edward III? Once more Richard's feigned religiosity is apparent, as when he swears "By holy Paul" and "By God's holy mother." It is a good touch also to have him voice sympathy and Christian forgiveness for Queen Margaret, who has scathingly denounced him.

Especially important is the role of Queen Margaret, who makes her first appearance in this scene. As has been pointed out in the discussion of her character above, actually she had died in 1482. Even if she had survived, the appearance of this one-time champion of the house of Lancaster among her enemies is quite fantastic. Nevertheless, her role is a key one. Margaret immediately establishes herself as a terrifying chorus whose violent curses, directed first to her successor, Queen Elizabeth, then repeatedly to Richard, and finally to Elizabeth's relatives, reveal her as a symbolic figure, "the doom of the House of York." At one point she denounces Richard as an "abortive, rooting hog." The reference is to his premature birth—evidence of his unnaturalness and perhaps the cause of his deformity—and to Richard's armorial crest, upon which was depicted a boar. The adjective "rooting" is meant to describe his destructive activities.

In this play, which has been called the most religious that

Shakespeare ever wrote, it is Margaret who repeatedly emphasizes the major theme: God's inexorable justice visited upon those guilty of the heinous sins of murder and perjury. Richard is first to be charged with unforgivable crime—the murder of Henry VI and Edward, Prince of Wales. And when Gloucester, recalling that his brother Clarence had forsworn himself by deserting Warwick, hypocritically implores that Christ forgive the sinner, Margaret bitterly calls for God's vengeance upon Clarence. Once more it is a mathematical kind of justice—the logic of which so appealed to Elizabethans—that she emphasizes when she summarizes her indictment of those responsible for the fall of the house of Lancaster. Her speech begins with these words addressed to Elizabeth: "Edward thy son, that now is Prince of Wales, / For Edward our son, that was Prince of Wales" (200–201). It ends with her fervent prayer: "That none of you may live his natural age, / But by some unlooked accident cut off!" (213–14). In the course of the subsequent action, vengeance will indeed be visited upon each of those whom Margaret indicts.

But what of this aged former queen who has suffered and is suffering so much? Richard reminds her of her own offenses—how she had deserved the Duke of York's curses and how the young Duke of Rutland had been killed by the Lancastrians. Familiar as they were with the history of these times, members of Shakespeare's audience would not fail to recall that Henry VI, although widely praised for his piety, was the grandson of a regicide and usurper, one who had seized the throne from the lawful, anointed King Richard II, from which deed all these troubles had stemmed. Did not the Bible say that the crimes of the father would be visited upon the children even unto the third generation?

Scene 4 is a highly dramatic scene that contains much that is doctrinally and thematically important. Clarence's long speeches addressed to Brakenbury follow the tradition established by that popular collection of tragical histories in verse entitled *Mirror for Magistrates*, a work of accretion, the first edition of which appeared in 1559. Other editions followed in 1571, 1574, 1575, 1578, and 1587. Significant is the fact that the *Mirror* dealt primarily with English history from the reign of Richard II to the fall of Richard III at Bosworth's Field in 1485. It mirrors the instability of fortune and the punishment of vice and, as we are told in one of the prose introductions, seeks "by example of other's miseries to dissuade all men from sins and vices." Successively the ghosts of fallen great persons tell their stories in long monologues, announcing their own guilt and usually stressing the theme of divine vengeance. In the development of this theme in Shakespeare's play, the supernatural, including portentous dreams, has an important place. In Clarence's terrifying dream appears the ghost of Warwick to denounce him as "false, fleeting, perjured Clarence."

In Scene 4, Clarence's first long speech (9–33) is, of its kind, quite superior as poetry. If indeed Shakespeare still writes a predominantly Marlovian type of verse, the lines of which are usually end-stopped, he incorporates specific details in a way hardly characteristic of Marlowe so that every line evokes a picture. Notable is the way in which the poet builds up to climaxes: "All scattered in the bottom of the sea" (28) and "And mocked the dead bones that lay scattered by" (33). Following each, the rhythm of Clarence's lines changes appropriately.

The second long speech (43–63) contains Clarence's outburst of self-incrimination, leaving no doubt of his particular guilt. But he remains a human being and invites our sympathy. Unselfishly he thinks of his family, and courageously he meets his violent death. Nevertheless, one must not lose sight of the fact that he is a grievous sinner who must endure the inevitable punishment of a just God in accordance with the orthodox doctrine that informs this play.

The two murderers are exceptionally well individualized. Their prose dialogue is most realistic and packed with grim humor. Note, for example, the second murderer's speech in which he indicts conscience on the grounds that "it makes a man a coward" (137–48). When asked scornfully if he is afraid, he replies: "Not to kill him, having a warrant; but to be damned for killing him, from which no warrant can defend me" (112–14).

The question is one regarding vengeance in general. The proper authority, functioning as God's minister on earth, as he is called in Romans 13, can and must execute public justice; but no one, however exalted his position, can rightfully execute private revenge. This is the import of Clarence's argument as he seeks to dissuade the murderer:

> Erroneous vassals! the great King of kings
> Hath in his table of His law commanded

> That thou shalt do no murder. Will you, then
> Spurn at His edict, and fulfill a man's?
> Take heed; for He holds vengeance in His hand,
> To hurl upon their heads that break His law.
>
> (200–205)

The second murderer, to whom these lines were addressed, has an answer: "And that same vengeance doth He hurl on thee / For false swearing, and for murder too" (206–207). Clarence argues that these crimes were committed for Edward's sake and that the king is therefore quite as deep in sin as is Clarence himself. He goes on: "If God will be avenged for the deed, / Oh, know you yet, He doth it publicly" (221–22). The king will observe the due process of law.

And then the doomed Clarence learns that these murderers serve his brother Gloucester, whose motive is criminal ambition, not revenge, public or private. What conclusions are to be drawn from all this? There is no doubt that Clarence deserved extreme punishment. But how to account for the fact that two murderers hired by an arch-villain perform the deed? Is this an example of God's inexorable justice? According to Tudor theory, it was exactly that. Just as God may permit the rebel to rage in order to punish a sinful ruler, so may He use even such sinners as Richard and, at a different level, the hired assassins to execute his justice against Clarence. They function as the Scourge of God. But, still in keeping with the larger concept of justice, they will be scourged in turn ultimately. In the previous scene, Margaret had implored God to punish Clarence: Her prayer has been answered. At the end of Scene 4, the second murderer acknowledges the fact that the two have "most grievous murder done," and he will have no share in the promised reward, the thought of which earlier had led him to spurn the urgings of conscience. There is, then, no contradiction, no inconsistency here in the sustaining of the play's major theme.

ACT II

Summary

The scene shifts to the palace. King Edward, whom we meet for the first time, has called the queen and members of the family and court to his bedside. He commands them to be reconciled to one another and to swear to refrain from enmity in the future. Successively Rivers, Hastings, the queen herself, Dorset, and Buckingham solemnly take the sacred vow. Only Gloucester is absent "To make the blessed period of this peace," to use the king's words. But Richard makes his appearance immediately, wishing all present "a happy time of day." When he is told that all differences have been settled and that hate has now given place to "fair love," he pronounces the king's action to be "a blessed labor" and, insisting that he desires "all good men's love," declares himself to be devoted to all present. He concludes by piously thanking God for his humility.

When Queen Elizabeth, anxious that the newfound amity be extended to all members of the court group, urges the king to pardon Clarence, Richard delivers the shocking news that Clarence is dead: Edward's reprieve had arrived too late. Almost at once Derby enters and begs that his servant's life, declared forfeit for murder, be spared. This request fills Edward with remorse as he contrasts the zeal of a master for a servant with the neglect of Clarence. Especially he remembers all that Clarence had done for him, and he blames not only himself but all others present, none of whom had interceded in Clarence's behalf. Edward concludes that he and the rest have rendered themselves subject to God's punishment. Calling Hastings, the lord chamberlain, to accompany him, he leaves with the queen and some members of the court.

Gloucester promptly takes advantage of the occasion to draw Buckingham's attention to what he describes as the guilty looks of the queen's relatives. He charges that they had urged the king to put Clarence to death, and he predicts that "God will avenge it." He then asks Buckingham to join him in comforting Edward.

In a mood consistent with Edward's remorse and sorrow, Scene 2 introduces the young son and daughter of Clarence, who suspect that their father is dead. They are talking to their grandmother, the Duchess of York, who is weeping not, as they think, for Clarence but for the mortally sick king. Richard has succeeded in convincing these children that Edward, influenced by Queen Elizabeth, is responsible for their father's death. He has assured them of his devotion to them and has told them to rely on him. Richard's mother, fully aware of her son's intent, laments that she has given birth to so foul a monster. But Clarence's young son finds it impossible to believe that his uncle could be such a villain.

Queen Elizabeth, grief-stricken and all disheveled, enters. All now learn that King Edward is dead, and a general chorus of grief ensues. The duchess weeps for her husband and two sons, the queen for her husband, and the children for their father. Dorset and Rivers try to comfort the queen, Rivers immediately introducing the comforting thought of her son, who should be summoned from Ludlow immediately to be crowned.

Gloucester comes in with Buckingham, Derby, Hastings, and Ratcliff. He is in good form as usual, offering words of comfort to Queen Elizabeth and asking his mother's blessing. Buckingham suggests that the Prince of Wales be brought from Ludlow with a small group of followers and succeeds in convincing Rivers that a larger group might lead to a new outbreak of trouble. All the while, Richard presents himself as one only too ready to cooperate in carrying out the will of the others. All except Buckingham and Gloucester retire to discuss the proposal. The exchange between the two makes clear the fact that Richard has been letting Buckingham play the man of action and do the talking and that there is an arrangement for them "to part the Queen's proud kindred from the Prince." They set forth for Ludlow.

Three London citizens meet in a street and discuss the news of the king's death. Each has a clearly marked character. The first citizen is optimistic, almost buoyantly so. The second citizen is not so confident as he voices the traditional fear that change, particularly in matters relating to the state, is not usually for the better. He places his hope in the conviction that Edward IV's young son will be guided wisely by his counselors. The third citizen, however, is a thoroughgoing pessimist. He predicts "a troublesome world," especially because the new king is "in his nonage"—that is, his boyhood. When Henry VI, then a mere child, came to the throne, virtuous uncles were at hand to give him prudent counsel. Not so now, for "full of danger is the Duke of Gloucester," and "the Queen's sons and brothers [are] haughty and proud." In a series of sententious lines, he concludes that it is wise to fear the worst. All three, instructed to appear before the justices, depart together.

The archbishop announces that the party bringing the young prince will arrive within a day or so. This begins a conversation about the appearance of the prince, whom the mother, grandmother, and younger brother are anxious to see. The queen hopes that he has grown; his grandmother has heard, however, that the nine-year-old duke has almost overtaken him. The boy hopes this is not so, for his uncle Gloucester has told him that "small herbs have grace, great weeds do grow apace." The old duchess retorts that, since Richard grew slowly, if this were so he should be full of grace, about which she ironically expresses her doubts. The precocious boy remembers a story he has heard that Richard was born with all his teeth and must have grown fast since he could "gnaw a crust at two hours old," a biting jest indeed for a boy of nine! Since getting teeth early was also believed to be a sign of villainous disposition, the two women recognize the boy's shrewdness, and his mother rebukes him for being mischievous.

Dorset enters with the upsetting news that Lord Rivers, Lord Grey, and Sir Thomas Vaughan have all been sent to Pomfret Castle, imprisoned by the "mighty dukes" Gloucester and Buckingham. Dorset does not know what accusation had been brought against them. The queen, rightly seeing the downfall of her house, bemoans the tyranny that preys on the young king's innocence. The Duchess of York cries out against yet another indication of the dreadful war of blood against blood and self against self for the crown. The queen takes the boy to sanctuary, led by the Archbishop of York, who gives the Great Seal into her keeping.

Commentary

Conflict is, of course, the essence of drama. In Act I, Richard emerged ahead in his conflict with a society, indeed with the state itself. Now events occur that suggest that the odds have shifted. The ailing king appears to have quieted the quarreling factions, as the first two lines of Scene 1 make clear. This is a solemn occasion for all concerned, for England's king is on his deathbed. As Tudor political philosophy had it, the subject, whatever his rank, is to the ruler as is the child to his parent. Vows made to a king are especially sacred, thus the import of Edward's admonition beginning "Take heed you dally not before your king" (13–15). Note that both Rivers and Hastings are vehement in their avowals, and so the rest. But most eloquent is Buckingham, who had been held blameless by the rapacious Queen Margaret. Each has committed himself irrevocably, inviting God's punishment if the oath is violated.

The ethical significance of Clarence's death is now made crystal clear: Inexorable justice is operating once more. Practically all of the characters in Scene 1 deserve or will deserve divine punishment. And in this connection, note that the last two lines of King Edward's long reply to Derby are portentous: "O God, I fear thy justice will take hold / On me and you, and mine and yours for this!" How ironical are Richard's words addressed to Buckingham, spoken as they are by the one who is directly responsible for Clarence's death: "God will revenge it" (138).

Score another point for the villain-hero, that master dissembler who had intercepted the orders countermanding the execution of Clarence. So far from amity flourishing, the split is greater than before. The immediate point is that God's justice continues to be administered and Richard continues to function as His scourge. Significantly, it is Buckingham who has the final line. If we had any doubts heretofore, we now know that he has committed himself to serve Richard for his own purposes.

The first part of Scene 2 serves to point up the tragedy that has befallen the house of York. There is much that is formally ritualistic here, and the pronounced religious tone is evident enough. Thus one of Clarence's children, having been led to believe that King Edward was directly responsible for his father's death, says, "God will revenge it, whom I will importune / With earnest prayers all to that effect" (14–15). And Dorset, seeking to comfort his bereaved mother, Elizabeth, voices the orthodox views on Christian forbearance in the passage beginning "God is displeased / That you take with unthankfulness His doing" (89–95). In this way, the major theme is kept to the fore.

To some, it may seem that the Duchess of York takes a rather heartless attitude toward the death of Clarence when she explains that she laments "the sickness of the King," not the loss of her other son: "It were lost sorrow to wail one that's lost" (11). But this is consistent with Christian teaching, certainly with that which flourished in Shakespeare's England. Elsewhere in Shakespeare, one finds expression of the idea that life is a loan from God to be repaid when He demands it, and Dorset's speech addressed to Elizabeth repeats this idea. Undue grief for the dead was thought to imply a question of God's dealings with mortals. Moreover, Edward is not only the duchess' son: He is the king, and she is one of his subjects. What happens to Edward is a matter of public concern; the welfare of the state is involved. And, of course, all this adds to the religious tone.

Queen Elizabeth, "with her hair about her ears," is the very symbol of tormented grief. In Scene 2, her first speech provides a good example of highly mannered, rhetorical style. This is typical of early Shakespeare, reflecting the influence of Seneca—at least the Seneca of the popular stage. In this connection, note the sententious elements in her speech, as when she exclaims, "Why grow the branches when the root is gone? / Why wither not the leaves that want their sap?" (41–42). Senecan also is the exchange between the children and the two queen-mothers beginning "Ah for our father, for our dear lord Clarence!" (72–79). These lines provide an example of *stichomythia*.

Edward did not die a violent death, as did Clarence. Nevertheless, his death is part of the larger pattern: The grievous sinner cannot escape God's justice.

While tracing the dominant theme in *Richard III*, we must not ignore the skill with which Shakespeare delineates the character of Gloucester, who early and late holds the interest of all readers and members of an audience, whether or not they be interested in or concerned about the major theme of the play. Consistently this Machiavellian villain who rejects God gives us a good example of his cynical humor in his aside after his mother complies with his expressed wish that she give him her blessing.

The action continues to rise, and an element of suspense is introduced in Scene 2. Rivers urges Queen Elizabeth to see to it that her son be crowned as soon as possible. Obviously, the coronation would be a great setback for the ambitious Richard and might make it impossible for him to advance his evil fortunes. But Richard is never to be underestimated. He has taken steps to forestall the coronation and to remove the prince from the protection and influence of the queen's family. And Gloucester, who more than once has made reference to his simplicity and humility, grossly flatters his dupe, Buckingham, speaking of himself as a child willingly guided by this "oracle" and "prophet." At his level, let it be remembered, Buckingham is no less selfishly ambitious than Richard.

Scene 3, a short scene, allows for the necessary passage of time for the arrests of which we learn in Scene 4. But its chief importance is to emphasize the fact that (as in all Shakespeare's chronicle history plays) the state is the real protagonist in the larger sense, for it is the welfare of England, the well-being of all subjects, that is of first importance. When the sententious third citizen exclaims, "Woe to that land that's governed by a child," he is paraphrasing Ecclesiastes 10:16 ("Woe to thee, O land, when thy king is a child"). The text is voiced twice by Buckingham in Edward Hall's chronicle history of these events (1548) and had long since become proverbial. Note that the third citizen expresses the conviction that, if England is to suffer as a result of Edward IV's death, it deserves to suffer since all things are in God's hands (36–37). This constant reference to God is a tacit reminder that His justice always is operative, whatever the conditions may be, and particularly so with reference to the state. The "virtuous uncles" of Henry VI (21) were the Dukes of Bedford and Gloucester, who prosecuted the war against France. The commoners of England, it is clear, are aware of the bitter rivalries at court, rivalries that may lead to violence and destruction at this time of the succession. And they can only voice their hopes and fears and remain passively obedient.

The young Duke of York's instinctive dislike and distrust of his uncle is a prelude to the news that Gloucester has struck his first blow against the princes. Having seen to it that the queen's son and brother, as well as Sir Thomas Vaughan, constant and faithful attendant on young Edward from the new king's infancy, are imprisoned in Pomfret Castle, Richard now has all active power in his hands. That Pomfret should be the place of imprisonment is in itself especially ominous, for there Richard II and many others had met their deaths.

Scene 4 derives, at least ultimately, from More's account, in which it is stated that the archbishop had been roused "not long after midnight" by a messenger from Lord Hastings, who had reported that Gloucester and Buckingham had taken young Edward V, then on his way to London, from Stony Stratford back twelve miles to Northampton. It has been argued that "if the Archbishop knew that the young king had been carried back to Northampton, he must also have known that the lords who accompanied him were sent to prison." Long since it has been pointed out, however, that Shakespeare deviates from historical truth in order to attain dramatic effect. As Shakespeare dramatizes the event, one must assume that the news of the return to Northampton made the archbishop so apprehensive that he hurried to the queen bearing the

Great Seal, without which the highest acts of state could not be ratified formally.

Summary

A flourish of trumpets announces the arrival of the young prince, followed by Gloucester and Buckingham, Cardinal Bourchier, Catesby, and others. From the first the prince is melancholy. He wants (that is, lacks) "more uncles" to welcome him and is not convinced when Richard implies that they were false friends from whom he is better protected. The lord mayor, appropriately attended, enters and greets the uncrowned king. The youth responds courteously and then again complains about not seeing his mother and brother.

As the prince further complains about the absence of Hastings, that lord enters with the news that the queen has taken the young Duke of York into sanctuary, he knows not why. Buckingham tells Cardinal Bourchier to fetch the boy by force if necessary, but that dignitary objects to violating the "holy privilege." Buckingham overcomes the objections by reasoning that the law of sanctuary is not valid in such a "gross" age and that the boy is too young and innocent to need or ask for sanctuary in any case. The cardinal is easily convinced, and he sets out, accompanied by Hastings.

The prince asks his uncle where he will stay until the coronation. Richard advises him to resort to the Tower, the thought of which does not appeal to the prince. Since Julius Caesar was then credited with having built the Tower of London, the prince and Gloucester engage in a dialogue concerning Julius Caesar and the nature of reputation and fame.

Hastings and the cardinal return, bringing with them the young Duke of York, who, after greeting his brother and referring to his father's death, quickly takes the opportunity to flout his uncle. He refers to his own growth, trying to make Richard repeat the compromising speech about the young king's idleness referred to in the previous scene. He next begs a dagger from his uncle and jests about the possibility of Richard's giving him his sword. This sharp speech culminates in the boy's joking allusion to his uncle's crooked shoulders. Buckingham expresses admiration for the young duke's precocity, but Richard apparently ignores it. He urges Edward and his brother to leave for the Tower. Meanwhile, he will entreat Elizabeth, the queen-mother, to join them there. The duke demurs, saying that he will not sleep quiet in the place where his uncle Clarence had been murdered. Edward, however, says that he fears no uncles dead. And to Gloucester's "nor none that live, I hope," he retorts "and if they live, I hope I need not fear." His thoughts, obviously, are about Lord Rivers. The children go unhappily to the Tower.

Buckingham again comments on the wit of the young duke, suggesting that he may have been incited by his mother to taunt Richard. Richard's reply, "No doubt . . . he is all the mother's," brings out at once the contrast between the two children and Gloucester's deep hatred of the queen-mother and her faction. Buckingham calls Catesby over and takes the initiative in sounding him out as to the possibilities of winning Hastings over to their side. Catesby suggests that Hastings' great loyalty to Edward IV will keep him from doing anything against the prince and that Stanley will do whatever Hastings does. Buckingham sends him off to sound out Hastings and summon him to the Tower to join the counsel in discussing the coronation. It is Richard who gives Catesby the final order: "Shall we hear from you, Catesby, ere we sleep?"

After Catesby has left, Buckingham wonders what will be done with Hastings if he proves unwilling to go along with their plots. As if there were no possible question, Richard says, "Chop off his head," and reminds Buckingham to ask for the earldom of Hereford and related properties when Richard becomes king. Buckingham replies that he will indeed claim the promised reward, and the two retire to sup and arrange their plans.

Scene 2 begins with the arrival of a messenger at Lord Hastings' house at four o'clock in the morning. The messenger comes from Lord Stanley, who has had a premonitory dream about "the boar" that destroyed his helmet. Stanley is so disturbed that he wishes Hastings to flee with him to the north. Hastings scorns the advice and sends the messenger back. He knows of the two councils that are to be held, but since he will be in one and his servant Catesby in the other, there can be nothing to fear. Moreover, "To fly the boar before the boar pursues / Were to incense the boar to follow us / And make pursuit where he did mean no chase" (28–30). Stanley is instead to rise and go with him to the Tower. As the messenger leaves, Catesby enters and cunningly tests Hastings' loyalty by saying that things will never be right in the kingdom until Richard wears the crown. Hastings remains loyal to the young prince and does not waver in his devotion even when told that his enemies, members of the queen's family, have been put to death at Pomfret. Not even if his life were at stake would Hastings move to prevent the "true descent" of Edward IV's heirs. The wary Catesby, his mission accomplished, sanctimoniously approves Hastings' declaration of loyalty: "God keep your lordship in that gracious mind!" (56).

The confident Hastings now begins to boast of those he will get rid of within a fortnight, relying as he does on the favor of Richard and Buckingham. Catesby encourages this opinion, but his aside makes clear that Hastings has, as it were, pronounced sentence upon himself and that Richard and Buckingham will see to it that Hastings is put to death as a traitor.

Stanley appears, still uneasy, and Hastings reasserts his buoyant confidence. Stanley reminds him that the lords imprisoned at Pomfret had been no less sure of themselves. When he is told that those lords are to be beheaded, he again voices his fears, suggesting that those who are to die may be better men than some who have brought charges against them. When Catesby and Stanley leave, Hastings continues to express his complete confidence in an exchange with a pursuivant whom he had met earlier when on his way to be imprisoned in the Tower. A priest enters and greets him. Hastings thanks him, acknowledges indebtedness for the priest's service, and promises to reward him on the next Sabbath. Buckingham enters and remarks that, unlike his friends at Pomfret, Hastings has no need for a priest—that is, no urgent need for confession and absolution. Hastings replies that the thoughts of Rivers, Vaughan, and Grey had indeed come to his mind as he talked with the priest. He then asks whether Buckingham is going to the Tower. The latter's reply is sinister enough, although Hastings is unaware of the fact: "I do, my lord; but long I cannot stay there. / I shall return before your lordship thence" (120–21).

Scene 3 at Pomfret Castle concludes the story of the queen's relatives. Ratcliff, one of Richard's henchmen, enters leading Rivers, Grey, and Vaughan to death. Rivers protests that he is dying "For truth, for duty, and for loyalty." Grey thinks of the prince and prays that he may be kept safe from this pack of bloodsuckers. As Ratcliff hurries them, Rivers speaks again, remembering that Pomfret was the scene of Richard II's murder. Grey thinks of Margaret's curse, and Rivers recalls that she cursed Hastings, Buckingham, and Richard also. He prays in one breath that those curses will be fulfilled and in the next asks God to consider the blood about to be shed enough to save Elizabeth and the prince. Again enjoined by Ratcliff to hurry, they embrace each other and leave to meet their doom.

Scene 4 contains the meeting at the Tower to which Hastings and Stanley have been summoned to discuss the date of the coronation. The Bishop of Ely suggests the following day, but as Richard is not yet present they hesitate to decide without him. Cunningly, Buckingham asks who is most intimate with Richard. To the bishop's reply that he himself is, Buckingham answers ironically that, unlike faces, hearts remain unrevealed. He then calls upon Hastings, who, confident that he stands high in Gloucester's affections, offers to speak for him. At that very moment, Gloucester enters, and Buckingham is careful to let him know what Hastings had said.

For no apparent reason other than unusually high spirits, Richard begs the bishop to send for some fine strawberries Richard had seen in his garden. When the bishop leaves, Richard calls Buckingham aside to report that Hastings will never consent to oppose the coronation of the prince. The two leave the stage. Lord Stanley (called Derby in this scene) expresses the opinion that the coronation should be postponed until the next day. The bishop returns, looking about for Richard, and Hastings remarks that Gloucester "looks most cheerfully and smooth"; he is sure that Richard's face reveals the heart of a man who is offended with no one. As Stanley, still uneasy, prays that this is true, Gloucester and Buckingham return.

Richard's mood has changed completely. He demands to know what should be done with those who have planned his death by means of witchcraft. Hastings has the answer: They should be put to death. Drawing back his sleeve to show his withered arm, Richard blames the queen and Mistress Shore. "If they have done this deed, my noble lord—," Hastings begins. He is not allowed to finish. Gloucester seizes upon the conditional *If* and denounces him as the "protector of this damned strumpet," Jane Shore. Hastings further hears himself declared to be a traitor and sentenced to death. Lovel and Ratcliff are ordered to carry out the sentence.

Only Hastings and his executioners remain onstage. In his dying speech, Hastings laments the fate of England and regrets his own foolish confidence, his ignoring of ominous portents. Even his horse, clad in ceremonial dress and proceeding at a walking pace, had stumbled three times on its way to the Tower, as if unwilling to carry its master to his death. He remembers the priest, whom he now needs for himself, and the pursuivant who had listened to him gloat over the impending deaths of Rivers, Vaughan, and Grey. He remembers also Queen Margaret's curse.

Ratcliff abruptly orders him to hurry in order not to delay Gloucester's dinner. Lovel rudely interrupts his final musings on the vanity of man and the shortness of life. Prophesying "the fearfull'st time" for England and the same fate as his for those who smile at him today, Hastings is led off to the block.

Outside the Tower, Richard and Buckingham come in wearing battered, rusty armor. They are engaged in further deception, namely to pretend that they are in terror of an attack on their lives. Richard instructs Buckingham to speak breathlessly and turn pale, and Buckingham replies that he can counterfeit like an experienced actor. Then the lord mayor enters, brought by Catesby. It is now apparent that the act is put on for his benefit. And it is a good act. The mayor witnesses an excited Richard rushing about as he gives incisive orders for defense against enemies who apparently are about to enter. Buckingham plays his role well enough as he exclaims, "God and our innocency defend and guard us!" (20). And then Ratcliff and Lovel—"friends"—enter with Hastings' head.

Richard protests his unsuspecting love for Hastings and talks of having confided in him and of being convinced of his innocence in other things since he frankly acknowledged his relations with Jane Shore. Richard and Buckingham convince the lord mayor that Hastings had plotted to murder the two of them that day and that only this extreme peril forced them to execute him before the lord mayor arrived. Gloucester is careful to point out that the "peace of England," as well as their own lives, was involved. Even after the mayor wholly agrees that Hastings fully deserved death, Richard protests that Lovel and Ratcliff had carried out his intentions too hastily, for he would have liked the lord mayor to hear the traitor's confession so that he, in turn, could reassure the citizens who might misinterpret Richard's action. After further assurances on both sides, the mayor leaves and Gloucester instructs Buckingham to follow and talk to the citizens at an advantageous moment. He is to imply that Edward IV's children are illegitimate, making the most of the late king's alleged notoriety in matters relating to sex. Further, Buckingham is to suggest that Edward himself was illegitimate. But the latter charge is to be handled skillfully since Edward's mother survives. Buckingham promises to do his work as well as if he were to gain the crown for himself. Thus having taken the necessary steps to prepare the populace to look on himself as the only true heir to the throne, Richard dispatches Lovel to a priest, Doctor Shaw, and Catesby to Friar Penker; both churchmen are to meet him at Baynard's Castle within the hour. Then he leaves to put Clarence's children out of sight so that no one will have access to them.

In the very brief Scene 6, a scrivener reads the indictment of Hastings which he has just copied so that it may be given a public reading at St. Paul's Cathedral without delay. It had taken him eleven hours to copy the original draft, which must have taken quite as long to prepare. Yet Hastings was executed only five hours ago. Obviously the whole proceeding is unjust. But the scribe departs, commenting that anyone with sense enough to see what is going on must also have sense enough to keep quiet about it.

Buckingham, returned from haranguing the mob, meets Richard at Baynard's Castle, as had been arranged. Richard asks at once about the reactions of the London citizens. Buckingham reports that they were silent and goes on to describe his own recital of Edward's engagements to Lady Lucy and the sister-in-law of the King of France before his marriage. He contrasted Edward's dissimilarity to their father and Richard's likeness and went on to dwell upon Richard's "discipline in war, wisdom in peace; . . . bounty, virtue, fair humility." When they said nothing, he asked the mayor the cause of their silence. The mayor explained that they were used to being spoken to on public matters only by the recorder, the chief legal authority of the City of London. At Buckingham's insistence, the recorder did report Buckingham's argument but took care to indicate that he was not speaking for himself. When he had finished, ten of Buckingham's paid followers cried, "God save King Richard!" Taking advantage of this, the duke thanked the multitude for their applause, complimented them on their wisdom, and came away. Buckingham explains that the mayor is coming and advises Richard to pretend to be afraid and to answer only after much urging. Richard is to retreat with two churchmen, while Buckingham makes out a case for his holiness. Above all, Richard is to appear most reluctant when he is requested to accept the crown. As a knock at the door is heard, Gloucester goes up the "leads" (the flat roof top) to prepare himself for his latest and perhaps most challenging role.

The mayor and the citizens enter, followed by Catesby, who tells them that Richard, "divinely bent to meditation," is in the company of "two right reverend fathers" and begs them to return tomorrow or the next day thereafter. Buckingham then directs Catesby to plead with Richard to come and talk with them. While Catesby is gone, the duke takes the opportunity to point up the contrast of Richard's holy occupation with the late king's self-indulgence. He concludes with apparent fear that Richard will not accept the kingship. "Marry, God defend his Grace should say us nay!" exclaims the mayor. Catesby comes back with the timely message that Richard is apprehensive as to the reason for the delegation that waits upon him. Again Catesby departs to convey Buckingham's reassurance. Just as the duke finishes a comment on the religiosity of men like Richard, the lord protector himself appears above, standing between two clergyman—"Two props of virtue for a Christian prince," as Buckingham is quick to point out. The duke implores Richard to pardon them for interrupting him in his holy devotions and to listen to their request. The soul of humility, Richard protests that it is he who is at fault for neglecting his friends. Or, he continues, he may have been guilty unwittingly of greater offense. Buckingham follows this cue: Richard's fault is his failure to rescue the country by becoming king at this time of crisis.

In a nicely contrived refusal, Gloucester protests that he would turn away in reproof except that they might misinterpret his action as "Tongue-tied ambition." He argues that, even though he were to receive the crown as his due, he does not consider himself to be worthy of such greatness; fortunately the young prince, who merits the crown, will receive it in due course. According to Buckingham, this nicety of conscience shows his integrity. But, he points out, the prince cannot be the real heir since Edward married his mother when she was a widow and Edward himself betrothed successively to Lady Lucy and to Bona, sister of the King of France. Thus, only by courtesy is young Edward called the prince; it is Richard's duty to save the kingship from an impure line. The mayor, Buckingham once more, Catesby—all plead with him, but again Richard refuses. Buckingham lauds him for the compassion and nobility that cause him to refuse but points out that they will not accept the prince in any case, so that Richard's refusal would mean the downfall of the house of York. "Come, citizens," he concludes. "'Zounds! we'll entreat no more." Gloucester greets this with a pious injunction against swearing. When Catesby and one of the citizens urge him to call them back and accept, he does so sorrowfully.

Richard is at pains to make clear that he is accepting the burden on their entreaty, though to do so goes against his conscience. All have returned to the stage now, and Richard tells them that they must shoulder the blame if he does not fulfill his office well since they urged him to it. Buckingham salutes him with the title of king and promptly suggests that the coronation take place the very next day. "Even when you please," says Richard, "since you will have it so." The arrangements having been concluded, they depart. And Richard returns to his "holy meditations."

Commentary

In Scene 1, we witness the always energetic Gloucester preparing for the removal of obstacles in his quest for the crown. The chief obstacles are, of course, the uncrowned boy, King Edward, and his brother, the Duke of York. But there are also Lords Stanley and Hastings to be considered, and they must be dealt with. Richard is nothing if not the capable executive. He leaves to the well-schooled Buckingham the task of making suggestions and arguments so that Richard himself usually appears as one seeking to be helpful and cooperative. Buckingham provides an interesting contrast to Catesby, who also serves Richard. Catesby awaits only instruction to carry out an order without question; he requires no special handling. But Buckingham is vain of his talents and responds readily to Gloucester's flattery, as when he is called "my thoughts' sovereignty"—king of my thoughts (2). He possesses considerable political ability and the powers of subtle contrivance. Sophistry characterizes his words to young Edward beginning "Sweet prince, the untainted virtue of your years / Hath not yet dived into the world's deceit" (7–15) and his reply to the cardinal, whom he finds to be "too senseless-obstinate, / Too ceremonious and traditional" (44–56). In pursuit of his own goal, he is not troubled much by conscience.

When Richard informs him that, if Hastings does not prove pliable his head must be chopped off, Buckingham thinks only of the promised reward: the earldom of Hereford, together with all "movables" (goods) that had been confiscated by King Edward IV.

Of interest also are the contrasting characters of the two royal brothers. Edward is grave, thoughtful, conscious already of his responsibilities; thus his rebuke to the Duke of York: "A beggar, brother?" (112). The ironic dialogue about Julius Caesar and the nature of fame leads him to express his own ambition to win renown: "I'll win our ancient right in France again" (92). The implication is that, if he be permitted to survive and to rule England, internecine conflict would no longer occur; rather, the ruler would win fame in fighting a foreign enemy. In the polemical literature of the age, the horrors of civil war were frequently contrasted with the glory to be won in a conflict legitimately waged against the country's foe. Tacitly suggested also is that Edward's villainous uncle will achieve not fame but infamy in the annals of history.

The Duke of York is a "perilous boy" (154)—that is, dangerously cunning from the points of view of Buckingham and Richard. He is "bold, quick, ingenious, forward, capable [intelligent]." Like his royal brother, he is deeply suspicious of his uncle Gloucester. Indeed, his instinctive dislike and distrust, established in the previous scene, is emphasized here. When he asks for his uncle's dagger, he means much more than that involved in a natural request made by a pert, forward lad; he intimates that Gloucester should be rendered harmless by being disarmed. Farther along in the dialogue he wittily alludes to Richard's deformity and tacitly calls him a fool. This is introduced with the play upon the word *bear* (127): "Because that I am little, like an ape, / He thinks that you should bear me on your shoulders" (130–31). In Buckingham's words, "With what a sharp-provided wit he reasons!"

In Scene 1, Shakespeare arouses the tragic emotions of pity and fear for the boy king and his brother. He does so particularly by means of the double meanings typically found in Richard's discourse, as when he says, "A greater gift I'll give my cousin" (115), and in his ominous asides: "So wise so young, they say, do not live long" (79) and "Short summers lightly have a forward spring" (94). Furthermore, established here are the probable positions of Hastings and Stanley.

The doctrinal element is not absent from Scene 1. That Bucking-ham, actually the voice of Richard, should reject the concept of sanctuary as a "holy privilege" and that Edward V is not to Richard a "dread sovereign" underscore the fact that the sins involved are sins against religion, against God—sins that invite His inexorable justice. For in accordance with politico-religious thinking in the Age of Eliz-abeth, the sovereign was indeed to be dreaded—to be held in awe or "feared" in the biblical sense. Again let it be remembered that the ruler was accepted as God's lieutenant on earth by the orthodox.

In *Romeo and Juliet*, the romantic tragedy that dates some two years later than *Richard III*, Shakespeare assigns these lines to Romeo near the end of the play: "How oft when men are at the point of death / Have they been merry! Which their keepers call / A light-ening before death" (V. iii. 88–90). "A lightening before death"— that is the theme of Scene 2, in which Hastings is the chief character. He remains merry and confident, unperturbed by the report of Stanley's ominous dream of the boar that razed the helmet. Since Gloucester's crest is the boar, the interpretation of this dream poses no problem: Those who stand in Richard's way invite death.

Shakespeare follows Holinshed in identifying Catesby as one of Hastings' servingmen. But already we have learned that Catesby had become dedicated to Richard, whose most recent orders he is now carrying out. As far as Hastings is concerned, the concept of tragedy in this scene is medieval. He is at the top of Fortune's wheel, supremely confident of his own well-being and future. Stanley's dream, the ironical comments and the aside of Catesby, the appear-ance of the priest, and Buckingham's sinister remarks—all are either ignored or misunderstood by Hastings. But they indicate that Fortune's wheel is about to turn once more. He seems to invite disaster when he gloats over the thought of the impending execu-tions of Rivers, Vaughan, and Grey, as well as to predict the down-fall of others. Nevertheless, in his unshakable loyalty to Edward IV and to Edward's heir, he appears to be an exemplum of righteous-ness. By implication, at least, Catesby acknowledges as much when he says, "God keep your lordship in that gracious [holy] mind." Catesby, who is in the process of violating his trust to his master, is not moved by such graciousness. Then why, one may ask, should Hastings be marked for death? The answer is that, as an active adherent to the Yorkist cause, he also is guilty. Recall that Queen

Margaret had identified him as one of the "standers-by" when her son had been "stabbed with bloody daggers" (I. iii. 210–12). All this, therefore, is part of the fulfillment of the curse upon the house of York.

In Scene 3, the careful reader may be surprised to find Ratcliff at Pomfret, which is in Yorkshire, since he appears at the Tower of London in the next scene. Obviously Shakespeare trusted to the imagination of his audience rather than to their geographical knowledge. This, to be sure, is a minor point. There are two major ones to be made. First, it is again made clear that the dethronement and murder of Richard II, a lawful, anointed king, started all these bloody events, for that was the prime action that invited vengeance upon the guilty members of the houses of Lancaster and York. Second, Gloucester, arch-villain though he is, continues to be the immediate instrument of divine justice. Grey acknowledges his own guilt and that of Rivers and Vaughan: All three had been accessories to the murder of Queen Margaret's son.

In Scene 4, Buckingham's reply to the Bishop of Ely's questions ("Who knows the Lord Protector's mind herein? / Who is most inward with the royal Duke?") sums up the whole extent of Buckingham's deception of others and of Richard's deception of him. It is, then, a prime example of irony in a scene packed with irony.

Richard's superior cunning, no less than his heartlessness, again is dramatized in Scene 4. With what skill he first presents himself plausibly as the man of good will. "I have been a sleeper," he explains to the "noble lords and cousins" assembled in the Tower (24). Richard a sleeper—he who continues to reveal himself as the most energetic character in the play! The apparently irrelevant bit relating to the strawberries in the bishop's garden, the details of which appear in More's account and in Holinshed, serves Shakespeare's purpose in this connection, for it shows Richard displaying affability and good humor, a careless ease in the midst of his crimes. Little wonder that Lord Hastings should be deceived completely. Hazlitt found Hastings' belief that "with no man here he [Richard] is offended" (58) to be one of the "finest strokes in the play," showing as it does "the deep, plausible manners of Richard." One conclusion to be drawn is that Hastings is not to be dismissed as incredibly naive, even if he is not wary as is Stanley. He is one of those individuals who, to borrow a line from another Shakespearean play, "believe men honest who but seem so." In no circumstance must one under-estimate Gloucester's skill as a dissembler.

After Edward IV's death, Jane Shore had become Hastings' mis-tress. It will be recalled that Richard had told Catesby to inform Hastings that his "dangerous adversaries" were to be executed and to bid him "give Mistress Shore one gentle kiss the more" (III. i. 185). The attractive daughter of a London goldsmith had indeed been accused of witchcraft, and Hastings' relations with her therefore worked to Richard's advantage. Shakespeare's audiences would not have considered the accusation to be absurd. Although skepticism was widespread, most Elizabethans firmly believed that witches existed and practiced their evil craft.

It need hardly be pointed out again that Richard functions as God's scourge, for Hastings also was guilty of heinous crime: He was among those who "stood by" when young Edward of Lancaster was stabbed at Tewkesbury. But Richard remains the most grievous sinner. In this instance, he takes vengeance into his own hands. Despite his title of lord protector, he has no right to act without due process of law; he makes use of a trumped-up charge.

Sir Richard Ratcliff and Lord William Lovel, whom we meet in Scene 4, survived to join Catesby as Richard's most confidential ministers during the usurper's short reign. The following lines were affixed to the door of St. Paul's Cathedral on July 18, 1484, at the instigation of William Colyngburne: "The Cat, the Rat, and Lord our dog / Ruleth all England under a Hog." Lovel became the king's chamberlain; Catesby, speaker in Parliament in 1484; and Ratcliff, sheriff of Westmorland. The last named was probably closest to Richard, as his role in this play suggests.

In his next-to-last speech in Scene 4 (98–103), Hastings moral-izes in a completely medieval manner. He pictures himself as one among the many who thoughtlessly sought the "momentary grace of mortal men" rather than "the grace of God." Such reflections are typical of those expressed by the tragic figures in Boccaccio's *De Casibus Virorum Illustrium* and its progeny, including the Elizabe-than *Mirror for Magistrates*, which is recognized as one of the sources for Shakespeare's *Richard III*.

In Scene 5, Shakespeare prepares for the scene in which Gloucester is offered the crown. Not without significance is the fact that it reveals a wary Richard who does not take into his confidence

Buckingham, the man whom he had called his "other self," his "oracle" and "prophet," his "thoughts' sovereign."

The stage direction, "Enter Gloucester and Buckingham, in rotten armor, marvellously ill-favored," derives from the First Folio (1623). It follows More's account: "And at their coming, himself [Richard] with the Duke of Buckingham stood harnessed in old ill faring briganders [body armor for foot soldiers], such as no man should when that they would vouchsafe to put on their backs except that some sudden necessity had constrained them." Obviously the two have dressed themselves appropriately for the roles they are about to play for the benefit of the Lord Mayor of London—that is, to make him believe that their concern is for the safety of the state.

At the beginning of Scene 5, we find Gloucester schooling Buckingham in the devices and methods of the Machiavellian villain. And Buckingham proves to be an apt pupil. His first speech (5–11) incorporates an interesting bit of dramatic criticism, a commentary on "ham" acting. This play is sufficiently melodramatic, one that lends itself to the rhetorical school of acting with all its excesses. But Shakespeare tells us thus early in his career that he recognizes such acting for what it is. It should be recalled that he himself was an actor as well as a playwright. The student will find relevant a more famous expression of dramatic criticism written by the mature Shakespeare in *Hamlet*, III. ii. 1–40.

The lord mayor was Sir Edmund Shaw (or Shaa), who had been elected in 1482. History reports that he indeed took an active part in influencing the succession of the crown on the death of Edward IV. The grateful Richard later made him a privy councilor. Doctor Shaw, whom Gloucester sends for at the end of the scene, was the lord mayor's brother. He was chosen by Richard to preach a sermon at St. Paul's Cross on June 22, 1483, wherein he impugned the validity of Edward IV's marriage to Elizabeth Woodville and even asserted that Edward and Clarence were bastards. More states that both Shaw and Friar Penker were great preachers but adds that both were "of more learning than virtue, of more fame than learning." He further states that the brothers Shaw were taken into the confidence of Richard and Buckingham after Hastings' death.

Although the audience already is fully aware of why Hastings has been rushed to his death, Shakespeare chose to emphasize the complete illegality of Richard's action. He does so in Scene 6 by introducing the professional writer of legal documents with his non-dramatic but pointed speech. Like the lengthy exchange between Clarence and his murderers (I. iv.), the scene underscores the fact that the Shakespeare of *Richard III* was especially interested in the theme of revenge and develops it from more than one point of view. Further, the scrivener gives expression to what one critic has called "the smothered feeling of indignation that boils in men's minds under a tyrannical dynasty." Recall how Shakespeare had used the three London citizens for a comparable purpose in Act II, Scene 3.

It may be argued that Scene 7, the final scene of Act III, is quite as contrived as is the scene in which Richard woos and wins Lady Anne (I. ii.), but in its way it is no less entertaining and theatrically effective. The element of suspense is first introduced. We learn that Buckingham has followed his directions to the letter but that there is little evidence of popular support for Richard, who inveighs against the citizens, calling them "tongueless blockheads." Yet this apparent setback is really a challenge that, ably assisted by Buckingham and Catesby, he meets successfully. He succeeds in making the mayor and his group believe that the office seeks the man, not the man the office, and that they must assume responsibility accordingly. The arrival of the mayor and others and the dramatic appearance of Richard aloft, standing between two bishops, provide first-rate spectacle.

Much already has been said about Richard's superior intellect and cunning; his entire performance in this scene substantiates all that. But Buckingham's accomplishments must not be ignored. As a matter of fact, they add to those of Gloucester, who picked and schooled him in the art of dissembling. Here Buckingham proves himself capable enough to coach his master on how to present himself to the lord mayor and the citizens. The duke has even picked up Richard's trick of using pious oaths, as when he swears "by the holy mother of our Lord" (2), which, in context, is deeply ironical.

Once more much is made of the allegation that Edward IV's heirs are not legitimate. Lady Elizabeth Lucy had been one of the king's mistresses, but there is no record of a betrothal despite Buckingham's assertion that the Duchess of York had been a witness to such a ceremony (180). But all chroniclers agree that Edward was secretly married to Elizabeth Woodville when the Earl of Warwick had already succeeded in obtaining King Louis of France's consent to the marriage of the Lady Bona. These events are dramatized in *Henry VI, Part 3*, Act III, Scene 3. In accordance with canon law that prevailed before the Reformation, Edward could not have married Elizabeth Woodville legally. But, of course, Edward remained in England and may not have had news of Warwick's action. More telling is the accusation of "loathed bigamy" (189). Bigamy, defined as either marrying two virgins successively or once marrying a widow, had been declared unlawful and infamous by canon law in the thirteenth century. The reader will recall, however, that Lady Anne was a widow when Richard wooed her. The essential point is that Buckingham marshals every possible argument in an attempt to prove that Richard is the rightful heir to the throne.

It should be understood that when he salutes Richard as "England's royal king" (240), he is using the term *royal* in a very special sense well understood by Shakespeare's generation. It meant that Richard was not merely royal in rank, having been chosen king, but royal in descent. Essential to Richard's purpose is that he be accepted as a lawful king, not as a usurper.

ACT IV

Summary

This act opens with a gathering of those whom Richard has wronged and who will suffer far more acutely in the future. Queen Elizabeth, the old Duchess of York, and Dorset enter from one side. They are on their way to visit the princes in the Tower. At the same moment, Richard's wife, Anne, Duchess of Gloucester, comes in leading Clarence's young daughter, Lady Margaret Plantagenet. They are also on their way to the Tower.

As they exchange greetings and make their errands known to one another, Brakenbury enters. Queen Elizabeth immediately asks how the princes are. He replies that they are well but that the king has ordered that they are to have no visitors. The reference to "the King" appalls Elizabeth, and she demands an explanation. Brakenbury begs her pardon and says that he means the lord protector. The women are now thoroughly alarmed, and each protests that she has special right to see the children. But Brakenbury insists that he cannot violate his oath.

The Earl of Derby (Stanley) enters and greets the Duchess of York as "the looker on of two fair queens," meaning, of course, Elizabeth and Anne. He has come to escort Anne to Westminster for the coronation. Both women express utter horror at the news. When Dorset tries to comfort his mother, she immediately thinks of his danger and commands him to join Richmond in Brittany. Stanley, stepfather to Richmond (to whom he refers as his son), strongly approves of her counsel. The old duchess curses the womb that brought forth Richard.

Stanley urges Lady Anne to hurry. She replies that she would rather be tortured by the ancient method of encircling her brow with red hot steel than be crowned queen. Elizabeth, so far from being offended at Anne, voices words of commiseration. Anne recalls how she had denounced Richard for making her a widow and had uttered a curse on the woman who married him. Now she realizes that she is the victim of her own curse, for she has not known a moment's rest since her marriage because of Richard's "timorous" dreams. She fears that Richard will do away with her. With grief and foreboding, the women part, the old duchess wishing for the grave and Queen Elizabeth remaining behind to look back at the rough outline of the Tower. She prays that it will use her young children well, knowing perhaps too well that her entreaty to the stones is useless.

In Scene 2, the climax of the play has been reached. Richard now wears the coveted crown. He enters the palace in pomp, acknowledges Buckingham, his right-hand man, and tries the duke's loyalty to the utmost by inciting him to arrange for the immediate murder of the little princes. The wary Buckingham does not pick up Richard's indirect suggestion, and the newly crowned king is forced to speak openly: He wishes the "bastards" dead. Now Buckingham's reply is circumspect, and when Richard taunts him, he asks leave to consider. Angry, Richard rails against Buckingham, saying he will speak only to unfeeling and thoughtless boys hereafter. He calls a page over to ask if he knows of anyone who would do murder for money. The page suggests one Tyrrel for whom "gold were as good as orators to tempt." While the page goes to get Tyrrel, the king resolves to confide no more in Buckingham.

Stanley enters with the news that Dorset has fled to Richmond. Without appearing to have heard, Richard orders Catesby to spread the rumor abroad that his wife Anne is ill and likely to die. He will make certain that she sees no one. Meanwhile he must find some commoner to marry and dispose of Clarence's daughter; Clarence's son poses no problem since he is weak-minded. Richard knows that to murder the princes and then to marry their sister Elizabeth, as he hopes to do, involves great risks: "Uncertain way of gain! But I am in / So far in blood that sin will pluck on sin" (64–65). Stanley, who had moved to one side, did not hear a word of this heartless speech.

Tyrrel enters and arrangements are made to dispose of the princes, whom Richard describes as foes to his rest and his "sweet sleep's disturbers." Buckingham, having considered the king's suggestion about murdering the children, returns. Richard ignores him and talks to Stanley, warning him to take care since Richmond is his stepson. The duke interrupts with a request for the rewards he has been promised, especially the earldom of Hereford. The king continues to ignore him. He recalls a prophecy of Henry VI that Richmond would be king and another made by an Irish bard that Richard himself would not live long after he saw Richmond. As Buckingham again interrupts, Richard asks the time and sarcastically compares the duke to the "Jack" on a clock, a mechanical figure that appears to strike the hour—in just such a way does Buckingham keep begging and interrupting Richard's thoughts. Left alone on the stage, the duke now fully understands his position. Recalling the fate of Hastings, he resolves to flee to his manor at Brecknock without his rewards but at least with his head.

In soliloquy in Scene 3, Tyrrel describes the murder of the children, which has taken place offstage. He is shaken with horror at the very thought of the bloody deed; even the underlings he had hired to do the actual killing melted with compassion. As he retells the story Dighton and Forrest had told him, he describes for the audience the children, sleeping in each other's arms, a prayer book lying on their pillow. For a moment, Forrest became conscience-stricken, but he recovered himself to join Dighton in smothering the innocent children. Now the latter is conscience-stricken and filled with remorse as he brings his report to the "bloody King."

Richard is pleased to learn that the princes are dead and buried. He instructs Tyrrel to see him after supper and give him all the details and receive the promised reward. As Tyrrel goes out, Richard summarizes his accomplishments: Clarence's son is in prison, his daughter "meanly . . . matched" in marriage, the princes are dead, Anne has "bid the world goodnight." And now, since Richmond wants to marry young Elizabeth, daughter of Edward IV, Richard must carry out his plan to marry her first. He is about to leave and to present himself to her as a "jolly thriving wooer" when Ratcliff enters.

Now the mood changes for Richard. Ratcliff brings the disquieting news that Ely has fled to Richmond and that Buckingham is gathering forces in Wales. The king is more distressed to hear of Ely's withdrawal. The news, however, instead of crushing him, fills him with a zest for battle. Urging speed, he goes off to muster men for the fight.

The first part of Scene 4, a long lament, opens appropriately with old Queen Margaret saying that she has lurked about and watched the waning of her adversaries. She is going to withdraw to France, confident that everything will continue as badly as it has begun. Queen Elizabeth enters with the Duchess of York, weeping for her children. Margaret declares that the loss is a deserved one since Edward IV, the children's father, had been a principal in the murder of Margaret's son Edward. When Elizabeth asks her when she could sleep when the little princes had been put to death, Margaret replies bitterly: "When holy Harry died, and my sweet son." The duchess, overcome with her own woes, sits down on the ground that has been "made drunk with innocent blood." Elizabeth wishes that the earth would open up and offer her a grave as easily as it offers her a seat.

Queen Margaret joins them, insisting that her sorrows have precedence since they are the oldest. She begins a long recital of their joint woes, identifying Richard III as the author. The Duchess of York interrupts to accuse Margaret of being responsible for the deaths of her husband (Richard, Duke of York) and Rutland, one of her sons. Margaret continues, insisting that the deaths of Edward IV, the young princes, and Clarence were debts paid for crimes committed against the house of Lancaster. So died the "beholders of this tragic play," Hastings, Rivers, Vaughan, and Grey—yet Richard, "Hell's black intelligencer," still lives. She utters a prayer that she may yet survive to say "The dog is dead."

Elizabeth recalls Margaret's prophecy that the time would come when she would ask for Margaret's help in cursing Richard, "That bottl'd spider, that foul bunch-back'd toad!" Margaret reminds her of what she had said at greater length about Elizabeth. She compares Elizabeth to a flag borne by a standard-bearer that attracts all shots: "Where is thy husband now? Where be thy brothers? / Where be thy two sons? Wherein dost thou joy? / Who sues, and kneels, and says, 'God save the Queen'?" (92–94). Just as Elizabeth once usurped her place as queen, so now she usurps a just share of Margaret's sorrow. When she is about to leave after this tirade, Elizabeth asks her to stay and teach her how to curse. Margaret gives her a grim recipe, and, on further urging, points out that woe will teach Elizabeth what she wants to know. Finally she leaves. The duchess asks why calamity should be so full of words. Elizabeth describes them as "Windy attorneys to their client woes" which "Help nothing else, yet do they ease the heart." The duchess urges Elizabeth to accompany her and smother Richard in the breath of bitter words since he had smothered Elizabeth's children. At this point, the king himself enters, marching, with drums and trumpets.

Richard asks who intercepts his march, whereupon the duchess and Elizabeth attack him for his wrongs. He threatens to drown his mother's words in a flourish of trumpets unless she speaks fair of him. When he shows his impatience, she states that she can think of no single hour, from his birth onward, when he has not been a source of trouble to her. She warns him that, though this is their last meeting, she leaves him with a "heavy curse": "Bloody thou art, bloody will be thy end." Elizabeth voices her amen to all that the duchess has said, but Richard nevertheless detains her.

When Elizabeth states that she has no more sons for Richard to murder and that her daughters will be "praying nuns, not weeping queens," the king begins his suit for the hand of her daughter Elizabeth, whom he praises as "Virtuous and fair, royal and gracious." Understandably, the queen-mother wonders what new torture Richard has in store for her, and she is provoked into a violent harangue against him. He protests that he means to do her good—he will marry her daughter if she will only forget past grievances and give her consent. Elizabeth is horrified. When he asks how to go about winning the young lady, she bitterly suggests that he has done everything calculated to win a girl's heart—murdered her brothers, her aunt (Anne), her uncles (Clarence and Rivers). Making use of all of his persuasive powers, the king claims that what is done cannot be undone; he will make up for the loss of the princes, her children, by making her daughter the mother of kings and herself the happy grandmother. Elizabeth obviously is moved by the proposal and agrees to let him know her daughter's mind shortly. This jolly, thriving wooer asks her to bear to the girl his "true love's kiss." Once she has left, however, he refers to Elizabeth with amusement: "Relenting fool, and shallow, changing woman!"

Ratcliff and Catesby come with the news that Richmond, with a powerful navy, is off the coast of Wales waiting for Buckingham's support. Richard orders Catesby to go immediately to the Duke of Norfolk, and Ratcliff to leave for Salisbury. Not until he has upbraided Catesby for delaying does he become aware of the fact that he had neglected to give instructions. Norfolk is to be told to raise the greatest possible "strength and power" and to meet Richard at Salisbury.

Lord Stanley (Derby) enters with the news that Richmond, aroused by Dorset, Buckingham, and Ely, "makes for England, there to claim the crown." Richard asks why should this be since the royal throne is occupied and no other heir of York survives. He accuses Stanley of planning to rebel against him and fly to his enemies. Stanley protests that he is loyal to Richard and promises to bring his forces down from the north. But the king still does not trust him; he insists that Stanley leave his son George as assurance of his loyalty.

As Stanley leaves, messengers enter successively with news of the revolt of Courtney and the Bishop of Exeter in Devonshire, and of the Guildfords in Kent—that is, risings in the southeast and southwest parts of the kingdom. Furious, Richard strikes the third messenger before he has a chance to speak and then learns that this time the news is good: Buckingham's forces have been dispersed by flood. Still another messenger reports that Sir Thomas Lovel and Dorset head a force in Yorkshire to the north. But this bad news for Richard is offset by the report that Richmond, his fleet broken up by a tempest and mistrusting those on shore who said they came from Buckingham, has hoisted sail and made for Brittany.

Catesby comes in to say that Buckingham has been captured but that Richmond had landed with a "mighty power" at Milford. "Away for Salisbury!" exclaims Richard. There is no time to reason: "A royal battle might be won and lost." His final order is that Buckingham be brought to Salisbury.

Derby (Lord Stanley) sends Sir Christopher Urswick to his step-son Richmond with the message that his son George is held captive. For fear of causing his son's death, Derby cannot send aid to Richmond immediately. He learns that Richmond now is in Wales. Supporting the claimant to the throne are many "of noble fame and worth." They are headed for London. Derby finally instructs Sir Christopher to tell Richmond that the Queen-Mother Elizabeth heartily has given her consent to the marriage of Richmond and her daughter.

Commentary

Scene 1 is important chiefly because we get the first hint of a possible turn of events that could lead to Gloucester's downfall. Queen Elizabeth says to Dorset, her son, "If thou wilt outslip death, go cross the seas, / And live with Richmond, from the reach of hell" (42–43). This is the first mention of Henry Tudor, Earl of Richmond. Since Shakespeare was dramatizing history, his audiences knew that Richmond would emerge as Richard's nemesis.

It is not without interest that Stanley, who had married the widow of Owen Tudor and is thus Richmond's stepfather, should endorse Elizabeth's advice so emphatically, although it is he who came to escort Anne to Westminster, where Richard is to be crowned King of England. His behavior here is quite consistent with what history tells us about the Stanleys. They flourished during the entire period of the Wars of the Roses by shifting loyalties when events seemed so to dictate to their advantage.

A turning point in the action is indicated also by the report of Richard's "timorous dreams." Here Shakespeare remained quite faithful to his sources. More reported that Gloucester was "sore weaned with care and watch, rather slumbered than slept, troubled with fearful dreams," and that he would sometimes leap out of bed and run about the chamber. Now, since Richard has been established as a Machiavellian villain devoid of conscience, some explanation is called for. It may be argued that conscience does not bother Richard at all but rather fear for his own life as he wades through blood on his journey to the crown. Or perhaps critic Stopford Brooke had the right answer: "Shakespeare, with his belief that in the far background of an evil nature the soul lives, but unknown, unbelieved in by its possessor, shows how it awakens at night when the will sleeps, and does its work on the unconscious man. Then, and only then, conscience stirs Richard. Then, and then only, fear besets him." What is most important is that Richard is suffering the unquiet mind. God's justice now is reaching out to him; his doom has begun even before he wears the coveted crown.

Never does Shakespeare let us forget the dominant theme of the play. Anne, who recalls how she had implored God that Richard's wife be made to suffer, again invites divine vengeance on herself when she exclaims, "Anointed let me be with deadly venom, / And die ere men can say 'God save the Queen'" (62–63).

Certain other points of lesser significance in Scene 1 require comment. Note the ritualistic quality of the duchess' farewell addressed successively to Dorset, Anne, and Elizabeth (92–94)— further evidence that the language is highly rhetorical throughout this play. Queen Elizabeth's outburst beginning "Oh, cut my lace in sunder" (34–36) has been cited as an example of sheer rant. But in Tudor England, the husks or corsets worn by fashionable women so tightly controlled their figures that one can understand the queen's need for drastic relief in this moment of great emotion.

When Anne refers to herself as having been made "so young, so old a widow" (73), she means that she had been made old in sorrow. The Duchess of York, indeed an elderly lady, makes reference to her "eighty odd years" (97). Had her husband lived he would have been just seventy-three; the duchess actually was sixty-eight. Shakespeare purposely exaggerated her age as one means of showing how utterly devoid of virtue Richard was. Reverence for age, particularly for an aged parent, was an essential part of Elizabethan order. At the family level, as at the political level, Gloucester destroys order.

In the climactic Scene 2, wherein Richard enters in state amid the sounding of trumpets, preparation is made for the murder of the little princes, the death of Anne, and the plan for Richard to marry his niece, Elizabeth of York. Even more important is the fact that the newly crowned Richard definitely begins his descent on Fortune's wheel. Crediting Buckingham for making possible this advancement to the throne, the king asks, "But shall we wear these glories for a day? / Or shall they last, and we rejoice in them?" (5–6). Anne's account of his "timorous dreams" told us that now Richard was a man beset with fears. Like Macbeth, he has murdered sleep. And as he explains to Tyrrel, the princes are foes to his rest and are his "sweet sleep's disturbers" (74). His words concerning how "sin will pluck on sin" anticipate those of Macbeth, the later Shakespearean tragic hero who also willfully embraced evil, driven first by inordinate ambition and then by fear: "I am in blood / Stepped in so far that I should wade no more, / Returning were as tedious as go o'er" (*Macbeth*, III. iv. 136–38). But Buckingham, the "deep-revolving [artful, cunning] witty Buckingham," who had been so pliant heretofore, cannot bring himself to be the agent in the murder of the princes. Such utter heartlessness belongs only to Richard, the self-avowed villain who would outdo Machiavelli. But surely this is not the sole answer. Buckingham knows quite as well as does Richard that here indeed is "uncertain way to gain."

For Richard, the disaffection of Buckingham is the first serious check in his fortunes. Shakespeare develops this part of the scene with consummate skill. When the king says "Edward lives" (10), he expects the duke to reply that Edward will not survive for long. Instead, Buckingham merely says, "True, noble prince." And Richard's vehement exclamation, "O bitter consequence, / That Edward still should live. True, noble prince!" implies that, in his opinion, the duke is acknowledging the prince's right to the throne.

The news of Dorset's flight to Richmond is additional evidence that Richard has begun his fall. That he should appear to ignore Stanley, who brought him this latest intelligence, and to proceed to instruct Catesby to spread the rumor that Anne "is sick, and like to die," and then to question and instruct the newly arrived Tyrrel as regards the little princes—all this is only new proof of his capacity for prompt action, for dealing with first things first. Earlier commentators suggested that, in view of Richard's words with Catesby, the king himself planned to poison his wife. However, it has been established that Anne was suffering from tuberculosis and that she had been crushed in spirit by the recent death of her son.

Henry VI's prophecy, recalled by Richard in Scene 2 (98–104), is to be found in *Henry VI, Part 3*, IV. iv. 68–74. The last of the Lancastrian rulers addressed young Richmond as "England's hope" and spoke of him as one "Likely in time to bless a royal throne." It is irrelevant that Richard himself was not present when the words were spoken, although he speaks of himself as "being by." The main thing is that Richmond is becoming an increasingly important figure, the very mention of whose name is ominous to Richard.

Authentic classical drama never included scenes of violence on the stage but depended upon reports usually made by a messenger. In Elizabethan drama, notably the Seneca of the popular stage, such scenes were presented in full sight of the audience. But Shakespeare was not influenced by classical tradition here. Surely a matter of good taste was involved. In Scene 3, the actual scene of the two children being put to death would have been intolerable even for audiences nurtured on scenes of violence. Actually, Tyrrel's recital is far more effective as a means of arousing the emotions of pity and horror. The utter bestiality of the crime is first emphasized by identifying Dighton and Forrest as two "fleshed villains, bloody dogs"—that is, they are like vicious animals that have been allowed to taste human blood. The description of the victims, "those tender babes," more than suffices for Shakespeare's purpose. Now we are fully ready emotionally to witness the bloody king's downfall. Richard's hurried questions—" . . . am I happy in thy news? . . . But didst thou see them dead? . . . And buried?"—and his concern to hear all the details of the murders reveal the state of his anxiety.

In the summary of his accomplishments that precedes the bad news he is to receive, we learn that Anne has died and the king is free to marry Elizabeth of York. Holinshed wrote that she died "either by inward thought and pensiveness, or by infection of poison, which is affirmed most likely." Richard's public reputation, made clear by the discourse of the two London citizens (II. iii.), is such that, whatever the true facts may be, he is suspect.

Richard, whose intellectuality is never to be underestimated, is perceptive enough to realize that, in seeking to marry Elizabeth, Richmond aspires to wrest the crown from him. Characteristically, he will not delay wooing her for himself.

John Morton, Bishop of Ely, who was among those present in the Tower of London to make arrangements for the coronation of Edward V (III. iv.), fled to join Richmond after plotting with Buckingham, according to Holinshed. News of his flight especially oppresses Richard. But once more the villain-hero proves himself to be a man of action above all else. "My counsel is my shield," he exclaims (56)—that is, he will waste no time in deliberation; he will fight.

In Scene 4, Queen Margaret makes her last appearance and once more, in a completely ritualistic manner, "tells o'er [the

Yorkist] woes again" by viewing her own. Her grim forebodings are now being fully realized, and she stresses that mathematical kind of justice that is involved—an eye for an eye, a tooth for a tooth. Probably most would agree with the Duchess of York. Queen Margaret *does* represent "Dead life, blind sight" (26); but she is also the "Brief abstract and record of tedious days" (28), the grim commentator upon bloody deeds who never tires of pointing out the inevitability of God's punishment for grievous sins.

As we follow her long discourse, which is briefly interrupted twice, we might well ask as does the Duchess of York: "Why should calamity be full of words?" (126) But Shakespeare forestalls criticism of Margaret's extreme volubility by providing Queen Elizabeth's explanation. In *Henry VI, Part 3*, this same Margaret, having just witnessed the slaughter of her princely son, had said: "No, no, my heart will burst an if I speak; / And I will speak that so my heart will burst" (V. v. 58–59). So in *Titus Andronicus*, the titular hero, who had sought to ransom his captive sons by cutting off his hand as directed and sending it to the emperor, voiced similar thoughts: "Then give me leave, for losses will have leave / To ease their stomachs with their bitter tongues" (III. i. 233–34). And in *Macbeth*, written late in Shakespeare's career, Malcolm counsels the distraught Macduff, who has just learned that his wife and children have been killed: "Give sorrow words. The grief that does not speak / Whispers the o'er-fraught heart and bids it break" (IV. iii. 208–09). The main thing, however, is that in her recital in Scene 4, Margaret brings focus upon Richard as the arch-criminal:

> I had an Edward, till a Richard killed him.
> I had a Harry, till a Richard killed him.
> Thou hadst an Edward, till a Richard killed him.
> Thou hadst a Richard, till a Richard killed him.
>
> (40–43)

Granted that later she indicts Edward IV and Clarence, along with Hastings, Rivers, Vaughan, and Grey, but the emphasis remains on the villain-hero who "yet lives" (71), the recipient of Margaret's most vehement curses. Once she leaves the stage, the Duchess of York and Queen Elizabeth read the catalogue of Richard's crimes in ritualistic manner, now addressing the king himself. The force of the duchess' words—"Bloody thou art, bloody will be thy end. / Shame serves thy life and doth thy death attend"

(194–95)—strikes home when one recalls her blessing of her son early in the play. Whether present or absent, then, Richard remains the center of interest.

As the king urges the queen-mother to let him marry her daughter, he argues that he will advance her "to the dignity and height of fortune, / the high imperial type of this earth's glory" (243–44). Here indeed is the key to Richard's own ambition that drove him to extreme cruelty and bloodshed. He was beset with the same "thirst and sweetness of a Crown" that motivated Marlowe's Tamburlaine and that made Macbeth willing "to jump the life to come."

There are similarities between this wooing scene and the earlier one. For example, at one point the king says, "Say I did all this for love of her," when Elizabeth denounces him for the murders of Clarence and Lord Rivers (281–88). Moreover, the same kind of one-line speeches (stichomythia) serves to link the two wooing scenes. Finally, Richard's last words (431) are somewhat reminiscent of those he spoke just after Anne had left him. How do the scenes differ? Chiefly in that sardonic humor finds no place in this later scene: Tragic gloom now pervades the action.

This has been called an "outrageous courtship." And so it is. In the chronicle histories, both Hall and Holinshed are appalled at the queen's inconstancy. They record that the queen-mother had already promised the princess to Richmond and later was persuaded by Richard to grant his suit. It may be added that in these prose histories Elizabeth even sends orders for Dorset to desert Richmond and return to England. But not until Scene 5 does Shakespeare let us know that the queen has "heartily consented to the match with Richmond." Judged solely by the action in this scene, Queen Elizabeth may indeed be a "shallow, changing woman" who is moved by selfish ambition. Or one may argue that she saw in such a match the only chance to bring an end to the bloody strife. Did not Richard argue: "Without her, follows to this land and me, / To thee, herself, and many a Christian soul, / Death, desolation, ruin and decay" (407–09)? If the villain refers to "this land" first, he makes reference to himself before he mentions others who will suffer. But perhaps Elizabeth is no less concerned about her own fate than is the egotistical Richard.

Again one must anticipate Elizabeth's action in Scene 5. Many critics conclude that Shakespeare intended us to believe that Richard is tricked in this, his second courtship. That this interpretation would seem to be the correct one is consistent with what we learn in Richard's talk with Catesby, Ratcliff, Stanley, and the messengers. Clearly he is losing his grip on himself. Note how he fails to instruct Catesby and how he changes his mind about Ratcliff's mission. Most of the news is bad now. As Richard hears the tidings, he cries: "Out on you, owls" (509). The owl, of course, is a symbol and portent of death.

There is one piece of good news for Richard. Buckingham's army has been dispersed and scattered by sudden floods. A bit later we learn that the duke himself has been captured. How does this fit into the scheme of things? Buckingham is a perjurer and an accessory to murder; it would not do to have him survive and fight on the side of righteousness. Again we recall Margaret's dire prophecy when Buckingham ignored her counsel and allied himself with one upon whom "Sin, death, and hell have set their marks" (I. iii. 297–301). No Tudor loyalist would have failed to see divine intervention evident in the sudden floods that were the immediate cause of Buckingham's downfall.

The latter part of Scene 4 provides a good illustration of how Shakespeare telescoped historical events for his purpose. Richard did lead a force toward Salisbury to meet Buckingham in October 1483. Cut off from his Welsh levies, Buckingham was captured and put to death on October 31. Shortly thereafter, Richmond embarked from Brittany with an invading army, but his ships were dispersed by a storm. He did appear in one vessel off Poole. Richard, endeavoring to lure him ashore, sent false information to the effect that the troops ashore were led by Buckingham. But Richmond did not fall into the trap; instead he returned to France. Not until two years later did he invade England. To help him repel this invasion, Richard sent for the Duke of Norfolk.

In Scene 5, the powerful forces mustered to oppose Richard are identified. Those who will join Richmond are led by such nobles as Sir Walter Herbert, son of the Earl of Pembroke, who had been a staunch Yorkist; Sir Gilbert Talbot, uncle to the Earl of Shrewsbury; and Sir William Stanley, Derby's brother. Derby's real feelings toward Richard are finally made clear, although he dares not openly oppose the king. Thus, by the end of this act, Richard is supported only by Ratcliff, Catesby, and Lovel. That Richard's last stratagem has failed is also revealed: Elizabeth of York will marry Richmond.

Derby's reference to Richard as "this most bloody boar" emphasizes the king's heartless cruelty, which has led him to the brink of ruin. The reader will recall that, in Act I, Scene 3, Anne had denounced him as a "hedgehog," the first insulting reference to Richard's crest of the wild boar. In Act I, Scene 4, the villain-hero had referred to Clarence as being "franked up to fattening for his pains." A frank is a sty for fattening hogs. But it is Richard himself, of course, who is bestial. Here, in the lines assigned to Derby, Shakespeare sustains the metaphor.

ACT V

Summary

As Buckingham is led to his execution at Salisbury, he is told that Richard will not grant him an audience. He thinks of Henry VI, Henry's son Edward, Hastings, Rivers, Grey, Vaughan, and others who had died "By underhand corrupted foul injustice." If from the other world they view his plight, he continues, let them mock his fate. It is All Souls' Day, and he recalls that on another such sacred day he had given Edward IV his pledge to remain at peace with the dying king's children and the queen's allies, inviting God's punishment if he broke that pledge. He then recalls Margaret's curse when he had scoffed at her warning. "Wrong hath but wrong, and blame the due of blame," he concludes. He is saying that this unjust death is only retribution for the unjust deaths he has been responsible for.

Scene 2 shifts to Richmond's camp near Tamworth. Richmond, entering with drums and trumpets, addresses his "Fellows in arms" and "most loving friends," inciting them against Richard, "that wretched, bloody, and usurping boar," who has placed upon them the "yoke of tyranny" and has despoiled their "summer fields and fruitful vines." He acknowledges the receipt of good news from Lord Stanley and reports that Richard is at Leicester, only one day away. In God's name, he urges them on. Oxford and Herbert predict that all Richard's friends will desert him since they are only friends through fear. "All for our vantage," exclaims Richmond, and again invoking God's name, he commands them to march onward.

On Bosworth Field, Richard, fully armed, enters with Norfolk, the Earl of Surrey, and others. He orders that their tents be pitched.

When Richard chides Surrey for looking sad, the earl assures him that his heart is light. Then the king rallies Norfolk, who agrees that they must give blows as well as receive them. Richard states that he will rest here for the night; where he will rest tomorrow, he knows not. Philosophically he adds: "Well, all's one for that." He has reason to be confident, for he learns that his forces outnumber Richmond's three to one. With characteristic vigor, he gives commands preparatory to the battle and calls for men of competent leadership.

On the other side of the field, Richmond enters, accompanied by several distinguished nobles. While some soldiers are pitching his tent, Richmond takes note of the sunset, which gives promise of a fair day tomorrow. Calling for ink and paper, he plans the deposition of his forces for the battle. Before parting from the rest, he sends Captain Blount off with an important message to Stanley, whose forces lie about half a mile south of the king's. As they withdraw into the tent to finish the battle plans, Richard, with Norfolk, Ratcliff, Catesby, and others, claim our attention.

It is now nine o'clock and time for the evening's repast, but Richard decides not to sup. His thoughts are solely on the fight with Richmond. He calls for ink and paper; he asks if his armor is in readiness; he orders Norfolk to check the sentinels. Next, the king instructs Catesby to send a herald's officer to Stanley, ordering that lord to bring his regiment before morning unless he wants his son's head to be forfeit. He asks about the "melancholy Lord Northumberland" and is somewhat cheered to hear that the earl and Surrey have gone among the soldiers encouraging them. But Richard concedes that his own spirits lack alacrity and his mind its wonted cheerfulness. Therefore, he calls for a bowl of wine. Having instructed Ratcliff to come about the middle of the night to arm him, the king asks to be left alone.

Now attention is attracted to Richmond, who is in his tent with various lords and attendants. Derby (Lord Stanley) enters, and the two exchange greetings. Derby brings blessings from Richmond's mother, who prays constantly for her son's welfare. He counsels Richmond to put his fortunes to the test in tomorrow's battle but explains that in view of his son's plight, he cannot openly join the claimant's forces. Regretting that the encroaching battle prevents them from more time together, Stanley leaves. Richmond prepares himself for sleep, aware that he must be rested before he fights the good fight. Alone, he solemnly prays for God's good will, and to Him he commends his "watchful soul."

As both Richard and Richmond sleep, they are visited by a procession of ghosts of those the king had killed. They come in order of their deaths—Prince Edward, Henry VI, Clarence, Rivers, Grey, Vaughan, the little princes, Hastings, Lady Anne, and Buckingham. Each ghost appears to Richard as an image of retribution, indicting him for his crime and telling him to "despair and die." In the words of Anne, each fills his sleep with perturbations. In contrast, each ghost offers praise and words of comfort to the sleeping Richmond: let him "live and flourish," for good angels guard him and fight on his side. The ghost of Hastings especially urges him to "Arm, fight, and conquer, for fair England's sake!" And the two princes urge him to "Live, and beget a happy race of kings!"

As the ghosts vanish, Richard starts out of his sleep. He has been dreaming of "bloody deeds and death." He cries out for a horse and for someone to bind his wounds. Realizing that he has been dreaming and that he is a victim of "coward conscience," he goes through a self-examination that ends in bitter condemnation of isolated and unpitied guilt. Ratcliff enters to rouse him for battle. Still unnerved, he tells Ratcliff his dream. Ratcliff tries to rally him, and Richard turns his mind to the question of his followers' loyalty. He leaves with Ratcliff to eavesdrop at their tent and see if any mean to shrink from him.

Attention is now directed to Richmond's tent, where nobles enter to greet their leader. He has rested well, having enjoyed the "sweetest sleep and fairest-boding dreams." He tells the lords how the souls of Richard's victims had come to his tent and "cried in victory." Told that it is now four o'clock in the morning, Richmond replies that it is "time to arm and give direction." There follows his formal address to his soldiers.

"God and our good cause fight on our side," he assures the troops, and adds that the "prayers of holy saints and wronged souls" stand before their faces. Even Richard's followers, he continues, want him to be defeated. Denouncing the king as "A bloody tyrant and a homicide," Richmond urges his men to fight against God's enemies and their country's foes. Then may they expect to thrive in a prospering land, their wives and children free from danger. Richmond declares that he himself will fight unto death if necessary. If he wins, all will share in the gain. He calls for drums and trumpets to sound "boldly and cheerfully." And with the stirring cry, "God and Saint George! Richmond and victory!" he leads the way offstage.

It is Richard's turn now to receive full attention. He asks what Northumberland has said of Richmond and is pleased to hear Ratcliff tell him that the earl thinks very little of Richmond's capacity as a soldier and that Surrey was no less pleased with Northumberland's opinion. Richard then asks the time of day. He takes notice of the weather and remarks that the sun should have risen an hour ago. At first Richard is dashed by the thought that the skies are lowering down on him, but he realizes that the sun is not shining on Richmond either. Aroused from these thoughts by Norfolk, Richard tells that noble his plan of battle. A vanguard of horse and foot is to be spread out in front, with archers in the midst. Norfolk and Surrey are to command the foot and horse. Richard will follow in the main battle, his power on each side well-winged with foot and horse. Norfolk approves all this but passes Richard a taunting note he has found on his tent that morning. Richard dismisses it from his mind and sends his captains to their commands. He is determined not to let "babbling dreams" disturb his soul nor his conscience to bother him. Strong arms will be his conscience and swords his law: "March on, join bravely, let us to't pell-mell; / If not to heaven, then hand in hand to hell" (312–13).

In his oration to the troops, Richard denounces the enemy as a pack of foreign vagabonds and robbers who threaten to devastate the land and attack wives and daughters. He makes much of their being French, reminding his soldiers that their fathers had beaten the French on French soil. He concludes with a stirring call to arms. At this moment, a messenger comes, saying that Stanley refuses to bring his forces in. Richard wants to have young George's head cut off at once but is persuaded to wait until after the battle since the enemy are already past the marsh. Crying "A thousand hearts are great within my bosom" and invoking the name of Saint George, the king charges into action.

The battle is in progress. Catesby is crying to Norfolk to rescue the king, whose horse is slain and who continues to fight on foot. Richard enters, crying out for a horse. Catesby urges him to retire. He refuses, for he is determined to risk all. He leaves this part of the field, still crying for a horse and seeking Richmond.

Richard and Richmond fight, and Richard is slain. Richmond retreats and returns, receiving the congratulation of his friends for the victory, which is now assured. Derby (Lord Stanley) is carrying the crown, which he has taken from Richard. He places it on the head of Richmond. To the new king's question about young George Stanley (Richmond's half-brother), Derby replies that the youth is safe in Leicester. Richmond asks the names of nobles on both sides who have been slain and orders that they be buried "as becomes their births." In accordance with his wishes, all soldiers who have fled are to be pardoned if they return in submission to him. After taking the sacrament, he will marry Elizabeth of York, Edward IV's daughter, thus uniting the Yorkists and the Lancastrians. The harsh wars that have caused so much grief and injury, even among members of the same family, are now over. God willing, England will enter a reign of peace and prosperity. His concluding words are a prayer that traitors may perish and peace reign now that civil wounds are healed.

Commentary

According to Holinshed, Buckingham made a full confession in the hope that Richard would agree to see him. He "sore desired" the meeting whether "to sue for pardon . . . or whether he being brought to his presence would have sticked him with a dagger." The execution actually took place in Shrewsbury.

Scene 1 again makes apparent that throughout the play Shakespeare never lets one lose sight of the major theme: the execution of God's judgment on those guilty of perjury and murder. To Buckingham's credit, let it be said, he acknowledges his own guilt, and his words add up to a justification of God's ways to man.

Scene 2 could easily be cut out. Shakespeare included it as essential to the theme he develops throughout the play and to point up Richmond's virtues. From a political point of view, never to be ignored in the chronicle history plays, Shakespeare now teaches the orthodox lesson: Richmond is the rightful heir to the throne, moving against a usurper and murderer. He fights in God's name to save England from the ravages of one who, for a time, had been permitted to function as the scourge of God.

In Scene 3, Shakespeare especially remained quite faithful to Hall and Holinshed in his account of Richard and Richmond just before the Battle of Bosworth Field. Now, so near to the end of the play, the conflict has become completely centralized. Early there is evidence that Richard's downfall may be imminent. Surrey looks sad, and his insistence that he is really light of heart is not convincing. A bit later the king inquires about the "melancholy Northumberland." He has reason to be doubtful about that noble. Holinshed reported that Richard suspected him, and later wrote that, when it came to fighting, Northumberland stood aside "with a great company and intermitted not in the battle." And Lord Stanley still poses a problem for the king. Nevertheless, Richard's soldierly courage is apparent, as when he says, "Here will I lie tonight. / But where tomorrow? Well, all's one for that" (iii. 7–8). More to the point is Norfolk's report that Richmond's forces are far outnumbered by Richard's.

Richmond, having risen from "sweetest sleep," is in his tent carefully drawing up his plan of battle. He makes reference to his "small strength" but says nothing that suggests doubt or fear. In fact, his opening lines reflect confidence and peace of mind: "The weary sun hath made a golden set / And by the bright track of his fiery car / Gives token of a goodly day tomorrow" (iii. 19–21). Richmond's prayer, voiced in formal, impressive language, is anything but humble in tone. To understand its full import, one must take the historical point of view. The most obvious point to make is that Shakespeare was writing about Elizabeth I's grandfather, the first of the Tudors, whose claim to the throne had never been wholly secure. Richmond is moving against the man who wears the crown. Throughout the sixteenth century and beyond, the doctrine of absolute obedience to the ruler was inculcated. Even if, like Richard of this play, he was a usurper and murderer, no subject legitimately could rebel against him. In *Richard II*, written two years later, the wise old John of Gaunt, uncle to the king and a voice of orthodoxy, replies to the Duchess of Gloucester, who has implored him to avenge the murder of her husband, Gaunt's brother, a crime attributed to Richard II:

> God's is the quarrel, for God's substitute,
> His deputy anointed in His sight,
> Hath caused his death. The which if wrongfully,
> Let Heaven avenge, for I may never lift

An angry arm against His minister.

(I. ii. 37–41)

Granted that Richard II was not an arch-criminal as is Richard III. But, according to the accepted doctrine, it was through God's sufferance that Richard III wore the crown; he functioned, for a time, as has been stated earlier, as the scourge of God. Now his time to be scourged approaches. Richmond presents himself as God's captain and prays that he and his followers may be "Thy ministers of chastisement." In other words, he now becomes the instrument of God's justice. Thus heralded, the ghosts appear, bringing blessings to Richmond ("Live and flourish!") and curses on Richard ("Despair and die!").

Admittedly the verse in this "ghost" part of the scene is mediocre; in such pageant-like scenes, Shakespeare never achieved his best poetry. His aim was to make the most telling use of the supernatural as a way of keeping his major theme to the fore. Since the ghosts appear in the order of their deaths, Shakespeare recapitulates, crime by crime, the whole catalogue. Richard's sleep indeed is filled "with perturbations," to use Anne's phrase. And as the last ghost vanishes, the king wakes in terror and calls for another horse. He has dreamed prophetically that "white Surrey" has been killed under him. His waking thoughts relate directly to the last words spoken by the ghost of Buckingham.

Things have come full circle now. Richard is a deeply troubled soul in contrast to Richmond, God's captain. When he first appeared in the play, the villain-hero revealed his over-powering egotism; he gloated that he was "subtle, false, and treacherous"; he had expressed his determination "to prove a villain." He spoke these words with an insolence that showed him to be utterly devoid of conscience. Now his words appear as overwhelming reproof as he makes his first—and last—homage to moral law. Especially the horror of his isolation from humanity oppresses him: "There is no creature loves me, / And if I die no soul shall pity me" (iii. 200–201).

"Cowardice conscience" afflicts him. Only when he slept and was dormant could conscience stir. In that sense it was cowardly. But so vivid had been his dream that he cannot immediately escape conscience even when he wakes: "O Ratcliff, I fear, I fear—," he exclaims. The fact that he feels impelled to eavesdrop on his troops illustrates his faltering confidence.

Richmond's oration to his soldiers requires only brief comment. If there has been any doubt up to this point, now that doubt is resolved: Richmond emerges unmistakably as the divinely appointed champion of justice opposing one who "hath ever been God's enemy." The action now assumes the character of a holy crusade, not against an anointed ruler but against a bloody tyrant who has enslaved true-born Englishmen.

When Richard re-enters, he has completely recovered himself. For one thing, it would not do to have the tragic hero collapse before the battle and prove himself to be a straw man. Like Macbeth, that other great criminal, he is the soul of courage, a worthy adversary. Does the sun "disdain to shine" on his army? It does not shine for Richmond either. Richard is his Machiavellian self again: "Conscience is but a word that cowards use," he now exclaims (iii. 309).

In the chronicle histories of Hall and Holinshed, Richard was made to confess the murders of the little princes and to express sorrow for the deed when he addressed his army. Not so in Shakespeare's play. In the king's oration, there is no place for regrets, despondencies, or sense of violated honor. We have here what has rightly been called "a masterpiece of bold mockery of the foe." Northumberland had reported that Richmond was "never trained in arms" (272); now Richard refers to his adversary as a "milk-sop, one that never in his life / Felt so much cold as over shoes in snow" (325–26). The epithet derives from Holinshed, and Shakespeare makes the most of it. Similarly, Richmond's followers are described in the most contemptuous terms—"overweening rags of France," "famished beggars," "poor rats," "bastard Bretons." No leader could have done more to instill confidence in his troops, to convince them that "Victory sits on our helms." If Richmond is to defeat Richard, God indeed must be on his side.

Of chief importance in Scene 4 is evidence of King Richard's unsurpassed courage and martial skill. He is depicted as one "enacting more wonders than a man." From one point of view, this goes far to enhance his stature as the tragic hero; from another point of view, it redounds to Richmond's credit, for the claimant is opposed by one who seems to be superhuman in courage and determination.

Richard's cry ("A horse! a horse! my kingdom for a horse!"), so stirring in context, is the best-known line in the play. It was much admired, quoted, and imitated by Shakespeare's contemporaries.

The line does not appear in either Halle or Holinshed. One close to it ("A horse, a horse, a fresh horse") is found in *The True Tragedy of Richard the Third*, a quite inferior version of the villain-hero's rise and downfall that, according to critical consensus, predates Shakespeare's historical tragedy. As one critic notes, "A stage-entry on horseback being impractical, such a cry was an effective one for a general entering on foot in a battle scene."

As regards the "six Richards in the field," Shakespeare employed the same device in *Henry IV, Part 1*, wherein several of Henry's knights were dressed like him in the Battle of Shrewsbury. Obviously it was a precaution since the leader's death often meant defeat.

Appropriately in the final scene there is a clearing of the moral atmosphere. The "bloody dog" is dead; order is restored. In hand-to-hand combat, Richmond slays the adversary who had performed apparently superhuman deeds on the battlefield. Everywhere the new king's moral superiority is emphasized: his concern for George Stanley; his chivalry in ordering that all nobles slain, enemies included, be given proper burial; his proclamation of an amnesty; his profound religiosity. Shakespeare lived and wrote in an England beset with repeated threats to peace: the Northern Rebellion (1569); the Ridolphi Plot (1572); the Babington Plot (1586); attempted foreign invasion and fear of a rising against a queen who had been declared excommunicate and deposed by the Papal Bull of 1570. In official sermon and numerous polemical tracts and ballads, the horrors of civil war and the heinous crime of treason were dominant themes. In the latter part of this scene, Shakespeare finds occasion to offer the same doctrine. To Elizabethans especially, Richmond's fervent prayer was most appropriate and inspiring.

1594

kING JOHN

KING JOHN

LIST OF CHARACTERS

King John

King of England because of his mother's maneuvering after the death of her elder son, Geoffrey. His claim to the throne, and thus England's security, is vulnerable. His two best characteristics in the play are his loyalty to England and his defiance of the pope.

Prince Henry

The son of King John; heir-apparent to the throne if his father successfully defends their line of succession. His only role in the play is as a unifying factor at the end.

Arthur

The Duke of Britain, a young boy who is the nephew of King John. As the pre-teen son of the previous king, he is the natural successor to the throne. As long as he is alive, he is a tempting rallying cause for civil war.

The Earl of Pembroke, the Earl of Salisbury, and the Lord Bigot

Three powerful members of English nobility who waver from loyalty to King John, to rebellion after Arthur's death, to loyalty to Prince Henry.

The Earl of Essex

A member of King John's court.

Hubert de Burgh

A trusted henchman of King John. He remains loyal to all orders of the king—except for the blinding and killing of Arthur.

Philip the Bastard

Raised as the elder son of Sir Robert Faulconbridge, he accepts the conclusion that he is actually the illegitimate son of the deceased King Richard Coeur-de-Lion and then assumes an important role as a member of the ruling family.

Robert Faulconbridge

Apparently, the only son of Sir Robert Faulconbridge.

James Gurney

A servant to Lady Faulconbridge.

Peter of Pomfret

A minor character who plays the role of a prophet.

Philip

The King of France. He first supports Arthur against King John, then interjects religion into the controversy and abandons Arthur's cause.

Lewis

The Dauphin of France, son of Philip. He marries Blanch, niece of King John, apparently achieving a union between France and England. He becomes the aggressor in a war against England when he is encouraged by Pandulph to take advantage of the weakness caused by King John's errors in judgment in controversies with the pope and with Arthur.

Lymoges

The Duke of Austria. When the play begins, he is an ally of France, in support of Arthur's cause. He is defeated and beheaded by the Bastard.

Cardinal Pandulph

The legate of the pope. He destroys Arthur's cause by instigating a religious war. Eventually, he helps arbitrate peace between England and France after France's forces are defeated in England.

Melun

A French lord who helps to convince rebel English lords to save their necks by abandoning their brief alliance with Lewis the Dauphin against King John.

Chatillon

A French ambassador. He tries to negotiate King John's surrender to Arthur's allies at the opening of the play.

Queen Eleanor

Mother of King John and the deceased Richard and Geoffrey. She uses her son John to continue her role as the power behind the throne.

Constance

Arthur's ambitious mother.

Blanch of Spain

Eleanor's niece. Because of her agreement to marry Lewis the Dauphin, she briefly serves an important role in an alliance between France and England.

Lady Faulconbridge

Mother of Robert Faulconbridge and Philip the Bastard.

SUMMARIES AND COMMENTARIES

ACT I

Summary

Chatillon opens the action by beating diplomatic war drums. Speaking for the King of France, who is acting on behalf of Arthur Plantagenet, he claims England and other specific territories. If John refuses to willingly relinquish his title to Arthur, France is prepared to enforce Arthur's rights through war.

King John listens to the entire presentation, then responds that he is ready for war. He then provides Chatillon with safe passage but warns him that he must hurry to warn King Philip before England's attack.

Eleanor scolds her son for not heeding her warnings about the ambitions of Constance, Arthur's mother. When John blusters that the throne is his because of the power of both possession and right, his mother admits that he possesses it, but he possesses it by power only—he did not rightfully inherit the throne of England.

Essex interrupts their conversation and says that he would like to introduce the Faulconbridge brothers. King John barely has time to decide to levy taxes against the Church (to pay for war expenses) before he patiently agrees to attend to the controversy about the Faulconbridge inheritance.

Philip introduces himself as the eldest son of Sir Robert Faulconbridge, a soldier who was knighted by Coeur-de-Lion. Robert introduces himself as the son and heir of Sir Robert Faulconbridge.

King John questions the authenticity of the mixed claims to the Faulconbridge title. The major question raised by Robert is whether or not his father is also Philip's. Technically, King John rules that Philip is the heir because old Sir Robert raised him as a son, thus legitimizing Philip; the evidence, however, indicates that Philip is illegitimate. The claim that Robert, on his death bed, dispossessed Philip as illegitimate falls too late in the chain of events according to John.

However, concerning the evidence that Richard Coeur-de-Lion visited Lady Faulconbridge while old Sir Robert was out of the country on court business and that Philip unquestionably resembles Richard, King John determines that Philip is probably his own illegitimate nephew. Eleanor then offers the Bastard the opportunity to claim his rights as a son of Coeur-de-Lion. When the Bastard declares that that offer is better than his decision to insist that he belong to the inferior Faulconbridge line, Eleanor praises his attitude and urges him to join the English cause against the French campaign.

Philip then renounces his claim to the Faulconbridge fortune and assumes his place as an illegitimate son of Coeur-de-Lion. King John presides at a hasty ceremony for the purpose of re-naming Philip as Sir Richard. The new Sir Richard enthusiastically embraces his identity as a Plantagenet; however, he is referred to throughout the play as the Bastard.

As the Bastard is savoring and adjusting to his new social status, his mother bursts in to demand an explanation for the public shame foisted upon her by her two sons. The Bastard convinces her to name his real father, who is, indeed, Richard Coeur-de-Lion. He assures her that she should not be blamed for succumbing to seduction by a king, and he thanks her for providing so fine a father. He then escorts his mother to meet his new relatives while assuring her that no one could behold his fine physique and declare her act a sin—without risking being killed by the Bastard.

Commentary

Conflict dominates this play from its opening lines. When Chatillon challenges King John in the name of King Philip, he introduces a number of conflicts: national unity versus civil war, English sovereignty versus the Church of Rome, York versus Lancaster, stability versus ambition, and world order versus chaos. Unfortunately, the conflicts are not carefully controlled, and so a central weakness of the play must be identified as Shakespeare's failure to establish a dominant conflict with clever counter-pointing of subplots. A component of *all* the conflicts that develop through characterization, however, is honor. Characterizations of honor include esteem and respect, good reputations, integrity, purity, and social courtesy.

For instance, when John's honor as a rightful king is challenged, his next scene involves an honorable resolution of the Faulconbridge dispute. He patiently unravels the legal and moral implications to reach a measured verdict in the dispute that, in itself, involves reputation, integrity, and the purity of Lady Faulconbridge. This scene is followed by the Bastard's soliloquy regarding the social courtesies that are attached to his new station in life. This sequence on honor ends with Lady Faulconbridge's outrage about the attacks on *her* honor.

Before this act ends, King John's character has been established as a patriotic king who is conscientious about his responsibilities. But his flaw has also been established: He maintains a willful hold on the crown in spite of the *legitimate* claim of Arthur.

The Bastard is emerging early in the play as a strong individualist. His honor and patriotism are just beginning to manifest themselves as he tests the meaning of his new relationship to the royal family. He does not cling to his Faulconbridge ties when he is given the opportunity to claim his rights as a royal bastard. Nor does he castigate his mother for her illicit liaison with the king; instead, he chooses to reinforce her sense of honor.

ACT II

Summary

King Philip takes charge of introducing the allies who have gathered just outside the gates of Angiers. He explains to Arthur that the Duke of Austria has volunteered to support Arthur's cause in order to make amends for killing Richard the Lion-Hearted, Arthur's late uncle. Since this death allowed King John's usurpation of the English throne, King Philip explains that the Duke of Austria feels obligated to aid the correct realignment of Richard's posterity.

Arthur extends an innocent, loving welcome and graciously declares that God will forgive his uncle's death in return for Austria's defense of the rights of the young Coeur-de-Lion, who has been wronged by John. Austria vows that he will not return home until Arthur is established with his rightful powers. Constance joins in the thanks and implies a more substantial reward once Arthur is king. Austria then aligns the cause with heavenly peace and justified war.

King Philip wants to attack Angiers immediately in order to initiate Arthur's territorial claims, but Constance wants to wait for Chatillon in case King John has peacefully relinquished the throne. She wants no unnecessary bloodshed.

Just as Constance finishes her request, Chatillon enters with the advice to forego the siege of Angiers in order to prepare for an attack from England. He explains that adverse winds delayed his passage, but those same winds speeded up the English army's advance, so an attack by a strong English army is imminent. Finally, Chatillon describes the royal English party as consisting of King John, the Queen Mother (whom he implies acts as an inciter of vengeance), Lady Blanch of Spain, and the Bastard. When the army's drums portend the arrival of the English army, Chatillon ends his report with the advice to prepare either to parley or to fight.

King Philip seems unprepared for the expedition, and so Austria urges the quick preparation of a defense, for which he thinks they are well-prepared. Before either can act, however, King John enters with his parley party to demand surrender from France—or else do

battle with England. He declares his action to be justified by an
agent of God.

King Philip responds by bidding peace to England, which he
claims he loves and represents in the cause of the rightful King of
England—Arthur. He cites the natural succession from John's
deceased elder brother, Geoffrey, to Geoffrey's son, Arthur. Thus,
King Philip concludes that Arthur's cause fits God's plan, *not* John's
unnatural succession.

King John questions King Philip's right to usurp authority and
declare himself to be Arthur's guardian and champion. Eleanor and
Constance then clash. Constance calls John a usurper, and Eleanor
calls Arthur a bastard. Constance retorts that Arthur emotionally
and physically resembles his father as much as John resembles
Eleanor in behavior, and she further implies that *Geoffrey* is more
likely to be a bastard considering the moral inconsistency of Eleanor. After they mutually criticize each other to the hapless Arthur,
Austria calls for quiet, and the Bastard concurs. Austria demands
identification of the Bastard, who responds by threatening Austria
for his wrongs against Richard Coeur-de-Lion. Both Blanch and the
Bastard refer to Richard's lion's robe, which Austria is wearing.

King Philip impatiently orders the "women and fools" to keep
quiet, then he asks King John if John will peacefully relinquish
England, Ireland, Anjou, Touraine, and Maine. King John defies
France, declaring that he would rather die. He then attempts to
seduce Arthur's loyalty with offers of love and rewards. Eleanor
urges the boy to come to his grandmother. After Constance causti-
cally comments that if Arthur gives up his kingdom to his grandmother, he will be rewarded with "a plum, a cherry, and a fig,"
Arthur cries out that he wishes he were dead instead of in the
middle of this "coil," whereupon Eleanor and Constance castigate
each other for shaming the boy. This time, King John demands
quiet. Constance adds that Arthur is being punished for Eleanor's
sin, and Eleanor retorts that she can produce a will that bars any
rights that Arthur might now claim.

Again, King Philip orders the two women to be quiet, and he
quickly calls for a summons to the men of Angiers to choose
between Arthur and John. A citizen appears and inquires who has
summoned him.

King John quickly responds; he says that England calls its

"loving subjects"; King Philip interrupts to call them "Arthur's subjects." King John interrupts Philip to point out that French cannons are aimed at the walls of Angiers and that the British army is there to protect Angiers; therefore, he requests entrance to the city in order to rest. King Philip follows with the reasonable explanation that he is there on behalf of their rightful ruler, Arthur, and he requests only Angiers' acknowledgment of that fact; otherwise he'll attack.

The citizen of Angiers diplomatically declares that his fellow citizens are loyal subjects of the King of England but that they have barred their gates until one of the two men proves clear title, whereupon the two kings prepare to battle. The Bastard insults Austria, continuing his own personal vendetta.

Heralds of both kings return to Angiers to report bloody battles and claim victory. The citizen of Angiers observes that the battles have been worthy but that they did not determine who could enter the city. The two kings verbally joust about imminent victory.

The Bastard persuades King John and then King Philip to combine armies against Angiers. His plan is to punish peevish Angiers for defying them, then to battle afterward for the right to rule the conquered city. King John chooses to attack from the west, Austria from the north, and King Philip from the south. The Bastard gleefully realizes that he can manipulate Austria and France into damaging each other by firing artillery into each other's opposite positions.

However, the citizen of Angiers suggests another compromise in order to save his city. Step by step, he leads the kings to consider a match between Lady Blanch of Spain, who is a blood relative of the Coeur-de-Lion, and Lewis, son of the King of France. Blanch's qualities include beauty, virtue, and bloodlines. Each can benefit from the wholeness that marriage provides for them as unfulfilled single people. Furthermore, for the marriage, the gates of Angiers will be unbarred; without it, Angiers will mount a stiff resistance.

The Bastard sullenly mutters that Angiers mounts barrages of words without any force to back its challenge to choose to recognize this proposed marriage or else be prepared to fight a bloody battle. At this point, Eleanor urges King John to grasp this opportunity to prevent King Philip's pursuit of Arthur's cause and thus secure the throne of England.

The citizen of Angiers urges a response from the separately conferring parties. King Philip wants England to speak first because

King John had opened the demands for Angiers to choose between them. King John responds by offering a dowry for Lady Blanch "equal with a queen." King Philip then asks Lewis for his reaction. The young prince gazes into Blanch's eyes and declares himself in love.

The Bastard mutters cynicisms about the love match. Lady Blanch promises to do as her uncle wishes, and, while stopping short of declarations of love, she does emphasize that she sees nothing in Lewis to hate. After Blanch confirms her willingness to marry and Lewis confirms his love, King John offers a dowry of the provinces of Volquessen, Touraine, Maine, Poictiers, and Anjou, plus "thirty thousand marks of English coin" to King Philip. The French king accepts the offer, and the young couple seals the betrothal with a kiss.

King Philip tells the citizens of Angiers to open the city gates for the imminent wedding. He then uneasily asks where Constance is, anticipating her disappointment about the arrangements. He asks King John for advice about how to handle the withdrawal. King John thinks that he can assuage Constance with an offer to elevate Arthur's current title to Duke of Bretagne and Earl of Richmond; then the citizens of Angiers will turn their city over to him. Both kings obviously hope to prevent another tirade from Constance.

The Bastard declares his contempt for the "Mad world! mad kings! mad composition!" Besides recognizing that King John offered an unnecessary compromise by giving Arthur part of John's kingdom and that King Philip betrayed an honorable cause, the Bastard recognizes that he himself has not benefited from the rules of "commodity" that he has just learned. A fast learner, however, he now pledges his loyalty to the personal benefits that will accompany his commitment to dealing in the rules of trade.

Commentary

Words engulf action in this long, potentially tedious act. Although conflicts seem to abound, the dialogue serves mostly as narrative.

For example, the citizen of Angiers opposes the warring factions and, at one point, incites the action of battle. However, the battle takes place offstage with its high points narrated for the benefit of the audience; it resolves nothing. That leaves the audience with nothing but the verbal confrontation, and, thus, we have little that is dramatic. The Bastard, who agitates for action to settle a conflict, any conflict, aptly summarizes this dialogue between Angiers and the kings when he blurts out, "Here's a large mouth, indeed, / That spits forth death and mountains, rocks and seas," and he disgustedly summarizes the situation: "Zounds! I was never so be-thumped with words / Since I first called my brother's father dad."

The war of words between Constance and Eleanor is vicious enough to make a boy (Arthur) cry and unsettle two kings, but it does not move the action forward. This is proven by the fact that when the combined efforts of the kings quiet the two women, nothing has changed. The only place in which it is dramatically effective is in Arthur's case; he is well characterized as a hapless pawn, for he is onstage and yet separated from all the parleys that will determine his sad fate.

Even the Bastard's conflict with Austria serves only as a belated exposition of the untimely death of Richard the Lion-Hearted. This untimely death is verbally structured as the fulcrum of the unbalancing of the Coeur-de-Lion's succession to power and, thus, the cause of the current conflict between King John's and Arthur's supporters.

No single, dominant conflict emerges. Like Act I, this act meanders without a clear focus. Honor, however, appears again as a central factor in characterization. Austria cites his obligation to Arthur because of his fatal wounding of Richard, albeit in battle, which disrupted the boy's future. Arthur is characterized as innocent and virtuous. Eleanor and Constance scrap over continence and legitimacy. At the opening of the act, Arthur's allies declaim their "just cause" and vow to fight until they win back Arthur's rights by defeating all the forces that John can muster because of his "unnatural succession." However, by the end of the act, the Bastard shares with us the lesson that he has learned:

> Commodity, the bias of the world,—
> The world, who of itself is peised well,
> Made to run even upon even ground,
> Till this advantage, this vile-drawing bias,
> This sway of motion, this Commodity,
> Makes it take head from all indifferency,
> From all direction, purpose, course, intent.

Honor has been engulfed by greed.

The Bastard admits his envy of the kings' lure by "commodity," while he himself has not had the opportunity to choose. As a "beggar," he condemns the vices of the rich, but he looks forward to the time when he can be rich and condemn the vices of beggars. Impressed by the power of "commodity," he vows to worship "gain." The lure of profit is thus added to his original thrill at the sudden power and possession of a title.

In this act, King John succumbs to his flaw—his willful hold on the crown in spite of the legitimate claim of Arthur. Instead of remaining conscientious about his responsibilities, however, he gives away large portions of English territory, hoping to shore up his crumbling powers.

ACT III

Summary

Constance opens the act by summarily rejecting a report of the betrayal of Arthur's cause: "Gone to be married! Gone to swear a peace! / False blood to false blood joined! Gone to be friends!" She flatly states that she will not accept the hapless messenger's report of the marriage alliance nor the king's gift of provinces since the messenger is a "common man," and she has "a king's oath to the contrary." She threatens the messenger with punishment for alarming her during her vulnerable state. After a series of descriptions of the physical actions of the messenger, who uses body language to support his words, she demands that he speak once more—and then only to confirm the truth of his report.

The messenger, who is Salisbury, does so. Constance, who well understands the implication of the destruction, condemns Salisbury for bringing such a message. Salisbury, trapped by the ill fate that comes to the bearer of bad news, tries to separate his report from his responsibility of the events, but Constance refuses to accept that logic.

Arthur begs his mother to "be content." Constance proclaims that if only he had not been so obviously fit to rule, she would be content, but Arthur is in every way so obviously a potential king. She condemns Fortune for whoring with King John and King Philip, and then she orders Salisbury to go berate the two kings and tell them they must come to her. Salisbury protests that he cannot approach them unless she accompanies him, but finally he goes in spite of his doubts.

The kings appear then, accompanied by others in the wedding party. King Philip proclaims the wedding day to be a "blessed day"; Constance contradicts that it is a "wicked day." King Philip protests that she has no cause to complain because he has pledged his "majesty" to her; Constance counters that his majesty is "counterfeit."

Constance indulges in a general expression of outrages that culminates in an insult to Austria. When Austria brags about what he would do if a *man* said that, the Bastard twice repeats the insult. King John interjects that he disapproves of the Bastard's speaking out of turn.

The entrance of the pope's legate, Pandulph, interrupts the squabble. He demands to know why King John has interfered with the pope's appointee as Archbishop of Canterbury. King John responds by denying the power of a mere pope over the King of England. Speaking for all of England, the king states that "no Italian priest" can usurp a power over English dominion that is held by heaven alone.

King Philip gasps that this is blasphemy. King John stoutly holds that although all other Christian kings may pay homage to "this meddling priest," *he* opposes the pope.

Pandulph immediately declares John to be cursed and excommunicated, and he offers blessings to all who revolt against John's rule. He also offers sainthood to anyone who kills John. Constance weaves an alliance with Pandulph although the cardinal seems reluctant to admit the similarity of their complaints against King John. Pandulph then orders King Philip to break his alliance with England if John refuses to swear allegiance to Rome. King Philip, for a moment, is unable to act while advice is heaped upon him, with Eleanor, John, and Blanch urging the maintenance of the marital alliance; Austria, Constance, and Lewis urge Philip to forego his pledge to England in order to avoid being cursed as a heretic. King Philip appeals to Pandulph for some gentle compromise to release him from his dilemma, for he is caught between betraying an order of the pope or betraying the vows of the marriage alliance.

But Pandulph offers no relief. Instead, he demands that King Philip either actively battle England in the name of the Church or expect a curse from the Church. He attacks King Philip's conflict with his conscience by arguing that Philip's vows to the Church take precedence over all other vows. Between Lewis' additional pressure and Pandulph's renewed threat of a curse, Philip succumbs and severs his alliance with England.

After another round of pro and con opinions, France and England prepare to battle. Scene 2 is composed entirely of a brief meeting between King John, Hubert, Arthur, and the Bastard, during which Hubert receives custody of Arthur and the Bastard assures King John that Eleanor is safe. Scene 3 features a disintegration of the English defenses and of King John's good judgment. King John falsely assures Eleanor that she will be safe if she stays where he is leaving her, and he assures Arthur that *he* will be safe, for he will be under royal protection. King John then dispatches the Bastard to precede them to England, where the Bastard is to amass funds for the war by raiding Church properties. The Bastard declares that "bell, book, and candle" (excommunication) shall not be a defense against his opportunity to amass valuables and money; he exits to carry out his assignment.

While Eleanor takes Arthur aside to try to calm him, King John woos Hubert's loyalty with praise and vague promises in order to persuade him to kill Arthur. All exit then toward their separate destinies—Eleanor to her guarded sanctuary and spy post, Arthur and Hubert to England, and John with the bulk of the army to Calais.

Scene 4 focuses on King Philip's gloom over France's setbacks. The French armada has been scattered, Angiers lost, Arthur captured, and the English forces successfully embarked for England after fortifying all captured territories. The French king cannot tolerate either Constance's remonstrances nor Lewis' assurances that all will eventually go well.

After Constance indulges in grief, Pandulph retorts that she is mad, not grief-stricken. Constance verifies that she *can* distinguish reality and that it is reality that has driven her to consider suicide rather than to exist with her unrelieved grief. King Philip tries to cajole her, then commands her to bind up the hair she has torn loose. Constance agrees, saying that her hair should not be free while her son is not. She then conjures for Pandulph a scene in which she and Arthur will meet again in heaven, but Arthur will be so disfigured from mistreatment that she will miss the opportunity for reunion because she will not be able to recognize him. Both

Pandulph and Philip criticize her fondness for grief. Constance then exits to be alone, and King Philip follows because he fears that she might attempt suicide.

Lewis indulges in melancholy, saying that life is as tedious as a "twice-told tale." Pandulph intrigues him with the prophecy that King John will kill Arthur, which, in turn, will open the way for Lewis and Blanch to claim all that Arthur now holds. Furthermore, they will be supported by all of the English citizens who will rebel because of Arthur's murder. Lewis is eager to believe the prophecy that a French invasion of England will be joined by a great army of rebels on English soil. He embraces the vision that he will lead this force to a glorious victory and future, and he exits with Pandulph, hoping to convince King Philip to press for the invasion of England.

Commentary

Unfortunately, the action halts again in the middle of what has already been a predominantly verbal play. Conceivably, Constance's strident speeches hold the focus, thereby countering the forward movement of the action with her ineffective arguments. She moves the other characters—not to action nor to listening—into the multi-role of a chorus, telling her to keep quiet.

Rhetoric for and against the marriage obscures the marriage's dramatic significance until Pandulph identifies it for Lewis late in the act. Blanch would be next in line if King John were defeated in battle and if Arthur were killed by his uncle. Because of the power of the male (that will be such an anathema to Queen Elizabeth I), Lewis would then rule England as Blanch's husband.

Another conflict, the religious issue, does move action into a new dimension. When King John refuses to acknowledge the Archbishop of Canterbury, who has been sent by the pope, King John takes a stand that was popular with Elizabethan Anglican audiences but that was fatal within the historic context of the play. He defies the conditions that Pandulph offers, and thus he destroys the new alliance and, thereby, structures the play's dramatic resolution. Pandulph breaks up the alliance by threatening excommunication and a curse for all who align themselves with John. Additionally, he sets up John for murder by declaring sainthood for anyone who can accomplish John's murder. By the end of the act, Pandulph convinces Lewis to invade England. But the focus of this act is blurry because King John is not the prime mover of events, as a protagonist should be. Other than defying Pandulph's commands, making some brief strategic decisions for the war, and planting the seeds for Arthur's accidental death, he does not initiate or focus the action. As a result, the act moves along awkwardly.

Character development is also weak. Pandulph is a stereotyped one-dimensional, ambitious Roman Catholic. Constance rants and raves from motivations that are so obscure that other characters in the play express confusion. King Philip wavers, the Bastard declaims, Lewis emotes, Blanch wheedles, Arthur mews, and Austria vegetates. Hubert alone has some moments of depth as he strives to understand and obey his king.

The only full character development occurs within King John. His character and fortune deteriorate when he persuades Hubert to kill Arthur. His assurances to Arthur turn into lies; he dishonors himself by promising protection to Arthur and then arranging the boy's murder. Thus, the king's flaw—the willful capture of the throne—corrupts the patient and wise leadership qualities that he displayed in Act I.

ACT IV

Summary

Hubert orders the executioners, who enter with him, to hide behind the arras until he stamps his foot. Upon hearing the signal, they are to rush out and bind Arthur to a chair. One executioner comments that he hopes Hubert's warrant legitimizes the act. Hubert retorts that the executioner should not voice unacceptable scruples and that he had better obey. The executioners exit then in order to hide.

Arthur enters when Hubert calls him, and he immediately notices that Hubert appears sad. He says that no one but himself should be sad, and he explains further that he could be happy anywhere but in prison and that he fears his Uncle John's intentions. He observes that it is not *his* fault that he is Geoffrey's son; he would much rather be Hubert's son so that Hubert would love him.

In an aside, Hubert agonizes over the compassion that is aroused by the boy's conversation. He braces himself to carry out his orders quickly, and even as Arthur expresses his love for Hubert, the burly servant thrusts King John's warrant at Arthur, tells him to read it, and complains in another aside about the tears in his eyes.

Arthur asks: "Must you with hot irons burn out both mine eyes?" Hubert declares that he must, and he will. Arthur reminds his torturer of the time when he bound Hubert's aching head with a princess' handkerchief without ever asking for its return and lovingly tended him throughout the night. Can Hubert remember that night and still blind the eyes that lovingly gazed upon him? Hubert growls that he must do as he promised the king he would. After another appeal for love and mercy from Arthur, Hubert stamps his foot to summon the executioners. Arthur begs Hubert to save him from "these bloody men," and he says that rather than being bound while the executioners blind him, he would rather have Hubert perform the deed. In return, Arthur promises to sit quietly and to forgive Hubert.

Hubert orders the executioners to leave, and one of them expresses relief for being excused from the order. Arthur realizes that he was mistaken when he ordered the compassionate executioner to leave, so he requests his return. Hubert commands the boy to prepare himself. Instead of keeping his promise to "sit as quiet as a lamb," Arthur incessantly begs Hubert to spare his eyes. The boy gains precious time when the fire needed to re-heat the cold poker goes out, and he calls upon Hubert to show as much mercy as the fire and the irons have.

Finally, Hubert relents and promises to keep the boy safe. Arthur goes to hide, and Hubert exits to spread false stories about Arthur's death in spite of the danger to himself for having refused a king's command.

In the following scene, King John and some of his advisers examine the current state of affairs. John hopes that his recent second coronation will prove effective. Pembroke remarks that the first should still be in force but that it was done when there were no symptoms of revolt. Salisbury adds that this second crowning is "wasteful and ridiculous excess." Pembroke and Salisbury comment further that the second coronation might serve only to awaken suspicion about a fault that would not have been noticed previously. Salisbury then oozes flattery for the king by indicating that although King John ignored their advice, they are always pleased to stand by whatever he wants.

King John responds that he shared some of his reasons prior to the coronation and will offer more when his fears have lessened. In the meantime, he is open to all suggestions for reform. Pembroke asks that Arthur be freed on behalf of all those who value the king's safety. The king grants this wish just as Hubert enters.

Pembroke knows that Hubert had a warrant from King John to blind and execute Arthur, and as he observes Hubert's mannerisms during a private conversation with the king, Pembroke believes that the bloody deed is already done. Salisbury also observes that the king shows signs of emotional distress. King John then announces that his desire to free Arthur cannot be carried out because Arthur has just died.

Both Pembroke and Salisbury mutter their fears that stories of the boy's sickness would end in death. King John asks why they frown at him as if he could control life and death. Salisbury blurts that Arthur's death was apparently the result of foul play, and he criticizes the king for it. He and Pembroke exit to find the poor dead child. They predict trouble. King John expresses his regret: "They burn in indignation. I repent."

A messenger enters to report bad news from France. A huge French army has been quickly assembled and dispatched. King John wonders aloud how such an event could escape his mother's knowledge. The messenger then reports that Eleanor died on April 1 and that, according to rumor, Constance died about three days before that.

King John pleads for time to mourn the loss of his mother, as well as the threat of the gathering French forces, until he can deal with his discontented lords. He is further upset upon learning that Lewis the Dauphin is leading the invasion force.

When the Bastard and Peter of Pomfret enter, the king begs to be spared from more bad news. The Bastard replies that if the king is afraid of "the worst news," then he has none to deliver. King John then composes himself and tells the Bastard to report whatever he wishes to report.

The Bastard says that he was successful in collecting money from Church coffers, but, everywhere, he found that people were possessed by unidentifiable fears. He has brought with him the prophet Peter of Pomfret, whom he heard predict that before the next Ascension Day at noon, King John would yield his crown.

King John orders Hubert to imprison the prophet until noon on Ascension Day, when he is to be hanged. Then, Hubert is to return to receive other instructions. After they leave, the king requests any news that the Bastard may have heard about the French army. The Bastard says that everyone is talking about the landing of the army. Furthermore, he himself met with an agitated group led by Bigot and Salisbury, who were searching for Arthur's body.

The king requests that the Bastard find the group and persuade them to come to him so that they can be persuaded to love him again. The Bastard says that he will. King John urges him to hurry because he cannot afford a domestic rebellion when a foreign army is invading. King John then sends the messenger after the Bastard in case messages need to be relayed; afterward, he grieves: "My mother dead!"

Hubert enters to report a natural phenomenon—four fixed moons with a fifth in "wondrous motion." People were awed by the sight and have begun to whisper about Arthur's death. The king is furious at the reminder of the people's fears and Arthur's death. He complains, "Thy hand hath murdered him. I had a mighty cause / To wish him dead, but thou hadst none to kill him."

Hubert protests that he merely followed orders. King John implies that Hubert *misunderstood* their conversation and acted without authority upon that misunderstanding. While Hubert produces the signed warrant, King John wriggles away from responsibility for the evidence. Instead, he blames Hubert for being there, for looking like a killer and thus inspiring him to think about the warrant. Hubert, he says, should have employed his conscience and resisted the order instead of turning the king's moment of weakness into a bloody deed. Furthermore, John says that a simple pause at the time he issued the warrant would have been enough resistance to stop him.

Since Hubert made the mistake of carrying out a flawed command, King John dismisses him with the warning to stay out of his sight forever. The king recognizes that his order to kill Arthur has resulted in "civil tumult" just when he needs a kingdom united against the French invasion.

Hubert then assures King John that he can arm the country against the invaders because Arthur is alive. He also complains that the king has misjudged by equating the quality of his conscience with his physical appearance. King John urges Hubert to go and report Arthur's survival to the angry lords, and then he apologizes for his angry criticisms of Hubert's rough looks.

In Scene 3, Arthur counters all efforts to save his life. While poised on the high prison walls, Arthur, disguised as a ship-boy, begs the ground below not to hurt him when he jumps. He conjectures that if he does not break any bones, he has many alternatives for his escape; if he dies, he believes that such a fate will be preferable to staying in prison. The jump is fatal.

Arthur dies just as the search party appears. Salisbury, Pembroke, and Bigot decide to accept an invitation to a meeting with Pandulph the next morning. At this point, the Bastard enters to deliver King John's request for an immediate meeting.

Salisbury composes a message for the Bastard to deliver: They will not serve a king with such a stained reputation. The Bastard cautions that whatever their thoughts, the lords should use "good words." Salisbury retorts that they are now ruled by grief, not good manners.

Just as the Bastard leads up to the good news that Arthur is alive, they discover the boy's body. Salisbury declares Arthur's murder to be the vilest in history. Pembroke extends this comparison into the future as a murder heinous enough to minimize all murders yet to be committed. The Bastard agrees it is damnable "if that it be the work of any hand." Salisbury dismisses the "if" and blames King John and Hubert, then vows dedication of his life to revenge. Pembroke and Bigot concur with this view.

Hubert suddenly bursts in to joyously announce that Arthur is alive. Salisbury draws his sword to convince Hubert to get out of their sight. A confused Hubert states that he will defend himself even against a lord of the realm. Bigot and Pembroke join the threats against Hubert; the Bastard urges them to "keep the peace." Salisbury and the Bastard then threaten each other with death. Hubert explains that he loved the boy, left him alive an hour before, and joins them in their mourning.

Salisbury warns his group not to be deceived by Hubert's cunning tears, and he calls for all who abhor such slaughter to leave with him. Bigot and Pembroke announce that they will leave for a meeting with the Dauphin at Bury; King John can find them there.

The Bastard then states how damned Hubert is if he so much as "agreed" to this vile murder, and he states further that he suspects that Hubert *was* involved. Once again, Hubert cannot utter a convincing word in his own defense. Finally, he declares that if he in any way contributed to the boy's death, hell can inflict its worst tortures, but "I left him well."

As ordered, Hubert picks up Arthur's body to carry it away for burial. The Bastard declares his amazement at "how easy dost thou take all England up!" With a clear vision of the turmoil that now threatens England, the Bastard leaves to join the king.

Commentary

Action finally moves forward with sudden dramatic focus in Act IV, although the action here, as in the previous acts, is composed of actions that seem complex. All events here center on John's willful hold on the throne.

As an example of improved dramatic focus, the conflict between King John and Arthur is better represented than earlier. Pembroke and Salisbury are more emotionally involved in Arthur's cause than were France and Austria, so they project more emotional tension to the audience. They are also more effective. Furthermore, the threat of civil revolt because of Arthur's death was an emotionally arousing theme for Shakespeare's contemporaries—even more rousing and fearful than a foreign invasion.

Obviously, the conflict between John and Arthur also becomes direct. The king orders the boy to be killed; the boy dissuades the executioners. On the other hand, when King John wants Arthur to live, the boy ironically thwarts the king's wish by his fatal, desperate leap for freedom.

France is still threatening to invade England, as it was when Act I opened, but by being separated from Arthur's cause, France is clearly defined as an enemy. The audience can now focus its sympathies *against* France and *for* England. France takes on a hateful image, a ghoul preying on reactions to Arthur's death.

Unfortunately, action is still sometimes slowed because of excessive verbiage. For example, the dramatic action of a sword fight between Hubert and Salisbury bogs down in speeches such as Hubert's:

> Stand back, Lord Salisbury, stand back, I say!
> By heaven, I think my sword's as sharp as yours.

> I would not have you, lord, forget yourself,
> Nor tempt the danger of my true defense,
> Lest I, by marking of your rage, forget
> Your worth, your greatness, and nobility.
> (IV. iii. 80–85)

And all of Arthur's lengthy appeals to spare his sight and life are melodramatically sentimental:

> O heaven, that there were but a mote in your
>   [eyes],
> A grain, a dust, a gnat, a wandering hair.
> Any annoyance in that precious sense.
> Then feeling what small things are boisterous
>   there,
> Your vile intent must needs seem horrible.
> (IV. i. 92–96)

In addition, two major structural flaws diminish tension and continuity of action. First, the conflict between King John against the pope, a popular stand for contemporaries of Shakespeare, is not continued from the previous act. Thus, an important link is missing. Second, this act features no human protagonist. Events turn and twist both King John and Arthur, the two featured characters, and although one could argue that England is the protagonist, the argument does not hold up well for the entire play.

If anything, the action in Act IV develops a convoluted philosophy about King John's flaw—his willful hold on the throne. His fearful second coronation arouses suspicions about his right to the throne. Although Shakespeare's contemporaries were aware that the Yorks employed suspicious means to gain and hold the throne of England, they did not believe that mere suspicions or disagreement justified civil rebellion. Rather, measured against a world order in which the kingship was established by God, people believed that no one had the right to overthrow the king unless that king were to issue an order that would demand that the citizens disobey one of God's commandments. Thereby hangs the significance of much of what is said and done in this act. King John's order for Hubert to kill Arthur is judged as heinous murder. Had King John's order been obeyed, the king would have been culpable, and the rebels would have acted correctly. However, since King John is guilty *only of the*

thought and Arthur kills himself by his own foolish, desperate decision, the rebels are wrong. Hubert and the Bastard take actions that
are correct for the sake of world order and England.

The Bastard's final line in this act, however, identifies the issue
as unresolved: "And heaven itself doth frown upon the land." Subsequent civil war upholds the opinion that England is not operating in
a manner that is acceptable to God. The play's historical context represents fearful memories of the thirteenth-century civil war and the
subsequent years of instability, which were caused by the conflicts
of the Yorks versus the Lancasters. The Tudor line was regarded as a
safeguard against civil war, and Queen Elizabeth I is remembered
for her obsession with peace.

Hubert successfully fends off all who would stereotype him as a
two-dimensional character who looks like and, therefore, is a murderer. His sense of honor emerges in the form of integrity, a quality
of which Hubert is proud. In fact, his sense of honor and conscience
responds to Arthur's appeals for mercy and creates an inner conflict
that eventually overwhelms the order of a king. Thus, Hubert
becomes a three-dimensional character during this act.

The Bastard continues to develop. In each previous act, he
learned and shared one important lesson. Act IV is no exception.
Here, he learns how fearful are disloyalty and disrespect (aspects of
honor) that are channeled into civil rebellion. Unlike the bold
embracing of new concepts that the Bastard exhibited previously, a
cold flailing against an unacceptable lesson emerges when he says,
"I am amazed . . . and lose my way." Thus, fear and doubt add
another layer to the Bastard's character. With loyalty stretched
almost to the breaking point by Arthur's death, the Bastard chooses
to support King John for the sake of stability, exhibiting again the
quality of honor that, although much shallower before, marked him
from his first appearance. The Bastard is now the most fully developed character in the play.

King John does not fare as well. Instead of developing the wise
and patient leadership qualities that he exhibited in Act I, he is now
deteriorating. His flaw now dominates every action, and it appears
to be toppling him from the height of his monarchy. Although still
patriotic to the extent that he wants to defend England against foreign invaders, he is no longer conscientious about his responsibilities. He does realize that he has contributed to a disastrous civil

tumult. And he refuses to accept responsibility for the death of Arthur. Instead, he blames Hubert, claiming that had Hubert only hesitated, the order would not have been signed. John's moral disintegration has diminished him to a shadow, a character who interacts with no one. His role is reduced to a symbol needed for national security.

ACT V

Summary

King John enters into a ceremony of contrition with Pandulph. Having handed over his crown to Pandulph, John receives it again with the blessings of the pope. In return, Pandulph promises to stop the war that he began. Pandulph marks the day of conversion as Ascension Day. After Pandulph leaves, King John remembers the prophecy and expresses relief that yielding his crown before noon was a voluntary act.

The Bastard brings bad news again: Kent has surrendered; London has welcomed the Dauphin and his troops; most of the English lords have joined the French forces. King John asks why the lords did not return to his service after they had learned that Arthur was alive. The Bastard tells the king of their discovery of Arthur's body. Upon learning that Hubert was mistaken about Arthur's survival, the king is overcome by despair. The Bastard then urges his king to display courage, to challenge his enemies, and to lead his remaining supporters to an attack.

King John announces the agreement that he arranged with the pope's legate. The Bastard remonstrates his king for this "inglorious" compromise; he disapproves of arranging a truce with the invaders, and he takes special exception to yielding to the arrogant young Dauphin. Again, the Bastard urges a brave defense, if for no other reason than to act as insurance in case Pandulph cannot deliver the promised peace.

King John assigns the fight to the Bastard's leadership. They leave as the Bastard exhorts his king to meet the odds with courage.

Scene 2 features the Dauphin and his followers. Lewis dictates to Count Melun the oaths sworn by the rebel English lords. Salisbury affirms his allegiance but regrets that he must kill his countrymen. He bewails the sickness within his government that has driven him to heal it by joining forces with invaders of his homeland, then excuses himself to weep.

Lewis praises Salisbury for both his decision and the war of conscience that he is fighting. The Dauphin declares that even he himself is moved by Salisbury's manly tears. He urges Salisbury to compose himself, to fight, and to look forward to the rewards. Seeing Pandulph, Lewis anticipates a blessing on their enterprise.

Instead, Pandulph announces King John's reconciliation with the pope as a cause for withdrawing the French attack. Lewis responds that he is too proud and "high-born" to be controlled by the commands of a secondary power. He says that Pandulph's voice kindled the war but that Pandulph is too weak to blow out the resulting flames. Lewis claims that John's peace with Rome has nothing to do with peace with France. Furthermore, the Dauphin claims England because of his marriage to Blanch. He wants to press the battles that have nearly guaranteed the prize. He denies that Rome has any jurisdiction over this campaign. Pandulph says that Lewis is considering only externals in this issue. Lewis declares that he will not return until he wins this war.

At this unfavorable moment, the Bastard arrives to inquire about the progress of the negotiations. Pandulph reports on the Dauphin's refusal to stop the war. The Bastard hurls brave challenges at both the Dauphin and the English rebels, painting a portrait of a brave King John who stands ready to lead his loyal countrymen in a successful defense.

Lewis dismisses both the Bastard and Pandulph, refusing to listen any more. He announces that war will win his arguments. The Bastard warns the Dauphin that his drums announce the beginning of the battle that will defeat the invaders.

Scene 3 consists of bad news for the British. Hubert informs King John that their forces are faring badly in the day's battle. King John tells Hubert that he feels ill. A messenger informs the king that the Bastard wants him to leave the battlefield. King John informs everyone that he is withdrawing to go to the abbey at Swinstead; he complains the fact that fever prevents him from celebrating the news that the French supply armada was wrecked at sea, and he orders a litter to carry him away.

In Scene 4, the rebel English lords worry about their setbacks. Salisbury expresses surprise at the number of supporters of King

John. Pembroke urges vigorous support for the French or they themselves will lose, and Bigot blames the Bastard for the astonishing defense.

A mortally wounded Count Melun manages to reach the group and urges them to join other English lords who have abandoned their cause in order to re-pledge loyalty to King John because Lewis has pledged to behead any rebels upon the moment of his victory. When the lords express doubt, Count Melun assures them that he tells the truth because he is dying and because his grandfather was English. In return, Melun requests help to assist him to a quiet place to die. The English lords agree both to help Melun and to rush back to King John.

In Scene 5, Lewis must cope with bad news about Count Melun's death, the English lords' defection, and the armada's destruction.

In the next scene, through a series of codes that lead one to believe that they cannot see each other in the black night, Hubert and the Bastard meet. Their exchange of news is also bleak. Hubert reports that the king has been poisoned, apparently by a monk, but has a slight chance of recovering. The good news is that all of the English lords have returned and been pardoned at Prince Henry's request. The Bastard, in turn, reports that half his fighting forces have been lost to a sudden, devastating turn in the battle. Having barely escaped on his fast horse, he asks Hubert to lead him to the king.

In the seventh and final scene, Prince Henry appears and takes charge. He reports that King John is dying. Pembroke adds that the king believes that he can recover if he is brought into the fresh air; he is more patient now and has been singing. When Prince Henry mourns death's deterioration of his father's body and mind, Salisbury assures him that Henry is well suited to fit the vacant throne.

King John is carried in. He praises the comfort of the open air for his fever and pain. He tells Prince Henry that he, John, has been poisoned, and he blames all around him for not supplying cold air to help him. Prince Henry offers his tears, but they are rejected as too hot and salty.

The king clings to a thread of life until the Bastard can deliver his news. This news is that the Dauphin is advancing against defense forces that were devastated by the unexpected turn in the battle. King John dies.

Salisbury urges Prince Henry to take over the monarchy. The prince is unnerved by his father's "demonstration of mortality." The Bastard appeals to heaven to aid him in avenging the king's death, after which he pledges continued servitude after death.

Salisbury says that Pandulph awaits within for acceptance of a tolerable offer of peace. The Bastard urges a strong defense first. But Salisbury convinces the Bastard that nothing else is necessary because the Dauphin has already prepared for the ceremony.

Commentary

Unfortunately, Act V does not maintain Act IV's improved focus. There is, however, a focal point—King John's deterioration and death occupy our thoughts. But that focus is not dramatic because it is not the center of conflict and tension. John, leader of England, is no longer opposing the rebellion. Instead, he assigns England's defense to the Bastard and withdraws eventually to Swinstead Abbey. After Salisbury's vacillation, all of the rebels return to the fold and await the death of the man whom they swore to destroy. But they do not act on King John's initiative, and so this entire conflict recedes in dramatic impact.

When word of France's peace offer arrives, no one even verifies the terms; they just grab what they can get. And this peace offer leaves a question: Why did the Dauphin give up the fight? After jeopardizing his immortal soul in a confrontation with Pandulph, Lewis reappears in one brief scene to hear some bad news. The next thing we know, he has given up—even though the Bastard dropped his defense.

In addition, the role of Pandulph deteriorates. We are left wondering whether or not he actually convinced Lewis to negotiate the peace (which would answer the question as to why Lewis gave up), or whether he has been reduced to the role of an emissary. Either way, Shakespeare fails to justify Pandulph's actions; Shakespeare thus withholds a potentially important dramatic change from the audience.

That failure and the failure to resolve the end of the rebellion through dramatic conflict are key weaknesses in this play. It is doubtful that anyone deeply cares when John, who is intended to be the central character in this play, faces failure and dies. His deterioration and death, the reuniting of England under Prince Henry, and the withdrawal of the French forces are merely catalogued in a series of narrative speeches. John's death serves the playwright's need to resolve all of the issues and set up Prince Henry as a reconciliation figure in order to end this play.

Because Shakespeare wrote a weak, forced conclusion that does not grow naturally out of events which preceded it, he could do little more than provide his characters with declamatory speeches.

Characterization fares little better than plot in Act V. As mentioned in the preceding summary, characters do not interact in order to develop conflict; they declaim. Prince Henry arouses curiosity, but he is a wooden figure without personality. Identified as the son of King John and as the only hope for England's unity, he nevertheless remains a dull character when he should be rousing hope and inspiring cheers.

Even the Bastard departs from the pattern of learning one important lesson per act. Here, he serves only to lead an unsuccessful defense and to deliver bad news. He is devastated when he is told to accept the peace.

One interpretation of this ending that can structure unity is that in the end, everyone must capitulate to political reality—the merciless, unyielding "policy" that overrules humanistic, passionate objections. Constance rebels against the system but hers is a hopeless, uncompromising protest that results in a frenzied death. In contrast, once the Bastard accepts the fact, he gains power. Once he comes to terms with political realities, he accepts without protest the French terms of peace, King John's death, and the need to prepare Prince Henry to take over the government. The spirited protester at Angiers is as dead as the illegitimate king.

That interpretation notwithstanding, plot and characterization, both of which displayed intermittent promise during the development of the play, diminish toward the conclusion of *King John*. Perhaps it was enough for Elizabethan audiences to witness the reuniting of England and the defeat of the French, but those events are not, in themselves, sufficient to stir modern audiences to cheers or catharsis at the climax of the play.

1595

RICHARD II

RICHARD II

LIST OF CHARACTERS

King Richard

Historically, he is said to be the handsomest man of his time; in the play, he has great charm and a love for beautiful things. His court is characterized outwardly by its luxury and refinement, but Richard's own particular favorites are greedy men who are interested primarily in the profits made from usurping land, excessive taxation, and fraud. Richard allows himself to be used by these men and, as a result, is deposed by one of his noblemen, whom he sent unfairly into exile.

Bolingbroke

Henry, Duke of Hereford and Lancaster; he takes revenge on Richard after the king unfairly banishes him from England and, moreover, claims all of Henry's family lands and wealth after Henry's father, John of Gaunt, dies. Bolingbroke is a "model" Englishman and, for that reason, is not entirely convinced that he has the right to usurp the crown from a man who *seems* corrupt even though he is supposed to be God's deputy on earth.

York

He is Richard's most powerful supporter; when Richard leaves with his forces to fight in Ireland, he leaves York in charge of England. York is honest and good throughout the play, and because of these qualities, he finally cannot condone Richard's unprincipled actions; thus he changes his allegiance to Bolingbroke and his supporters.

Aumerle

York's headstrong son remains loyal to Richard throughout the play despite the fact that this loyalty threatens his relationship with his father. He even becomes involved in a plot to assassinate Bolingbroke, but at the pleading of his mother, he confesses his deed and is pardoned by Bolingbroke.

Queen Isabella

She appears four times in the play and, each time, is characterized by her gentleness and her devotion to Richard. Moreover, there is a feeling of helplessness about her. Her grief becomes despair when she realizes that her husband has been deposed. She tries, however, to goad him into at least a *show* of valor and resistance when she speaks with him on his way to prison.

Mowbray

Clearly, he had a hand in the murder of Gloucester even though he denies it. Richard exiles him for life, probably in order to remove this hand-chosen assassin from the country. Mowbray dies abroad during one of the Crusades.

Northumberland

A powerful and aggressive character; his allegiance is early aligned with Bolingbroke. He fights alongside Bolingbroke and arranges for Richard's surrender. It is he who breaks up the last of Richard's conspirators.

Percy

Northumberland's son. He is an eager soldier, chivalrous, and an active supporter of Bolingbroke.

Duchess of Gloucester

It was the murder of her husband that caused Bolingbroke to accuse Mowbray of assassination and treason. She begs old Gaunt to take revenge on Richard; her anger is fiery and passionate. She dies of grief for her husband.

Duchess of York

Her loyalty is, foremost, to her son, who is loyal to Richard. Her whole character revolves around Aumerle's safety. She herself is fearless before Bolingbroke, but she fears the latter's power to silence her son's seemingly treasonous words and deeds.

Surrey

He is sympathetic with Aumerle and refutes Fitzwater's claim that Aumerle, in Fitzwater's presence, did take credit for Gloucester's death.

Carlisle

He is ever-loyal to Richard because he sees Richard's role as one that was heaven-ordained. He rails against Bolingbroke but, importantly, also chides Richard for the kind of king he has been. In the end, Bolingbroke pardons him because of his unusually high character.

Abbot of Westminster

He hears Aumerle's wish to revenge himself on Bolingbroke and, therefore, invites Aumerle home so that the two of them can make further plans.

Ross and Willoughby

Representatives of the followers of Bolingbroke.

Fitzwater

He swears that he heard Aumerle take full credit for Gloucester's murder. Surrey takes issue with this statement, and Fitzwater challenges him to a duel.

Exton

Believing that Bolingbroke wishes him to kill Richard, he does so; immediately afterward, however, he is sure that he acted rashly. Bolingbroke banishes him.

Salisbury

Richard leaves him in charge of the military forces while he fights in Ireland. He is upset when he discovers that he has no Welsh support for Richard when he knows that Bolingbroke and his supporters are ready to attack Richard.

Scroop

He announces to Richard that the common people have championed Bolingbroke as their favorite. He appears only in Act III, Scenes 2 and 3.

Berkeley

In charge of the troops guarding Bristol Castle, he is rebuked when Bolingbroke confronts him, and he refers to Bolingbroke as Hereford—and not as Lancaster.

Bushy and Green

They are followers of Richard, but they are neither heroic nor staunch in their loyalty. They plot, connive, and flee at the approach of danger. Bolingbroke corners them finally and has them killed. They are representative of the low-class flatterers whom Richard surrounds himself with.

Bagot

He has a part only slightly larger than Bushy and Green; otherwise, he is not distinguishable from them.

SUMMARIES AND COMMENTARIES

ACT I

Summary

King Richard II opens the play by asking old John of Gaunt if he has brought John's son, Henry Bolingbroke, to substantiate charges of treason that he has made against Thomas Mowbray, Duke of Norfolk. After asking Gaunt if he has already questioned his son on the matter, Richard orders that the two men be brought before him; Richard greets them formally, and then he asks Henry Bolingbroke to clarify his case against Mowbray. Bolingbroke charges Mowbray with being a "traitor and a miscreant," but before he can finish speaking, Mowbray breaks in and offers a counter-accusation: "I do defy him and I spit at him, / Call him a slanderous coward and a villain." Mowbray suggests that they settle their quarrel by dueling at Coventry, and Bolingbroke throws down his glove as a symbol of his counter-challenge according to the rites of knighthood.

After Mowbray retrieves the glove and accepts the challenge, the king asks Bolingbroke to explain his accusation against Mowbray. Bolingbroke levels the charges: "All the treasons of these eighteen years" have their origin in Mowbray; he did plot the murder of the Duke of Gloucester. Mowbray responds that he committed *one* grave sin in the past—laying an ambush for old Gaunt's life, but he has since repented it. He denies killing Gloucester. The king tries to calm them both with the words "Forget, forgive; conclude and be agreed," and he appeals to old Gaunt for help in the matter. Gaunt cannot decide what to do, and so he exits. Meanwhile, Mowbray refuses to withdraw the challenge. "The purest treasure," he says, that "mortal times afford / Is spotless reputation." Therefore, he tells Richard, the king can command his life, but not his shame; Bolingbroke's reply is similar: "Shall I seem crestfallen in my father's sight?" Richard seemingly cannot determine which of the men is lying and, therefore, refuses to arbitrate any longer; he orders that the duel shall take place at Coventry on Saint Lambert's Day (September 17): "There shall your swords and lances arbitrate."

Scene 2 takes place at the London palace of John of Gaunt; old Gaunt is talking to the Duchess of Gloucester, who is paying him a visit. The duchess is very upset; she wants revenge and she hopes that old Gaunt will see to it that revenge is exacted because Gloucester, her husband, was Gaunt's brother. Gaunt advises his sister-in-law that they can't do anything against the "butchers of [Gloucester's] life." They had best leave the "quarrel to the will of Heaven." The duchess is shocked at Gaunt's apparent lack of will to take vengeance for her "dear lord." Her husband's blood was Gaunt's own blood, she emphasizes. Likewise, she tells Gaunt that her murdered husband and Gaunt shared the same womb, but Gaunt refuses to submit to her tactics. The duchess, however, continues; she argues that "to safeguard thine own life / The best way is to venge my Gloucester's death." Gaunt explains that his hands are tied; the king, "God's deputy," caused the murder, hence revenge must be left to heaven. One cannot defy God's appointed deputy in England, he insists. The duchess appears to acquiesce and bids

Gaunt goodbye. She hopes that at least right will triumph when Bolingbroke and Mowbray fight at Coventry, and that Bolingbroke's spear "may enter butcher Mowbray's breast!" Weeping, she bids Gaunt farewell.

Richard and his knights arrive at Coventry, on a field prepared for single combat, and enter to the sound of trumpets. Then Mowbray enters with a herald. The king bids the Marshal to "demand of yonder champion" the cause of the present quarrel. After Mowbray is asked the cause of his being here, he repeats his case, promising to prove himself true and, furthermore, promising to prove Bolingbroke "a traitor to my God, my King, and me." Trumpets are heard again, and Bolingbroke, armed like his counterpart, enters the scene. Richard asks the Marshal once again to inquire the cause of complaint. The Marshal does so, and Bolingbroke repeats his previous accusation: Mowbray is a traitor, "foul and dangerous." Bolingbroke then asks permission to bid farewell to the king by kissing his ring. The king acknowledges the request and descends from his seat to "fold him in our arms." Richard states that despite whose blood will be shed, no revenge will be taken.

Bolingbroke then takes leave of the king, his kinsmen, his followers, and finally his father. He bids them to shed no tears and promises to perform valiantly for his father's sake. His father, in turn, bids him to "be swift like lightning" in the fight.

Mowbray then has his turn to bid farewell to the king, claiming to be a "loyal, just, and upright gentleman" who will fight without boasting about it. "As gentle and as jocund as to jest / Go I to fight," he says, for "truth hath a quiet breast."

Before the fight begins, however, King Richard throws his baton to the ground as a signal to halt the proceedings. "Let them lay by their helmets and their spears," he says, "and both return back to their chairs again." Richard explains that he does not wish to see blood spilled by his countrymen, as in civil war, and therefore will banish the two contestants from England. Bolingbroke is not to return for ten years, while Mowbray is banished for life. The two men accept their sentences gracefully, though Mowbray, who is never to return, expresses a deep sadness that he will not be able to speak the English language again; he feels condemned to a "speechless death."

As the two turn to leave, Richard stops them and makes them lay their hands on his royal sword and promise never to come into contact with one another again nor to engage in any treasonous act; never are they "to plot, contrive, or complot any ill." Both swear accordingly, but Bolingbroke has a parting word with Mowbray; he asks him—now that he is banished and free from other punishment—to confess the crime against the state that he has committed. Mowbray replies that he'd rather be "from heaven banished" than admit to such a thing. He exits then.

Richard turns to Gaunt and immediately reduces old Gaunt's son's sentence from ten years to six years because Gaunt's old eyes betray a "grieved heart." Bolingbroke gratefully accepts the commutation of his sentence and muses on the ease with which Richard can change the course of another man's life: "Such is the breath of kings." Gaunt also thanks the king but remains saddened because he is an old man who may not live the six years before his son returns. When the king cheerfully reminds him that he is in good health and will live many more years, Gaunt stops him short by saying that even the king "cannot buy my breath." The king questions Gaunt, wondering why he did not defend his son more vehemently. Gaunt replies that he was urged to speak as a judge and not to argue "like a father." His duty to the judgment process forced him to remain as objective as possible, and now he must suffer privately for it.

In the last minutes of Scene 3, Bolingbroke and his father take leave of each other. Gaunt tries to cheer up his son by saying that it won't be too long before he returns and that if he keeps his mind on other things, the time of exile will pass quickly. Bolingbroke, however, asks,

> O, who can hold a fire in his hand
> By thinking on the frosty Caucasus?
> Or cloy the hungry edge of appetite
> By bare imagination of a feast?
> Or wallow naked in December snow
> By thinking on fantastic summer's heat?
>
> (294–99)

He departs, swearing that wherever he wanders, he can at least boast that "though banished, [he is] yet a trueborn Englishman."

Scene 4 opens shortly after the last. Richard is subtly trying to test the loyalty of Aumerle, the son of the Duke of York, and, at the same time, to find out from him what Bolingbroke said on his departure, for Aumerle escorted Bolingbroke away. Aumerle says that

Bolingbroke said only "Farewell." Clearly, he does not like Boling-broke and did not enjoy escorting him away, feigning feelings of fond farewell. Richard does not want to seem villainous, and so he reminds Aumerle that Bolingbroke is "our cousin." He then explores another avenue of conversation; he says that he has had certain of his men—Bushy, Bagot, and Green—observing the country people, and they report that the banished Bolingbroke is popular among the commoners. He ponders,

> How he did seem to dive into their hearts
> With humble and familiar courtesy,
> What reverence he did throw away on slaves,
> Wooing poor craftsmen with the craft of smiles.
>
> (25–28)

To Richard, it seems "as were our England in reversion his."

Green then speaks up and reminds Richard that, at least, Bol-ingbroke is out of the way; now they must turn their attention to the pressing problem of the Irish rebellion. Richard decides to go into battle himself against the rebels, and he plans to do so with the greatest assurance of success. To that end, he decides that he must first fill his coffers with riches borrowed from (and demanded from) his country's nobles. At that point, Bushy rushes in with the news that Gaunt is extremely ill, probably dying. Richard wishes the old man "good speed" (to death). In fact, his comment is quite mercenary: "The lining of his coffers shall make coats / To deck our soldiers for these Irish wars" (61–62). They all exit then to go to Gaunt's bedside.

Commentary

As is the case with Shakespeare's other history plays, this play has as its central concern a civil strife that threatens a country with a weak government. Thus, *Richard II* opens with a scene that graphi-cally illustrates the point: Two nobles are locked in bitter argument over who is most loyal to the crown, and the only logical outcome would seem to be a physical struggle, even to the death. The best that the king can do is agree to let them fight.

The character of old Gaunt is important here because he is referred to several times as an "old" man and is therefore supposed to be a "sage" man. Richard appeals to Gaunt to help settle the argument but with no success; neither the ruler nor he who possesses the wisdom of age can calm the troubled waters in Scene 1; only a decision based on formal violence will decide the issue.

Note in particular the chivalric atmosphere of Scene 1. When the challengers speak to the king and to each other, they use a very formal style of address. For example, Bolingbroke first speaks to his king:

> In the devotion of a subject's love,
> Tend'ring the precious safety of my prince,
> And free from other misbegotten hate,
> Come I appellant to this princely presence.
>
> (31–34)

And Mowbray, when he accepts the challenge, also speaks in a formal manner:

> I take it up; and by that sword I swear
> Which gently laid my knighthood on my shoulder,
> I'll answer then in any fair degree
> Or chivalrous design of knightly trial.
>
> (78–81)

The formal speech patterns and the chivalric code of behavior in Scene 1 act as metaphors for order and control. These men are preparing to kill each other, but they are going about it in a gentlemanly way. Such formal patterns exist, according to Shakespeare's orthodox belief, in the world of government too. There is always an attempt—even when it becomes a struggle—to keep the most violent passions regulated within a pattern.

Speaking of formal patterns, we must not ignore the real passion and invective in some of the remarks that the opponents hurl at each other. Take, for example, Bolingbroke's promise to tear out his own tongue and "spit it bleeding" in Mowbray's face rather than withdraw from the fight. This is naked, unbridled passion. But it is spoken within the formal context of a verbal tournament, preluding the tournament at Coventry. And, in reference to passion, there is an important, implicit clue as to the murderer of Gloucester. Mowbray has indeed had a hand in killing him (and that's what Bolingbroke accuses him of), but Mowbray did it at Richard's request. When Bolingbroke utters the words "the death," Mowbray says, "I slew him not; but, to my own disgrace / Neglected my sworn duty in that case." Mowbray swore, without a doubt, to Richard to see to it that Gloucester was either killed by his hand or by Mowbray's order.

One more matter that should not be neglected in any discussion of language in Scene 1 includes the fact that the language, besides being mostly chivalrous and formal, suggests a religious theme in several places: Such words as "miscreant," "innocent souls," "rites of knighthood," and "our sacred blood" occur frequently. This language will be of even more importance later in the play.

Shakespeare's plays were written for performance without any breaks between the scenes or the acts. The flow of the scenes, their placement, and the effect that was created by contrasting elements in the scene constitute his chief technical resource. In Scene 1, for example, Richard tries to arbitrate a dispute between two peers of his realm. The issue is one of state—loyalty to the king—and also a personal matter of honor between two men of arms. The tone of the opening scene tells us that something is wrong in the state of England. Scene 2, appropriately, personalizes this wrongness, this grief, by showing us a woman lamenting aloud both the loss of her husband and the fact that she is likely not to see proper vengeance done. That she is suffering personally is certain, and her confusion is clear in her last speech, for she finds it difficult to say farewell to old Gaunt:

> Commend me to thy brother, Edmund York.
> Lo! this is all: nay, yet depart not so;
> Though this be all, do not so quickly go.
> I shall remember more. Bid him . . . Ah! What?
> With all good speed at Plashy visit me.
>
> (62–66)

The phrasing—"Lo! . . . nay, yet depart not . . . Bid him . . . Ah! What?"—tells more about her distraught state of mind than the words themselves.

At the beginning of Scene 2, when the duchess tries to play on Gaunt's feelings for his murdered brother, her language echoes Christian and biblical phrases. She refers to the patriarch: "Edward's seven sons, whereof thyself art one, / Were as seven vials of his sacred blood, / Or seven fair branches springing from one root" (11–13). As she continues, her emotion wells up: "But Thomas, my dear lord, my life, my Gloucester, / One vial full of Edward's sacred blood / . . . / Is hacked down . . . / . . . / Ah, Gaunt, his blood was thine!" (16–22). The effect of this speech is to reinforce her feelings of loss by emphasizing the "sacredness" of their common father's blood. The irony, and a serious religious and political problem for Shakespeare's age, is that another father-figure, one who is also "sacred," is Richard II, the king, and he has had a hand in perpetrating the crime. Gaunt has relatively few lines in this scene, and for good reason. He, like others around him, feels impotent before this impossible dilemma. This old and sage Gaunt, in his helplessness in the face of personal and public grief, is an important early theatrical image in the play. He can only lamely repeat the formula: "God's is the quarrel; for God's substitute, / His deputy anointed in His sight, / Hath caused his death" (37–39).

Notice the progression of Scene 3. It begins as a highly formal, almost ritualistic display in the chivalric tradition. The accused and the accusing parties are announced; they state their cases, make their farewells, and prepare to fight. It ends with a father and a son, Gaunt and Bolingbroke, saying goodbye for six years, or, considering Gaunt's age, maybe for the last time in their lives. The scene moves from the affairs of state in a public ceremony to the intimate details of personal, familial relationships. That very pattern, you will recall, was the pattern of Scenes 1 and 2. Here it is repeated with continuous focus on the principals in the drama.

When Richard pronounces the words "orderly proceed" at the start of Scene 3, he is, of course, sounding the keynote to all of Shakespeare's history plays again. The ritual of this hand-to-hand combat, though it is enacted to resolve a passionate dispute and may end in bloodshed, will be carried out according to mutually acknowledged rules. One must imagine the start of this scene as being filled with suggestions of the spectacle of a medieval tournament. Representatives of the opposing camps march in, present themselves to the king, speak their pieces, and take up positions on an elaborate stage tableau. The picture onstage and the accompanying regular trumpet blasts are clear metaphors for a kind of order. And at the center of this ordered world is, of course, King Richard, who is stationed upstage to observe the proceedings. When he descends from his raised platform (which was traditional) and walks downstage to stop the proceedings later in the scene, he travels quite a distance (the depth of Shakespeare's stage was about 25 feet), reinforcing his pivotal place on the stage and in the political picture.

The language of Bolingbroke, describing himself and Mowbray as two men who "vow [to take] a long and weary pilgrimage," continues the religious imagery that is germane to the subject of this play. Bolingbroke wants to take a long farewell with his father because it may be their last farewell. But before he launches into his private farewell, he is embraced by the king, a poignant moment when one considers the scene later in the play when the two of them meet again—when Richard renounces his throne to Bolingbroke. Richard hands him the crown then. Here, the father of the nation, as it were, embraces one of his "sons"; later, that "son" will depose him. Bolingbroke bids farewell to his faithful followers, then to his actual father, Gaunt.

Notice, too, the way that Shakespeare contrasts the characters of these opponents by suggesting a difference in their bearing in these scenes. When they first encountered one another in the first scene of this act, Mowbray made a point of contrasting his own response to the situation with Bolingbroke's. Implicitly, he is claiming that Bolingbroke is somewhat hot-headed and, therefore, less creditable than himself. There he said:

> Let not my cold words here accuse my zeal.
> 'Tis not the trial of a woman's war,
> The bitter clamour of two eager tongues,
> Can arbitrate this cause betwixt us twain;
> The blood is hot that must be cooled for this.
> (I. i. 47–51)

He has apparently listened to Bolingbroke's enraged words and has decided to respond with a posture of perfect reasonableness. In Scene 3, he strikes the same theme when he says, "Truth hath a quiet breast." The reason for this relatively calm bearing might be his quiet confidence that the king is on his side, and, therefore, he shall come to no harm. Whatever the reason, the posture of one combatant being more feverish than the other is important for dramatic reasons. Besides adding variety in characterization, this contrast prepares for a similar contrast later during the deposition scene (IV. i.). Notice there how quietly Bolingbroke endures the lengthy diatribes of King Richard II.

An important dramatic facet in Scene 3 is Richard's decision to stop the combat and to exile the opponents. All of the spectacle and verbal exchange in the scene is leading up to a violent combat that show of suffering. The matter of loyalty to the king is important with regard to Aumerle because of his actions later in the play when he is chided by his father for behavior disloyal to the new king, Bolingbroke. In the end, of course, Bolingbroke pardons Aumerle, but that pardon will seem all the more magnanimous because of the memory of this early scene in which Aumerle is quite clearly a loyal ally of Richard's and a foe of Bolingbroke's.

Consider the dramatic effect when Richard sarcastically bids his followers to come with him to the dying Gaunt's bedside: "Come, gentlemen, let's all go visit him. / Pray God we may make haste, and come too late!" And they reply, to a man: "Amen!" The contrast with the closing of the previous scene is a powerful one.

ACT II

Summary

Scene 1 takes place at Ely House in London, where Gaunt lies ill. His first speech forms a sort of "bridge" between the end of the last scene and this act. Speaking to his brother, the Duke of York, Gaunt asks, "Will the King come, that I may breathe my last / In wholesome counsel to his unstaid youth?" Clearly, Gaunt is worried about conditions in England. York, however, has no easy words of consolation; he thinks that the king is beyond listening ("all in vain comes counsel to his ear"); he thinks that the king listens only to young men who are more concerned with aping Continental fashions than coping with England's political troubles. Still, however, Gaunt hopes that his advice won't be wasted. He reasons that dying men are listened to more carefully because it is recognized that their words are precious because they are so scarce.

Acknowledging that he probably sounds like an Old Testament prophet, Gaunt charges Richard with the sin of wasting himself in a "rash fierce blaze of riot" which "cannot last." He is determined to convert the erring Richard to a better life worthy of his role as king. He appeals strongly to the patriotic sentiments of the audience as he rhetorically describes England: "This royal throne of kings, this sceptred isle, / This earth of majesty, this seat of Mars, / This other Eden, demi-paradise" (40–42). Then Gaunt reverses the imagery and speaks of the shame that has been brought to England of late, how Richard turned this paradise into a shameful place and turned

never takes place. Why does Shakespeare have Richard stop the fight? For one thing, Richard is, in fact, indebted to Mowbray for being instrumental in eliminating a potential enemy (Gloucester). For another, to allow the combat to go forward and risk the life of the apparently popular Bolingbroke would be a poor political move. It seems best to appear the wise and kind ruler by preventing any civil bloodshed at all. Notice that Richard also manages to banish Mowbray, the one who has evidence against him, for life, while commuting the sentence of Bolingbroke from ten years to six years, further mollifying his potential political opponents. Rulers in Shakespeare's age would have been familiar with Machiavelli's famous *Prince*, a popular and rather cynical manual for rulers, and would have known that it is always wiser to appear harsher at first, making severe punishments all at once, and then to soften one's stance with mercy. The mercy, however, is not received quite as Richard had expected, and this irritates him.

There is a serious undertone of antagonism between Richard, on the one hand, and Gaunt and his son, on the other. Richard knows very well what he is doing in commuting the sentence as he does, and he is hoping that Gaunt will receive this lordly gesture appropriately. When Gaunt takes up his son's cue on the words "such is the breath of kings" and tells the king that though he can easily send a man into exile or even cut a man's life short, he *still* does not have the power to add one minute to a man's life, he is raising a very sensitive issue and one very important to a central theme of this play. In a play in which the deposition of God's appointed minister, the king, is a central action, it is a highly charged dramatic moment when the matter of the limitation of the power of the king is raised. None of this by-play is openly acknowledged by the speakers, but their words are certainly spoken with an awareness of all connotations. What Gaunt is saying, in effect, is that although Richard may be God's anointed and appointed deputy, he is certainly *not* God Himself. One wonders if the conversation that he had with his sister-in-law in the previous scene, coupled with the present sorrow of saying goodbye to his son, has given him some of the courage that the Duchess of Gloucester found wanting.

That Gaunt's remarks have the desired effect on Richard is clear from the way in which the king exits, with two clipped lines reiterating the sentence just meted out: "Cousin, farewell; and, uncle, bid him so; / Six years we banish him, and he shall go" (247–48). The last moments of Scene 3 are especially important for their emotional tone. There is speed in the delivery of the lines between Gaunt and his son, Bolingbroke, that belies the feelings underneath. Bolingbroke is silent at first, until his father urges him to speak:

Gaunt:	O, to what purpose dost thou hoard thy words, That thou return'st no greeting to thy friends?
Bolingbroke:	I have too few to take my leave of you, When the tongue's office should be prodigal To breathe the abundant dolour of the heart.
Gaunt:	Thy grief is but thy absence for a time.
Bolingbroke:	Joy absent, grief is present for that time.
Gaunt:	What is six winters? They are quickly gone.
Bolingbroke:	To men in joy; but grief makes one hour ten.
Gaunt:	Call it a travel that thou tak'st for pleasure.

(255–64)

This scene seems very genuine psychologically. Gaunt's distress is shown by the fact that he is using "arguments" to make his son feel better, which he had, just a few minutes before, rebuked the king for using—that is, that the exile really won't be so long, that it really is only a temporary absence. In addition, it is as if the rush of words they exchange is a way of covering up feelings they would rather not have to cope with. There is an irony in the remark that Gaunt makes to his son, telling him that his absence will serve as a foil to his coming home and make the coming home that much more joyous. In a way, this is true, for Bolingbroke's return will eventually lead to his becoming king, albeit reluctantly. His return *will* seem greater because of the absence. Also, Richard's behavior, by comparison, will make Bolingbroke seem greater. Interestingly, this metaphor of

a *foil* carries on into the *Henry IV* plays. There, we find Bolin an older and a wearier man, now the king himself, having with a recalcitrant son, Prince Hal. Throughout the play, Hal pades with the lower orders of society are described in such that they can be seen as setting his "true" (princely) self off as is set off by the less precious metal leaf which serves as back it in a setting.

There is superb humaneness in old Gaunt as he gives some conventional fatherly advice at the end of Scene 3. He is to be perfectly reasonable and allay his son's fears: Don't thi the king has banished you, but rather think that you have ba the king; try to think that a foul pestilence sits in the land a are better off out of the country. In a sense, there *is* a truth in that there is a less-than-perfect king on the throne, but Bolin can answer only from his heart, and none of his father's arg makes him feel any better. Who can "wallow naked in De snow / By thinking on fantastic summer's heat?" he asks. The of banishment will be so painful that he won't be able to himself for a minute into believing otherwise. At the very las ever, Bolingbroke exits with an important, manly, and p flourish: "Where'er I wander, boast of this I can, / Though ba yet a trueborn Englishman" (308–309). These, undoubtedly, words of a hero.

In Scene 4, we see Richard in close-ups; he is a man accustomed to exploiting his countrymen, and in this scene marked contrast to the "trueborn Englishman" who bade us f in the previous scene. Shakespeare shows Richard quite ope paring to take his country's wealth to spend on a foreign v also hoping for an early death for the venerable old Gaunt. rather bold characterization, somewhat melodramatic, an typical of Shakespeare's early plays than his later ones. The question at this point where an audience's sympathies lie.

Note also the character of Aumerle in this scene. He is a man, the son of the Duke of York, and naturally enough he loyalty to his king. He is proud of having successfully feign at Bolingbroke's departure, and he happily joins Bagot and C the king's side. Shakespeare will later sound this note of grief when Richard gives up the crown. There, it will be broke who sarcastically commends Richard for putting on

this fortress-like isle into a prison. As the king enters, York hastily warns Gaunt to temper his rage, saying that "young hot colts being raged do rage the more."

Richard, with his favorite courtiers, approaches Gaunt and is amazed at the old man's invective. Gaunt charges that Richard is the sicker of the two men, and he extends the idea of sickness and infection to include England itself: "Thy death-bed," he says, "is no lesser than thy land / Wherein thou liest in reputation sick." He points to the covey of political sycophants whom the king surrounds himself with; the crown of England cannot encompass all these "thousand flatterers," Gaunt warns. Richard is no king; Richard is no more than a greedy landlord to his country.

Richard loses his composure and abruptly stops the old man: If Gaunt were not the brother to great Edward's son, he would soon have his head separated from his body. Gaunt is not impressed. He reminds the company that that sort of scruple didn't bother Richard when he ended Gloucester's life. As Gaunt is taken out, he turns and hopes that "these words hereafter thy tormentors be!"

Gaunt's death is announced shortly thereafter by Northumberland, and the Duke of York is distressed to hear Richard almost gloat over "the plate, coin, revenues, and moveables" of old Gaunt. What is to become of the entire system of allegiance and inheritance, he asks, if Richard can so capriciously take the lands and property of Gaunt, which rightfully belong to Gaunt's son, Bolingbroke? If Richard does this, York warns him that he "pluck[s] a thousand dangers on [his] head." Richard is unmoved; he means to immediately "seize into our hands / His plate, his goods, his money, and his lands," and to that end he orders Bushy to arrange the transfer of possessions.

When the king is gone, Northumberland, Willoughby, and Ross discuss the state of the nation. Northumberland fears that banishment will be the punishment if one of Richard's flatterers chooses to decide to denounce him. Ross points to the grievous, unjust taxes now levied on commoners and nobles alike, and Willoughby mentions the plethora of blank checks and forced loans. The three men see no hope for England; "unavoided is the danger now." The times demand revolt, and Ross urges Northumberland to lead the revolt. Northumberland then gives them the news that already he has had news from Bolingbroke; Gaunt's son has gathered a large number of highly placed sympathizers who have ships and some "three thousand men." As soon as Richard leaves for Ireland, Bolingbroke means to fight to reclaim what is his. Moreover, Northumberland promises them that they personally will soon have a chance to "redeem . . . the blemished crown, / Wipe off the dust that hides our sceptre's gilt, / And make high majesty look like itself."

At Windsor Castle, deep in conversation with Bushy, one of the king's favorites, the queen is trying to discover the source of her deep depression. The king has departed for Ireland, and the queen feels that something ominous is about to occur: "Yet again, methinks, / Some unborn sorrow, ripe in fortune's womb, / Is coming towards me" (8–10). Her "inward soul" persuades her that there is something amiss causing her anxiety, something more than mere separation from the king, although that separation is indeed a source of pain to her.

Green hurries onstage as they are talking and proves the queen's premonition correct by delivering the news that Bolingbroke has landed with his army in the north of England. York enters then and laments the fact that he was left by Richard to uphold the royal forces, to "underprop his land." There is no money left to fight a successful campaign against the rebels, and even if there were, it seems apparent that the popular figure in the country is *not* the king but his adversary—Bolingbroke. Adding to the general woe that has befallen the present company, a messenger enters with the news that the Duke of York's sister-in-law, the widow of the late Duke of Gloucester, has died. "God for his mercy! what a tide of woes / Comes rushing on this woeful land at once," cries York in despair. He is thoroughly confused; he is duty-bound (by conscience and kinship) to defend the nation against the rebels, but his sympathies are with his nephew Bolingbroke, whom the king has wronged.

The queen and York leave, and Bushy, Bagot, and Green remain behind to discuss their plans. Bagot decides to go to Ireland and join the king, while Bushy and Green decide to seek refuge at a sympathetic castle in Bristol. The three of them are convinced that the Duke of York's chances of repelling the rebels are slim. The task of defending Richard's crown, Green likens to "numbering sands, and drinking oceans dry." Convinced that they may never meet again, they exit.

Somewhere in Gloucestershire, once more in England, Bolingbroke questions Northumberland about the way to Berkeley. These "high wild hills and rough uneven ways" have exhausted them both. Northumberland replies that Bolingbroke's "fair discourse" and his good conversation have made the journey seem light and easy. Bolingbroke replies graciously that his companion's words have special value for him.

Northumberland's son, Henry Percy, comes onto the scene and pledges his services to Bolingbroke for life. Northumberland and Bolingbroke then discuss the military situation and are soon joined by the forces of Willoughby and Ross, and both men reaffirm their pledge to right the wrongs done to Bolingbroke in his absence. The Lord of Berkeley enters then, bearing a message from the Duke of York. Berkeley addresses Bolingbroke as "My Lord of Hereford," and Berkeley is rebuffed by the rebel leader, who tells Berkeley to address him by his proper title—Lancaster—if he wants an answer.

The Duke of York, unattended, enters next and is greeted formally and respectfully by Bolingbroke, who kneels to him. York, however, will have none of this formality and tells his nephew to "Grace me no grace, nor uncle me no uncle; / I am no traitor's uncle, and that word 'grace' / In an ungracious mouth is but profane" (86–88). York reminds Henry and his rebels that "in my loyal bosom lies his [King Richard's] power," but Bolingbroke stands firm in his claim that he has every right to be doing what he is doing. He was banished as Hereford, but now that his father is dead, he returns as Lancaster to claim what is his and "to rouse [Richard's] wrongs." He further entreats old York to think of him as a son ("methinks in you / I see old Gaunt alive"). He continues the kinship argument, trying to persuade York that if the situation had been reversed and it was *York* (instead of Gloucester) who had been killed by Richard, it is certain that old Gaunt would have backed *Aumerle* (York's son).

Northumberland reiterates the point that *all* of them are concerned primarily with righting the wrongs that have been done to Bolingbroke, and Bolingbroke asks York to join them in attacking Bristol Castle, where the "caterpillars of the commonwealth," Bushy, Bagot, and their accomplices, are hiding. York finds the argument to be strong, and he says, "It may be I will go with you. . . . Things past redress are now with me past care."

A short scene closes this act. In a camp in Wales, the Lord of Salisbury is speaking with a Welsh captain and is worried that he has heard "no tidings from the King." The captain is ready to disperse his troops but is urged by Salisbury to maintain his forces one more day. The captain, however, refuses; he believes the rumor that "the King is dead." Unnatural omens and portents seem to prove the supposition and "our countrymen are gone and fled." Salisbury, likewise, laments Richard's dying glory—"like a shooting star." Symbolically, Salisbury sees the sun set "weeping in the lowly west."

Commentary

Scene 1 begins with the individual rage of an esteemed old man who is soon to breathe his last, and it ends with the suggestion that the rage has spread to large numbers of people who are prepared to do something about it. The situation is a potentially revolutionary one, and Shakespeare traces the development of political turmoil by first allowing one man to speak his frustration and bear the insults of a capricious ruler, and then showing the effect of this scene of humiliation on those who have witnessed it. When Northumberland, Ross, and Willoughby conspire at the very end of the scene to join forces with the rebellious army of Bolingbroke, we have a feeling that there is a rightness to their decision. We not only hear about Richard's ill-treatment of deserving countrymen, but we witness that ill-treatment. Shakespeare's dramatic strategy is at its most effective here.

In the first conversation between York and Gaunt in Scene 1, Gaunt is perhaps a symbol for the sickly state of the nation, for there is the suggestion that what is symbolically best about the nation is languishing at the moment. After York prepares the ground with references to corrupt foreign influences and herds of flatterers, it is Gaunt who delivers the rousing patriotic speech that is the emotional center of the entire scene. By the end of the speech, it is as though Gaunt is identified with all that is good and noble and blessed about England. The scene gains further dramatic significance by the fact that these are the words of a dying man. Point for point, the features of England that Gaunt mentions in his rousing speech are those features that are being misshapen by the actions of the king and his court. "This seat of Mars"—England—a proud, warring nation, has become so craven that it gains more and spends more from its cleverly concluded truces than it does from the actual spoils of war. And when Northumberland and his friends speak at the end of the scene, it is clear that they loath the new set of priorities that Richard has set for the nation.

Even the war fought in Ireland is fought on borrowed, extorted, and stolen money, and it is fought for a purely imperialistic purpose—that is, to fill the coffers of the profligate king. Gaunt's charges are keen and forceful: "This fortress built by Nature for herself," "this precious stone set in the silver sea," has become instead a prison "bound in with shame" and an object to be pawned, "now leased out." Gaunt is responding to the corruption of his England in the interests of the private indulgence of a bad king, and Shakespeare, for his part, like many of his contemporaries, is here making unhappy reference to changes in the economic system that were taking place in Elizabethan England. The new order for England would be the order of a profit-oriented world. Shakespeare also sounds the religious note of the play anew in this scene when he makes reference to the "Christian service and true chivalry" of the former "royal kings" of England. At the end of Gaunt's speech, one can imagine the old man being somewhat exhausted, especially when he utters the lines, "Ah! would the scandal vanish with my life, / How happy then were my ensuing death!" (67–68). His own strength is diminishing in strong contrast with the swift and lively entry of Richard and his queen and courtiers.

Richard, true to his reputation, always travels "in style," as it were. Whenever he comes onto the scene, it is always with a verbal flourish and an entourage. He is a man who likes "entrances," a man with a special penchant for acting. Consider the situation when Gaunt utters his last tired breath at the end of his patriotic tirade, and Richard bursts onto the scene. Notice the way in which Richard speaks to the old man. His speech is short and clipped, and his treatment of Gaunt is disrespectful, to say the least. First, there is the exchange between them on the subject of Gaunt's punning comment on the state of his health and the meaning of his name—gaunt, sickly, and thin. Richard's words are, at first, questions, one after the other—"What comfort, man? How is it with aged Gaunt?"; "Can sick men play so nicely with their names?"; "Should dying men flatter with those that live?" But when Gaunt loses patience, as an old man deprived of the comfort of having a son near him as he himself nears death, he launches a direct attack on the king and his court. The king, in turn, responds viciously.

Gaunt's reference to the "thousand flatterers [who] sit within thy crown" and more specifically to the fact that Richard is dangerously close to deposing himself strikes a raw nerve within Richard. Earlier, he entered the scene self-assured and confident that Gaunt was no threat to him because of his illness; he has come to Ely House in the first place to collect the old man's wealth, but now he loses his composure at these words and suddenly attacks the old man:

> A lunatic, lean-witted fool,
> Presuming on an ague's privilege,
> Dar'st with thy frozen admonition
> Make pale our cheek, chasing the royal blood
> With fury from his native residence.
>
> (115–19)

This attack adds cowardice and foolhardiness to the list of Richard's faults. One should remember, however, that Richard's response to any attack on himself is, in orthodox terms, justified; he *is* the king and, therefore, an entity apart from ordinary mortals. The complication in this scene, and indeed in the play as a whole, is that this king seems unworthy of the divine office he occupies. His attacker, old Gaunt, especially after the emotional "this other Eden" speech, is much more the "kingly" figure to be identified with England's virtues than the actual king himself.

Before Gaunt exits, he virtually accuses the king of the murder of Gloucester, and he warns him that these words will later haunt him: "Live in thy shame, but die not shame with thee! / These words hereafter thy tormentors be!" (135–36). The words will haunt him, and we should recall them when we witness the last scenes of the play, when the king faces death and despondency—as old Gaunt now does.

One reason for Shakespeare's writing the next part of Scene 1, between Richard and York, is that it offers a point of contrast between the two "old" men (York and Gaunt) in their responses to the king. We have already witnessed the conversation between York and Gaunt, and we know that York is unhappy with the state of England, though he is less likely to become infuriated and risk any treasonous act or statement. He tried to conciliate old Gaunt, tried to calm him in the face of the king, and now he uses the words of a diplomat to quell the king's anger toward Gaunt: "I do beseech your Majesty, impute his words / To wayward sickliness and age in him"

(141–42). York has a careful nature here; clearly, he knows just how explosive the situation is and doesn't want anyone to risk upsetting whatever equilibrium prevails. He will retain this role throughout the entire play, even after the rebels prove successful in deposing Richard.

It is significant that this "normative" figure, York, has his patience tried when Gaunt's death is announced, and the king, without the least trace of remorse, makes plans to immediately collect the booty he came for in the first place. The king's words, ironically, point to his own future situation: "The ripest fruit first falls, and so doth he; / His time is spent, our pilgrimage must be. / So much for that" (153–55). The king himself is "ripest" in the sense that he is most nearly "rotten"; and the king will indeed follow Gaunt on a "pilgrimage"—to humiliation and death. Richard breaks off these thoughts in mid-sentence and turns his mind to Gaunt's "plate, coin, revenues." It is here that York approaches exasperation: "How long shall I be patient?" he asks and begins a lengthy discourse on the falseness of Richard's conduct. One must imagine Richard's demeanor through all this long speech of York's. His interrupting words are: "Why, uncle, what's the matter?" The tone is almost certainly sarcastic because it couldn't fail to be clear to anyone exactly *what* the matter is.

York continues his desperate argument, completely unaware that, at best, the king is merely tolerating his words. York concludes his argument about succession: Since Richard is violating rights of inheritance and succession by seizing Gaunt's goods, he is putting the very idea of succession in jeopardy:

> Take Hereford's rights away, and take from Time
> His charters and his customary rights;
> Let not tomorrow then ensue today;
> Be not thyself.
>
> (195–98)

Indeed, in being a bad king, Richard is *not* being himself, kingship being by definition divine and therefore good. Richard is totally unmoved by this speech and, single-mindedly, repeats his intentions: "Think what you will, we seize into our hands / His plate, his goods, his money, and his lands" (209–10). York departs in despair, a mood that will change to hope in the rebellious persons of Northumberland, Willoughby, and Ross.

Remember that these three men have been present for most of
the foregoing scene and have witnessed the behavior of the king—
both to Gaunt and to York. At first, their plight seems to be the same
as York's. They dare not open their mouths for fear of the repercus-
sions. That foul injustice has been done to Gaunt and to his son Bolingbroke is without doubt, but they must tread lightly when
considering what action to take. The dialogue is written in such a
fashion as to emphasize the volume of wrongs that the king has
done. One after another of his deeds is catalogued, all those things
we have already heard Gaunt and York accuse him of. The reason
for the repetition is to indicate just how widespread the discontent
with the king is; in addition, it serves as a way of allowing these individual nobles to garner the courage to decide to commit what will
be, after all, treasonable acts. They list all the wrongs, then they
pause to consider their weight, and Northumberland speaks for
them all when he expresses fear at his own thoughts: He "dares not
say" what they can do to set things right in England. It is important
to realize that there is something conspiratorial about this scene in
that the three nobles are aware of the gravity of the situation. But
when they decide at the end to join forces with Bolingbroke's forces,
they do so with conviction:

> . . . we shall shake off our slavish yoke,
> Imp out our drooping country's broken wing,
> Redeem from broking pawn the blemish'd crown
> [and]
> Wipe off the dust that hides our scepter's gilt.
>
> (291–94)

Note in these words of Northumberland's the reference to Richard's
financial dealings ("redeem from broking pawn") and the pun on the
word "gilt," which refers to both the golden scepter, the symbol of
the crown that has become besmirched by the king's behavior, and
the actual "guilt" which lay on Richard's head, presumably for the
murder of Gloucester. The irony is heavy with significance.

The dramatic strategy of Scene 2 is similar to that which Shakespeare uses elsewhere and which he will bring to its most perfect
execution in *Macbeth*. He builds suspense and tension by having a
figure of some importance in the play, here the queen, articulate her
premonition of evil things to come, then after a suitable interval in
which another character, Bushy, tries to dissuade her from her

gloomy thoughts, he has the news announced that her intuition was correct; shortly thereafter, woe upon woe is to be visited upon all present. It is interesting to note that in the queen's immediate response to Green's information about the rebel forces, she even uses a form of imagery that Shakespeare will later have Lady Macbeth use to great effect:

> So, Green, thou art the midwife to my woe,
> And Bolingbroke my sorrow's dismal heir;
> Now hath my soul brought forth her prodigy,
> And I, a gasping, new-delivered mother,
> Have woe to woe, sorrow to sorrow, joined.
>
> (62–66)

The image of giving birth in the context of sorrow and political intrigue (birth given to a monster-prodigy) and all as if first conceived in the imagination (the soul brought forth the monster) is of special importance to this play. First, there is the general theme of legitimacy and inheritance to consider: The play is about a deposition and an unlawful succession to the throne, and for all of its consideration of the inadequacy of the king in question, the process shall bring forth misery as its heir.

Another motif, which Shakespeare makes much of in the last acts of the play, is that of the relationship between one's experience of suffering and the imagination. Later, Richard is isolated in his prison cell and will meditate on the "populous" world of his thoughts and how they breed: "My brain I'll prove the female to my soul, / My soul the father; and these two beget / A generation of still-breeding thoughts" (V. v. 6–8). After Bushy's advice to "despair not," the queen continues with her theme and uses phrases that relate the current state of sorrow to their immediate causes:

> Who shall hinder me?
> I will despair and be at enmity
> With cozening hope. He is a flatterer,
> A parasite, a keeper-back of death,
> Who gently would dissolve the bands of life,
> Which false hope lingers in extremity.
>
> (67–72)

Hope, she says, is a flatterer and a parasite and keeps even death at bay; she is speaking these lines to the very characters in the play who have been identified (by most of the sympathetic characters) with the flattery and corruption that will drag Richard down to his doom.

When Bushy is first speaking to the queen, before Green enters with the news about the rebels, he also uses language that prepares us for several later scenes in the play when Richard will become more of a central focus. In a later scene, Richard has an important moment in which he asks for a mirror and then, gazing at his image, meditates publicly on his situation as king and as an ordinary mortal. Here in Scene 2, Bushy uses a metaphor that obliquely prepares us for that important dramatic moment:

> Each substance of a grief hath twenty shadows,
> Which shows like grief itself, but is not so;
> For sorrow's eye, glazed with blinding tears,
> Divides one thing entire to many objects,
> Like perspectives, which rightly gazed upon
> Show nothing but confusion.
>
> (14–19)

Again, the key idea is that there is a difference between what you *think* you perceive and what is *actually* there, and beyond that, there is the natural distortion that a confused emotional state will bring to one's perceptions. Here the idea is graphically expressed in the image of an eye filled with tears through which one's experience is refracted. As this might be true of the queen in this scene, it is also true to a certain extent of Richard in a later scene. There it will be Bolingbroke who comments sarcastically about the difference between true emotion and "shadows." This idea is one that fascinated Shakespeare throughout his life, perhaps because he was so closely associated with the stage, where it is the business of a good actor to convey the *substance* of true emotions through mere *shadows* (acting) of those emotions. As a concluding note on this idea, consider the following two brief passages: "Howe'er it be, / I cannot but be sad; so heavy sad / As, though on thinking on no thought I think, / Makes me with heavy nothing faint and shrink" (30–32). These lines are spoken by Richard's queen here in Scene 2. And the following is spoken by another of Shakespeare's mentally tortured heroes, Prince Hamlet, speaking of Denmark: " . . . for there is nothing either good / Or bad but thinking makes it so. To me it is a prison" (II. ii. 255–56).

With the announcement of the arrival of the rebel forces and the death of the Duchess of Gloucester, all talk of imaginary worries ceases. It would be foolhardy to ignore the signs of things to come. An important figure in Scene 2 is the Duke of York, for he has lost a sister-in-law and is dissatisfied with the king, yet he has been appointed to be the guardian of the realm in the king's absence. His feelings are divided:

> Both are my kinsmen:
> Th' one is my sovereign, whom both my oath
> And duty bids defend; t'other again
> Is my kinsman, whom the King hath wronged,
> Whom conscience and my kindred bids to right.
> (111–15)

His last words of confusion make it absolutely clear that there is no hope of any real resistance to Bolingbroke, but because he is duty-bound, the Duke of York will, for now, fight for the king.

The last moments of Scene 2 are given over to the three representatives of Richard's court still remaining—Bushy, Bagot, and Green. They present a picture of expedience and cowardice, Bagot being the only one who will go to join the king in Ireland. There is no question concerning whether or not they will join the Duke of York in his battle against Bolingbroke's army. These men are like rats, leaving a sinking ship; here, the ship is England, the ship of state.

Bushy, Bagot, and Green had the last words in Scene 2 as they prepared to escape to Ireland, in Bagot's case, or to ensconce themselves in Bristol Castle, as Green and Bushy decided to do. By the end of Scene 3, the forces of Bolingbroke will be preparing to go to Bristol themselves to clear the land of these "caterpillars of the commonwealth." Scene 3 itself is almost melodramatically opposed to the one that precedes it, setting off the forces of good against their evil opponents.

The way in which Bushy, Bagot, and Green disport themselves is in striking contrast to the behavior of the Bolingbroke faction. Even their lines are overdressed, somewhat genteel and effete, in comparison with the speeches of Bolingbroke and his men. For example, the soldiers have been on their feet for some time. They speak of the hard road they have traveled and the distance they have yet to go, but as befits their heroic status, they do not complain too loudly. Of particular importance here is the implied reason for their forbearance in these hard times. Notice the way, for example, in which Northumberland speaks to Bolingbroke. It is as though Shakespeare wants to prepare us in advance for Bolingbroke's ascent to the throne. Explaining his renewed energy despite the physical hardships, Northumberland claims that the "noble company" of Bolingbroke has been its chief source. This way of speaking about someone is usually closely associated with a *royal* personage; the impression given is that the very presence of royalty—in this case, Bolingbroke—emanates some life-giving source. When Henry Percy comes onto the scene and tenders his service to Bolingbroke, one almost imagines him bending his knee and pledging himself as one would to a king. With the arrival of Willoughby and Ross, the effect is redoubled: Shakespeare has these various entrances strung out in this way to give the dramatic illusion of great numbers of people supporting the king-to-be. It is as though Bolingbroke will almost *have* to become the new ruler by popular acclaim. Though no admirer of democracy himself, Shakespeare's idea here is that there is a will of the people (albeit the nobility) that might, in some cases, supercede the divine right of kingship.

When Bolingbroke, in mid-sentence, decides to use his new title of Lancaster, we get the feeling that the popular support *might* have had some effect on this leader of men. But at this point, Bolingbroke still feels uneasy about his position, and he is never too actively in pursuit of power, as, for example, Richard III is in Shakespeare's play of that name. There is a feeling in this scene that circumstances are mounting that are likely to force certain kinds of commitments from the nobility and, specifically, from Bolingbroke. One should be alert to various shades of indecisiveness and commitment in this scene. This element is used as dramatic material throughout the play.

With all of these "royal indications" in mind, imagine the dramatic effect when Bolingbroke kneels to the Duke of York and calls him "my gracious uncle." It is clear that the duke is the king's representative, but it would be unlikely that Bolingbroke would at this point be thereby showing obeisance to the *king*. Bolingbroke is testing both himself and his uncle with the irony and the seriousness of their situation, and the ensuing conversation between the duke and Bolingbroke is quite serious. Treating issues of importance to the country, Bolingbroke argues soundly that he has been wronged, and in so arguing, he uses language that strikes the central theme of rights of inheritance:

Will you permit that I shall stand condemned,
A wandering vagabond, my rights and royalties
Plucked from my arms perforce, and given away
To upstart unthrifts?
. . . .
I lay my claim
To my inheritance of free descent.

(119-36)

The last lines of Scene 3 voice the central dilemma in the words of Bolingbroke and York: Bolingbroke speaks of "weeding" the country of what is choking it, and York grapples with his own conscience over what this weeding entails:

It may be I will go with you, but yet I'll pause,
For I am loath to break our country's laws.
Nor friends nor foes, to me welcome you are.
Things past redress are now with me past care.

(168-71)

Scene 4 serves in place of a stage battle to tell us that Richard's cause has been lost. The language used by Richard's allies is conventional in its reference to the natural elements being somehow in harmony with the momentousness of the occasion. When great men fall, so goes the popular belief, the echoes of that fall are heard in the earth's crust itself. The tradition can be traced back at least to the time of the crucifixion of Christ, at which time earthquakes and natural calamities were witness to the event. Shakespeare, along with his contemporaries, uses this idea fairly frequently; it is an important motif in all of his history plays. Salisbury's comment on the fall of Richard being "like a shooting star" makes reference to the particular image of Richard in the play as someone who does possess, however one may judge it, a kind of style or romantic glory. This is how he is known and how he knows himself. It is also a conventional metaphor for the "tragic" fall from greatness by a heroic or noble figure.

ACT III

Summary

Bolingbroke makes his first public, political act. Standing before the castle of Bristol, he passes sentence on Bushy and Green. (Bagot went to Ireland.) He gives a long account of the men's wrongs, including the charges that they "misled a prince, a royal king . . . [and] made a divorce betwixt his queen and him." Furthermore, they seized Bolingbroke's lands, ruined his parks, and removed the coat of arms from his property, and, finally, they unjustly urged Bolingbroke's exile. Bolingbroke has had to live in a land not his own, where he "sighed [his] English breath in foreign clouds, / Eating the bitter bread of banishment." Bolingbroke has not proclaimed himself king, but his actions are very much like those of a king, and the lords present all recognize his authority. He orders the execution of Bushy and Green forthwith. But before the two men allow themselves to be led proudly away, believing their cause to be just, Bushy defiantly proclaims that "more welcome is the stroke of death to me / Than Bolingbroke to England." Green adds that he is confident that "heaven will take our souls."

Bolingbroke then turns to the Duke of York and asks him to see that the queen is looked after and kindly commended. York assures him that he has already dispatched a messenger to her. Bolingbroke then announces that he will set out for Wales, where the king has joined Glendower.

Bolingbroke was right; Richard has indeed landed back in Wales and is now at Carlisle with his army. He is joyous to be back in his native country again, especially after a difficult crossing of the Irish Sea. He weeps for joy and is convinced that his presence will be enough to deter the rebel forces. In a highly emotional soliloquy, he declares,

> Dear earth, I do salute thee with my hand,
> Though rebels wound thee with their horses'
>   hoofs.
> As a long-parted mother with her child
> Plays fondly with her tears and smiles in meeting,
> So, weeping, smiling, greet I thee, my earth,
> And do thee favours with my royal hands.
>   (6–11)

He bids the land itself rear up and attack Bolingbroke and his men, but the Bishop of Carlisle wisely suggests that they do something more practical than prattle. "That Power that made you king," he says, will "keep you king in spite of all"; he admonishes that "the means that heavens yield must be embraced, / And not neglected." Aumerle, York's son, agrees "that we are too remiss, / Whilst Bolingbroke, through our security, / Grows strong and great in substance and in power." Richard does not catch their meaning, however, and reiterates his faith that "The breath of worldly men cannot depose / The deputy elected by the Lord."

Salisbury enters with the bad news that the Welsh army, believing that the king was slain, disbanded. He says that Richard stayed too long in Ireland; had he returned only a day earlier, Salisbury could have brought him an army of twelve thousand Welshmen. Hearing this, the king falls into despair. "Time hath set a blot upon my pride," he moans; Aumerle turns and reminds him that he should carry himself like a king. Recovering his poise, Richard proclaims confidence in York: The crown *will* be preserved.

Scroop, a loyal follower of Richard, comes on the scene with yet worse news. He announces that the entire British nation, including women, old men, beardless boys, and clergymen, has risen up in arms against the king. He also tells the king that Bushy and Green have made their peace with Bolingbroke, but before he can explain what he means, Richard launches into an attack on his fickle friends. (Of course, what actually happened was that those who were captured were executed, but Scroop is unable to reveal this to the king until Richard's tirade is over.)

Aumerle asks a very practical question: "Where is the Duke my father?" York, remember, had been left in charge of the kingdom. The king ignores Aumerle, however, and launches into an extended monologue about the sad fate of kings in this transitory world: "For God's sake, let us sit upon the ground / And tell sad stories of the death of kings" (155–56). Carlisle then begs Richard not to be so morbidly self-absorbed but to put his fear of the foe to good use in opposing him. Richard accepts this chiding and says that he has already taken control of himself: "This ague fit of fear is over-blown; / An easy task it is to win our own." Richard's mood, however, is reversed when Scroop continues his report with the information that the Duke of York has joined the rebels who are backing Bolingbroke. Richard plunges once again into despair, and Aumerle is unsuccessful in coaxing him out of it. As the scene ends, Richard says darkly that he will go to "Flint Castle; there I'll pine away." He orders his officers to send their troops home.

Bolingbroke's forces have marched the hundred miles from Bristol to Flint Castle on the northeastern coast of Wales when Scene 3 opens. Now Bolingbroke stands before the castle with York, Northumberland, and their attendants. He has sent Northumberland's son Henry Percy into the castle. When Percy returns, he announces that Richard is inside, along with Aumerle, Lord Salisbury, Scroop, and the Bishop of Carlisle. Bolingbroke instructs his lords to deliver a message to Richard that Henry wishes to speak to him. "On both his knees," he instructs them to tell Richard, he will lay his "arms and power, / Provided that [his] banishment [be] repealed / And lands restored again be freely granted."

First Bolingbroke, and then York, notices Richard on the castle wall, and both of them describe his majesty. Bolingbroke sees "the blushing discontented sun" peeking out from "envious clouds"; York urges Bolingbroke to notice Richard closely. To York, Richard still "looks . . . like a king! Behold, his eye, / As bright as is the eagle's."

Richard speaks first to Northumberland and upbraids him for not showing the requisite courtesy of bending his knee to the king. He wonders if some act of God has dismissed him from his "stewardship." He further instructs Northumberland to tell Bolingbroke that his very presence on English soil is in defiance of the king's express command and that it is, therefore, treasonous. He accuses Bolingbroke of instigating "the purple testament" of civil war, and he warns him that "ere the crown he looks for live in peace, / Ten thousand bloody crowns of mothers' sons / Shall ill become the flower of England's face." Northumberland tries to soothe Richard's ire, and he tells him that it is *not* Bolingbroke's intention to use force in any way: "His coming hither hath no further scope / Than for his lineal royalties." Richard answers that "all the number of his fair demands / Shall be accomplished without contradiction." He then turns to Aumerle in shame and wonders aloud if he should send back a defiant answer to Bolingbroke instead. Aumerle advises him to remain calm, that they would do better to give themselves time to find allies before attempting a fight. Richard then cries out in agony, "O that I were as great /As is my grief, or lesser than my name!" When he hears that he has a message from Bolingbroke, he begins an extended, self-mocking monologue, stripping himself in words of all the accouterments of his royal household and position of power: "I'll give my jewels for a set of beads, / My gorgeous palace for a hermitage, / My gay apparel for an almsman's gown" (147-49). At the end of this heavily ironic speech, he refers to his adversary as "King Bolingbroke," asking "Will his Majesty / Give Richard leave to live till Richard die?"

Bolingbroke shows deference to the office of king by kneeling before Richard and addressing him as "My gracious lord." Richard refuses to accept Bolingbroke on bended knee with an offer of obeisance, however, and he bids him rise; he says that he will give him what he wants, adding "Your own is yours, and I am yours, and all." Richard then says that he will ride to London; the kingship, it is understood, will be decided on there.

Back in the Duke of York's garden, the queen is waiting for news of her husband, and her two lady attendants are trying to distract her gloom. No matter what they suggest as diversion, though, the queen sighs that it would only remind her that the world is cruel and that her sorrow is too heavy to be lifted. While they are walking and she is weeping, they notice a gardener and his men. The queen decides to spy on them in the hope that they might have something to say about the nation and its problems ("They'll talk of state; for every one doth so").

The gardener gives elaborate instructions to his apprentices about how to prune and trim the plants which they are working on in order to ensure the proper growth and governance of their garden, to prevent its being choked by weeds, and to save it from being in a state of chaos. The servants speak up and make explicit reference to England being like a garden, and they compare Richard and his followers to weeds that once threatened its health. Bolingbroke is named as the one who has "plucked up" those weeds, "root and all." Bolingbroke, they say, "Hath seized the wasteful King. O, what pity is it / That he had not so trimmed and dressed his land / As we this garden!" (55-57). The queen holds her silence as long as she can; then she comes forward and accuses the gardener of being beyond his station in talking of the deposition of a king: "Dar'st thou, thou little better thing than earth, / Divine his downfall? Say, where, when, and how, / Cam'st thou by this ill tidings? Speak, thou wretch" (78-80). The gardener defends himself by telling the queen that what he has just said is nothing more than common knowledge; all she needs to do is go to London and she will find things exactly as he has described them. The queen decides to do this and departs.

After she has left, the gardener tells his servants that "in the remembrance of a weeping queen," he will plant a "bank of rue" where the queen's tears have fallen to the earth.

Commentary

In order for Bolingbroke's character to assume sufficient dramatic stature, he must be seen to grow into the role of king. Although the entire play is not devoted to the "education of a king," as it is in Shakespeare's *Henry IV, Part 1*, it is an important element here, for the proper sympathies must be aroused. Two simple things, therefore, take place in Scene 1, both involving Bolingbroke in something of a public role. We first see him as a dispenser of justice, and it is right that we discern some righteous indignation in his manner of dispatching Bushy and Green. He has good cause to be angered by these corrupters of the king. Note that this is where the emphasis is—on the tempters and not on the tempted. In *Henry IV, Part 1*, Shakespeare returns to this idea in much more complex form. The play involves some of the same characters as this one. Bolingbroke is there the aging King Henry IV, and it is his son, Prince Hal, who must learn to be the next king. The great worry of King Henry is that his son is being led astray by the low company he is keeping, chief among them being Jack Falstaff.

As benefits the good ruler, the last item that Bolingbroke attends to shows him to be a compassionate man: "For God's sake, fairly let her be entreated," he instructs his companions regarding the queen. He can dispense harsh justice when necessary, but he also has an expansive heart. Compare Bolingbroke's behavior here with the cunning of Richard's public dealings earlier in the play. Shakespeare is writing some rather effective propaganda for Henry Bolingbroke and his successors.

Richard has been absent from the stage for quite some time by the beginning of Scene 2, so it is necessary for Shakespeare to use bold strokes in re-establishing the character of the king. The number of times that Richard vacillates in his mood and apparently changes his mind in this scene is a clear indication that he is *not* what one would conventionally think of as a solid and inspiring leader. Throughout, he is cajoled and rather babied by his companions. There is sorely lacking in him a sense of manly resolve and rightness.

His first long speech seems promising, however; it is patriotic and rather cock-sure, but too often Richard is fond of "poeticizing." There is something slightly absurd in his entreaty to the *elements* to do his fighting for him. "But let thy spiders," he tells his England, "that suck up thy venom, / And heavy-gaited toads lie in their way, / Doing annoyance to the treacherous feet / Which with usurping steps do trample thee. / Yield stinging nettles to mine enemies." The king is supposed to be divine, according to conventional wisdom, but he is also meant to be a natural warrior and a leader. The problem with this theory is that the mortal king who fills the role isn't always up to the standard of the idea, and here, Shakespeare does seem to be indicating the weakness of this theory.

The other men around Richard are good, strong soldiers and are ill at ease when their sovereign indulges in his romantic ecstasies. This is especially clear as the scene progresses, and they must repeatedly insist that he stop acting the weakling.

This would be very simple characterization indeed if it weren't for the fact that Shakespeare gives to Richard, here and elsewhere, such grand lines of poetry that it is difficult to dismiss him as "just" a whining incompetent. This man, who is also a king, deeply feels his inadequacy, and perhaps the absurdity of his situation, but, more importantly, he seems to observe himself perform. This, at times, renders him virtually immobile. He seems childishly subject to the passing change in fortunes, exchanging phrases like "Have I not reason to look pale and dead?" for "Awake, thou coward majesty! . . . / Is not the King's name twenty thousand names?" It is true that he indulges himself and cries his woes aloud, and often the tone seems self-indulgent, but on many occasions, he does reach majestic poetic stature:

> Let's talk of graves, of worms, and epitaphs;
> Make dust our paper and with rainy eyes
> Write sorrow on the bosom of the earth.
> . . . .
> For God's sake, let us sit upon the ground
> And tell sad stories of the death of kings:
> How some have been deposed, some slain in war;
> Some haunted by the ghosts they have deposed;
> Some poisoned by their wives; some sleeping
> killed;

> All murdered: for within the hollow crown
> That rounds the mortal temples of a king
> Keeps Death his court, and there the antic sits,
> Scoffing his state and grinning at his pomp,
> Allowing him a breath, a little scene,
> To monarchize.
>
> (145–65)

Richard is guilty of "monarchizing" but, one might say, with *style*. Richard is quick, however, to attack the friends he thinks have turned on him—"O villains, vipers, damned without redemption"—although when he learns that he has misjudged them and that they have been executed as his allies, he doesn't show the remotest sign of remorse. This leaves a strong impression on us, and most likely such actions do not pass unnoticed by his present associates. Richard's fickleness, they would note, can have dangerous consequences for themselves. This, combined with the almost-certain victory of the armies of Bolingbroke, who have the entire nation in their sympathy, leaves the king a pitiful figure by the end of Scene 2.

The most striking detail in Scene 3 is the appearance of Richard on the castle wall. There must be something majestic about Richard's entrance for the scene to have any power. That Shakespeare wanted it that way can be seen in the reactions that he ascribes to the first two people who see the king. They both see him in a *glorious* aspect, perhaps seemingly more glorious because he is seen from above and from afar. His position above, high above the others, on the castle wall, says as much as the words he speaks. Notice that he presents a strong position to those below him when he speaks to them as the king but that he weakens visibly in his indecisive aside to Aumerle towards the end of the scene.

After the strong buildup of Bolingbroke as a natural leader, it comes as somewhat of a reversal to see the king back in a position of power even if it is largely a symbolic position. But the emphasis here is on the fact that Bolingbroke, unlike Richard, is *not* an ambitious man, and he is still rather awed by the idea of majesty and its present physical manifestation. He remains apart throughout most of this scene, as if to emphasize the fact that he does not feel entirely legitimate in his present role. Remember, it is to be characteristic of Bolingbroke that he feels uneasy about his stewardship of the nation. Thus, it is a stroke of dramatic genius to have him appear hesitant about confronting the king, who has just appeared high on a castle wall. Richard's strong warning that the crown will not rest easily on a usurper's head is not lost on Bolingbroke. This theme of ill-fitting royal garments is one that Shakespeare will use again and again in the great tragedies, especially in *Macbeth*.

In this regard, it is important to note that before Richard makes his appearance, we witness a conversation between the Duke of York and Bolingbroke in which the duke reminds him of the importance of what is about to transpire, and that there was a time when had Bolingbroke dared to act as he now is, the king would have wasted no time in having him executed. Bolingbroke's answer, tellingly, is rather ambiguous:

> *York:* Take not, good cousin, further than
> you should,
> Lest you mistake the heavens are o'er
> our heads.
> *Bolingbroke:* I know it, uncle, and oppose not
> myself
> Against their will.
>
> (16–19)

"Oppose not myself / Against their will" is the key phrase here. If Bolingbroke emphasizes "oppose not myself," the meaning would be that he is acting in his own self-interest, as he perhaps has the right to do. But there are other shades of meaning apparent if one pauses between "myself" and "Against their will." In that case, his reply could be taken to mean that the heavens themselves would favor Bolingbroke's cause; all it needs is an emphasis on the "against."

When Richard does appear above, Bolingbroke's confidence obviously seems to weaken. His words express a certain awe before the majesty of the king:

> See, see, King Richard doth himself appear,
> As doth the blushing discontented sun
> From out the fiery portal of the east,
> When he perceives the envious clouds are bent
> To dim his glory and to stain the track
> Of his bright passage to the occident.
>
> (62–67)

The phrase "envious clouds" could, of course, refer to Bolingbroke himself, intentionally on his part or not, but that doesn't remove from the passage itself the feeling that we are in the presence of some glorious being, far above us. Earlier, Gaunt made a similar reference to Richard in a negative sense—as one who would expend himself in a "fierce blaze of riot." Here, coming out of "the fiery portal of the east," the context makes him seem heroic.

In Richard's two long speeches in Scene 3, one finds reason for the awed responses of the spectators. There is an authority and dignity with which he speaks to them at first, upbraiding them for their failure to show proper respect for the office of king. When Richard continues, however, his characteristic self-pity begins to take over. What prevents it from descending into mawkishness is a sarcasm in his tone of voice. When Bolingbroke bends his knee to the king, Richard greets him with these words:

> Fair cousin, you debase your princely knee
> To make the base earth proud with kissing it.
> Me rather had my heart might feel your love
> Than my unpleased eye see your courtesy.
> Up, cousin, up; your heart is up, I know,
> Thus high at least, although your knee be low.
>
> (190–95)

Here, stage directions are inserted after "Thus high at least." The actor playing Richard is instructed to point to the crown on his head. Bolingbroke, reminded of who addresses him, is rather tight-lipped during this scene, as he usually is in the presence of the king. Thus his awkwardness in the situation leaves him no option but to allow the king to do the speaking. The king, at the very end of the scene, plays on Bolingbroke's reticence and more or less *forces* him to give an order:

> *Richard:*   Set on towards London, cousin,
>   is it so?
> *Bolingbroke:* Yea, my good lord.
> *Richard:*   Then I must not say no.

Scenes like Scene 4 in Shakespeare's plays have a very special function: There is something contemplative about them, as if Shakespeare wants the audience to have sufficient time to consider some of the issues—political and individually human—that are at stake. That is not to say that there is no emotion in Scene 4, for we witness the queen's distraught state of mind and her forced silence while the representatives of the common people discuss the demise of Richard; there is clearly an emotional strain in her bearing and in the delivery of her lines in this scene. Also, it is not to be assumed that the gardeners are without feeling, either to the queen or to the nation's desperate condition. The core of the scene, nevertheless, is the long discourse on the sort of care needed to keep a garden at its most productive, a clear and very common metaphor for the kind of governance necessary to keep the nation functioning at its most productive. There is a definite solemnity with which the gardener gives the instructions:

> Go thou, and like an executioner,
> Cut off the heads of too fast growing sprays,
> That look too lofty in our commonwealth;
> All must be even in our government.
> You thus employed, I will go root away
> The noisome weeds, which without profit suck
> The soil's fertility from wholesome flowers.
>
> (33–39)

The gardener is by no means advocating democracy in any form when he says "all must be even in our government"; he is referring to those members of the nobility who have gained excessive favor with the king and who therefore have too much power. To bring things back to "normal," with the proper hierarchy assuming its natural function, these excessive "weeds" and "caterpillars" (an image already referred to) must be removed. Richard is accused only in that he was wasteful and because he did not aid nature in this political pruning operation. The common people, or at least the artisan class as here represented, are perfectly orthodox in their beliefs, recommendations, and wishes:

> Superfluous branches
> We lop away, that bearing boughs may live;
> Had he done so, himself had borne the crown,
> Which waste of idle hours hath quite thrown
>   down.
>
> (63–66)

Scene 4 began, remember, with the queen's attending ladies trying to divert her with various trifling games and songs, but these delights are ineffectual in her present state. It is interesting that one feature of Richard's reign was his delight in courtly entertainments and glamorous display. Starting this scene with oblique reference to "entertainments," inappropriate entertainments at that, it is a subtle variation on one of the themes of this play. The gardener refers to "some few vanities" that will be the only things to weigh in the balance with Richard against Bolingbroke. The vanities are also references to his frivolous entertainment-filled lifestyle.

When the queen speaks of "old Adam's likeness" in referring to the gardener and later asks, "What Eve, what serpent, hath suggested thee / To make a second fall of cursed man?" she is continuing the religious thread that runs throughout the play. As well as describing England as a garden, Shakespeare has her invoke the idea of the Garden of Eden to make it clear that more is at stake than just the *ordinary* affairs of an *ordinary* man. The very act of pruning the garden, if it involves also pruning the king of his power, is an act against God's divine will. The queen reminds us of this point. The gardener would probably agree, but he is really just a powerless man reporting what has happened. Yet the gardener remains a sympathetic character. Even though he is from a lower order of society, he responds to events very much like old Gaunt and perhaps York in his better moments. At the very end of Scene 4, it is significant that Shakespeare has the queen curse the gardener—"Pray God the plants thou graft'st may never grow"—but the gardener feels no spite; rather, he feels pity for her. This pity that Shakespeare evokes for the queen acts as a prelude and a cue to our response to her husband when we see him in his fallen state later in the play. The gardener's last words understandably evoke sympathy from us:

> Poor queen! so that thy state might be no worse,
> I would my skill were subject to thy curse.
> Here did she fall a tear; here in this place
> I'll set a bank of rue, sour herb of grace.
> Rue, even for ruth, here shortly shall be seen,
> In the remembrance of a weeping queen.
>
> (102–107)

ACT IV

Summary

This act has only one scene, and it takes place in London, in

Westminster Hall, about forty days after the king's surrender at Flint Castle. It focuses on a meeting in Parliament, held to decide the matter of kingship and also to discuss Bolingbroke's actions, as well as those of Richard and his accomplices. Among those present for the council are Bolingbroke, Aumerle, Northumberland, Percy, the Earls of Fitzwater and Surrey, the Bishop of Carlisle, and the Abbot of Westminster. Bagot, who escaped earlier to Ireland and thereby escaped execution at Bristol, has now been captured and is now being questioned about Richard's actions.

Bolingbroke wants to know, first of all, who is responsible for Gloucester's death. Bagot's answer is immediate; he points to Aumerle, the son of York. Aumerle, he says, once boasted that he could dispose of his uncle Gloucester and, moreover, that not even one hundred thousand crowns would be enough to bribe him to help return Bolingbroke to England; England, indeed, would be "blest" if Bolingbroke were killed. Aumerle, of course, denies the charge, but the Earl of Fitzwater, Henry Percy, and another lord substantiate Bagot's accusations. Aumerle is defended by the Earl of Surrey, but Fitzwater charges Surrey with lying and swears that he heard the banished Mowbray say that it was Aumerle who arranged for Gloucester's assassination.

Mowbray, as it turns out, cannot affirm or deny the charges. The Bishop of Carlisle informs the group that Mowbray was killed during a crusade to the Holy Land. The Duke of York enters then and announces that Richard, "with willing soul," has yielded up his "high sceptre" to Bolingbroke. To Bolingbroke, he says, "Long live Henry, fourth of that name." Hardly has Bolingbroke accepted the throne, however, than the Bishop of Carlisle objects: No one but God, he says, can judge Richard. He objects to Richard being tried for "apparent guilt" without even being present. Bolingbroke's "trial" of the king, he says, is a "black, obscene" deed, and he prophesies that if Bolingbroke is crowned king, "The blood of English shall manure the ground, / And future ages groan for this foul act." The civil wars that follow, he vows, will be worse than the Crucifixion itself. Northumberland interrupts the bishop's tirade and orders him arrested and charged with treason.

When Bolingbroke speaks, he calls for Richard to be brought before them so that he himself can surrender "in common view." When Richard is brought in, he remarks on the many once-friendly

faces that are now ready to condemn him; Christ had only one
Judas. Yet he tempers his emotion when he hands his crown to
Henry. He reminds him of the many "cares" that go with the crown;
he then renounces his claim to the throne and wishes Bolingbroke
"many years of sunshine days."

Northumberland, not swayed by Richard's poignant words of
fatalism and resignation, demands that Richard read aloud the
charges against him—"Committed by your person and your followers . . . [so that] men / May deem that you are worthily deposed."
Richard, however, says that his tears prevent him from seeing the
list of charges. He sobs that he is nothing—a king of snow, melting
before "the sun of Bolingbroke." He asks only to "be gone and trouble you no more." Bolingbroke, therefore, orders him to be taken to
the Tower of London; the coronation will be performed on the
coming Wednesday, he says as he exits.

Alone with the clergymen, Aumerle proposes a plot to do away
with Bolingbroke, and the Abbot of Westminster invites Aumerle to
his home for further talk. Together, they will conceive such a plot
that will "show us all a merry day."

Commentary

Shakespeare sets up a parallel here with the opening scenes of
the play. This simple scene, you should note, comprises the entire
fourth act. You will recall that the first words of the play were Richard's: He asked Gaunt to bring forth his son, Bolingbroke, to explain
charges of treason that he leveled against Mowbray. The situation
has virtually reversed itself by Act IV. Here it is Bolingbroke who is
doing the ordering and the judging of the cases. He asks Bagot what
he knows about the death of Gloucester, significantly the same issue
that preoccupied Richard and the nobles in the first scene of the
play. The fact is, Richard was conducting something of a sham
inquiry in the earlier scene—that is, he was only trying to keep the
facts of the matter under cover while not allowing his nobility to
become embroiled in too open a dispute. Bolingbroke accused
Mowbray—and justifiably so—of treason, and later we find out that
it was indeed Mowbray who had a hand in the assassination of
Gloucester. Yet the upshot of that first dispute was the exiling of Bolingbroke and Mowbray—on Richard's orders. Years have passed
since then, and it is only after suffering the loss of his father, old

Gaunt, and the humiliation of having his property unlawfully seized that Bolingbroke now finds himself in the position of one who can see the full truth revealed concerning what Richard has done and what kind of a man and a king he truly is. Bolingbroke is a victim of grave injustice. Politically it is important for Bolingbroke to raise this issue of Gloucester again so that it be publicly known that he has been wronged—he did not deserve banishment—and that the king and his henchmen have been involved in shady actions.

The main accusation in this act is against Aumerle, York's son, who allegedly had involved himself in the plot against Gloucester. Shakespeare constructs the scene in such a way as to emphasize the heated feelings and potentially anarchic situation of the nobles. Aumerle defends himself against first one, Bagot, and then another, Fitzwater, and then yet another, a nameless lord. The repeated attacks on Aumerle and his challenge to fight all of them for his honor are a graphic representation in miniature of the chaos that has been predicted in the event that the anointed king might be deposed. Surrey and Aumerle are pitted against Fitzwater, Bagot, and a nameless lord.

Bolingbroke is silent through much of this bickering, waiting for the opportunity to quell the stormy atmosphere. This he does by seizing on a detail of Fitzwater's report—"I heard the banished Norfolk [Mowbray] say / That thou, Aumerle, didst send two of thy men / To execute the noble Duke"—and announcing that all previous disputes and challenges are now concealed until the noble Mowbray returns from abroad. Bolingbroke's cleverness as an arbitrator is obvious here. One way of forcing all those present to cease their arguments is to make the outcome of the argument hinge on the words of someone who is absent and who won't be able to return for some time.

The Bishop of Carlisle's report that Mowbray died in Italy after spending some time abroad fighting the "black pagans, Turks, and Saracens" changes the tone yet again. All in the company are made to consider the fact that he is buried on foreign soil; this should bring them back to an awareness of the wrongs done to many nobles like him who were forced into exile by King Richard. With the question of Gloucester's assassin conveniently put aside for the moment, Bolingbroke utters a prayer-like commendation of the late Duke of Norfolk; he also ends the dispute for the time being:

Sweet Peace conduct his sweet soul to the bosom
Of good old Abraham! Lords appellants,
Your differences shall all rest under gage
Till we assign you to your days of trial.

(103–106)

The next lines in the text announce Bolingbroke as the new king, Henry IV, but before he can gracefully accept York's bid to ascend the throne, the Bishop of Carlisle delivers a long speech warning of the consequences. Remember, here, that it was York in the earlier scenes who delivered this sort of warning. Here it is someone else, a clergyman, warning Bolingbroke and the rest that what they are doing goes against God's will:

O, if you raise this house against this house,
It will the woefullest division prove
That ever fell upon this cursed earth.
Prevent it, resist it, let it not be so,
Lest child, child's children, cry against you "woe!"

(145–49)

The heated exchanges and challenges to armed combat that opened this scene are almost a case in point, proving the credibility of the bishop's prophecy.

This speech is an important one because of where Shakespeare positions it in the play. At this point, we have to wonder how Boling-broke will respond to it. He is aware of the gravity of consequences, and he is not wholly convinced of the rightness of what he is doing. Remember, he is not characterized as an overly ambitious man. He remains quiet throughout Carlisle's speech, and it is Northumber-land who orders the bishop arrested for treason. Bolingbroke doesn't respond in words to the speech, but his first words after it are firm: "Fetch hither Richard, that in common view / He may sur-render" (155–56). Foremost here, we should note Bolingbroke's attentiveness to the bishop's words.

The second part of this act belongs to Richard, with Bolingbroke staying largely in the background. Now one should profitably think of Richard in three ways: first, as a king, one who is aware of the behavior appropriate to the office; next, as a man who is suffering the humiliation of defeat; and, finally, as an actor, as a performer with an awareness of situations and specific audiences. It is exactly where these three "roles," as it were, overlap that Shakespeare is at his finest as a dramatist. During Richard's speeches in this act, we should always consider where the "performing" and the "reality" become interchangeable. Since we know that Richard is intensely introspective, we need to be aware of clues in his speeches that suggest that we are hearing the "real" Richard, as well as the one who is "putting on a show" and, finally, the Richard who is aware of himself as such. This is a complicated matter but one that deserves attention.

When thinking of Richard as an "actor," we should recall the two central props that Richard uses in this scene: the crown itself and a mirror that he asks to have brought on especially for him. These are the props of a practiced performer, and he uses them well.

After the first fifteen lines, in which Richard describes himself as a Christ who has more treacherous "apostles" than Jesus did, he asks to hold the crown. During these fifteen lines, he pointedly reminds everyone present that they have, not too long ago, all responded to him as king. In former times, the gathered multitude would utter an "Amen" or a "God save the King" after Richard declared his "God save the King." Here, however, there is no response, and Richard has made his point dramatically: "Will no man say amen?" he asks sarcastically of the silent nobles.

He takes the crown in his hands and bids Bolingbroke take it from him. They hold the crown on either side while Richard teases his successor with the moment:

> Give me the crown. Here, cousin, seize the crown.
> Here, cousin,
> On this side my hand, and on that side thine.
> Now is this golden crown like a deep well
> That owes two buckets, filling one another,
> The emptier ever dancing in the air,
> The other down, unseen, and full of water.
> That bucket down and full of tears am I,
> Drinking my griefs, whilst you mount up on high.
> (181–89)

Here, Richard holds the crown on one side, with both hands, and Bolingbroke on the other, also with both hands. These two possessors of the crown look at each other in all of their manifestations: one on the way up, the other on the way down; one virtually a king, one virtually an ex-king. Here, one might profitably jot down the ways in which they are alike, the ways in which they are dissimilar, and the ways in which this crown (used in this way) is like a mirror into which each looks into his soul and into the soul of his counterpart.

In cataloguing the process of his deposition, Richard is no doubt forcing his audience of nobles to be clearly aware of what they are doing, and he also seems to be working his way up to an emotional outburst. The formality of the repetition makes the speech seem less spontaneous than some of his outbursts, but it prepares the way for something else in the next speech.

> With mine own tears I wash away my balm,
> With mine own hands I give away my crown,
> With mine own tongue deny my sacred state,
> With mine own breath release all duteous oaths.
> All pomp and majesty I do forswear;
> My manors, rents, revenues I forgo;
> My acts, decrees, and statutes I deny.
>
> (207–13)

Here, Richard is the king stripping himself of all the trappings of his office. In the next speech, he is an ordinary man who is embarrassed that he is to be forced to read an account of his transgressions in public:

> Must I do so? and must I ravel out
> My weaved-up follies? Gentle Northumberland,
> If thy offences were upon record,
> Would it not shame thee in so fair a troop
> To read a lecture of them?
>
> (228–32)

When Carlisle was defending the king's divine right of rule in the first part of this scene, he used a word that is associated with the pattern of natural imagery running throughout the play. One thinks of the gardener's speech when Carlisle describes the king as God's "captain, steward, deputy elect, / Anointed, crowned, planted many years." Now that Richard is being forced to step down, he describes himself in relation to Bolingbroke in natural imagery that was conventionally associated with royalty: "O that I were a mockery king of snow, / Standing before the sun of Bolingbroke, / To melt myself away in water drops!" (260–62).

The command to see his own face in a mirror that he may better contemplate himself is perhaps Richard's greatest historical posture. His language is highly poetical, even at one point reminiscent of the famous "face that launched a thousand ships" speech from Marlowe's popular tragedy *Dr. Faustus*. Richard says,

> Was this face the face
> That every day under his household roof
> Did keep ten thousand men? Was this the face
> That, like the sun, did make beholders wink?
> Is this the face which faced so many follies,
> That was at last out-faced by Bolingbroke?
> A brittle glory shineth in this face;
> As brittle as the glory is the face,
> For there it is, cracked in a hundred shivers.
>
> (281–89)

Just before the last line, stage instructions indicate that the actor playing Richard should fling the mirror to the floor. Clearly, Richard is suffering here, but one wonders if he doesn't relish this opportunity for his self-pitying display. Note Bolingbroke's response to the display and Richard's response to that response: "The shadow of your sorrow hath destroyed / The shadow of your face," says Bolingbroke, after remaining silent through all of Richard's soliloquy. This is a biting remark, for it accuses Richard of play-acting, dealing with "shadows" and pretense instead of showing real emotion. This remark is the more effective because of Bolingbroke's previous long silence. Notice the clipped few words with which Richard responds to this accusation. He is obviously caught off guard:

> Say that again.
> The shadow of my sorrow! Ha! let's see.
> 'Tis very true, my grief lies all within;
> And these external manners of laments
> Are merely shadows to the unseen grief
> That swells with silence in the tortured soul.
>
> (293–98)

This witty answer comes only after Richard has bought himself time to recover with "Ha! let's see."

The last exchanges between Richard and Bolingbroke are in the form of short sentences. Richard's rhetorical flourishes are at an end;

he wants to bring the whole sordid business to a conclusion. His lines are the last ironic gasps of a defeated, once-lordly sovereign:

Richard:	Being so great, I have no need to beg.
Bolingbroke:	Yet ask.
Richard:	And shall I have?
Bolingbroke:	You shall.
Richard:	Then give me leave to go.
Bolingbroke:	Whither?
Richard:	Whither you will, so I were from your sights.

(309–15)

Richard puns on the word "conveyors" in his exit line, calling them all thieves who "rise thus nimbly by a true king's fall."

The scene and the act do not end, however, with the exit of the deposed Richard and the man who has just announced his own coronation date. Shakespeare presses the point that civil strife is in the air after the deposition by having the last people onstage act and sound like conspirators. The Abbot of Westminster, the Bishop of Carlisle, and Aumerle remain behind. The abbot's last line is: "I'll lay / A plot shall show us all a merry day." The play is not yet over. Richard's spirit of greed and power has infected even a man of the church.

ACT V

Summary

The last act opens with Richard on his way to the Tower. The queen is onstage, waiting for her husband to pass by so that she may tell him goodbye. When she sees him, she likens him to a "beauteous inn" that houses grief; she likens Bolingbroke to a common "alehouse." She urges her husband to stand tall; it pains her to see him not only deposed but physically bowed. She wonders if Bolingbroke has also usurped Richard's intellect, for he seems, truly, a ruined man. Richard begs her not to grieve and urges her to leave England and to enter a convent in France.

Northumberland enters and tells Richard that Bolingbroke has changed his mind: Richard is to go to Pomfret and not to the Tower. The queen, he says, has been ordered to France. Richard turns to Northumberland and compares him to a ladder that Bolingbroke used to ascend to Richard's throne. He warns Northumberland that fear and hate will soon separate him and Bolingbroke. But Northumberland refuses to argue with Richard, and he also refuses to allow the queen to follow her husband to Pomfret or him to follow her to France. With deep sorrow, Richard turns to his wife and pleads that their goodbyes be brief, for they make "woe wanton with this fond delay." They part, then, for the last time.

In Scene 2, two or three months have elapsed since Richard was taken to Pomfret. The Duke of York is telling his wife what has happened—how Richard and Bolingbroke arrived in London, how the crowd "threw dust and rubbish" on Richard's head, and how Bolingbroke was hailed with many welcomes and blessings. He thinks that "Heaven hath a hand in these events," and he says that he has sworn allegiance to Bolingbroke.

York sees his son, Aumerle, approaching and says that not only has Aumerle been reduced in rank but that he himself has made a pledge in Parliament for Aumerle's loyalty to Bolingbroke. When York and his wife speak to their son, Aumerle is clearly out of sorts: He does *not* know who the favorites are at court ("the violets now / That strew the green lap of the new come spring"), nor does he care, and, furthermore, he tells his father that he does *not* know who's jousting at Oxford. His spirit pales, however, when his father mentions to him a sealed paper that he has spied in Aumerle's pocket. A quarrel ensues, and York seizes the paper and reads it. He loudly denounces his son for being a traitor, and he calls for his boots. Despite his wife's pleas and protestations, he means to reveal what he has learned to Bolingbroke. He and his wife quarrel bitterly over Aumerle's treason. York's wife calls her husband unnatural for disclaiming their son, and he calls her a fool for her blind love. After York leaves, his wife pleads with Aumerle to get to the king before York does. Meanwhile, she herself will saddle up and try to delay York: "And never will I rise up from the ground / Till Bolingbroke have pardon'd thee."

Bolingbroke, now Henry IV, laments to Henry Percy that Prince Hal, the heir to the throne, is wasting his life with dissolute companions and that it has been "full three months since I did see him last."

Aumerle suddenly rushes onstage and asks for a private audience with the king, and when it is granted, he proceeds to beg forgiveness for his involvement in an assassination plot against the crown. With the door locked, Aumerle is prepared to confess, but before he does so, the Duke of York comes to the door and demands that the king should beware of the traitor in his midst. The door is opened, and York dashes in and loudly accuses his son.

"O heinous, strong, and bold conspiracy!" shouts Bolingbroke, "O loyal father of a treacherous son." Before any action can be taken, however, the Duchess of York arrives and begs forgiveness of the king in behalf of her son. The king throws up his arms and responds to the turn of events by saying that "Our scene is altered from a serious thing, / And now changed to 'The Beggar and the King'" (79–80). The duke and duchess then revive the family squabble of the previous scene and fall on each other in front of the king; they all kneel, making their various pleas, until the king silences them with his decisive judgment: "I pardon him, as God shall pardon me." Bolingbroke then declares that he will execute all of the other conspirators. Quietly, the duchess takes her son in hand and they leave the stage. She vows to Aumerle that she will pray until "God make thee new."

Scene 4, consisting of only eleven lines, takes place a few months later. In Windsor Castle, Sir Pierce of Exton is speaking to his servant; he interprets Bolingbroke's words "Have I no friend will rid me of this living fear" to mean that Bolingbroke wants someone to kill Richard and put an end to all thoughts of a counter-coup in the country. He explains to his servant that Bolingbroke uttered these words twice—and looked at Exton "as [if he would] say, 'I would thou wert the man.'" Exton's servant confirms Bolingbroke's words and his actions. Exton says finally, "Come, let's go. / I am the King's friend, and will rid his foe."

Scene 5 opens as Richard is sitting alone in his cell at Pomfret Castle. His only companions, he says, are his thoughts. Thus he speaks aloud. He "peoples" the world with his thoughts and plays in one person many people in his imagination. When he hears music from outside his prison cell, it disturbs him: "How sour sweet music is, / When time is broke and no proportion kept!" The music maddens him, for the giving of this music to him is a sign of love in the giver, and, to Richard, love "is a strange brooch in this all-hating world."

His soliloquy—in which he compares himself with a clock measuring time, his thoughts being the minutes, his eyes being the dials, and his groans being the striking of the hours—is interrupted when a groom, one of his former servants, enters. The groom remembers having tended to Richard's horse during happier days, and he would like to talk to his former king, but Richard becomes irritated when he hears that Bolingbroke now rides proudly on Richard's "roan Barbary." Richard curses his horse, then speaks words of forgiveness.

A keeper breaks off their conversation and offers Richard his meal. Richard, however, says that he won't eat until the food is first tasted by the guard; he is afraid of being poisoned. The keeper says that Sir Pierce of Exton "commands the contrary."

Exton enters with henchmen and a fight breaks out. After killing one of the would-be assassins, Richard is killed by Exton, but before he dies, he curses his killer: "That hand shall burn in never-quenching fire / That staggers thus my person" (109–10). Richard's dying words affect Exton; "O would the deed were good!" he says. Clearly he fears the consequences of what he has done.

Some days after Richard has been killed, Bolingbroke is talking with York, and he tells him that rebel forces have consumed with fire a town in Gloucestershire, and it cannot be ascertained whether or not the rebels themselves have been killed or captured. But there is good news, for Northumberland announces that the heads of Oxford, Salisbury, Blunt, and Kent have been sent to London. It is next Fitzwater's turn to speak: "The heads of Brocas and Sir Bennet Seely," men who were involved in the Oxford plot to kill Bolingbroke, have also been sent to London. Henry Percy enters then and tells them that the "grand conspirator," the Abbot of Westminster, "hath yielded up his body to the grave," and that Carlisle is being brought as a captive before them. The king sentences Carlisle to life imprisonment; he spares his life because of the "high sparks of honour in thee have I seen."

Exton enters then and presents Richard, lying in his coffin, to Bolingbroke and is rebuked by the king. Exton declares that he killed Richard because of Bolingbroke's own words, but Bolingbroke is deaf to these excuses. He banishes Exton and vows to "make a voyage to the Holy Land" to expiate the guilt that he has accrued to himself.

Commentary

In Scene 1, we see Richard in a close-up portrait with his wife, and the emotional quality of the scene balances that of the one that preceded it. Then, he was a man of display before his former subjects; here, he is a private man saying goodbye to his wife. The queen's lines, in which she describes him, at the beginning of the scene set the tone. Richard is a man to be pitied, a shadow of his former self, a "withering rose." When she compares him to Bolingbroke, she uses a metaphor that characterizes Richard as something elegant and special, while Bolingbroke is common. There is an irony here, of course, as it is Bolingbroke's very "commonness" that accounts in part for his transition to the throne. Earlier in the play, Richard commented on Bolingbroke's popularity with the common people. This will be picked up again in the *Henry* plays, in which Bolingbroke's son, Hal, is noted for having "the common touch," in the best meaning of the phrase.

A curious thing happens in Scene 1. Not only does the queen's pity set the tone in general for this scene, but the fact that her pity finally becomes annoyance is also significant. She becomes angered by what seems to her to be Richard's too-easy compliance with his fate. Although it is a piteous sight to gaze on greatness fallen low, to her it is also loathsome to see that former greatness going to its slaughter like a lamb. She uses the conventional symbol of the proud lion to make her point: Richard should act like the king of beasts and continue to struggle to the end. This is not the first time that Shakespeare presents Richard within the framework of this metaphor, but one should resist the temptation to label him too quickly; the author's characterization of Richard is a complex one, and Shakespeare doesn't allow a simple progression of responses to the king.

While we can sympathize with Richard in his private suffering, it is a fact that this private suffering occasionally degenerates into self-pity. It seems as though Richard almost enjoys the fantasy of imagining weeping, aged women sitting around a fire during a deep winter's night and telling the woeful and lamentable story of poor King Richard.

With relief, we finally see Richard seem to spring to life during his verbal attack on Northumberland in the next part of Scene 1. His first two lines, calling Northumberland a mere "ladder" that Bolingbroke used to climb to the throne, open an attack upon Northumberland and express a warning to him and those like him: Treason and distrust will breed more of the same, and none of those involved will see a happy end to this business. This is really the first time in the play where Shakespeare has Richard sound this theme so forcefully and explicitly, and Northumberland's easy dismissal of the advice—"My guilt be on my head, and there an end"—betrays a suspiciously cocky and over-confident attitude.

An important point about the conclusion to Scene 1 is the physical action that Shakespeare adds to it. Where it may be difficult to sympathize unqualifiedly with Richard, especially when he is dramatizing his own situation, it is easy to imagine him kissing his wife farewell, then kissing her farewell again, as if to delay the inevitable parting. The farewell is poignant, the tone much like that when Gaunt parted for the last time from Bolingbroke: "One kiss shall stop our mouths, and dumbly part; / Thus give I mine, and thus take I thy heart" (95–96).

There is something oddly farcical about Scene 2 in an otherwise humorless play: We get a glimpse into the household of one of the minor actors in the political drama where the strife of the outside arena is seen in miniature.

Earlier, York was a defender of Richard and the divine right of kingship. When the situation became intolerable, he switched his allegiance to Bolingbroke. This was an important switch because it was not done capriciously. York had difficulty in coming to his decision, and although one might be tempted to see York as a political time-server, it doesn't seem that Shakespeare wanted him to be judged too harshly. York's heart seems to be in the right place, and the interests of the nation at large seem to have motivated him to do what he did. In this scene, we see that his son, Aumerle, has remained faithful to the previous ruler. Why not? His father's sympathies had been there too at one time. Aumerle's personal loyalty supercedes his questionable duty to the new king. Questionable, in fact, is the only word we can use concerning loyalty in this case because one must remember that the new king's legitimacy as a monarch is in doubt.

The struggle between the father and son seems serious enough because finally Aumerle's mother has to break in and try to make her husband leave the matter alone and put all thoughts of their turning their only child over to the authorities completely out of his head. They struggle over his boots, most likely (this is not completely clear from the text); she tries to keep them from him, and he tries to put them on so that he can ride to inform Bolingbroke of the plot against his life. Her lines are those of a distracted mother: "Strike him, Aumerle. Poor boy, thou art amazed." His are those of a perhaps over-zealous patriot: " . . . were he twenty times my son, / I would appeach him."

The purpose of Scene 2 is twofold: First, it shows the results of the political uncertainty and impending chaos at the local level, where most ordinary humans would experience it. (A family spat is a civil war in miniature.) And second, it presents the odd games that fortune plays with political loyalties and political necessities. Who is correct in his loyalty? The father's loyalty to the newly crowned king, or the son's loyalty to the man whom he has served? Shakespeare raises the question without answering it. Aumerle's part in the plot and the outcome of his mother's appeal will feature importantly in the next scene.

One final note on Scene 2 should be made concerning the description of Richard, again the performer. This is important as a prelude to Richard's final scene and his now-famous soliloquy. York describes him thus:

> As in a theatre, the eyes of men,
> After a well-graced actor leaves the stage,
> Are idly bent on him that enters next,
> Thinking his prattle to be tedious;
> Even so, or with much more contempt, men's eyes
> Did scowl on gentle Richard.
>
> (23–28)

One thing this speech does is identify Bolingbroke as the next "actor" in the role of king. The two men gazed into each other's faces through the hollow crown in an earlier scene; we shall see that in more ways than one they will prove to be "mirror images" of one another.

Bolingbroke is now the leader of the nation. What does that mean? For one thing, as Richard predicted, he will never be fully secure for the rest of his days. There is a conspiracy afoot, the first of many, one supposes. And, to make matters worse, as is brought out in the first part of the scene, the king has an unregenerate son, Prince Hal, who whiles away his time with Sir John Falstaff (particularly in the *Henry IV* plays of the tetralogy).

Another errant son, York's, breaks onto the scene as the agent of the conspiracy. One must imagine Bolingbroke taking the threat when it is revealed to him by York quite seriously. There is a real danger to the throne. But when the duchess enters the scene, a bit of the farce of the previous scene spills over into this one. Bolingbroke is now involved in a petty domestic dispute, or what seems like such. There is a pronounced difference between the glamour associated with rulers and ruling and the tedious reality of this sort of administration and arbitration on a daily basis. This does seem to be Shakespeare's point, or at least one of them, because this scene is in such marked contrast with the rather philosophical heaviness of the entire play up until now. Our last view of Richard was a philosophical one; Shakespeare focused primarily on the idea of kingship and what it was. Here, the reality is exposed, with all its boring, melodramatic features. Richard was aloof. That was one reason for his downfall. Henry is not aloof; for that reason, one can easily imagine (from Scene 3) the price that he will pay for keeping himself caught up in petty embroilments.

The vehemence with which York denounces his son seems odd, as if Shakespeare wanted to discredit an over-zealous patriotism. York's words, echoing the theme of civil strife, are harsh:

> If thou do pardon, whosoever pray,
> More sins for this forgiveness prosper may.
> This festered joint cut off, the rest rest sound;
> This let alone will all the rest confound.
>
> (83–86)

The wisdom is politically sound perhaps, but in reference to his own son, it is certainly extreme. Bolingbroke pardons the son as an act of mercy, showing himself the good ruler in this, but he also dispatches the other conspirators without hesitation: "Destruction straight shall dog them at the heels." He seems to believe firmly in justice and mercy—as a good ruler must—and Shakespeare *did* want to show him as a good ruler.

Scene 4's action is short and straightforward: Sir Pierce Exton interprets Bolingbroke's words "Have I no friend will rid me of this living fear?" to mean that he wants someone to kill Richard and put an end to all thoughts of a counter-coup in the country. He explains this to another man and they go to kill Richard. Because of this information, our reception of Richard's final soliloquy will be that much more acute.

In Scene 5, we see Richard at his most naked and honest. His thoughts, he says, could fill this little world in place of people. During his reign, he needed people as audiences and companions; this explains the flatterers in his court, those who contributed to his downfall. But even the world of thoughts, like the world of people, has a falling out with itself: There is not one single thought that enters his head that cannot be immediately countered with its contrary. Even the Bible is not immune to this fact of contradiction. "Come, little ones," says the word of God, but the same book also says that it is as hard to "come" as it is for a camel to pass through the eye of a needle. The association between contrary thoughts, opposing ideas, and the topsy-turvy turn of events in England and in Richard's life is apparent here:

> Thoughts tending to content flatter themselves
> That they are not the first of fortune's slaves,
> Nor shall not be the last; like silly beggars
> Who, sitting in the stocks, refuge their shame,
> That many have and others must sit there;
> And in this thought they find a kind of ease,
> Bearing their own misfortunes on the back
> Of such as have before endured the like.
>
> (23–30)

Optimistic or rationalizing thoughts, then, are false flatterers to themselves and serve no useful purpose in the end. Richard recapitulates his experiences succinctly: "Thus play I in one person many people." He has played many people and many roles throughout the course of this play, and now in his imagination, he re-runs the gamut of the types. He has played the king, and he quakes from fear of treason; he has played the beggar, and he feels crushed by penury into thinking he was better off as king. The end result of this "logic" is that he *would* be better off dead:

> But whate'er I be,
> Nor I nor any man that but man is
> With nothing shall be pleased, till he be eased
> With being nothing.
>
> (38–41)

The chords of music heard from outside the cell have a marked effect on Richard. Scene 5 is the most contemplative in the play, and its "philosophy" speaks of a different kind of concern to Shakespeare in this part of the play from what has gone before. Compare the tone of this scene with the "petty squabbling" found in the two preceding ones. In evoking this difference, the music serves the function of being a mood setter. As an art form, music seems able to "articulate" things that cannot be expressed in any other way. Richard's melancholy is thus underscored. Also, the perfect measure and construction of the phrases of music jar on Richard's ear because they unhappily remind him of his own discordant state of mind:

> And here have I the daintiness of ear
> To check time broke in a disordered string;
> But for the concord of my state and time
> Had not an ear to hear my true time broke.
> I wasted time, and now doth Time waste me.
>
> (45–49)

The play on words—"time" in music, in the sense of measured duration, and "Father Time"—leads to Richard's observation on his own demise: "So sighs and tears and groans / Show minutes, times, and hours" (57–58). At the end of the speech, Richard seems to grow energetic in his anger, shouting, "This music mads me." As he is not so predisposed, music cannot exercise its calming effect on him.

Shakespeare presents the interlude with the groom as a way of reminding Richard of former, better times, and therefore redoubling the pain of his present state. The groom also serves to show that among some of the common people, there is still respect and feeling for Richard. In addition, the groom has secret thoughts that are perhaps rebellious in nature: "What my tongue dares not, that my heart shall say."

To impress us with the villainy of murdering the king, Shakespeare has Exton recoil in horror from his own accomplishment:

> As full of valour as of royal blood!
> Both have I spilled. O would the deed were good!
> For now the devil that told me I did well
> Says that his deed is chronicled in hell.
>
> (114–17)

The tradition that regicide originates in hell is here repeated.

The last scene of the play swells with details of civil horror: a razed town, six beheadings, one life imprisonment, one banishment, and the corpse of a murdered king. The prophecies of doom seem to be fulfilling themselves. Bolingbroke thanks "gentle Percy" for his part in fighting the rebels. (In *Henry IV, Part 1*, Shakespeare shows Henry Bolingbroke's armies in pitched battle against this same Percy.) The mercy that Bolingbroke shows Carlisle, in sparing his life, attests to the general misery of the scene momentarily, but no sooner is the sentence of life imprisonment offered than Exton arrives with Richard's coffin. The note of damnation and possible regeneration through penance that Bolingbroke's last speech contains concludes the play in the religious imagery that has been threaded throughout.

1597

henry iv
part 1

HENRY IV, PART 1

LIST OF CHARACTERS

King Henry IV

The eldest son of John of Gaunt, Duke of Lancaster, and grand-son of Edward III, Henry had returned from banishment on July 4, 1399, to claim the rights of inheritance denied him by Richard II. As these events were dramatized in Shakespeare's *Richard II*, he led a revolt against the crown, forced Richard to abdicate, and became the first of the Lancastrian rulers of England; subsequently he had the hapless Richard put to death. In Shakespeare's *Richard II* and on occasion in *Henry IV, Part 1*, he is referred to as Bolingbroke, from the place of his birth. History reports him as a brave, active, and temperate man who had been welcomed to the throne by all classes, pledging "to abandon the evil ways of Richard II" and to govern "by common counsel and consent." He is further described as being a good soldier, a careful administrator, and a wise statesman. Never-theless, his position was insecure and trying because of the manner in which he attained kingship. Bitter experience was to make him somewhat suspicious and calculating.

Henry, Prince of Wales

Prince Hal, as he is usually called in this play, the high-spirited eldest son of Henry IV, had indeed been a carefree, boisterous youth, and the "wild prince" stories were circulated beginning in his own lifetime. History records also that he distinguished himself in the Welsh wars and gained valuable experience in government. Holinshed, Shakespeare's chief source, says: "Indeed he was youth-fullie given, growen to audaucitie . . . But yet . . . his behavior was not offensive or at least tending to the damage of anie bodie." That he did become alienated from his royal father is historical fact. Again in the words of Holinshed, "The king after expelled him out of his privie councell, banisht him the court, and made the duke of Clarence (his younger brother) president of the counsell in his steed." Reconciliation followed, but much later than in Shakespeare's play. In the *Henry IV* plays, the dramatist depicts the apparent waywardness of the prince and the profound concern of the king, both happily resolved by Hal's chivalry and heroism at Shrewsbury.

Henry Percy, surnamed Hotspur

Son of the Earl of Northumberland and nephew of the Earl of Worcester, Hotspur emerges as the impetuous leader of the northern rebels. Again it was Holinshed who provided the basic elements of his character; but it remained for Shakespeare to so develop that character, consistent with his purpose of providing a strong contrast primarily to Prince Hal and secondarily to King Henry, that the Hotspur of this play is almost an original creation. He is identified only as "Percy" in *Richard II*; in the present chronicle-history play, he is a major figure whose name suggests that he is indeed, in the words of Holinshed, "a capteine of high courage" spurring on the horse that carries him into battle.

Henry Percy, Earl of Northumberland

Hotspur's father, the titular head of the House of Percy, most powerful baronial family of the North Parts. He appears as he did in *Richard II*—cold and politic, in marked contrast to his son, a man who is, from the royalist point of view, certainly "a haughty, insulting" enemy of the crown.

Thomas Percy, Earl of Worcester

Brother of the Earl of Northumberland and uncle of Hotspur, it is he who has especially influenced his impressionable young nephew. According to Holinshed, his "studie was ever . . . to procure malice, and set things in a broile." So he appears in this play.

Owen Glendower

First referred to as "the irregular and wild Glendower" (I. i. 40), he was a Welsh nobleman, descended from Llewellyn, last of the Welsh kings. It was he who defeated and took captive Edmund Mortimer, Earl of March, who married one of Glendower's daughters. Incensed because Henry IV had not provided him redress against a grasping neighbor in a quarrel over landed property, Glendower led a great following of his countrymen against English rule. Traditionally, certain supernatural powers were attributed to him.

Edmund Mortimer, Earl of March

Mortimer is presented in this play as the son-in-law of Glendower, the brother-in-law of Hotspur, and claimant to the throne of England. For the record, it was his nephew, a younger Edmund, who married Glendower's daughter and who, as son and proclaimed heir of Roger Mortimer, Earl of March, was claimant to the throne of England. By taking liberties with history here, Shakespeare magnified the dangers faced by Henry IV.

Prince John of Lancaster

Younger brother of Prince Hal, he appears in the very first scene and on the battlefield at Shrewsbury, where he is distinguished for his courage. To some extent he functions as a foil to his older brother, the Prince of Wales.

Archibald, Earl of Douglas

This "ever-valiant and approved Scot," as he is called by the Earl of Westmoreland (I. i. 54), was a leader of the forces defeated by Hotspur at Holmedon. He then became an ally of the Percies in their revolt against Henry IV.

Sir John Falstaff

Knight of the realm, enormously fat and white-bearded, he is the companion of the carefree Prince Hal. Falstaff is concerned largely with pleasures of the flesh and cheerfully rejects conventional ideas and behavior especially suitable to his rank and age. He emerges as the most paradoxical character in all fiction, dramatic or non-dramatic. His irrepressible humor and superior wit, by means of which he retrieves himself from embarrassing or difficult situations, make it practically impossible for one to pass moral judgment on his character.

The Earl of Westmoreland

One of the noblemen who lead the king's army.

Sir Walter Blunt

Another nobleman loyal to King Henry and a commander of the royal forces at Shrewsbury. He functions especially as an emissary for the king.

Sir Richard Vernon

His role is exactly that of Sir Walter Blunt, but he serves the rebellious Percies, not the king.

Richard Scroop

The Archbishop of York and an ally of the Percies in the rebellion.

Sir Michael

A follower of the Archbishop of York.

Poins

Prince Hal's companion at Boar's-Head Tavern in Eastcheap, it is he who devises the plot to gull Falstaff at Gadshill. His special relationship with Prince Hal suggests that he, in contrast to Peto and Bardolph, comes from a genteel family.

Gadshill, Peto, Bardolph

These three are the riotous and rascally associates of Falstaff. The first (whose name is identical with that of the scene of the robbery) serves as advance man among the rogues, the one who ascertains all the necessary facts relating to the planned robbery; the last named functions as a kind of parasitical serving man to Sir John Falstaff.

Lady Percy

Hotspur's sprightly, affectionate wife, she is the sister of Mortimer.

Lady Mortimer

Daughter of Glendower and wife of Mortimer, who dotes upon her. She speaks no English and her husband speaks no Welsh.

Mistress Quickly

This is the kindly, if rather stupid and disreputable, hostess of the Boar's-Head Tavern in Eastcheap.

SUMMARIES AND COMMENTARIES

Summary

An exhausted King Henry describes the horrors of civil strife that his realm has endured during the twelve months that he has ruled England. At last he will be free to lead a united force of English soldiers to fight the enemies of Christendom in Jerusalem. But the Earl of Westmoreland brings news that forces the king to postpone this crusade. In Wales, Mortimer's forces have been badly defeated by Glendower, and Mortimer himself has been taken captive. Furthermore, English troops led by young Henry Percy, "the gallant Hotspur," are engaged in a battle at Holmedon against the Scots commanded by Douglas. The king has already learned the outcome of this battle, thanks to the services of Sir Walter Blunt. Young Percy has won a great victory and taken many prisoners. This is indeed, as Westmoreland states, "a conquest for a prince to boast of." The king sadly replies that he wishes his own derelict son were more like the valiant Hotspur. He is concerned also because that admirable son of the Earl of Northumberland refuses to turn his prisoners over to the crown, especially because many of them are ranking nobles. Westmoreland informs him that Hotspur's arrogance is the result of his uncle's influence: "This is his uncle's teaching; this is Worcester, / Malevolent to you in all aspects." The king announces that he will hold council at Windsor and instructs Westmoreland to order the Percies to be present.

The action now shifts to the prince's apartment in London, and the participants are Prince Hal himself, Sir John Falstaff, and Poins. Prince Hal, far from engaging enemies of the crown in armed combat, is amusing himself in witty verbal exchange with Falstaff. The subject of this discourse ranges from drinking to purse-snatching. The two vie with each other in trading amusing insults. Falstaff shows little deference for the prince, twitting him about his lack of grace and his devil-may-care attitude and behavior. Hal, whose

initial speech provides a full-length portrait of the knight as a glutton and lecher who is too "fat-witted" to be concerned about the
time of day, proves to be a rather worthy opponent in this combat of
wits. But Falstaff matches him in rebuttal; indeed, some critics
argue that the fat knight excels him.

Since the subject of robbery has been introduced prior to the
arrival of Poins, the way has been prepared for details about the
Gadshill enterprise in which Hal and Falstaff are asked to participate. Hal amuses himself at Falstaff's expense. First he refuses to go
along with the others even "for recreation sake"; then, after listening
to Falstaff's denunciation of him, he changes his mind; and finally
he refuses once more to be one of the thieves at Gadshill. After Falstaff has departed, the prince learns from Poins that the robbery will
provide a wonderful opportunity to gull Falstaff. Let Sir John, Bardolph, and Peto rob the travelers; then Hal and Poins, disguised, will
rob the robbers. The great sport will be to expose Falstaff as a
coward and liar. Prince Hal cannot resist such a good chance to trick
his old companion; he will take part in the robbery at Gadshill.

All the dialogue so far has been in prose. Left alone, the prince
now soliloquizes in blank verse. He makes it clear that he is fully
aware of the character of his chosen companions, likening them to
"contagious [poisonous] clouds." He states that he chooses for a time
to remain in their riotous company for recreation's sake but will, at
the right moment, surprise and gratify the world by standing forth
in his true character.

A determined King Henry strongly reproves the Earls of
Northumberland and Worcester, and Hotspur, who have obeyed his
summons to appear before him. His threat to use force if necessary
to curb their opposition leads Worcester to remind him that they,
the Percies, were largely responsible for his rise to the throne. The
king promptly orders Worcester to leave. Now it is Northumberland
who addresses Henry IV, voicing words of conciliation. Hotspur, he
states, has been maligned, for his son never intended to ignore a
royal command. Hotspur himself explains what happened. Battle
weary, he found it impossible to respond affirmatively to the
request made by the king's messenger, a pretentious, unmanly cox-
comb. Although the loyal Sir Walter Blunt puts in a good word for
Hotspur, the king does not accept this excuse. He is convinced that
young Percy intended to use the Scottish prisoners in bargaining

with him for the ransom of Mortimer, Earl of March, Hotspur's brother-in-law, whom he denounces as one who foolishly betrayed the forces he led and now has married the daughter of his captor, "that great magician, damn'd Glendower." Hotspur vehemently defends Mortimer, but the king refuses to believe that he is not a traitor. Ordering Hotspur to talk no more of the Earl of March, he adds: "Send us your prisoners, or you'll hear of it." The king and members of his retinue leave.

Hotspur is beside himself. Even though he risks his life, he will not obey King Henry. Just as Northumberland urges his son to control himself, Worcester returns to hear another outburst from his nephew. When Hotspur says that the king turned pale at the very mention of Mortimer's name, Worcester replies, "I cannot blame him." And this leads to a review of past events: Richard II's designation of the Earl of March as his heir to the throne, the role of the Percies in Bolingbroke's successful revolt, and the ignominious position in which this proud and ungrateful Henry IV has placed the members of the House of Percy.

Worcester interrupts to announce that he has a plan, one "deep and dangerous," which he will reveal to his kinsmen. Hotspur is exhilarated by the very mention of a dangerous exploit to be carried out in the name of honor. Henceforth, he declares, he will dedicate himself solely to opposing "this Bolingbroke" and the Prince of Wales. Only after Northumberland has succeeded in calming his son can Worcester proceed. Hotspur is to pacify Henry IV for the time being by turning the prisoners over to the crown, but he will make peace with Douglas and soon will ally himself with Glendower and Mortimer. Augmented by the Scottish and Welsh forces, the Percies will then confront the usurper Henry IV.

Commentary

The titular hero, King Henry IV, whom we meet and hear in the opening scene making what amounts to a formal address, had made the vow to fight the infidel in the Holy Land shortly after his usurpation of the throne from Richard II and the death of his predecessor, for which Henry himself was responsible (*Richard II*, V. vi. 30–52). Primarily, therefore, it is Henry, the sinner, the man guilty of the heinous sins of usurpation and regicide, who appears here—one who hopes to atone for his sins by going to the Holy Land. From a doctrinal point of view, never to be ignored in Shakespeare's chronicle-history plays, Henry is already enduring divine punishment, although, under God's authority, he rules England and merits the obedience of all subjects. This was the orthodox Tudor, sixteenth-century view that informs this play.

Understandably, then, in Scene 1, King Henry appears "shaken [and] wan with care" (1), as he tells us in his speech, dwelling with vivid detail on the "furious close of civil butchery" (13). The rising of the Welsh led by Glendower points to the fact that Henry will not yet be given the opportunity to do penance for his sins. And with these internal troubles, there remains the threat from Scotland, still an independent kingdom. The seriousness of this threat is apparent: Sir Walter Blunt has ridden hard to bring the news of Hotspur's victory.

As he did in the last act of *Richard II*, Shakespeare introduces the contrast between "young Harry," the king's eldest son and heir, and the dedicated, courageous Hotspur. The former's brow is stained with "riot and dishonour" (85); the latter is "the theme of Honour's tongue, / Amongst a grove the very straightest plant" (81–82). Little wonder that the distraught Henry would like to exchange sons with the Earl of Northumberland, especially since Hotspur has been winning glory not in civil strife but in fighting a foreign enemy.

In view of the second reference to the postponement of the king's "holy purpose," that of leading a crusade to Jerusalem, it follows that the reported failure of the Prince of Wales is part of Henry's punishment for his sins. So Shakespeare's generation would conclude.

The titular hero has been introduced in Scene 1, and we have gained an insight into one aspect of his character; the connection between this chronicle-history play and the preceding one has been indicated tacitly; and the dominant theme of rebellion has been established. Although neither Hotspur nor the Prince of Wales has made an appearance, the two have been set in opposition, and as a result the secondary but important theme of honor has been set forth.

Appropriately, prose is the medium used in Scene 2, which is the first scene of the broadly comic subplot wherein matters of state have no immediate place. But one should note that, colloquial though it is predominantly, it is the prose of upper-class, sophisticated speakers. Occasional vulgarisms in the man-to-man exchange between Falstaff and Hal should not mislead the reader. Sir John here, and throughout the play, is a speaker of superior prose, prose marked by a vivacity, brilliance, and finish evidenced from the very beginning in his first two speeches with their balance, antitheses, and allusive elements. Hal, and even Poins, uses the same general style, which provides a significant contrast to that used, for example, by the lowly carriers in Act II, Scene 1.

But most important in Scene 2 are the characters of Falstaff and Prince Hal. What is learned about Falstaff as he exchanges spontaneous, good-natured insults with the prince? He is, to be sure, a knight of the realm, apparently a not unfitting associate of the prince, whom he meets not in a disreputable tavern but in the prince's London apartment. If, for the moment, we take literally what Hal says about him in his first speech (2–13), Falstaff emerges as one devoid of any sense of responsibility. Time, a symbol of the ordered life as used here, could not possibly concern one whose hours are spent largely in drinking sack (a strong sherry-type wine, especially popular in the days before gin and whiskey), overeating, and wasting half the day in sleep induced by gluttony. Add to all this Falstaff's alleged interest in bawds and houses of prostitution. Quite an indictment, and one that Falstaff does not refute: "Indeed, you come near me now, Hal," he replies (14). Yet he is anything but embarrassed. Is his way of life unknightly, ignoring as he does *noblesse oblige*, the obligations of rank? Well, let Hal remember that Falstaff "take[s] purses by moonlight" and thus does not follow "Phoebus, he, 'that wand'ring knight so fair'" (16–17). Here, demonstrating for the first of many times his upper-class learning, he provides a brilliant rhetorical commentary on gross reality and, as always, is fully aware of what he is doing. Moreover, only a superior wit could accomplish all this in such an adroit way, effectively answering what may well be a serious indictment of his character. Cheerfully, he adds to his offenses: He is one who engages in robbery by night and thus goes "by the moon," not by Phoebus the sun. The figurative language here admits to interesting interpretation relevant in a play, the main theme of which is rebellion.

Traditionally, the sun is a common symbol of royalty; in this instance, it represents the king, who stands for law and order. Rhetorically and poetically, the moon may represent more than one thing; here it is unmistakably a symbol of instability, not only because it does not remain the same size to one's eyes as time passes but because (as Hal points out) it governs the tides of the sea, which ebb and flow. One of the leaders of the Northern rebels of 1569, a later Earl of Northumberland, was denounced by loyalists as "the wavering moon." As a knight who follows the moon, then, Falstaff is a rebel (though a comic one) against law and order. And this conclusion finds support in his witty, elegant circumlocutions and epithets: When Hal becomes king—and Falstaff is always aware of Hal's status as heir-apparent—let robbers be honored; let them be called "squires of the night's body," not "thieves of the day's beauty" (27–28). The opposition of day and night is that of order and disorder. "Diana's foresters, gentlemen of the shade, minions [favorites, darlings] of the moon," which is described as "noble and chaste," are other refined terms used by Falstaff to describe criminal activity.

When Hal's reply makes this very point, Sir John is quick to change the subject, or to try to do so. But the reference to the gallows and hanging, the usual punishment for robbery in Shakespeare's England, has been introduced by the young prince, who will not, for the moment, let his lively companion ignore it, thus the reference to the "buff jerkin" worn by sheriffs officers and to "durance," meaning not only "long lasting" but "imprisonment" (48–49). The culmination of Falstaff's rejection of law and order comes in his comic plea to the prince, urging him to have nothing to do with "old father antic [buffoon] the law" and to honor thieves, who are admirable men of "resolution" (65–70).

Here in Scene 2, Hal obviously enjoys his repartee with Falstaff, who indeed is, as he will say later, not only witty in himself but the cause of wit in others. The young prince lays a verbal trap for the knight: As king, he will not hang malefactors; Falstaff shall. Immediately Falstaff pictures himself as a learned judge—and then is told that far from being elevated to the bench, he will function as the common hangman. Wit rescues him from this ignominious position as he makes a play upon the word *suits* (petitions or solicitations made at court; suits of clothing). This is grim humor, appropriately like a jest on the gallows itself, for in Elizabethan times the hangman received the clothes of his victims and therefore was referred to ironically as the best-dressed man in England.

Wit or no wit, the subject of hanging is not a pleasant one, and Falstaff changes the subject and mood. He is "as melancholy as a gib cat or a lugg'd bear." And Hal matches him simile for simile. Falstaff's reply, "Thou hast the most unsavoury similes and art indeed the most comparative, rascalliest, sweet young Prince" (89–91), underscores at once his favored position as a kind of privileged jester and, surely, a genuine affection for the prince.

This by no means exhausts the facets of his complex character. Earlier in Scene 2 (54–60), it was made clear that Falstaff willingly let the prince foot all the bills at the tavern. Now, having been matched by Hal in the combat of wits, he adopts another role. For the moment, he becomes the penitent old sinner, acknowledging that he is "little better than one of the wicked." The style he adopts is that of the pulpit, biblical in its simple parallelisms and repetitions (95–98). How serious, how repentant he really is becomes clear at once. In mock sorrow, he, this white-bearded old man, attributes his moral downfall to young Prince Hal, whose use of biblical paraphrase in reply reveals his continued awareness of Falstaff's comic tricks.

But once more Sir John's ludicrous statement has made him vulnerable. When Hal suddenly asks, "Where shall we take a purse tomorrow, Jack?" (111), Falstaff responds with enthusiasm: "'Zounds, where thou wilt, lad; I'll make one." And yet once more his wit saves him when Hal dryly comments on this sudden shift from "praying to purse-taking." Thieving is Falstaff's profession; is it not proverbial that the wise man should follow his own vocation?

When Poins arrives with the details relating to the proposed robbery, we learn more about Sir John. He declares that if Hal does not join in the enterprise, Hal lacks honesty, manhood, and good fellowship; in retaliation, Falstaff himself will be a traitor when the prince rules England. Ostensibly finding such virtue in thieves, Falstaff sustains the force of his earlier reference to robbers as "squires," "gentlemen," and "Diana's foresters." If one chooses to analyze this amusing reversal of values closely, it becomes apparent that Falstaff and all who willfully engage in robbery as a vocation are rebels against the crown. Thus, much of the action in this comic subplot stands as a parody of the serious, public action in the main plot; moreover, the theme of rebellion is common to both. "Comic relief" will not suffice to describe the action in the subplot; there is much more.

Finally, as regards Falstaff, there is the question of cowardice, one much debated by commentators early and late in view of the knight's behavior later in the play. From Poins' remark made to Hal alone in order to persuade him to join in tricking Falstaff, one may conclude properly that cowards are not all of one piece. Peto and Bardolph are "true-bred cowards"; Falstaff is a coward on principle, a practical realist, as it were, who will fight no longer than he sees reason (207–208). Nor will he prove to be an ordinary liar; he will tell the most "incomprehensible lies" about his experience at Gadshill.

How does Prince Hal appear in Scene 2? In popular tradition, he is connected with various escapades including robbery; thus the early introduction of the theme of robbery would be immediately understood by Shakespeare's audiences. But the dramatist handles this subject carefully as far as the prince is concerned. It is Hal who is rather insistent in reminding Falstaff that thieves end up on the gallows. When asked to participate in the Gadshill robbery, the prince asks: "Who, I rob? I a thief? Not I, by my faith" (154). And we are to understand that he goes along only for the sake of duping Falstaff.

So amusing is Sir John that there is danger of underestimating Hal's wit. Falstaff indeed is the cause of wit in others, but time and again it is a remark made by the prince that provides Falstaff with the opportunity to scintillate. Surely one of the reasons that these two enjoy each other's company so much is that they share in the exhibition of verbal wit. For example, when Falstaff expresses his willingness to be hangman rather than judge because it "jumps with [his] humour as well as waiting in the court" (77–78), Hal gets the point immediately. "For obtaining of suits?" he asks. His last words addressed to the fat knight in this scene are brilliant: "Farewell, thou latter spring! Farewell, All-hallown summer!"

Prince Hal's final soliloquy in Scene 2 has disturbed many readers. Some find it "priggish and hypocritical," and one may well conclude that it leaves the reader with an unflattering impression of Hal. Perhaps it is best here to remember that Shakespeare is dealing with a beloved, honored historical character whose youthful escapades and subsequent reformation had become part of treasured tradition. In a sense, the speaker is not Hal, Falstaff's "sweet wag," but Henry, Prince of Wales, who one day will lead English troops to victory over the traditional enemy, France. Here in Scene 2, he functions as a kind of chorus. But once he gets beyond the indictment of his unprincipled associates as "contagious clouds" and "foul and ugly mists," his charm and breadth come through: "If all the year were playing holidays, / To sport would be as tedious as to work" (227–28). These lines rescue him from the charge of calculation or hypocrisy.

In Scene 3, the action in the main plot has risen to the point where the conflict is brought into the open. Following the audience with the king, the Percies are on the verge of rebellion. The danger to the crown is very great indeed as Hotspur's speech beginning "Send Danger from the east unto the west" (195–97) makes clear. Henry faces not only the opposition of the most powerful baronial family in the North but also, if the rebels' plan succeeds, the forces of Mortimer (legal heir to the throne according to the will made by Richard II) and the fearsome Glendower.

King Henry is represented not as the sinner, weary and wan with care, but as the forceful, competent ruler determined to maintain order within his kingdom as he faces baronial opposition. Yet he has been politic. The opening lines of his first speech tell us that he has sought to placate troublesome subjects, who nevertheless must respect him as one "mighty and to be fear'd" (6) if they prove recalcitrant. In the language of sixteenth-century political philosophy, Henry is a man gifted with the "specialty of rule." Nor does this conclusion rule out the fact that, in the words of Hotspur, he is a "subtle king"—one capable of calculation, as a successful head of state has to be, at least in an era of power politics.

But this does not mean that Henry's crimes are to be forgotten. To Hotspur are assigned speeches in Scene 2 that recall the sins of usurpation and regicide. For these the king and the Percies alike "wear the detested blot / Of murderous subornation" and must suffer "a world of curses" (162–64). In counsel with his father and uncle, young Percy frequently disdains to refer to Henry as king; rather, he is "cank'red [malignant] Bolingbroke," a thorn or canker in comparison to the lawfully anointed Richard II, "that sweet lovely rose." In the plant kingdom, the rose is the appropriate symbol of royalty, just as the lion is in the animal kingdom.

All this may confuse the modern reader. Who actually is in the right, King Henry or the Percies, if either? The only way to answer this question is by recourse to Tudor political policy that informs this play. Henry remains a sinner; usurpation and regicide cannot be justified. But now a just God permits him to rule England. God may permit the rebel to rage as part of the punishment of a sinful ruler, but the rebel himself is guilty of mortal sin for his revolt against the crown. A perceptive student may recall Richmond's leading a revolt against Richard III and emerging triumphant as Henry VII, first of the Tudor monarchs. Loyalists of the sixteenth century had an answer: Richmond (grandfather of Elizabeth I, ruler of England during the larger part of Shakespeare's lifetime) was the divinely appointed savior of the country and thus not a rebel. Perhaps it is well to remember that what most Englishmen cherished was stability—law and order within the kingdom. Richard II, in his latter years, was guilty of gross misrule; his successor, Henry IV, proved to be a strong, capable ruler.

Hotspur's basic character is firmly established in Scene 3. His high spirits and undoubted courage, and his forthright answer to King Henry make him appear admirable. Unlike his uncle, the crafty Worcester, architect of the planned revolt, he is completely aboveboard. His sincerity is not to be questioned when he inveighs against "half-fac'd fellowship" (208) and the alleged ingratitude of the king. He is dedicated to winning new laurels in the only way he knows how; craft and selfish motive have no place in his character.

But Hotspur lives up to his name in more ways than one. Patience and contemplation are foreign to his nature; only in violent action is he at home. Time and again either his father or his uncle must rebuke him. Will he obey the king's order to relinquish the prisoners? "An if the devil come and roar for them, / I will not send them," he exclaims (125–26). Northumberland's rebuke is hardly exaggerated: "What, drunk with choler?" No less revealing are Hotspur's words when Worcester first broaches his "deep and dangerous" plot: "O, the blood more stirs / To rouse a lion than to start a hare!" (197–98). This Hotspur of the North is dedicated to winning honor after honor and now relishes the prospect of facing his major opponent, the king himself. Again it is his father's remark that provides telling comment on his son's limitations as a leader: "Imagination of some great exploit / Drives him beyond the bounds of patience" (199–200). In martial affairs, this young man is indeed the soul of courage, but he lacks discretion; he is too impetuous. Subsequent lines with reference to plucking "bright Honour from the pale-fac'd moon" emphasize once more Hotspur's special concern with honor as he conceives it (and about which, perhaps, he talks too much). In the words of his uncle, "He apprehends a world of figures here, / But not the form of what he should attend" (209–10).

To be noted also is that Hotspur is again pitted against "that same sword-and-buckler Prince of Wales," as he contemptuously calls Hal. By the end of Scene 3, in which we learn that the Percies will be allied not only with Mortimer and Glendower but possibly with the disgruntled Archbishop of York, second ranking churchman in England, Hotspur can hardly contain himself: "O, let the hours be short / Till fields and blows and groans applaud our sport!" (301–302). His choice of the word *sport* referring to bloody conflict is as revealing as anything else as regards his character. Hal, we recall, has been manifesting a far different attitude toward what constitutes sport; he is about to engage in an enterprise that is against law and order within the kingdom ruled by Henry IV.

ACT II

Summary

Two carriers complain about the accommodations of the inn at Rochester as they prepare to drive their pack horses to the market in London. Gadshill, the professional thief to whom Poins had made reference, enters and asks to borrow their lantern, but the wary carriers refuse to lend it and leave. At Gadshill's call, the chamberlain, an informer, appears. He confirms what he told Gadshill earlier: A franklin (middle-class landowner) with three hundred marks in gold will be among the travelers soon to depart from the inn. Unlike the chamberlain, Gadshill has no fear of the hangman because he is joined in the robbery by Sir John and, to paraphrase his own words, persons of higher rank.

Prince Hal and Poins appear together on the highway near Gadshill. Poins has succeeded in depriving Falstaff of his horse, and the fat knight himself arrives calling for Poins, who has withdrawn into the darkness. Hal offers to find Poins, and Falstaff is left alone to complain about Poins' perfidy. When the prince returns, Sir John is no less voluble in his denunciation of any one who would so "colt" (fool) him. When Hal refuses to serve as Falstaff's groom—that is, get his horse for him—the knight unrestrainedly and wittily excoriates him.

Gadshill, Bardolph, and Peto enter. The victims of these robbers are now coming down the hill; all must put on their masks and be ready for them. Prince Hal instructs all but Poins to confront the travelers in the narrow lane, while he and Poins wait farther down the hill, ready to waylay their victims if they escape the first encounter. Falstaff has a moment of trepidation but agrees to stand fast. Hal and Poins leave to put on the disguises that will serve their purpose later.

Rendered helpless, perhaps chiefly by the verbal explosions of Falstaff, the travelers are quickly robbed and bound. The thieves are about to share the loot when the disguised Hal and Poins set upon them. Bardolph and Peto take to their heels at once; Falstaff remains only to strike a blow or two and then runs off, leaving the loot. The thought of the corpulent Falstaff footing it all the way to London delights Hal and Poins.

At Warkworth Castle, Hotspur reads a letter from a noble whom he has asked to join in the rebellion. The noble advances one excuse after another for declining the invitation. Young Percy is indignant and scornful of the writer, who ignores the fact that the Percies have powerful allies, some of whose forces already have set forth for the place of assembly. Hotspur suspects that this timorous lord may betray the plot to the king. Vehemently he expresses his defiance.

Lady Percy enters. She is deeply worried about her young husband, whose preoccupation with some serious business has made him neglect her and most normal activities. Hotspur will tell her nothing, and she suspects that he faces great danger. He does assure her, however, that she will join him at an unidentified destination.

At the Boar's-Head Tavern, Prince Hal and Poins are entertaining themselves. Hal tells his companion that he has won much honor by being accepted as "sworn brother" to the lowly tavern servants. He engages Francis, one of them, in a bewildering game with Poins' help. First the prince, then Poins, calls for poor Francis, who, striving to please both, runs up and down stairs in a ridiculous manner, answering each call with "Anon [at once], sir." Hal makes the newly arrived Falstaff and the rest of the thieves wait at the door while he comments on the significance of Francis' behavior, curiously shifting to a comparison of himself with "the Hotspur of the north."

Falstaff and his companions enter, the fat knight complaining bitterly about the prevalence of cowardice and calling for sack. He then tells how courageously he fought at Gadshill against enemies who, first said to number one hundred, are successively reduced to six or seven; and, as he testifies, two particular ones in buckram suits become successively four, seven, nine, and finally eleven. Hal and Falstaff exchange derogatory epithets. At last the prince gives the true account of what happened and challenges Falstaff to explain away the fact that he has proved himself to be a coward and liar. Falstaff, in his special way, does exactly that. Valiant though he is, never would he be one to kill the heir-apparent, whom he recognized immediately by instinct. His spirits are uplifted, for he now knows that Hal has the money taken from the travelers. Let all be merry, he exclaims and suggests a "play extempore"—a bit of amateur play acting—as a source of amusement.

A messenger from the king is announced. At Hal's request, Falstaff leaves to "send him packing." During Sir John's absence, Bardolph and Peto tell how the old knight coached them to back up his preposterous story. When Falstaff returns with news of the revolt of the Percies, the prince seems almost totally unconcerned. The names of renowned Hotspur ("that same mad fellow of the north," as Falstaff calls him), Mortimer, Douglas, and "that devil Glendower" leave him unperturbed; unlike Sir John, he cannot be a coward.

But Hal must appear before his royal father, and this provides the subject for the play extempore, a kind of rehearsal, in which the prince and Falstaff play alternate roles.

The arrival of the sheriff and "all the watch" at the tavern door interrupts this merriment. At Hal's request, Falstaff hides behind the arras and the others go upstairs, leaving the prince with Peto to face the law. The carrier who accompanies the sheriff into the tavern identifies one of the thieves as a gross fat man—"as fat as butter." Hal assures them that the man is not present and that he will answer personally for any charges made.

After the sheriff and the carrier have left, Falstaff is discovered fast asleep and snoring behind the arras. "Search his pockets," says Hal to Peto, who finds only a tavern bill for a bit of food and vast quantities of sack. On inspiration, Hal decides to pester Falstaff by giving him a command of foot troops that he will have to lead against the rebels. Hal himself will report to his father in the morning and will see that the stolen money is returned.

Commentary

The inn-yard setting in Scene 1 is a little masterpiece of vivid writing. It is picturesque in the literal sense, evoking a memorable picture—the darkness of a winter's morning with Charles' Wain (the constellation of the Great Bear) visible over the chimney, and the flea-infested inn itself. The note of homely realism is enhanced by the reference to the death of Robin Ostler, his passing lamented by the lowly carriers, whose colloquial discourse provides an interesting contrast to that between Prince Hal and Falstaff. And all this has its place in a play, the theme of which is rebellion. The carriers are representative of a goodly portion of the English people, going about their work in their unglamorous way. The quarrel between king and lords affects all Englishmen, including these carriers concerned about the comfort of their poor horses and getting their produce to market.

Gadshill, appropriately named after a stretch of road notorious for robberies, and the unscrupulous chamberlain provide the contrast to the hard-working, honest subjects of the crown. Gadshill's speech is laced with the jargon of the Elizabethan underworld; consider, for example, the references to "foot land-rakers" (footpads) and "long-staff sixpenny strikers" (thieves who will bash a person on the head for a pittance). But more important is his reference to the exalted company who are to join him in the robbery; they are ones who "pray continually to their saint, the commonwealth; or rather, not pray to her, but prey on her, for they ride up and down on her and make her their boots" (88–91). His sardonic words unmistakably are applicable to the Percies with their plot against the commonwealth, represented by the king, just as they are to Falstaff and Prince Hal. One may well recall the words spoken by Henry IV at the beginning of this play. Speaking of the grave civil disturbances that have occurred in the commonwealth during the first year of his reign, he said, "No more shall trenching war channel her fields, / Nor bruise her flowerets with the armed hoofs / Of hostile paces" (I. i. 7–9). Again the thematic connection between main plot and subplot is made clear.

In Scene 2, one may wonder how it happens that the travelers, including the well-heeled franklin, are not mounted and proceed afoot. Obviously, Shakespeare, actor and shareholder in his company, was the practical man of the theater; stage entries on horseback were impractical. Not only does he deprive the travelers of horses; he capitalizes on this necessity by having Hal and Poins deprive Falstaff of his horse.

In this scene, farcical action, the broadest type of comedy, is dominant: Falstaff is the victim of Prince Hal, aided by Poins, and is paying the price for his enormous girth and brave words, but Shakespeare does not permit him to become the object of derisive laughter. Again his lines are superb of their kind. Here especially he is the master of witty paradox. He will be "accurs'd to rob in that thief's company" (10); hourly during the past twenty-two years he has vowed never to endure Poins' company again. Yet he cannot bring himself to forego "the rogue's company." He calls down a plague upon all thieves who cannot be true men. Paradox is carried even further. This corpulent old man, for whom twenty-four feet up hilly ground is the equivalent of seventy miles for any one of his companions, is the personification of vitality when he confronts the travelers. His best line is "What, ye knaves! young men must live" (95–96); here is the Falstaff who, despite his advanced years and white beard, is the very spirit of carefree youth.

From one point of view, Hal and Poins function as the wits who so manipulate events that folly is exposed—specifically, the folly of Sir John. But a serious crime *has* been committed, and it is not easy to dismiss all this as no more than an escapade in which the prince amuses himself prior to his promised reformation. For the time being, however, judgment must await the outcome of the gulling of Falstaff.

Some readers may be disturbed by Hal's refusal in Scene 2 to show any pity for Falstaff, who "sweats to death, / And lards the lean earth as he walks along" (115–16). But that would be sheer sentimentality; there is no occasion to conclude that Sir John is in great discomfort. He is enduring comic punishment, as it were, for his sin of gluttony.

An occasional earlier commentator has argued that Scene 3 may be justified largely on the grounds that we must be given a recess from Falstaff. This is a wholly unwarranted conclusion. First, the scene reveals the progress of the rebellion planned by the Percies in the first act; second, it adds appreciably to what is now becoming a full-length portrait of Hotspur, the "theme of Honour's tongue," as Henry IV called him at the beginning of the play.

Young Percy's choleric asides, filled with contemptuous epithets ("lack-brain" . . . "frosty-spirited rogue" . . . "dish of skim milk") are sufficiently revealing. In writing to the unidentified noble, Hotspur has eliminated any possibility of surprise; inevitably the king will be informed. Enraged to the point where he could "divide [himself] and go to buffets" (34), he nevertheless will brook no delay; he will set forth that very night, still convinced that the revolt is an "honourable" action. The figure of speech he uses to reassure himself is admirable: "out of this nettle, danger, we pluck this flower, safety" (9–10). Especially characteristic is his rough yet good-natured sparring with his wife. Declaring that this world is not one for playing with mammets (dolls) or tilting lips, he adds, "We must have bloody noses and crack'd crowns, / And pass them current too. God's me, my horse!" (96–97).

It is hard to imagine anything that could be more revealing and graphic than Lady Percy's speech describing her husband's obsession with thoughts of armed conflict—a set speech, replete with rhetorical questions and balanced lines: "Of sallies . . . Of palisadoes . . . Of basilisks . . . Of prisoners' ransom" (40–67). But another side of Hotspur's character comes through strongly, one that is most attractive—a bluff manliness and wit of sorts. No one can doubt that he deeply loves his Kate, just as she dotes on him. His last words to her echo the well-known passage from the Book of Ruth and leave no room for doubt concerning the relationship between this attractive young couple: "Whither I go, thither shall you go too." There is irony in the fact that he will not tell her what the "heavy business" exactly is: He indiscreetly wrote all about it to a fellow nobleman.

The broadly comical Scene 4 is at once one of the most hilarious in all literature and also one of the most significant in this play. No reader will want to miss any part of the fun; but no careful reader should be so carried away by Falstaff's superb performance as to miss the ideas relating to the theme and to the characterizations.

First to be explained is the import of Hal's remarks about his relationship with the tavern tapsters and apprentices, to whom he refers as "loggerheads" (blockheads) and "a leash (a pack, as of leashed animals) of drawers." To many, this episode hardly reflects favorably upon the character of Prince Hal, particularly the trick played upon the lowly Francis. Perhaps Hal's exploits with the drawers may be considered "miserable attempts at mirth" introduced "to show the quality of the prince's wit when unsustained by Falstaff's," the whole comprising "a very strange incoherent rhapsody" best explained by the prince's volatile nature and by the fact that he has "spent several hours drinking with the drawers." This is the view taken by an early commentator. More recent Shakespearean critics have taken a far different view and have found coherence and relevance in this episode.

With the prevailing tendency to create Shakespeare in our own image, it is easy to go astray in Scene 4. For one thing, contemporary sources tell us that the gallants in Renaissance England took a sort of pride in being on quite familiar terms with drawers and that only favored guests were invited to the cellar to sample the wine in the hogsheads. Democratic sentiments must not mislead us. The prince of Shakespeare's *Henry IV* is at the highest rung of the ladder in a hierarchical society; in contrast, the drawers, worthy subjects of the crown, are at the lowest rung. Yet Hal has won their admiration and affection, and they compare him favorably to Falstaff, that "proud Jack." In so conducting himself, he has "sounded the very base string of humility." This could well be the best way to prepare for the day when he will rule all the people of England, all levels of society. In a word, in the first part of this comic scene, we are given an insight into the education of the prince, one who will lead an English army to France and be able to move freely among his soldiers on the eve of the decisive battle of Harfleur, listening to and understanding their conversation. From this point of view, Prince Hal has won a certain kind of victory. In *Henry IV, Part 2*, the Earl of Warwick, seeking to console the dying King Henry IV, who again has great reason to worry about his son's behavior, has this to say:

> My gracious lord, you look beyond him quite.
> The Prince but studies his companions
> Like a strange tongue, wherein, to gain the
>   language,
> 'Tis needful that the most immodest word
> Be looked upon and learned.
>   (IV. iv. 67–71)

As Hal explains to Poins in Scene 4, the trick played on Francis is a "precedent" (36), or example, one in which he has proved himself to be a man of "all humours." That is to say, he is willing to indulge himself in all the varieties of life, including the present kind of merriment. His devastating burlesque of Hotspur (114–25) logically follows. Young Percy, according to Hal, is like Francis in his concentration on one narrow field of human activity, for Hotspur is obsessed by thoughts of carnage in battle—with "crack'd crowns and bloody noses." Indeed, there is much special pleading here; Hal has been and still is a truant from noble exercises. He has yet to prove himself and to make good the promise he made at the end of Act I, Scene 2. Virtue must manifest itself in positive action.

To compare Hal's wit with that of Falstaff in this scene, or elsewhere in the play for that matter, is wholly irrelevant. Whatever Falstaff's limitations may be, no one can deny him preeminence in the realm of wit.

Falstaff is in rare form as he enters, denouncing Hal and Poins as cowards and identifying himself as one endowed with true "manhood," as one of the few "good" men left in a bad world. He manifests again his constant awareness of Hal's status as heir-apparent and his own status as privileged jester by declaring his intent to beat Hal out of his kingdom with a wooden dagger and drive Hal's subjects before him like a flock of geese—including, to be sure, the lowly ones whom Hal has just been winning over.

When Sir John brazenly denies that he has had a single drink, although we have seen him quaff a cup of sack almost as soon as he entered the tavern, the way is prepared for his gargantuan lies concerning the number of assailants at Gadshill. His immediate reply to Hal, who points out that Falstaff's lips are still wet with wine (170), provides a key to the old knight's tall stories: "All's one for that" (What difference does it make?). Surely it is futile to waste one's time debating whether or not Falstaff expects Hal and Poins to believe him. He remains the great wit at his calling; exaggeration, as is apparent here, can be wonderfully amusing.

And so when, with assumed solemnity, he justifies his conduct at Gadshill, having been exposed as a liar and coward. As Hal knows, he is "as valiant as Hercules; but beware instinct; the lion will not touch the true prince." In identifying himself with the great exemplar of strength and courage in classical mythology and with the lion (here a symbol not of royalty but of courage and ferocity in the animal kingdom), Falstaff illustrates another aspect of his complex character. Here he is the braggart warrior, a well-known type character in classical comedy, long since naturalized in Renaissance

European drama, including English. But let us give Falstaff credit; he is aware of the full import of his words.

The nobleman at the door, an emissary from the king, is dismissed by Falstaff as "Old Gravity"; the elderly, white-bearded knight in whose life seriousness has no place is glad to "send him packing" (328). The epithet Falstaff uses here is at one with "old father antic," which he used earlier to describe the law. The implication is the same: He has no use for responsibility, for law, for order. They interfere with life conceived as a perpetual holiday.

There follows an exchange between Hal and Bardolph and then between the prince and Falstaff; these have some special interest in the realm of the comedy of physical appearances (340–60) and also have some thematic relevance. Bardolph's flaming nose invites Hal's witty comment; it provides a constant glow that should have served Bardolph as well as his sword during the Gadshill robbery, and yet Bardolph ran away. Perhaps, in contrast to Falstaff's undisturbed good humor, there is rancor in Bardolph's reply: "My lord, do you see these meteors? Do you behold these exhalations?" (351–52). But Shakespeare is making a typical play on words here. On one level, meteors and exhalations stand for drunkenness and poverty; on a second level, not to be ignored in a play about rebellion, they stand for violation of law and order.

In the comedy of physical appearances, Falstaff's enormous girth, which invites Hal's merciless comments (357–61), provides much fun. "Bare-bone" Falstaff, Hal suggests, has been blown up by bombast, implying that the old man is devoid of real substance. There is, perhaps, pathos to be found in Sir John's reply: If he has not been able to see his own knees since he was a youth of Hal's age, once, long ago, he was becomingly slender. And, to be sure, he has his own explanation for his corpulence—"a plague of sighing and grief" has blown him up "like a bladder." We are not allowed to sentimentalize; Falstaff's wit drives away sentimentality.

The subsequent dialogue relating to the fearful opponents of Henry IV is especially revealing of Hal's character. Despite all that Falstaff says to undermine the courage of the young prince, Hal remains nonchalant and (thanks probably to the presence of Falstaff) quite witty. What should come through, especially since Hotspur dominated the previous scene and his character has had an important part in the present one, is that Prince Hal finds no occasion to become voluble and boastful about what he intends to do. News of impending conflict does not drive him beyond the bounds of patience. Deeds, not words, are called for, certainly not advertisement of one's self.

The "play extempore," culminating in Falstaff's brilliant defense of himself and his way of life, is a comic masterpiece. Sir John's genius is fully revealed here as he throws his considerable self into the role of an irate father and king reproving an errant son and heir. He is especially appreciated by the hostess of this disreputable tavern, whom he calls, in lines of heroic verse, his "sweet . . . tristeful queen." Earlier, attention has been called to Falstaff's rather wide range of knowledge, to the fact that his discourse reflects an education appropriate to a knight of the realm. This aspect of his character is again shown, as when he speaks of "King Cambyses' vein," a reference to the ranting style used by Thomas Preston in the widely popular tragedy *Cambyses*, written some twenty-eight years before *Henry IV, Part 1*. More emphatically, it is shown by Falstaff's matchless burlesque of euphuism, the highly contrived style used in the even more widely popular and influential prose romance *Euphues* (1579), by John Lyly. That style, which for a time was widely imitated, is marked by interminable parallelisms and antitheses, rhetorical questions, maxims, and curious allusions and similes that derive from the *Natural History* of Pliny, classical mythology, and the bestiaries of the Middle Ages. All these stylistic devices Falstaff makes use of in his speech, which includes insulting and even scandalous comments on the royal family. He concludes with words of highest praise for "a virtuous man" with whom the prince keeps company. Ah, yes—now he remembers the name. It is Falstaff. Let Hal "him keep with," the rest banish.

When Hal asks that they exchange roles, Falstaff asks, "Depose me?" And he challenges the prince to match him in gravity and majesty. At this point, some will be reminded of Hal's solemn promise to break "through the foul and ugly mists / Of vapours that did seem to strangle him" (I. ii. 225–26). If he is to do so, this king of jesters must be deposed.

Actually, Prince Hal, in the role of his father, makes no attempt to rival Falstaff; he makes use of this change to berate the fat knight as (among other things) "that grey iniquity, . . . that villainous abominable misleader of youth, Falstaff, that old white-bearded Satan"

(449–509). Then Falstaff, suddenly serious and dutiful in tone as he plays the role of the young heir to the throne, makes his memorable reply, one that is so eloquent, so appealing that generations of theatergoers and readers have taken Falstaff to their hearts—and uncritically have kept him there, whatever his actions have been or will be. Here indeed is verbal brilliance if any is to be found anywhere in literature, dramatic or non-dramatic.

There is fine irony in his first statement: He sees no more harm in Falstaff than he sees in himself. He follows this with an appeal for charity. Falstaff is old, he is white-haired; but let no one say he is a whoremaster! It is the strait-laced Puritan who is tacitly denounced in the reference to sack and sugar, fondness for which Falstaff does not deny. Here one of several biblical references used by the knight in the course of the two *Henry IV* plays serves his purpose. Are Pharaoh's lean kine to be loved? And then the incremental refrain on "Jack Falstaff" serves as the peroration. Banish all the other hangers-on at the Boar's-Head Tavern, but banish not Falstaff—the sweet, the kind, the true, the valiant, if old, Jack Falstaff from the prince's company: "Banish plump Jack, and banish all the world."

The commentator who dares to say a word against Sir John at this point of the action risks the charge of lacking a sense of humor (perhaps the most damning charge that can be made against an individual), with the resultant misunderstanding of Falstaff's worth. And yet he has been established as a glutton, one who is devoted largely to the pleasures of the flesh. As Shakespeare has occasion to say elsewhere, wine, used wisely, is a good companion (*Othello*, II. iii. 313). In this play, the evidence is complete: Falstaff uses wine in great excess. Nor are all the references to his gray hairs and white beard necessarily intended to invoke pity. Shakespeare's generation believed that age should bring wisdom and a sense of decorum. Carefree escapades may be amusing, even excusable in youth; but in an older person, one who is a ranking member in a hierarchical society, they cannot be laughed away—despite the fact that the rebel latent in many people applauds Falstaff's defiance of the establishment and the sheer brilliance of his defense.

It is with all this in mind that one must evaluate Hal's one-line response after Falstaff has said, "Banish plump Jack, and banish all the world." Says the prince: "I do, I will." Thus, playing the role of king in this play extempore, the heir-apparent embraces law and order; not for long can life be no more than a holiday for him; he has a sacred obligation to fulfill, one that affects the lives of all Englishmen.

Little explication needs to be added. Understandably Falstaff hopes that Hal will not permit the sheriff to enter his tavern sanctuary. His reply to Hal, who once more accuses him of being "a natural coward," is worth brief comment. "I deny your major," he says (544). Falstaff thus spontaneously uses the vocabulary of formal logic, again displaying the range of his knowledge. Moreover, he is not a *natural* coward, as are Bardolph and Peto; he is a coward on principle—that is, when self-interest and self-preservation are involved. He falls asleep behind the arras, confident that the prince will take care of troublesome people like the sheriff.

There is no need to belabor the point relating to the "intolerable deal of sack" consumed by Falstaff—and still not paid for. By the end of this comic scene, preparations are being made for another enterprise involving Hal and his tavern companions, one that will offer a marked contrast to the Gadshill affair. And we learn that Hal, who had told Falstaff that he would not be a thief (I. ii. 154) yet had gone along with the rest, will return the money with interest to the travelers.

ACT III

Summary

In Bangor, Wales, Hotspur and Worcester confer with Glendower, their host, and Mortimer. Young Percy and the Welsh leader, after exchanging compliments, engage in a personal dispute and are interrupted by Mortimer. A map is produced, whereupon the rebel leaders proceed to divide England into three parts—the north going to the Percies, the west to Glendower, and the south to Mortimer. It is Mortimer who explains the immediate action to be taken. He will set forth with Hotspur and Worcester to meet Northumberland and the Scottish forces at Shrewsbury; Glendower, who will need time to muster his forces, will join them later.

Hotspur expresses his dissatisfaction with the division, insisting that the course of the River Trent be changed so as to enlarge his share. Glendower protests, but the two reach an accord.

Mortimer's wife is desolate because her husband must leave

her. The couple try to communicate, although neither speaks the other's language. She then sings a Welsh song to the accompaniment of music invoked by Glendower's magic. Hotspur promptly urges his wife to join him in an amorous interlude, and they exchange witty remarks devoid of sentimentality. In short order, however, Hotspur puts an end to this interlude. He will sign the articles of partition and depart for Shrewsbury within two hours.

At the palace in London, Prince Hal appears before his father, who dismisses members of his court so that he can speak alone to his son. He passionately censures the heir-apparent for "inordinate and low desires" and for indulging in "such barren pleasures" in the company of such "rude" individuals, ignoring his status and obligations as a prince. The king seems to believe that Hal's dereliction may be evidence of God's punishment for "some displeasing service" he (the king) has done. Hal does not claim to be blameless, but he states that busybodies and scandalmongers have exaggerated accounts of his behavior.

The king voices his deep concern at considerable length. Hal has absented himself from councils of state, letting his younger brother take his place. If the king himself had chosen, as Hal has done, to cheapen himself in "vulgar company," he never would have won the allegiance of Englishmen. He especially sees in his son the same fatal weaknesses that led to Richard II's downfall. At that time, the king himself was like young Percy, who, no older than Prince Hal, commands "ancient lords and reverend bishops" into battle and has won "never-dying honour" by capturing the renowned Douglas. To Henry IV, it seems that Hal is his greatest enemy, not the Northern rebels and Mortimer.

Chagrined by this strong reproof, Prince Hal urges his father not to believe those who have led the king to misjudge him. He solemnly promises to "redeem all this on Percy's head"—that is, he will prove his loyalty and worth by performing glorious deeds in opposition to the valiant Hotspur.

Overjoyed, the king declares that Hal will be placed in command of royal forces. The king himself, joined by Westmoreland and Prince John, will lead another army, which will join Hal's in the north.

Sir Walter Blunt arrives with the news that Douglas and the English rebels even now have assembled their troops at Shrewsbury.

In Scene 3, Falstaff deplores his alleged physical decline resulting from lack of activity since the Gadshill "action." Bardolph's frank
comment on the knight's corpulence leads him to a rhetorical exercise, the subject of which is Bardolph's flaming nose. When Mistress
Quickly enters, Sir John accuses her of having picked his pockets,
and he refuses to pay his bill for wine, food, and even items of clothing. The hostess has occasion to mention the prince, whereupon Falstaff calls him a "Jack" (knave) and declares that he would cudgel
him if he were present.

The prince enters, marching with Peto. Falstaff joins them, playing on his truncheon (a short staff) as if it were a fife. Falstaff then
renews his altercation with the hostess, but when Hal tells him that
he directed the search of Sir John's pockets, the old knight magnanimously forgives her.

Falstaff is much relieved to learn that all matters relating to the
robbery have been settled. Yet the news of Hal's reconciliation with
the king hardly elates him, particularly when he is told that he is to
command foot soldiers. A serious Prince Hal then gives orders to
Bardolph, Peto, and Falstaff, all relating to their services in opposing
the rebels.

Commentary

Scene 1 is the "division" scene; in terms of political doctrine, it is
especially important. Conceivably some members of Shakespeare's
audiences, like many today, had their doubts about the titular hero
of this play, Henry IV, recalling not only the illegal manner in which
he came to the throne but also finding him too much the politician,
too calculating. For them, Falstaff's comic rationalizations of his
own actions to some extent parody those of the king. But few, if any,
Englishmen would have tolerated even the thought of division of
their country. Their sympathies inevitably would have been on the
side of the crown. Therefore, however valid any complaint by the
Percies may have been, their present action, in which they are
joined by Mortimer and Glendower, cannot be justified. In opposing
them, the king and his son will emerge as saviors of England.

Fortunately, the heavily doctrinal elements here and elsewhere
in the play are rendered sufficiently palatable, thanks largely to
superior character portrayal. Not only does Hotspur continue to
attract, especially because one sees him in contrast to Prince Hal,

but others, including Glendower and Mortimer, interest reader and audience alike. Glendower, it may be noted, is anything but the wild, barbaric figure of the prose histories. And, of course, the scene includes a delightful romantic interlude with music.

Appropriately, it is the character of Hotspur that receives greatest attention in Scene 1, and his very first speech is revealing. One may question the ultimate worth of a leader who, even momentarily, cannot recall whether he has forgotten or mislaid the important map. This would suggest that he is hardly the one for planning an action, however capable he may be in other areas. Most serious is young Percy's absolute inability to restrain himself or to tolerate what he considers to be conceit and superstition in Glendower, his host and ally and a man of genuine military greatness. Well along in Scene 1, Worcester lectures his headstrong nephew, and his words are weighty with import:

> In faith, my lord, you are too wilful-blame;
> And since your coming hither have done enough
> To put him [Glendower] quite besides his patience.
> You must needs learn, lord, to amend this fault.
> Though sometimes it show greatness, courage,
>   blood,—
> And that's the dearest grace it renders you,—
> Yet oftentimes it doth present harsh rage,
> Defect of manners, want of government,
> Pride, haughtiness, opinion, and disdain;
> The least of which haunting a nobleman
> Loseth men's hearts and leaves behind a stain
> Upon the beauty of all parts besides,
> Beguiling them of commendation.
>
>   (177–89)

"Loseth men's hearts": One recalls that in the previous scene, Prince Hal had been winning men's hearts!

This is not to say that Hotspur loses one's sympathy in Scene 1. Quite the contrary. There is graciousness and good heartedness in his reply to his uncle: "Well, I am school'd. Good manners be your speed!" The reader enjoys his satiric thrusts, well illustrated by his reply to Glendower, who claims the ability to "call spirits from the vasty deep": "Why, so can I, or so can any man; / But will they come when you do call for them?" (54–55).

Young Percy is no less amusing, but just as tactless and intolerant, when he comments on "lovely English ditties" and Welsh airs and what he calls "mincing poetry." These cultivated subjects have no place in the life of the Hotspur of the North. Although at one point Lady Percy says that her husband is "governed by humours" (237), it is really the single humour insisted upon by Prince Hal in the previous scene that rules him. Compared to either Mortimer or Glendower, whose cultural as well as military accomplishments receive attention, Hotspur is a personable barbarian. It may be added that although Glendower probably would have had serious difficulty in calling up devils from the vast deep, Shakespeare does give some evidence of his supernatural powers; it is Glendower who magically provides the music for the Welsh love song. But, admittedly, the dramatist introduces this rather casually; perhaps, like Hotspur, we are not much impressed.

Something more can be said to the credit of Hotspur in Scene 1. As in Act II, Scene 3, his relation with the lovely Lady Kate, who affectionately calls him a "giddy goose" (232), is delightful. His boyish attractiveness comes through strongly. Moreover, gallantry and fair-mindedness remain prominent in his character. When Glendower agrees that the Trent must be "turn'd," Hotspur replies, "I do not care. I'll give thrice so much land / To any well-deserving friend" (137–38).

In Scene 2, the climax and turning point are reached. Because of Hal's vow and his appointment as supreme commander of one large force, the way is prepared also for the shift in the comic subplot. The thematic relationship between main plot and subplot is sufficiently clear, for the reader has come directly from the scene in which this meeting between prince and king has been parodied.

To some, King Henry may appear especially calculating in parts of Scene 2. Why, for example, should he say to his son:

> I know not whether God will have it so,
> For some displeasing service I have done,
> That, in his secret doom, out of my blood
> He'll breed revengement and a scourge for me.
>
> (4–7)

Perhaps, it is argued, he is not sure that Hal's apparent failure is a sign of God's displeasure, but he is well aware of the "displeasing service" he himself had done—usurpation and regicide. Moreover, his second and much longer speech (29–91) is practical instruction on how to influence people—the right people—what with his remarks on dressing himself "in such humility / That [he] did pluck allegiance from men's hearts" (51–52). The point of view represented here is surely not to be ignored, but it may do Henry IV less than justice.

In the first place, it is primarily Henry IV, upholder of law and order, not Henry the sinner, who appears here and in the rest of the play—quite logically, since increasing attention has been paid and will be paid to the rebels. He is the man who, unlike his unfortunate predecessor, is gifted with the arts of kingship. If indeed, according to sixteenth-century political philosophy, the ruler was God's lieutenant on earth, responsible ultimately only to God, he nevertheless must "pluck allegiance from men's hearts," which means that he must win their respect and hold it if his reign is to be successful. The many contemporary discussions of kingship made all this abundantly clear. The king/father has heard only scandalous reports about his son's behavior. His concern about the succession to the throne is deep and proper; it was a dominant concern of Shakespeare's generation in an England ruled by the Virgin Queen.

Most emphatically now, Prince Hal is pitted against Hotspur. Earlier young Percy had been praised by the king as the "theme of honour's tongue" (I. i. 81); in Scene 2, he is "Mars in swathling clothes"(112), a youth no older than Hal who leads high-ranking subjects (a reference to Northumberland, Mortimer, and the Archbishop of York, who are all mentioned in lines 118–19), and who defeated the great Douglas.

At the end of Act I, Scene 2, Hal promised to redeem his tarnished reputation, but he spoke in soliloquy, voicing his secret thoughts, as it were. Now he makes his pledge directly to his king and father. This is not the casual, debonair Prince Hal of the Boar's-Head Tavern speaking. His father's words have penetrated deeply. The very simplicity of his first line underscores his sincerity and determination: "Do not think so; you shall not find it so" (129). He takes his oath "in the name of God" (153). Most readers share the king's elation: "A hundred thousand rebels die in this" (160).

In Scene 3, Falstaff's reference to "this last action," a term commonly used for military activity, serves to remind the reader of the connection between the comic subplot and the main plot in this chronicle-history play. One hardly needs the testimony of Bardolph to know that Falstaff has not "dwindled," not "fallen away," either physically or mentally. He is his redoubtable self. His answer to his own questions that begin this scene, complete with witty similes ("like an old lady's loose gown . . . like an old apple-john"), tells us as much. Like an old apple, he keeps his flavor; unlike it, he is not shriveled. We have seen him before in a mood of apparent repentance like the one that follows and are not at all surprised to hear him attribute his fallen state to "company, villainous company," no more than we are surprised to witness the sudden revival of his spirits thanks to his recourse to hedonist philosophy. When Bardolph remarks that he cannot live long, Sir John replies: "Why, there is it. Come sing me a bawdy song; make me merry" (15–16).

But it is his brilliant comments on Bardolph's physical appearance (27–59) that dominate the first part of Scene 3. This is an unsurpassed example of the comedy of physical appearance and of words—more specifically the "comedy of noses" (See Rostand's *Cyrano de Bergerac*, wherein the titular hero expounds wittily on the subject of his own nose). To put it another way, this is a comic aria, a bravura piece, all action stopping to give the performer his special opportunity to demonstrate his virtuosity. His evoking of the image of hell's fire (and making another accurate biblical reference) is especially effective; at this point, he sounds like a zealous preacher putting the fear of the Lord into the hearts of his listeners.

One additional point may be added. Falstaff has provided the wine for Bardolph for some thirty-two years, we are told (51–55). The time element, probably exaggerated to add to the fun, is not applicable, but the Falstaff of this play has depended upon Hal for the same courtesy. Thus the parasitical aspect of his character again receives notice. As a matter of fact, the interlude involving Mistress Quickly develops this. One learns that the old knight has been victimizing the kindly hostess, who has provided him with drink, food, and clothing.

In this kind of skirmish, or action, be it with the lowly tavern mistress or with the prince himself, Falstaff shows a kind of military genius. His method is to attack; that, quite often, is the best defense. Not irrelevant in this connection is the amusing military pantomime when Hal and Peto march in.

Falstaff is no less accomplished in his responses to the prince.

When the hostess reports that Sir John had claimed Hal to be in his debt to the extent of one thousand pounds (a fortune in Shakespeare's day), Falstaff has an unanswerable reply: His love for Hal is worth millions. Nor does he hold the prince in awe, for that emotion is properly to be reserved for the king. He caps all this, tacitly admitting that his pockets had contained only "tavern-reckonings, memorandums of bawdy-houses, and one poor penny-worth of sugar-candy" (178–80). He reminds Hal that Adam, progenitor of the human race, fell from a state of innocence, proving that all flesh is weak—and does not he, Falstaff, have more flesh than any other man? Clearly, it will not do to see Falstaff as symbolic of Prince Hal's irresponsible youth any more than it will to reduce him to a single comic-type character. He is uniquely himself.

But that is not to say that his wit absolves him from all faults. His status as privileged jester makes it possible for him to urge Hal to "rob . . . the exchequer" at once now that the prince is on good terms with the king, to suggest that Hal steal a horse for him so that he will not have to lead his soldiers afoot, and to praise rebels on the grounds that they offend only "the virtues" (205 ff.). But the course of life cannot be determined by the atmosphere of an Eastcheap tavern—not if one is to follow it honorably. Unlike Prince Hal, Falstaff is unwilling to give up life as a long series of holidays even though the fate of the nation is at stake. Quite in character, then, he has his own way of applauding the prince's stirring call to arms ("The land is burning; Percy stands on high"): "Rare words! brave world! Hostess, my breakfast, come! / O, I could wish this tavern were my drum!" (229–30). His sensitive appetite must be satisfied under all circumstances. And it is suggested that he would like to transfer the tavern to the battlefield. Perhaps, in a metaphorical sense, he will do exactly that.

ACT IV

Summary

The scene now shifts to the rebel camp near Shrewsbury, where Hotspur, Worcester, and Douglas appear. Young Percy and the Scottish warrior exchange compliments. A messenger arrives with news from the Earl of Northumberland. It seems that Hotspur's father is ill and cannot lead his followers to Shrewsbury. Shocked to hear this, Hotspur quickly recovers himself and finds reasons to remain confident: It would be bad strategy to risk his strength in a single encounter; moreover, a victory by the reduced rebel army will redound all the more to their credit, helping to convince the populace at large that the revolt will be successful. Douglas readily endorses these opinions.

Sir Richard Vernon brings news concerning the royal forces. The Earl of Westmoreland and Prince John lead seven thousand soldiers toward Shrewsbury, and the king himself has set forth with another army. Hotspur remains undaunted; he welcomes the opportunity of opposing the royal power. But what, he asks, of Prince Hal? Where is he? Vernon then describes the young heir-apparent "all furnish'd, all in arms," also headed toward the field of battle. Hotspur interrupts Vernon; he cannot bear to hear such words of praise about his royal contemporary. Nevertheless, he now can hardly restrain himself, so anxious is he for the conflict to begin.

There is more news. Vernon reports that Glendower needs more time to muster his power. Worcester and even the fearless Douglas concede that this is the worst news of all. Not Hotspur. When Vernon tells him that the royal forces number 30,000, he exclaims: "Forty let it be!" Douglas joins him in challenging death itself.

Falstaff and Bardolph appear on a public road near Coventry, followed by a newly enlisted company of soldiers. Sir John orders Bardolph to replenish his supply of sack and to tell Peto to meet him at the town's end. He dislikes the idea of marching his men through the town in their rags and tatters. Abjectly impoverished, not one of them could pay him, as so many others had, for release from military service. In Falstaff's own words, "No eye hath seen such scarecrows" (41).

Prince Hal and Westmoreland meet him on the road and comment on the poor creatures whom Falstaff leads. The knight remains undisturbed and is philosophical in the face of this criticism. And, for that matter, the prince seems amused rather than indignant. All are to make haste, says Hal, for Percy is already in the field.

Worcester and Vernon try to convince Hotspur that the rebel forces should not attack at once. Douglas sides with young Percy. The sound of a trumpet announces a parley, and Sir Walter Blunt enters "with gracious offers from the King." This gives Hotspur the occasion to review the story of how Henry was helped by the Percies when he returned from exile and how he then usurped the throne. Now, says the young rebel commander, Henry has proved ungrateful to his benefactors and has ignored the proper claims of Mortimer. When Blunt asks if this is Percy's final answer, he is told that it is not. In the morning, Hotspur will send Worcester to hear the king's terms and to present their own.

The Archbishop of York instructs Sir Michael to deliver in all haste certain written instructions and information to his allies and relatives who have a substantial number of followers. The archbishop has learned that Hotspur faces the king's power without the support of Northumberland, Glendower, and Mortimer. Convinced that young Percy will be defeated, he knows that the king will then move against him for his part in the conspiracy.

Commentary

Although the Battle of Shrewsbury is yet to be fought, the action in the main plot, having reached its climax in Act III, Scene 2, is now falling, structurally speaking. The fortunes of the Percies have been in the ascent prior to this act. Now the three items of intelligence mark the turn toward adversity: Neither Northumberland nor Glendower will appear with his troops to join those led by Hotspur; the Prince of Wales, having done no more than voice his good intentions, is now acting positively.

The Hotspur in Scene 1 is something more than the limited individual who deserved to be the object of Prince Hal's satire in Act II, Scene 4. He emerges as more than the vain, rather boastful (if courageous) warrior. Although the initial exchange between him and the Earl of Douglas may suggest that the Scotsman is young Percy's alter ego, it is Douglas, not Hotspur, who is the exemplar of unreflecting dauntlessness. Perhaps this difference is implicit in the fact that Douglas is hailed for his courage, Hotspur for his honor. But it is explicit in Hotspur's reaction to the adverse reports— the first brought by the messenger, the second and third by Sir Richard Vernon.

When he learns that his father will not arrive because of "inward" illness (an intentionally ambiguous term), young Percy recognizes the extent to which the odds have shifted and momentarily loses heart: "This sickness doth infect / The very life-blood of our enterprise" (28–29); it is "a perilous gash, a very limb lopp'd off"

(43). But as a leader, he knows that he cannot appear daunted. Promptly he recovers himself and advances reasons for complete confidence in the success of the enterprise. And, of course, Douglas can be depended upon to second him. This is equally true of their reaction to the news about Glendower's inability to muster troops in time, although he had assured the Percies that he would not need even fourteen days. Perhaps there is significance in the Scotsman's reply when Hotspur declares that all goes well: "As heart can think," he says (84). Emotion, not intellect, is his guide.

Vernon's description of the Prince of Wales and Hotspur's reaction call for special comment. From the start, these two have been set in opposition to each other. Young Percy is endorsing little more than the public reputation of the prince (who appropriately is never called "Hal" in these serious scenes of the main plot), one that had been held by King Henry prior to the reconciliation, when he, Percy, refers to him as the "nimble-footed madcap . . . that daff'd [thrust] the world aside / And bid it pass" (95–97). Up to the end of Act III, the prince in this play has completely ignored public responsibility, so far as positive action is concerned.

Vernon's portrait is that of the Ideal Prince, one that might have been depicted in a rich medieval tapestry. The prince and his followers, wearing the ostrich feather, heraldic emblem of the Prince of Wales, are endowed with spirit and ardor. The prince himself is compared to the Roman god Mercury, a tribute to his prowess: Certainly vaulting into the saddle with ease when armor-clad is an impressive accomplishment! Superior horsemanship, it may be added, was an essential accomplishment of the ideal Renaissance man.

Now it is Hotspur alone, not he *and* his comrades, who is momentarily crushed by this report of a battle-ready Prince of Wales: "Worse than the sun in March, / This praise doth nourish agues," he exclaims (111–12). When he recovers himself, his words comprise a challenge for individual trial by arms: "Harry to Harry shall, hot horse to horse, / Meet and ne'er part till one drop down a corse" (122–23). In a word, the conflict in the main plot is now assuming the characteristics of a medieval tournament, with an admirable centralizing of the action.

In Scene 2, Sir John Falstaff, knight of the realm and an officially appointed commander of troops, is off to the wars. A new Falstaff, then? Not at all. This latest "action" provides another occasion for plunder, another chance to show what he thinks of "old father antic the law." Well he knows that the soldier must have his provisions; therefore his first concern has to do with a bottle of sack. In his brilliant soliloquy (12–52), he practically boasts of the disreputable means he has employed to fill the ranks of his company. Nor has he spent a farthing to outfit the beggarly creatures. He had been careful to demand in the king's name those men who would, by one means or another, be able to pay for their release. Then, thanks to the cooperation of minor local officials, he filled the ranks with jail birds—which does not mean that any had been guilty of any serious offense since roving beggars were subject to arrest in sixteenth-century England. And so these ragged specimens of humanity "march wide betwixt the legs, as if they had gyves [fetters] on" (43–44). Led by the corpulent, well-fed Falstaff, these bare-boned, lowly subjects are a grotesquely incongruous sight, all the more so if one recalls the splendor of the prince and his fellow warriors in their plumes and glittering gold coats, as described by Sir Richard Vernon in the preceding scene. These "pitiful rascals," as the prince calls them, will win no glory, no honor in the wars. In Falstaff's callous words, they are just "food for powder" (72).

If Falstaff remains a speaker of brilliant prose in Scene 2, his humor now is grim. Here he is not victimizing a tavern hostess or engaging in robbery devoid of physical violence; he is dealing with the lives of his fellow men, but again he is concerned only with personal gain. He remains "as vigilant as a cat to steal cream" (65). Falstaff must be allowed to follow his course with logical consistency. Significantly, the Prince of Wales does not reprove him; he is permitted to proceed on the march to Shrewsbury.

The Hotspur in Scene 3 is admirable; he is anything but the foolhardy, impetuous youth. As supreme commander of the rebel forces, he reasons well. Already facing a numerically superior power, he knows that the odds against him will increase unless he commits his troops immediately. In his recital of grievances, he invites understanding and sympathy. He expresses a willingness to negotiate if the terms are honorable. The scene thus ends on at least a faint note of hope.

The consensus is that Scene 4 is to be justified solely on the grounds that it looks forward to the main action in *Henry IV, Part 2*, wherein royal forces indeed move against the archbishop and Lord

Mowbray, his most powerful and dependable ally. Yet there is some reason for its inclusion here strictly with reference to *Henry IV, Part 1*. It provides Shakespeare with the opportunity to summarize major events, to foreshadow the rebels' defeat, and to emphasize the seriousness and magnitude of the entire action.

The Sir Michael of Scene 4 does not find a place in history. He may well be a priest since priests often were given the courtesy title of "Sir."

ACT V

Summary

The Earl of Worcester and Sir Richard Vernon arrive as emissaries at the king's camp near Shrewsbury. Present are the king himself, the Prince of Wales, John of Lancaster, Sir Walter Blunt, and Falstaff. As Hotspur did earlier in his reply to the king's emissary (IV. iii.), Worcester voices at some length the grievances of the Percies, chief of which is Henry's alleged perfidy when, returning from exile, he assured them that he sought no more than the restoration of confiscated Lancastrian estates. The king does not deign to answer this charge; instead he dismisses it as no more than a pretext for rebellion against the crown. He refuses to permit the Prince of Wales to settle the dispute in single combat with Hotspur. Instead, he offers the rebels free pardon if they will lay down their arms. After Worcester and Vernon leave, the prince states that both Hotspur and Douglas, supremely confident and proven warriors, will reject the offer. The king agrees and orders all officers to their posts.

Falstaff shows little desire to risk his life in any kind of conflict. He asks Hal to keep an eye on him and to help him if necessary. Alone, he soliloquizes on the subject of honor and finds no profit in being a dead hero.

Back in the rebel camp, Worcester insists that Hotspur must not be told that the king has offered all of the insurgents free pardon. He argues that although his young nephew's trespass will be forgiven, Henry IV will never place his trust in the elder leaders of the rebellion. Vernon reluctantly agrees to remain silent. Accordingly, Worcester tells Hotspur that the king is merciless. Like Douglas, the youth is ready to fight.

When Worcester then tells Hotspur that the prince has challenged him to single combat, the young rebel fervently expresses his wish that such a meeting could take place. He remains skeptical regarding the worth of the prince even though Vernon describes the latter's chivalric behavior and becoming modesty.

Learning that even now the "King comes on apace," Hotspur exhorts his companions to fight nobly, and then he embraces them as the trumpets sound the start of the conflict.

On the battlefield, Sir Walter Blunt, wearing armor the same as that of the king, meets Douglas, who has slain the Lord of Stafford, similarly arrayed for the obvious purpose of misleading the foe. Now the Scotsman is convinced that it is Henry IV himself whom he faces, and he demands that Blunt surrender. Sir Walter does not reveal his true identity. The two fight and Blunt is slain.

Hotspur enters, speaking words of high praise to the jubilant Douglas, who believes that now "All's done, all's won" (17). Young Percy recognizes Blunt and disillusions his fellow warrior. Both leave to renew the fight elsewhere.

There is the sound of sudden attack. Then Falstaff appears alone. He finds things quite different from what they had been in London; it is not so easy to get off "shot-free" on the battlefield; he may have to pay the bill, which is a rather steep one. Looking down at the body of Sir Walter Blunt, he finds new reason to believe that seeking honor has its grave limitations. From his soliloquy, it is learned that he led his ragged "troops" into the heart of battle and that all but two or three have been slaughtered.

Now it is the prince who arrives. His mood of complete seriousness and dedication to duty is established at once as he sternly rebukes Falstaff for idleness and asks for the use of his sword. Falstaff boasts about his alleged valor and even claims to have taken care of Hotspur. When Hal assures him that the young rebel survives to slay Falstaff, the fat knight refuses to relinquish his sword but offers to give Hal his pistol. It is a bottle of sack, not a weapon, which he draws from the case. Hal seizes it, strongly reproves Falstaff, and throws the bottle at him.

Alone once more, Falstaff declares that he will slay Percy if that fearsome enemy survives. But he makes it clear that he is not about to go out of his way to find such "grinning honour" as that possessed by the dead Sir Walter Blunt. Clearly, Hotspur will survive to old age as far as Falstaff is concerned.

The king bids the Prince of Wales and his brother, John of Lancaster, to rest. Despite his wounds, the prince will not do so: " . . . God forbid a shallow scratch should drive / The Prince of Wales from such a field as this, / Where . . . rebels' arms triumph in massacres" (11–14). He has high praise for his younger brother, whose courage inspires them all. The two depart.

Douglas enters, faces Henry IV, and exclaims: "Another king!" He identifies himself and demands to know the true identity of his foe. The king expresses his regret that, until now, the Scottish warrior has met only "his shadows"—nobles whom he mistook for the king. While his son seeks out Percy, Henry will take on Douglas.

The king is in danger of defeat when Prince Hal enters. The latter identifies himself as the heir-apparent, engages Douglas in single combat, and forces his adversary to flee for his life. King Henry is particularly touched by this evidence of his son's courage.

After the king leaves, Hotspur enters, addresses the prince by name, and identifies himself. Now at last Harry *does* meet Harry face to face in combat. Falstaff appears to cheer Prince Hal, who will, as he says, "find no boy's play here" (76). At this point in the action, Douglas re-enters and engages Falstaff, who soon falls down as if he were dead. Just as Douglas leaves, Hotspur himself is wounded and falls.

In moving words, young Percy begins to recite his own epitaph but dies before he can finish. It is the prince who, in generous terms, completes it.

The prince sees the fallen Sir John Falstaff. Believing his old companion to be dead (if one takes his words literally), he now provides an epitaph for "Poor Jack," referring to him as "so fat a deer" and declaring that he will see him "embowell'd" (103–10). Hal departs.

Falstaff promptly revives and rises up. As in earlier, far less serious episodes, he indulges in witty rationalization for his unheroic behavior—specifically, in this case, counterfeiting death. Next, he expresses his fear of "this gunpowder Percy," who is apparently dead. Perhaps, he says, young Percy is "counterfeiting" as Falstaff himself did. He decides to "make him sure"—and then to claim that it was he who killed the valiant rebel leader. No living person is nearby to see him, so he stabs the corpse of the fallen Hotspur. He lifts the body onto his back just as Prince Hal and John of Lancaster re-enter.

Prince John is puzzled: Did not Hal tell him that the old knight had been killed? Hal replies that indeed he saw Falstaff "dead, / Breathless and bleeding on the ground" (137). Sir John, he concludes, is not what he seems.

Indeed he is not, replies Falstaff. As conqueror of the great Percy, he looks to be made either an earl or a duke. He is deeply shocked to hear the prince claim to have slain Hotspur. Prince Hal is not perturbed; he is not concerned with refuting Sir John. As he says to his brother, if a lie will serve Falstaff, he will not interfere.

A trumpet sounds retreat. All know that the rebels have been defeated. The two princes leave to find out how their comrades have fared. Falstaff will follow—for his reward, as he makes clear.

The insurrection having been repressed, King Henry orders the execution of Worcester and Vernon. The fate of the other rebels will be decided later. Prince Hal intercedes on behalf of the Earl of Douglas, and his life is spared. Prince John of Lancaster is given the honor of setting the Scotsman free. The king then announces that he will divide his forces. One army, led by Prince John and the Earl of Westmoreland, will move against the forces assembled by Northumberland and Archbishop Scroop in northern England. Accompanied by Prince Hal, Henry himself will march to Wales to fight Glendower and Mortimer.

Commentary

The opening lines help establish the mood of Scene 1, the action of which takes place not long before the battle starts. There is rather obvious irony in the speeches of both Worcester and the king. The former makes much of Henry's violation of an oath to the effect that he sought only redress of grievances and not the throne of England, implying that the Percies had no intention of becoming traitors to Richard II. But the reader will recall Hotspur's words spoken early in the play. Northumberland and Worcester "wear the detested blot / Of murderous subornation . . . Being the agents or base second means, / The cords, the ladder, or the hangman rather" who made possible the crowning of Henry (I. iii. 162 ff.). His solicitude for the fallen Richard, coming so tardily, does not conceal the basic selfish motives of the House of Percy.

It is no less evident that Henry, not content with retrieving the confiscated Lancastrian estates, was strongly motivated by self-interest, specifically with ambitions toward the throne. But the overwhelming fact now is that he is England's king and has not been guilty of gross misrule as was his predecessor. He is in the process of suppressing "pell mell havoc and confusion"; he seeks to restore law and order in England. If one keeps in mind the view that, in the larger sense, the State is the greater protagonist in the chronicle-history plays, there is a logic here.

Some commentators see calculation in the king's refusal to let his son meet Hotspur in single combat, arguing that Henry is too adroit to take a risk of this sort when he has numerical superiority. Certainly such a conjecture is admissible, but there is also the fact that the demands of recorded history weigh upon the playwright: A Battle of Shrewsbury *must* be fought.

Prince Hal's demeanor is admirable in Scene 1. His offer to meet the renowned Hotspur in single combat is motivated not by a desire to win personal glory but the wish to save lives. His gracious, magnanimous praise of young Percy (85–93) is in the best chivalric tradition, and there is not a hint of false modesty in the deprecatory remarks he makes about himself. Calmly he accepts the fact that death is a constant of armed conflict; he knows that he, like all mortals, "owest God a death," and he will not seek to postpone payment.

Not so Falstaff. Yet his soliloquy on honor, as he conceives it, is a thought-provoking piece in which he develops his theme with such telling particulars that one's immediate reaction may be to endorse his view wholeheartedly. As much as any of his speeches, this one illustrates his wit and verbal skill. Nor can one logically deny the major premise upon which his argument is based. For at the personal level, the utter pathos, even futility, of all armed conflict is exposed. But note that it is the strictly personal, the individual, that concerns Falstaff. Thus, this gifted comic presents at best a half-truth, and perhaps not even that if one recalls this same knight's bland unconcern about the lives of the poor wretches whom he recruited to fight for king and country.

There have been many references to honor in this play: Hotspur's concept of honor to be won and held largely in warfare; Hal's concept, not explicitly defined but implicit in his burlesque of Hotspur (II. iv.), and in the restrained way in which he vowed to make young Percy his "factor" (III. ii.). Now Falstaff, who in the comic scenes found occasions to speak of his valor, has given us his concept of honor, one based on self-interest to the exclusion of all else.

In Scene 2, Worcester's decision to keep from Hotspur the "liberal and kind offer of the King" (2) is wholly dishonorable, a monstrous act of treachery against his own flesh and blood, against the unselfish, if misguided, youth who has risen to the position of supreme commander of the insurgents. It is not by mere chance that this episode immediately follows Falstaff's soliloquy on honor. In comparison to Sir John, the Earl of Worcester is high in the baronial ranks of England; his is an act of betrayal on the grand scale. If the reader has been tempted to accept Falstaff's view of honor as realistic and eminently practical, he may find occasion now to reassess that view. Even in terms of self-interest, Worcester's act of infamy will prove to be impractical.

Vernon's agreeing to go along with Worcester is disappointing, for he has earned the reader's respect and sympathy by his chivalrous conduct. Indeed he does so in Scene 2 by making the generous report of Hal's demeanor (52–69). He too will pay a great price for his compliance.

The character of the Prince of Wales continues to be elevated, thanks to the testimony of Sir Richard Vernon—the testimony of a hostile witness, as it were. The prince's claim made to his royal father, namely, that he had been maligned (III. ii. 130–31), is supported here. Vernon states that the prince has been the victim of envy, or malice, and will be England's "sweet hope"—that is, the Ideal Prince—if his true character is revealed to all.

But the elevation of the prince is not achieved by the denigration of Hotspur's character. If young Percy finds it hard to accept Vernon's flattering description of the prince, he makes use of no term of contempt for his royal rival. In appropriate lines, Percy's courage and honor, as he conceives it, make him an attractive and a worthy opponent. Aware as the reader is that the Percy forces are outnumbered, Hotspur's brief but stirring battle oration (93–101) and his embrace of his fated companions elicit admiration and sympathy.

In Scene 3, the report of Douglas' slaying of the Lord of Stafford, his actual slaying of Sir Walter Blunt, and Hotspur's report that the insurgents "stand full fairly for the day" have the important effect of at least equalizing matters relating to the two opposing forces despite the fact that the royalists outnumber the rebels. In other words, suspense is sustained; it is still touch and go.

Nothing could be much more incongruous, more grotesque, than the appearance of the corpulent, white-bearded, unheroic Falstaff on the battlefield. His brash claims to valor, which are at one with those made in the Boar's-Head Tavern after the Gadshill affair, and his irrepressible verbal wit ("Ay, Hal; 'tis hot, 'tis hot. There's that will sack a city") provide a counterbalance to the heroics in Scene 3, which, by themselves, might well be given such emphasis as to be a bit ludicrous—excessively melodramatic in dramatic fiction.

Falstaff *has*, in a metaphorical sense, brought the tavern to the battlefield. The bottle of sack, in place of the pistol in the case, is emblematic. The braggart warrior, one of the facets of his complex character, finds expression here when he assures the prince that "Turk Gregory" never matched his deeds in arms. The allusion, in all probability, is to Pope Gregory VII, noted for ferocity, here given the title of "Turk" since the Turks were held to be exemplars of cruelty.

Now in the midst of battle, the prince has no occasion to indulge in the slightest witticism in his exchange with Falstaff. Sternly he rebukes Sir John: "What, is it a time to jest and dally now?" (57). Certainly the knight's sense of timing is lamentably bad.

Although another scene follows, Scene 4 provides the essential resolution of the action. From the start, the character of Prince Hal is enhanced. He refuses to leave the battlefield despite his wounds; he demonstrates at once his humility and his magnanimity in praising the deeds performed by his younger brother. Even more impressive is the fact that he saves the life of Henry IV, exponent and symbol of law and order in the realm. That the father should be deeply touched comes as something of a surprise. He had distrusted his son, believing that Hal wanted him to die. Now the reader knows how malicious indeed were the slanders against the spirited young prince who had chosen to play the truant for a while.

Although the battle necessarily is presented in a series of separate episodes, the encounter between Prince Hal and Hotspur is the climactic one, for it conveys the impression that the prince's triumph ended the conflict. It will be recalled that Douglas, believing that he had slain the king, was convinced that his action meant total victory for the rebels. Young Percy was the leader of the insurgents.

Hotspur, whose high courage and gallantry have received increasing emphasis, invites one's whole-hearted sympathy as he falls before the prince's sword; his indeed was a "great heart." Surely no one would care to gloat over the fact that this same Hotspur had spoken contemptuously of Hal, refusing to believe that the prince was capable of serious action. For one thing, it was not life *per se* but his matchless reputation as a great warrior that concerned him most. Nor does this suggest undue vanity. He had been no braggart warrior; his titles had been won honestly. Like other dying great men elsewhere in Shakespeare, but perhaps unexpected in this heretofore unreflecting young soldier, Hotspur philosophizes in almost a medieval fashion, seeing himself as "time's fool." Those near death were thought to have the gift of prophecy; Hotspur, had he time, could prophesy. What could he foresee? Unquestionably the triumph of Henry V over the numerically superior French—the emergence of Prince Hal as hero-king of England. Just as Hotspur's courage, sense of honor, and gallantry were stressed increasingly in the later scenes, so Prince Hal's preeminence is emphasized. Young Percy has been established fully as the most worthy of all opponents; his conqueror emerges as a completely heroic figure, one almost larger than life itself. Appropriately, there is no suggestion of personal triumph in Hal's words. Magnanimity determines their tone, for he dwells on young Percy's knightly virtues, his breadth of spirit, the high respect merited by one of such "great heart."

If valid military honor is the subject of this episode, the Falstaffian one that follows provides a grimly comic exercise on bogus military honor. When Hal sees Falstaff lying on the battlefield, he has a valediction for him, one no less appropriate than the one for Hotspur. The prince's statement that he could have "spar'd a better man" (104) probably is purposely ambiguous. For holidays, those occasional times when care may be put aside, there is no better man than Falstaff in the sense of being more entertaining. But life, certainly for the heir to the throne, cannot remain a perpetual holiday. It follows that the prince is not so much in love with "vanity" as to be crushed by the end of all that Falstaff represents.

There is another possibility here. "I know you all," the prince soliloquized at the end of Act I, Scene 2; and his remarks to and concerning Falstaff throughout the play have left no doubt that he does fully understand his amusing companion. With this in mind, it may be argued that he is fully aware now that Falstaff is up to his old tricks again. Perhaps his play on the words *heavy* ("O, I should have a heavy miss of thee") and *deer* ("so fat a deer") and the reference to "embowelling" may well be taken as an indication that Hal knows Falstaff hears every word spoken. But admittedly all this is conjecture.

The Gadshill episode established the fact that Falstaff was a coward on principle, not a born coward like Peto or Bardolph. So he is in Scene 4, as his famous line, "The better part of valour is discretion; in the which better part I have saved my life" (120–22), makes clear. To be sure, there is an important element of truth in what he says, just as there was in his comments on honor. But there is also a cynical perversion of an abiding truth. Young Percy, prior to the Battle of Shrewsbury, well could have employed discretion without sacrifice of valor, for he was far above self-centered consideration. Discretion to Falstaff means self-preservation and no more.

There was sufficient falling off in the character of Falstaff, with reference to his recruits; there is more now. Sir John Falstaff, knight of the realm, stabs the fallen Hotspur in the thigh, an act that involves complete renunciation of the chivalric code. It is an act of monstrous desecration, absolutely inexcusable.

One may presume that Falstaff no more expects to be believed when he claims to have slain Hotspur than he had expected Hal and Poins to believe his story of what happened at Gadshill, for one cannot deprive the witty, knowledgeable Falstaff of ordinary common sense. Hal had tricked him there; now he tricks Hal. And, if on principle he is cowardly where physical action is involved, in the realm of rhetoric he is dauntless. "There is Percy," he exclaims, throwing the body to the earth (142)—a salvo defying refutation. With the same confidence, he expects great reward. At the end of Scene 4, he says: "I'll follow, as they say, for reward. He that rewards me, God reward him" (166–67). That too has been a great part of his life's philosophy; throughout the play, he has followed for reward.

But Falstaff will not permit us to dismiss him scornfully, for his superior wit never deserts him, and, in a sense, he has considerable capacity for self-criticism. The thought strikes him that should he be elevated to a dukedom, actually he will "grow less," for such high rank has its obligations: The king of jesters would have to abdicate.

One other point relating to Falstaff's conduct needs to be settled.

Those who refuse to find any fault in this man, who is to them the true hero of this play, make much of his statement that he led his men into the heart of battle. This, it is argued, is irrefutable proof of his personal valor. But is it? Did he actually place himself at the head of his company when he committed it to battle? And did he then, thanks to great martial prowess, survive without a scratch despite his enormous girth? In the next episode, he counterfeits death as a means of escaping once more "shot-free." Perhaps that was not the first time in which he employed the ruse. Certainly Elizabethans would not interpret the word "led" as proof of Falstaff's courage—not in view of the frequent charges made against leaders who committed their troops to battle but avoided danger themselves. These charges may well provide a revealing insight into Falstaff's actions—and may be at one with his having "misused the king's press damnably" in recruiting his soldiers.

Prince Hal deserves the last word. His superiority and his magnanimity are well illustrated by his refusal to argue with Falstaff or to show the slightest concern about being deprived of the credit for the defeat of a great adversary. He is quite willing to humor this knight of the "latter spring." Nevertheless, it is worth noting that since Shakespeare indubitably had the sequel to this play in mind, Falstaff cannot be rejected at the end of *Henry IV, Part 1*.

"Thus ever did rebellion find rebuke." This opening line of Scene 5, spoken by the titular hero, summarizes the major theme of the play. Another line spoken by the king at the end of this scene points to the theme of *Henry IV, Part 2*: "Rebellion in this land shall lose his sway" (41).

Henry's strong words indicting the Earl of Worcester serve a two-fold purpose. First and most important, these leave the impression at the end of the play that Henry IV is a strong yet fair-minded ruler, one who gave the rebels every chance to embrace law and order before he moved against them. Second, if a villain is to be found in the main plot, he must be Worcester, who was largely responsible for schooling young Percy and who, as Henry reminds him, had not borne "true intelligence" from the king to the other rebel leaders at Shrewsbury.

Hal now is the Ideal Prince. Properly, it is he who saves the life of the "noble Scot, Lord Douglas," and who delegates to John of Lancaster the "high honour" of freeing Douglas without ransom. Since

Vernon has been depicted as no less noble and admirable, one may question why the prince's generosity did not extend to him. It is to be remembered, however, that Douglas, a valiant foe, is not an Englishman, not a rebel against a king to whom he had sworn allegiance.

1598

henry iv
part 2

HENRY IV, PART 2

LIST OF MAIN CHARACTERS

Henry IV

In this play, the titular hero, who does not make his appearance until late in the play, although frequent reference is made to him, is much as he was in Act I, Scene 1, of the earlier play. He is a man worn by the cares and troubles of ruling an England torn by civil dissension. He is also a man who is tortured by the knowledge that he himself had been a rebel: He had deposed Richard II and been responsible for his death.

Prince Henry

Although Hal appears chiefly in the scenes of the comic subplot, he is never the madcap youth who ignores responsibility. Instead, he is an unusually poised and gifted young man, the breadth of whose character is emphasized again and again.

Sir John Falstaff

The credits in Falstaff's character are sufficiently impressive, and one can understand why Prince Hal found him so entertaining. His brilliant wit and contagious high spirits make it altogether too easy, perhaps, to ignore the debits.

Prince John, Duke of Lancaster

The role of this third son of Henry IV is not one that invites the sympathy of modern audiences, but he is presented as the relentless foe of disorder in the kingdom. His determined attitude toward the northern insurgents and his sound estimate of Falstaff's behavior mark him as one devoted to public duty. He is not depicted as a warm, human person like his gifted elder brother, Prince Hal, but he must be recognized as a pillar of law and order. In this respect, he fulfills his function in the play.

The Earl of Westmoreland

He is one of the characters who, in his capacity as Prince John's emissary to the rebels, functions as the voice of political orthodoxy in this play: No subject, however exalted, has the right to "lift an angry arm" against God's representative on earth, the king. Unflinchingly he carries out the order of his superior; it is he who places the rebels under arrest for treason at the end of the parley at Gaultree Forest in Yorkshire.

Mowbray

The second Duke of Norfolk is an astute and courageous warrior who proves his worth. From one point of view, his action contrasts with that of the Earl of Northumberland, who fears to commit himself in the struggle against Henry IV. From another point of view, he provides a contrast to the unrealistic Lord Hastings and even the Archbishop of York, who in his optimism rejects Mowbray's sound counsel.

The Earl of Northumberland

The elder Henry Percy is depicted as one who is at first determined to avenge himself upon Henry IV after the defeat at Shrewsbury and the death of his son. He emerges as one who is concerned primarily about his own safety and welfare.

The Archbishop of York

Richard Scroop is a man who owed his advancement to high ecclesiastical office to Richard II and who never forgets that Henry IV was the one who ordered the execution of his brother. He is the determined leader of the active rebel force in the northern parts. But it is not merely personal grievances that motivate his bold challenge to the crown. His consideration and acceptance of the terms offered by Prince John indicate that basically he is a man of good will, anxious to bring a just settlement to issues that have led him to rebel against the king.

Lord Chief Justice of the King's Bench

He is the noble, serious pillar of the law, properly devoted to the execution of justice.

Warwick

Richard de Beauchamp, Earl of Warwick, remains almost constantly at the side of Henry IV, serving as the trusted and capable counselor and attendant. In this play, he is remembered especially for his insight into the character of Prince Hal when he seeks to reassure the troubled king. However, late in the play, he joins those who fear that Hal will not follow the wise path of his father.

Lord Hastings

One of the representatives of the northern aristocrats who actively opposed the rule of Henry IV, he proves to be a bad counselor to the Archbishop of York, for he is over-confident and easily deceived by the royalist leaders. He thus provides an interesting contrast to the sagacious Mowbray.

Bardolph

Falstaff's serving man proves his worth to his master in numerous ways. Under instructions, he attempts to underwrite the knight's credit with tradesmen; he is ready to draw his sword when Fang, the sheriff's officer, declares Falstaff to be under arrest; and he expertly carries out the business of accepting bribes from the Gloucestershire recruits.

Pistol

A humorous character who has a special idiosyncrasy that makes him ridiculous. He serves as emissary to Falstaff, who ironically addresses him as "Captain Pistol."

Poins

One of the regulars at the Boar's-Head Tavern with whom Prince Hal chooses to associate for a time.

Shallow

Master Robert Shallow, Esquire, the Gloucestershire justice-of-the-peace, is essentially a caricature—and a good one.

Silent

Kinsman of the wispy Shallow, the bare-bones Silent, himself a justice-of-the-peace, provides an amusing contrast to the loquacious squire.

Mistress Quickly

Hostess of the Boar's-Head Tavern and, according to Falstaff, a widow, she is among those victimized by Sir John. She endears herself to the audience chiefly because of her genius for misusing big words of which she is so fond.

Doll Tearsheet

Falstaff's Helen of Troy, as Pistol calls her, is another representative of unlicensed behavior. She is generally depicted as a harridan addicted to shrill vocal outbursts.

SUMMARIES AND COMMENTARIES

INDUCTION

The induction, a device rarely used by Shakespeare, is a forty-line prologue that serves to link the two parts of *Henry IV*. It is spoken by Rumour, an allegorical figure who appears before Warkworth Castle in Northumberland "painted full of tongues," as described in part by Virgil in the *Aeneid*. Rumour's function is to confuse all and sundry as to what actually was the outcome of the Battle of Shrewsbury. At first, Rumour tells the truth: King Henry's forces had crushed the rebels. Then Rumour spreads false reports: Hotspur killed Harry Monmouth (Prince Hal); the Earl of Douglas subdued King Henry; and the rebels won an overwhelming victory.

ACT I

Summary

Scene 1 first reveals how well Rumour has done its work. The setting is Warkworth Castle, seat of the House of Percy, the head of which is the Earl of Northumberland, who had remained "crafty sick" at home rather than join his son and brother at Shrewsbury. Lord Bardolph arrives and jubilantly tells Northumberland that the rebel forces commanded by the earl's son have triumphed. According to him, King Henry was wounded and is near death; Henry Percy had slain Prince Hal and taken prisoner John of Lancaster; the Earl of Douglas had killed Sir Walter Blunt. Northumberland is assured that this information came from "a gentleman well bred and of good name," who had just come from the site of the battle. At this moment, Travers arrives with a far different story, which he had learned from another who claimed to have been an eyewitness. His report is that the rebels suffered a crushing defeat and that Northumberland's son had been killed. Although Lord Bardolph is willing to wager his barony on the truth of his report, the earl does not know which to believe. All doubts are settled when Morton arrives direct from Shrewsbury and gives his firsthand account. The king had indeed triumphed. Hotspur had been slain; the Earls of Worcester and Douglas are captives. Moreover, Morton states that even now John of Lancaster and the Earl of Westmoreland lead troops against Northumberland and his faction.

For a moment, the earl gives way to stormy passion. But Travers and Lord Bardolph urge caution and restraint. Morton in particular advises him to remember how many lives are at stake and how necessary it is to wait until a large force is mobilized. A telling point is his reminding Northumberland of the great risk Hotspur had taken with his father's approval. But there is no question of flight. Lord Bardolph concedes that, in the first venture, the risk was great, but he points out that the possibility of gain was no less great. In ringing words he voices the sentiments of all: "Come, we will all put forth, body and goods." Morton is quick to concur, for now he has good news. The Archbishop of York has raised a force to oppose King Henry. Northumberland states that he was aware of the powerful archbishop's activities, and he directs his followers to waste no time in seeking the best counsel in order to insure safety and revenge.

In Scene 2, the opening dialogue between Falstaff and his newly acquired page deals successively with the latter's report on three matters and with Falstaff's reaction to each report. The first is the doctor's diagnosis of the knight's physical condition, which is hardly flattering. Falstaff, remarking that many take pride in gibing him, cites the latest prank played on him by Prince Hal—sending him the page whose diminutiveness offers such a comic contrast to the fat knight. But Falstaff, never at loss for words, expresses his views at length, concluding that the prince is now almost out of grace with him. Next, the page says that the tailor from whom Falstaff had ordered twenty yards of satin has refused to honor the knight's credit, particularly when Bardolph was his security. Finally, the page reports that Bardolph has gone to buy Falstaff a horse. And this bit of intelligence gives Sir John another chance to display his wit.

At this point, the little page announces the arrival of the Lord Chief Justice of England, identifying him as the man who had sent the prince to prison for attempting to circumvent justice on behalf of Bardolph after the Gadshill robbery (see *Henry IV, Part 1*, Act II). Falstaff pretends that his new appointment as a commander of troops moving against the northern rebels makes it impossible for him to concern himself with other matters. But the Chief Justice will not be put off. As he reproves the knight for ignoring his summons to appear before him, Falstaff attempts to avoid the issue by expressing concern for the Chief Justice's health and then, at greater length, for the king's—even going so far as to offer a diagnosis. In so many words, Falstaff is denounced as a wastrel, as one who has misled the young prince, and as one who defies convention and the principle of decorum befitting an elderly man. All this serves only to inspire audacious, witty replies. Falstaff concedes that Prince Hal should not have boxed the ears of the Lord Chief Justice, adds that he had "checked him for it," and concludes that the prince remains unconcerned, as obviously does Falstaff himself. Then he confirms the report that he has been asked to serve his king once more by joining the royal forces against the Archbishop of York and the Earl of Northumberland. And when the Chief Justice gives his blessings on the enterprise, Sir John brazenly asks him for a loan of a thousand pounds.

Alone with the page, Falstaff voices a complaint on his near-empty purse. In order to raise money, he sends the page with letters to John of Lancaster, to Prince Hal, and to "old Mistress Ursula," whom he weakly had promised to marry. As he concludes, "A good wit will make use of anything."

Present at the palace of Richard Scroop, Archbishop of York, are the archbishop himself, Lord Hastings, Mowbray (Earl Marshal of the North Parts), and Lord Bardolph. This is a council of war to determine the course of events. The archbishop has explained the reason for the move against the king and indicated what forces are at his disposal. Mowbray, at one with Scroop as regards grievances, questions if the insurgents are strong enough to oppose the king. Lord Hastings reports that already 25,000 men have been mustered and that reinforcements from Northumberland are expected. Judiciously, Lord Bardolph points out that the basic question is whether or not the rebels can survive without reinforcements. His own position is that it would be foolhardy for the rebels to commit themselves until they are sure of Northumberland's help. The archbishop agrees: They must not make the fatal mistake that Hotspur made at Shrewsbury. It is Lord Bardolph who sums up the argument, emphasizing the fact that they seek "almost to pluck a kingdom down / And set another up." Caution, he concludes, must be the watchword.

But Lord Hastings argues that the present force is large enough, and he has good reasons to support his case. King Henry faces danger from the French and from the Welsh led by Glendower, as well as from the northern insurgents: "So is the unfirm King / In three divided." Moreover, Hastings reports that the royal treasury is depleted.

This argument seems irrefutable. It is agreed that Henry IV cannot possibly commit all his forces against the Scroop-Percy faction and leave the realm defenseless against the Welsh and the French. Once more the audience learns that Prince John of Lancaster and the Earl of Westmoreland lead the royalists northward, and the king and Harry of Monmouth (Prince Hal) will move against the Welsh. Who will oppose the French if they should attack England is not known.

The archbishop then urges that the insurgents publish their list of grievances in which the king's government will be indicted for misrule. Both Mowbray and Hastings, fired with enthusiasm, call for prompt action: "We are Time's subjects, and Time bids be gone.

Commentary

In Scene 1, we are introduced to the Earl of Northumberland, Henry Percy the elder, father of Hotspur. As leader of the House of Percy, the most powerful baronial family in northern England, he had led the triumvirate that included his brother and his son in support of Henry Bolingbroke and was largely responsible for placing Henry on the throne. Later, he and his faction accused the king of failing to keep his promises to them and rose in revolt. Pleading illness, he had absented himself from the battlefield at Shrewsbury and had survived to threaten the king with rebellion once more. We also meet Lord Bardolph, a noble mentioned by Holinshed, who is a leading member of the Percy faction, and Travers and Morton, two loyal retainers of the Earl of Northumberland who, like so many in the north parts of England, "knew no Prince but a Percy."

Scene 1 establishes the basic theme of the main plot; clarifies the relationship between the first and second parts of *Henry IV*; introduces the leader of the rebellious Percy faction and identifies important adherents to its cause; provides the inciting incident that in a technical sense starts the action rising toward its climax; and impresses upon the audience the momentousness of the issues involved—the new dangers that now face Henry IV and all England.

In Scene 2, we are introduced to Sir John Falstaff, the most famous comic character of Shakespearean drama, who has won a place in the company of Prince Hal because of his matchless wit and incessant gaiety, his unfailing ability to incite laughter. Indeed, so gifted is he that generations of audiences have taken him to their hearts, often refusing to believe that he has any basic shortcomings and that his derelictions are all part of a game he plays for the sake of merriment. It may be argued that, in a sense, Falstaff embodies the rebel against seriousness and authority that is latent in many of the most respectable people. Grossly fat and white bearded, he appears as the very spirit of irresponsible youth. His final line in this scene very well sums up his philosophy of life.

The Lord Chief Justice of the King's Bench is England's premier legal official, an elderly, sober, dedicated man intent on seeing to it that order and justice in civil life are maintained within the realm. In Scene 2, he functions as a foil to Falstaff and helps to provide the link between the first and second parts of *Henry IV*.

The purposes of Scene 2 include the following: to start the subplot and introduce the theme of order therein; to present a full-length portrait of Falstaff; to make clear the fact that, despite the king's injunction, Falstaff and Prince Hal will soon appear together again; and to keep to the fore the major theme of rebellion and thus to link main plot and subplot, which is not to be considered as mere "comic relief."

In Scene 3, Archbishop Scroop—Richard Scroop, to whom important reference was made in Scene 1—emerges as a powerful opponent of Henry IV. He has been able to muster a force of 25,000 men. If one recalls that Henry V led a force of only 15,000 against the French and that Henry VIII's forces opposing the rebels of 1536 numbered less than 9,000 men, he can appreciate the seriousness of the threat against the crown. The archbishop wisely invites and listens to contrary points of view before making up his own mind on what action should be taken.

Mowbray, the second Duke of Norfolk, was the elder son of Thomas Mowbray, first Duke of Norfolk, who had been banished by Richard II because of his quarrel with Henry Bolingbroke, the man who now rules England. Perhaps because, for a time, he had been excluded from his father's honors, he joined the archbishop and the Percies in the treasonable action of the year 1405. Anything but foolhardy, he is a determined, strong adversary.

Lord Bardolph, whose adherence to the Percy cause was well established in Scene 1, now represents the Earl of Northumberland and shares the latter's sense of caution.

Scene 3 advances the main plot by presenting the council of rebel leaders, who, after an estimate of all factors, voice their determination to take to the field, and introduces personally the powerful Archbishop of York, co-leader of the northern insurgents. The scene makes even clearer the grave dangers confronting King Henry IV: The odds are weighted heavily against him in view of the threats from Wales and France.

ACT II

Summary

On a London street, Mistress Quickly, Hostess of the Boar's-Head Tavern, asks Fang, the sheriff's sergeant, whether or not he has served notice of the legal action she has brought against Falstaff. He assures her that he has done so. Snare, the sergeant's man, appears on call and is ordered to arrest the knight. When Snare voices concern for his life, the hostess urges caution. In lines packed with *double-entendre* hardly complimentary to her own character and to Falstaff's, she recalls how she had been victimized. Vocally, at least, Fang is all courage and determination; he cares not his (Falstaff's) "thrust."

The hostess fills in the details in lines marked by the repeated misuse of words. Falstaff, she insists, owes her one hundred marks (about seventy-eight pounds). He may be expected to appear in one of three public places. And at this moment Falstaff indeed appears, along with Bardolph and the page.

Falstaff demands to know what all the fuss is about: "Whose mare's dead?" Fang promptly declares him to be under arrest. Lively action ensues. Falstaff calls upon Bardolph to cut off Fang's head and to throw the hostess in the gutter. First crying out "Murder, murder!" Mistress Quickly then adds her voice to that of Fang in an appeal to passers-by for help—although it would seem that she is doing very well without assistance. The page adds to the din, scurrilously denouncing her, just as the Chief Justice and his men arrive on the scene.

The Chief Justice upbraids Sir John for street brawling, particularly at a time when he should be hurrying to join the royalists in Yorkshire. He is then told that Falstaff has imposed grievously upon Mistress Quickly, using worthless promises as the coin of the realm. Asked if he is not ashamed of himself for imposing upon a poor widow, Falstaff calmly asks the hostess for a bill of particulars. A new charge against him is included in her reply: As she had dressed the head wound he had received from Prince Hal for insulting the king, he had promised to marry her, had even kissed her—and had borrowed thirty shillings.

Falstaff assures the Chief Justice that the poor woman is demented, in proof whereof he states that she had declared her oldest son to be the very image of the Chief Justice. How to account for her sad state? Once prosperous, now indigent, she had lost her wits. Magnanimously, he does not bring charges against her. But as for Fang and Snare, that is a different matter.

The Chief Justice refuses to be misled by what he calls Falstaff's "impudent sauciness," pointing out that long since he has been familiar with the knight's behavior. He orders that Falstaff make restitution and mend his ways.

Sir John, unmistakably irritated by this "sneap" (insult), as he calls it, moves to the attack. He is not impudent; he is honorably bold. Nor will he curtsey to the Chief Justice or deign to be a suitor. Instead, he claims immunity on the grounds that he is engaged in the urgent business of the king.

As the Chief Justice firmly tells Falstaff to pay his debt, Gower, a messenger, enters with news for England's leading legal official: The king and Harry, Prince of Wales, are near London. Falstaff and the hostess hold the center of the stage while the two converse.

Now Falstaff uses all his wit and gives the audience a demonstration of his skill in victimizing the hostess and, incidentally, substantiating her charges against him. He succeeds in getting her to agree to sell treasured furnishings of the tavern in order to raise money for him. "Will you pay me altogether?" she asks, not without pathos. "As I live," replies Falstaff, and in an aside he instructs Bardolph to go with her and see that she does not change her mind. Before she leaves, however, she agrees to have Doll Tearsheet join the knight at the Boar's-Head, where he will continue to indulge himself and stretch his credit.

Falstaff and the Chief Justice now remain alone onstage. In their final exchange, it is revealed that the king has sent 1500 foot troops and 500 horses to augment the force led by the Duke of Lancaster. Falstaff is unable to learn whether or not the king plans to return to London at once.

Patently ignoring the Chief Justice, Sir John twice asks Gower, the messenger, to dine with him. The Chief Justice reproves him for loitering in London streets at a time of national peril and for a display of bad manners. Voicing his pride in his ability at verbal dueling, Falstaff says in effect that the Chief Justice had been his teacher as far as manners were concerned. "Thou art a great fool" replies the latter as Scene 1 ends.

In Scene 2, Prince Hal and Poins appear on a London street and engage in an exchange characterized by light, brilliant wit. In the amusing backchat between the two, it is made clear that Hal, very much aware of what he is doing and what the public reaction will be, chooses again to seek out the company of regulars at the Boar's-Head Tavern.

Ironically, the prince remarks that he should not be sad because the king, his father, is sick. And cynically Poins replies that Hal's grief cannot be very deep. Still in good humor, Hal protests that his reactions to such circumstances are not to be confused with those of Falstaff or of Poins. He adds that his heart bleeds inwardly, despite the fact that, in such "vile company," he makes no outward show of grief. Poins flatly states that tears would be a sign of hypocrisy in one who associates with Falstaff. The prince reminds him that he is no less guilty of association with Poins, and the latter makes a defense of his character just as Bardolph and the page enter.

The prince greets Falstaff's serving man as "noble Bardolph" and remarks that the page has been transformed into an ape. Again Bardolph's "malmesey nose" becomes the source of comedy. The page declares that, seen through the red lattice windows of the tavern, Bardolph's face was indiscernible. A scurrilous interchange follows, and the prince, amused by the page's wit, gives him a crown, to which sum Poins adds sixpence.

When the prince inquires about Falstaff, Bardolph hands over a letter addressed to Hal. Both the prince and Poins have a choice selection of epithets for and comments on Sir John as they read the letter. Beginning in an excessively formal manner, Falstaff has written a warning to Hal. Poins, he insists, boasts that his sister Nell is betrothed to the prince. He then urges Hal to report "at idle times" and adds a self-laudatory close to the letter. The incensed Poins vows that he will soak the letter in sack and force Falstaff to eat it. "Well, thus we play the fools with the time, and the spirits of the wise sit in the clouds and mock us," the prince concludes.

Hal learns that Falstaff is at the Boar's-Head Tavern in company with the old group as well as Mistress Quickly and Doll Tearsheet. About the latter's unsavory character neither Hal nor Poins is in any doubt. The two agree to "steal upon them," and Bardolph is warned not to give advance notice that the prince is now in London.

Alone, the prince and Poins discuss how they can arrange to eavesdrop on Sir John without being discovered. The ingenious Poins has the answer: They will disguise themselves as lowly drawers in the tavern.

Before Warkworth Castle, the Earl of Northumberland, Lady Northumberland, and Lady Percy seriously discuss the earl's plans. The two ladies vehemently urge Northumberland to avoid participation in the rising against Henry IV, but he replies that his honor is at stake since he has given his word to join the insurgents. Lady Percy reminds him that honor had not prevented him from failing to appear at Shrewsbury when Hotspur sorely needed his father's help. Describing her late husband as the "miracle of men," she bitterly argues that with half the number now led by the archbishop and the Lord Marshal (Mowbray), he would have defeated the royalists and have survived.

Lady Northumberland urges her husband to hurry to Scotland and to remain there until he learns how the insurgents fared in battle. At first unable to make up his mind, the earl then agrees to follow her counsel.

From the conversation of two lowly drawers at the Boar's-Head Tavern, the audience learns of another way in which Prince Hal had baited Falstaff by giving him five apples with wrinkled skins and identifying the knight as the sixth. They further learn that, at Doll Tearsheet's request, musicians have been sent for and that the prince and Poins will soon appear and borrow the drawers' jerkins and aprons.

The hostess and Doll Tearsheet enter, the former complimenting Doll on her improved health—that is, on having recovered from the excessive drinking of wine. Next, Falstaff makes his appearance singing a ballad. He is solicitous about Doll's health, and the two engage in their respective types of badinage, often a bit scandalous. The hostess is an appreciative audience, and her comments admit to interpretation at two levels, one inadvertently uncomplimentary to both parties. At the end of this verbal exchange, Doll remarks that she will remain friends with Falstaff since he is going to the wars.

The First Drawer announces the arrival of Pistol, who wants a word with Falstaff. At the mention of Pistol's name, Doll vociferously denounces him as a "swaggering rascal" and a "foul-mouthed rogue." The hostess, once more striving to keep up the appearance of respectability, vows that no swaggerers are welcome in her establishment. Falstaff then identifies Pistol as his "ancient" (a standard-bearer for a leader of troops) and states that he is a "tame cheater" (confidence man) who is as gentle as a puppy. After the hostess engages in another exercise in the misuse of words, Pistol is called for. He enters with Bardolph and the page.

Falstaff invites Pistol to drink a toast first to the hostess and then to Doll. But the latter will have none of it. She and the ancient have a virulent interchange, Doll excoriating Pistol and Pistol making blood-curdling threats to avenge himself. It remains a question of which is the more devastating—the foul language that pours from the lips of Doll or the ranting of Pistol.

The disguised Prince Hal and Poins now follow the musicians into the room. Completely unaware of their presence, Falstaff talks freely and most indiscreetly to Doll Tearsheet, who is seated on his lap. He blandly informs her that the prince is a shallow fellow fit only to be a pantryman and that Poins (that "baboon") is tolerated only because he is young and wild like the prince. Hal and Poins exchange witty and appropriate remarks on the slander and on Falstaff's behavior with Doll Tearsheet.

At last Falstaff notices the two drawers and makes unflattering remarks on their resemblance to the prince and to Poins. Hal's denunciation of the fat knight gives the show away, and the hostess welcomes Hal, as does Falstaff in his own brash style. But Doll, who had lauded Falstaff as a valorous man, now denounces him as a coward for permitting Hal to insult him.

Poins warns the prince that Falstaff will surely extricate himself from his predicament if there is any delay in attack. Flatly stating that he had overheard every word, Hal ironically adds that plump Jack, no doubt, will revive the specious argument he had used after running away at Gadshill and claim that he was aware of Hal's presence all along. But the knight, well aware that such a story will not serve him now, calmly admits that he did not recognize the prince. He has a new, original defense: So far from abusing the prince, he had sought to defend him from the wicked. If he, Falstaff, had voiced praise, they would have fallen in love with the heir-apparent. Hal seizes upon the word "wicked." Who are these "wicked" Falstaff speaks of? Surely not this "virtuous woman," Doll Tearsheet; surely not the Hostess! Did the knight then mean Bardolph, "whose zeal burns in his nose"? Or the page, perhaps?

Falstaff's wit does not desert him. He argues that all named are, in one way or another, wicked—even the little page, despite the "good angel about him." The hostess, once more sensitive about her reputation, protests, and the two engage in an amusing colloquy.

Peto enters with important news. The king is at Westminster, and messengers have arrived from the north. Moreover, no less than a dozen captains have been asking for Falstaff. Prince Hal reproves himself for wasting time, calls for his sword and cloak, and bids Sir John goodnight. Poins, Peto, and Bardolph leave with him.

Bardolph returns immediately with the news that the captains are waiting at the door for Falstaff, who must leave at once for court. Sir John says his farewells to the hostess and Doll Tearsheet, urging them to note "how men of merit are sought after." Both women are distraught as he leaves. But a moment later they hear Bardolph call from another room: "Bid Mistress Tearsheet come to my master." "Oh, run, Doll, run," blubbers the hostess.

Commentary

Mistress Quickly, the credulous, kindly hostess of the Boar's-Head Tavern, has been victimized by Falstaff in more ways than that relating to pounds, shillings, and pence. A devout lover of long words, she has her difficulty in getting them right and thus provides first-rate comedy of words. She strives to hang on to some reputation for respectability, insisting in Scene 1 that Falstaff had promised to marry her and using such phrases as "saving your manhoods" (29), which were usually voiced after inadvertently making an improper remark.

Master Fang, the sheriff's sergeant, is charged with the duty of delivering notices of action in civil cases and insuring the appearance of the accused in court. The obtuse Fang repeatedly strives to impress others with his efficiency and courage. Snare, the sergeant's assistant, provides a comic contrast to the apparent valor of his superior. Like Fang, and for that matter most of Shakespeare's characters at this social level, he is a realistic, well-delineated individual, despite his minor role.

Falstaff, remaining his unique self, once more demonstrates his utterly carefree attitude, his mental resiliency, his wit—and his impudence when confronted by the Chief Justice. At one point, however, Falstaff's animosity toward the latter nearly causes him to lose his usual self-confidence. The Lord Chief Justice again serves as severe critic of and foil to Sir John Falstaff and as the voice of order and respectability. His character is developed somewhat in Scene 1, for he finds the opportunity to vie with Falstaff in punning and comes off quite well.

Scene 1 gives further insight into the character of Falstaff, whose disregard of law and order is emphasized by his cavalier attitude toward the Lord Chief Justice, and introduces the hostess of the Boar's-Head Tavern in person. The way is prepared for the re-appearance of Prince Hal. Also, the scene adds expository details relating to the action against the insurgents and in this way keeps to the fore the theme of rebellion.

In Scene 2, we see that Prince Hal, the heir-apparent, again chooses to tolerate the unrestrained behavior of Falstaff and his cronies. Despite his keen wit and apparently devil-may-care manner, he is not without deep concern for his royal father nor unperturbed about affairs in the realm. Consistent with his character as drawn in *Henry IV, Part 1*, he appears as a man of "all humors that have showed themselves humors since the old days of goodman Adam" (See II. iv. 104 in the earlier play).

Poins, Hal's companion at the Boar's-Head, delights no less than does the prince in trapping Falstaff. It will be remembered that it was he who proposed to trick the fat knight in connection with the Gadshill robbery. In view of the accusation made in Falstaff's letter, Poins now has special reason for baiting Sir John.

The purposes of Scene 2 include the following: to reintroduce Prince Hal and Poins, filling in the outlines of character, particularly that of the former; to start the action involving comic conflict between Hal and Falstaff; and to provide expository details regarding the king's health.

In Scene 3, the elder Earl of Northumberland's decision to leave for Scotland after having given his word to lead his forces in support of those raised by the Archbishop of York points to the conclusion that the same concern for his own safety explains his failure to appear at Shrewsbury, where Hotspur, his son, faced the royal forces. Lady Northumberland, wife of the earl and mother of the slain Hotspur, is understandably concerned for the safety of her husband. Lady Percy, sister of Edmund Mortimer, Earl of March, and widow of Hotspur, demonstrates her deep love for her dead husband, well established in the earlier play, in this scene.

Scene 3 advances the main plot, making clear the fact that the numerically inferior troops led by John of Lancaster at least will not have to deal with forces mustered by Northumberland. The scene also provides another link between the first and second parts of *Henry IV* by reference to Hotspur and to events dramatized in the earlier play.

In Scene 4, Falstaff is revealed as one devoted to the pleasures of the flesh and as a gargantuan liar—but also as one who is indeed not only witty in himself but the cause of wit in other men. It is to be noted that however much he has taken advantage of the hostess and used Doll Tearsheet, both are devoted to him.

For the first time, the audience meets Pistol, one of Shakespeare's "humors" characters, a man who is comically unbalanced in a particular way. Pistol's humor is that he poses as a man who is a ferocious warrior, laconic but startling in speech. Shakespeare uses him partly to burlesque characters in plays notable for bombast which had wide popular appeal. Close students of Elizabethan drama recognize many verbal echoes in Pistol's lines. For example, when he speaks of the "pampered jades of Asia," he borrows a phrase from Christopher Marlowe's *Tamburlaine, Part II*. There are several more inferior plays presented by a rival company. Actually this "fustian rascal" is a poltroon, an arrant coward. Thus Shakespeare makes the most of comic incongruity.

Doll Tearsheet is a prostitute who is "as common as the way between Saint Alban's and London," to borrow Poins' words (II. ii. 184–85). She is a spirited character who is never at loss for words, usually invectives. If her charms are usually for hire, she nevertheless reserves a special place for Falstaff in her affections.

At the comic level, Prince Hal, who had vindicated his honor at Shrewsbury, once again crosses swords with Falstaff. Perhaps some will call the encounter a draw. But one should observe how Hal urbanely controls himself and, once more endorsing the precept that life should have its lighter moments, joins with Poins in gulling Sir John.

Scene 4 presents the initial encounter between Falstaff and Prince Hal, one that balances the Gadshill episode in *Henry IV, Part 1*. The scene advances the action of the comic subplot and at the same time does not lose sight of the theme of rebellion. Also, it develops the characters of the newly created Doll Tearsheet and Pistol and adds to the characterization of Prince Hal and Mistress Quickly.

ACT III

Summary

It is past midnight. Henry IV, now at the palace in Westminster, instructs a page to call in the Earls of Warwick and Surrey to consider the import of the news received from the north. Ailing and exhausted, the king invokes sleep and laments the fact that its soothing balm, freely enjoyed by the lowliest of subjects, is denied him: "Uneasy lies the head that wears a crown."

The two earls enter and, in reply to the king's question, state that they have studied the letters and are aware of the "rank diseases" that now infect the realm. Warwick reassures the worried Henry, arguing that good advice and little medicine will effect a cure—that is, Northumberland (whose decision to go to Scotland they know nothing about) will be subdued. Henry exclaims that if one could see into the future and become aware of the perils that await, not even the happiest youth would choose to live. These thoughts lead him to recall earlier events relating to Richard II, Northumberland, and himself, most of which were dramatized in Shakespeare's earlier chronicle history *Richard II*. He speaks of how Northumberland, once loyal to Richard, had joined forces with Henry himself against the reigning monarch. Especially Henry recalls Richard's ominous prophecy that the day would come when Northumberland would turn traitor again. Warwick discounts the possibility of there being anything supernatural in Richard's prophecy. The king replies that since such events seem to be unavoidable, they must be accepted. But he remains deeply troubled, for he has heard that the northern rebels now have a force of 50,000 men. Again Warwick reassures him. The report is rumor, which always exaggerates. He expresses confidence that the royal army now in the field will defeat the insurgents. And he has one piece of good news: Glendower is dead. Warwick then urges the king to rest. Henry accepts this counsel and declares that once order is restored, he and his lieutenants will leave for the Holy Land.

Before his home in Gloucestershire, Shallow greets Silent, his fellow justice and kinsman. He inquires about the health of Silent's wife and daughter and about the progress of son William, a student at Oxford. William, he says, must go on to the Inns of Court, the law schools in London. Shallow himself had attended Clement's Inn, and he is confident that his reputation as a wild young fellow still survives there. Among the roisterers whom he recalls is Sir John Falstaff, whom he identifies as one-time page to Thomas Mowbray, Duke of Norfolk. It is this same knight who will arrive soon to obtain recruits, so Shallow informs Silent. And he rambles on, commenting on Falstaff's prowess in brawling when both were young. He continues to talk now of the inevitability of death, now of the price of livestock.

Bardolph and another of Falstaff's men enter. When Shallow identifies himself, Corporal Bardolph (such is his new military title) conveys his master's greeting. The delighted justice lauds Falstaff as an expert with the backsword and inquires about the knight's health and that of "my lady his wife." Bardolph replies that a soldier is better accommodated than with a wife. Shallow is enchanted by the expression "better accommodated." Respectfully, the corporal points out that it is not a phrase but a word—a soldier-like word. And he defines it in terms of itself. Accommodated, it seems, means accommodated.

Falstaff enters and is effusively welcomed. When Shallow introduces him to Justice Silent, the knight remarks that a man with such a name is well fitted to administer the law. Then to business. Shallow assures Sir John that he has a dozen fit men among whom good recruits may be found. Four are successively called to be questioned, and the name of each gives Falstaff wonderful opportunity to display his wit.

The first is Ralph Mouldy, described as "a good-limbed fellow; young, strong, and of good friends." Falstaff remarks that Mouldy should indeed be put to use. Shallow, anxious to prove that he is not obtuse, explains the joke—things mouldy lack use. Despite Mouldy's protests that his wife will object, he is chosen as the first recruit.

Next is Simon Shadow, who helpfully identifies himself as his mother's son, giving Falstaff the chance to make the inevitable conclusion that Shadow is the natural son of some unknown male. Sir John approves of the name, however, for he needs man "shadows" to complete his roster. So Simon becomes the second recruit.

Thomas Wart, the third to be considered, does not pass muster; he is far too ragged—a "very ragged wart," indeed.

Francis Feeble next steps forth and is identified as a woman's tailor. Falstaff ironically observes that he will be "as valiant as the wrathful dove or most magnanimous mouse." He is accepted as the third recruit.

Then comes Peter Bullcalf, protesting that he is a "diseased" man. But his explanation that he had caught cold while ringing bells on Coronation Day does not help him. Falstaff curtly states that Peter will "go to the wars in a gown"—that is, whether he is sick or not.

Shallow interrupts to invite Sir John to dine with him, but Falstaff politely refuses, adding that he is most happy to see his old friend. With this cue, the harmlessly vain justice recalls more wild episodes in which the two had been involved during their student days. At last Silent manages to say something. He remarks that fifty-five years have passed since his kinsman was at Clement's Inn. Humoring Justice Shallow, Falstaff exclaims, "We have heard the chimes at midnight," and he leaves the stage in company of the two.

Immediately both Peter Bullcalf and Ralph Mouldy offer money to Bardolph to secure their release from duty. Peter argues that he is not concerned about himself; it is just that he does not want to go to the wars. In fact, he would rather be hanged. Ralph has a better reason. His wife is old and needs his help. Surprisingly, the "most forcible Feeble" proves to be the soul of courage. "A man can die but once," he declares, and adds that "no man's too good to serve his prince."

When Falstaff and the justices return, the knight is pleased to learn that Bardolph has had three pounds from Peter Bullcalf and Ralph Mouldy. He acts promptly. Although Shallow includes the names of these two in his list of those selected, Falstaff releases them. The perplexed justice cannot understand why, but Sir John makes everything clear: Spirit, not appearance, is the test. Ragged Wart (rejected earlier), thin-faced Shadow, and Francis Feeble—they are the men for him. Ralph must be a man of spirit since he obviously has nothing else. As for Shadow, the enemy will find him a very poor target. And Feeble, fleet of foot, will prove first-rate for retreating.

Satisfied with this explanation, Shallow once more reminisces about the good old days. Then Falstaff expresses his thanks to both justices and orders Bardolph to give coats to the new recruits. Shallow urges the knight to return and renew their old friendship, and Falstaff commands his corporal to march the men away.

In soliloquy, Falstaff makes it clear that he will indeed return to capitalize on the credulity of Shallow, whom he describes as an inveterate teller of tall tales about the past. He had remembered the justice as one who was "like a man after supper made of cheese-paring." And yet, says Falstaff to himself (and to the audience), this same Shallow is now a squire who speaks familiarly of John of Gaunt. He will prove an easy victim; Falstaff will snap him up.

Commentary

In Scene 1, Henry IV, the ailing King of England, is exhausted by loss of sleep and beset by worries. As was true in the earlier play, Shakespeare presents him as a ruler who, determined and capable though he is, suffers the "unquiet mind" of one who is guilty of usurpation and regicide. It is necessary for one to recognize the two-fold point of view here. Henry *is* a sinner, and that he should endure rebellion is part of his punishment; yet he wears the crown on God's sufferance. Those who rebel against him are in turn grievous sinners who have invited God's vengeance.

The purposes of Scene 1 include the following: to introduce the king personally and to show how he suffers from the problems of conscience and kingship; to review some of the events dramatized in *Henry IV, Part 1;* and to emphasize the elements of conflict in the main plot, notably those relating to the grave dangers that threaten Henry's government.

In Scene 2, the audience now witnesses Sir John as he carries out, in his own way, initial duties as a royalist leader. It will be recalled that in *Henry IV, Part 1,* he had performed the same task; but the actual recruitment was not dramatized. As he led his ragged army to Coventry, he said to Bardolph (IV. ii. 12–15):

> If I be not ashamed of my soldiers, I am a soused
> gurnet. I have misused the King's press damnably.
> I have got, in exchange of a hundred and fifty sol-
> diers, three hundred and odd pounds.

Now Shakespeare lets the audience see exactly how the artful Falstaff capitalizes on his commission to raise troops. After all, had Sir John not said that "a good wit will make use of anything"? Yet however much one may deplore Falstaff's action, he cannot avoid being vastly entertained by the wit and ingenuity. And so with the suave manner in which the knight manages his old school fellow, the gullible Justice Shallow.

Justice Shallow is a country squire—that is, a well-born member of a prosperous county family, whose title (esquire) places him just below the rank of knight. He flourishes as justice-of-the-peace in Gloucestershire, the small county just south of Shakespeare's Warwickshire. Advanced in years, as is Falstaff himself, he lacks Sir John's incisive mind and spirit of perpetual youth. He has reached the stage where he lives much in the past, and it is his loquaciousness and uncertain re-creations of the past that result in good comedy.

Justice Silent, Shallow's admiring kinsman and fellow justice-of-the-peace, provides comic contrast to the volubility of Shallow because of his inarticulateness.

Scene 2 presents Falstaff in his capacity as one of the king's officers exercising his commission to raise troops. It introduces and develops two new, original comic characters, Shallow and Silent, and prepares for one of Falstaff's later escapades, which will be carried out at the expense of Justice Shallow. Additionally, the scene satirizes actual malpractice relating to the recruiting of soldiers in Elizabethan England.

ACT IV

Summary

At Gaultree Forest in Yorkshire, the rebel leaders await the return of scouts who have been sent out to ascertain the size of the royal forces led by Prince John of Lancaster. The Archbishop of York tells his lieutenants, Mowbray and Hastings chief among them, that he has received more news from Northumberland. The earl has written that since he has been unable to raise a large force as befits his rank, he has retired to Scotland to wait until times are more favorable. He has only good wishes to offer the rebel leaders.

A messenger then reports that the royalists, in good formation and 30,000 strong, are no more than a mile to the west. Mowbray, noting that the insurgent's own estimate of size has thus been confirmed, is anxious to meet the enemy at once.

The Earl of Westmoreland enters. He brings greetings from his "general, The Prince, Lord John and Duke of Lancaster," and a message for the archbishop. But first he has words of reproach for the latter: Why has the "reverend father," a man of position, learning, age, turned rebel? The archbishop concisely states his case. Using the metaphor of "disease," he indicts the rule of Henry IV and argues that the same affliction had fatally infected the deposed and now dead Richard II. He further argues that so far from being an enemy of peace, he is one that seeks redress of grievous wrongs. He complains that although articles of grievance had been offered to the king, false counselors had seen to it that no audience had been granted.

When, asks Westmoreland, had the appeal been denied? Who

had stood in the archbishop's way? In a word, he argues that there is no valid reason for such a gross misuse of high ecclesiastical office. The archbishop then charges that Henry IV had been responsible for the death of his brother. But the prince's emissary insists that Scroop has no need for personal redress. Mowbray breaks in to say that *all* need redress of grievances. Westmoreland goes as far as to concede that in view of the general lawlessness, some injustices may have been inevitable. But he denies that the king is to be held responsible. He goes on to point out that the title and the estates of Mowbray's father (Duke of Norfolk) had been restored. The mention of his father's name leads Mowbray to recall the quarrel between the late duke and Bolingbroke, now Henry IV, which had led to the banishment of both parties. He insists that had Richard II permitted them to settle their differences in the lists of Coventry, Richard would not have lost his crown and life. But Westmoreland will have none of this. According to him, if the late Duke of Norfolk had defeated Henry in single combat, he would not have lived to leave Coventry, so great was public opinion aligned against him and in favor of Henry. All this, he adds, is mere digression. He has come to learn exactly what are the complaints of the rebels and to inform them that Prince John not only will give them audience but, if the demands are just, great redress.

Mowbray voices the first of his suspicions, arguing that this offer may be a trick. Westmoreland insists that it is an honest one, the motive for which is mercy, not fear. The royal army, confident and strong, he states, is better led than is that of the rebel leaders. In reply to a question by Lord Hastings, he assures them that as the king's general, Prince John has full authority to act in this serious matter.

Having listened to arguments on both sides, the archbishop requests Westmoreland to take the articles of grievance to the prince. He promises that if each is satisfactorily settled, the insurgents will disband. Westmoreland agrees to do so and says that the decision will be made while both armies await within eyesight.

Again Mowbray objects. He is sure that the king will not forget their action against him and will find an excuse to punish them. But the archbishop shares Hastings' optimism. He believes that Henry is tired of "petty" grievances and has learned that the death of one traitor leads to the birth of two others. Moreover, he argues, Henry is well aware that those who oppose him are closely allied to his friends; he dares not offend the latter. Hastings adds that having had to commit forces elsewhere in the kingdom, Henry is now a "fangless lion." Further to conciliate the wary Mowbray, the archbishop assures him that if the peace does not endure, the rebel power will be all the greater.

So when Westmoreland returns with the information that John of Lancaster will meet the insurgent leaders at a place equidistant between the two armed camps, the archbishop and his lieutenants leave promptly. "My lord, we come," are the archbishop's final words.

In Scene 2, Prince John of Lancaster courteously greets Mowbray, the archbishop, and Hastings as the three arrive for the parley arranged by Westmoreland. As his emissary had done in the previous scene, the prince deplores the fact that chief among the enemies of the crown is the Archbishop of York, who appears not in the vestments of his religious calling nor in the act of explaining God's Word to his flock but in armor and in the act of "turning the Word to sword and life to death." The archbishop concedes that he now appears in an unnatural form but insists that he is not the king's enemy. He repeats his earlier argument: the articles of grievance that he had sent to the court never received consideration; if those "most just and right desires" are honored, the insurgents will prove their loyalty to the king. Mowbray interposes the statement that if the wrongs are not righted, the rebels stand ready to fight to the last man. Hastings adds that they have reinforcements to back up their demands and warns that if the parley fails, members of their families will take up the quarrel. Prince John expresses doubt that Hastings possesses the wisdom and power to see into the future and then, at Westmoreland's suggestion, gives his decision regarding the articles of grievance. He states that he is well pleased with them and insists that his father is not to blame for any injustice: The royal intentions have been misunderstood and some officials misused his authority. The prince vows that "these griefs shall be with speed redressed." If the rebel leaders accept his assurance, he continues, let the armies be disbanded at once and peace and friendship restored.

The archbishop is quick to take John of Lancaster at his word, and Hastings promptly orders a captain to report the news to the rebel troops: "Let them have pay, and part." The leaders of the opposing factions now exchange courtesies. When shouts from the jubilant rebel forces are heard, Mowbray states that the sound would have been pleasing if it had signaled a victory.

The prince orders Westmoreland to see to it that the royal troops are disbanded and then asks that the rebels pass in review before their dismissal. Hastings leaves to make the arrangements for carrying out the request. Westmoreland reappears and reports that since the men had been ordered by the prince to stand fast, they will not leave until they receive direct orders from him. They know their orders, says the prince significantly.

When Hastings returns with the news that the men had lost no time in leaving for their homes and places of amusement, Westmoreland immediately declares that Hastings, Mowbray, and the archbishop are under arrest for treason. Orders are also given for the apprehension of any stragglers among the dispersed rebel forces. Protests regarding justice and honor and good faith are of no avail. The prince bluntly tells them that he had pledged no more than a redress of grievances—a pledge that he will keep. As for the three leaders, he concludes, let them expect to receive the punishment that awaits all traitors. "God, and not we, hath safely fought today," he adds as he orders the traitors to be brought to the "block of death."

In Scene 3, noise of armed conflict is heard as Falstaff and a stranger enter. In response to questioning, the latter identifies himself as Coleville of the Dale, a knight. Falstaff charges him with being a traitor who belongs in a dungeon. Asked if this is not Sir John Falstaff who addresses him, the fat knight goes no further than to say that he is as good a man; and he demands that Coleville surrender rather than suffer "fear and trembling." Coleville, convinced that this is Sir John, agrees to submit. His captor then reflects on the fact that his enormous girth always reveals his identity.

Prince John of Lancaster, the Earl of Westmoreland, and one Blunt arrive. The prince orders the earl to assemble the troops since the fighting is over and then asks Falstaff where he had been, pointedly making reference to the knight's "tardy tricks"—his gift for turning up only when the danger is over. Falstaff is injured innocence personified. Heretofore, he states, he had not known that rebuke and check were the rewards for valor. He insists that he had exhausted many post horses in his dash to the battlefield. Now he is here, "in . . . pure and immaculate valor," the captor of a dangerous enemy. Comparing himself to Caesar, Falstaff concludes that he came, he saw, he conquered. But the prince is sure that Coleville's courtesy, not Sir John's bravery, explains the capture. Falstaff remains Falstaff. As he turns Coleville over to the prince, he demands that his valor be celebrated in a broadside ballad illustrated with a picture of Coleville kissing Falstaff's foot. Then he will be sure to get true credit, outshining all others. There follows a brief colloquy between the prince and Coleville, who conducts himself with courage and dignity. Falstaff interrupts on three occasions, anxious to make good his latest fabrication.

Westmoreland returns to report that the prince's orders have been carried out and the royal forces are now re-assembling. The prince then orders his men to take Coleville and all other captives to York for immediate execution. Joined by his chief lieutenants, he himself will leave for court, where his father lies ill. Falstaff asks permission to return by way of Gloucestershire and urges the prince to report him favorably at court. Bidding him farewell, John of Lancaster says that he will speak better of Falstaff than the knight deserves.

Alone, Falstaff soliloquizes. He is aware that Prince John has little use for him. And little wonder. This "sober-blooded boy" drinks no wine; all such abstainers are notorious weaklings—and usually fools and cowards. Falstaff then expounds the virtues he finds in sherris sack. According to him, it enters the brain, making a man lively, inventive, witty; it warms the blood, giving him courage; it illumines the face, which then serves as a beacon warning the whole man to arm himself. And this moves the heart to direct the performance of valorous deeds. Thus it is, Falstaff continues, that Prince Henry is valiant. Like Prince John, he had inherited cold blood from his father, but good wine had transformed him. If Falstaff had a thousand sons, each would be taught the virtues of sack.

Bardolph enters and tells his master that all the soldiers have been discharged and dispersed. In effect, the knight says, "Good riddance." As for him, he will waste no time in seeking out Master Robert Shallow, whom he has already softened up for his purpose.

King Henry IV lies ill in a room known as the Jerusalem Chamber. Two of his sons, Princes Thomas of Clarence and Humphrey of Gloucester, enter with the Earl of Warwick and others. Addressing the group, the king states that if civil dissension has been surpassed and his health improves, he will lead the flower of England on a new crusade to the Holy Land. The ships and troops are ready for such an enterprise. He then asks Humphrey where Prince Henry is. The younger prince can only reply that his elder brother may be hunting in Windsor Forest. Learning that Thomas of Clarence is present, the king then asks why he is not with his oldest brother, who always had favored Clarence. He urges him to cherish the affection so that he can help his brother when the latter assumes regal authority.

All this leads King Henry to comment on the heir-apparent's character: If Prince Hal is humored, he is gracious and kind of heart; if aroused, he can be like flint. Therefore he must be carefully studied. The younger brother must reprove him when he is unduly mirthful but must do so tactfully. In this way, Clarence will prove to be a strong support to Prince Hal.

When the king learns that Hal is actually dining in the company of Poins and other lowly associates, he grieves for his son and heir, using the metaphor of "weeds" to describe those whom the prince now seeks out. What will happen to England, he asks, if Hal's "headstrong riot has no curb?" Warwick speaks up and argues that the king misjudges his son. According to him, the prince is schooling himself to understand even the lowliest subject. He predicts that Hal will turn past evils to advantage. Sententiously the king expresses doubts about the probability of sudden reformation.

Westmoreland enters and is welcomed as the bearer of happy tidings. Harcourt immediately follows and reports that Northumberland and Lord Bardolph are captives of the Sheriff of Yorkshire. But such good news does not improve the health of the now physically weak king. All try to comfort him. Warwick is sure that he will soon recover. But Thomas of Clarence is more realistic. He points out that incessant care and labor have brought his father close to death. When Humphrey voices his concern about possible trouble among the king's subjects incident to the succession, Thomas of Clarence is reminded that the river Thames had overflowed its banks three times, just as it had done when Edward III lay at death's door. At last the king revives and asks to be removed to another chamber.

Attending the ailing king is the same group who were present previously. Henry, oppressed by the respectful silence, asks for "some noise" and specifically for some music to minister to his weary spirit.

As Warwick gives the order for music to be played in the next room, the king directs that his crown be placed on a pillow next to him.

Prince Henry enters and learns that his father is gravely ill and now disposed to sleep. All leave except the heir-apparent, who says he will keep watch at his father's bedside. Observing the crown, he philosophizes about it as a symbol of care and anxiety. On his father's lip he notices a feather that, he assumes, would not remain stationary if the king were breathing. He therefore concludes that his father has died. In soliloquy, the prince states that he owes his father heart-felt grief and will pay the debt, and that his father owes him the imperial crown. Young Henry then lifts the crown and places it on his head, reflecting that just as he lawfully inherits it from his father, so he will pass it on to his heir and thus maintain unbroken the line of succession. He leaves the chamber through a door not leading into the one where the others await.

Suddenly awaking, the king calls for Warwick, Gloucester, and Clarence, who immediately enter. He learns that his eldest son has been in the chamber. Correctly assuming that Hal had taken the crown, he orders Warwick to find the heir-apparent and "chide him hither." To the king, his son's action is as great a cause of suffering as is the illness that has brought him close to death. He points the moral in words addressed to Gloucester and Clarence: Gold leads sons to turn against fathers who have exercised every care in their training and welfare. Warwick returns to report that Prince Henry is in the next room washing tears of grief from his face. When the prince enters, all others are asked to leave.

Prince Henry's first words are that he had not expected to see his father alive—words that the king interprets to mean that his son had hoped to find him dead. In a touching speech, he reproves the prince for being so impatient to wear the crown. Thus, says the king, the prince has proved that he had no love for his father, and adds that unruly behavior all along had pointed to such a conclusion. He urges young Henry to dig his father's grave and order the ringing of "merry bells" announcing the crowning of a new ruler. As for himself, the king sadly concludes, let him be buried and forgotten. In despair, Henry IV then predicts what he is sure will ensue: Vanity and misrule will flourish; wise counselors will be dismissed; "apes of idleness" and ruffians will flock to the court. The new ruler will give license to disorder and vice.

At last the prince speaks. Had he not been choked by grief, he says, he would not have remained silent so long. Kneeling before the king, he declares that the crown belongs solely to his father, and he expresses the fervent hope that his father may live long to wear it. He assures the king that he respects Henry IV's honor and renown and remains his obedient subject. Prince Henry goes on to explain that he honestly believed that his father had died and that the very thought had chilled him to the heart. He insists that if his words are false, he himself should not survive to realize his father's hope for reformation. Young Henry further explains that he had taken the crown, symbol of royal power and awful responsibility, and had upbraided it: The crown had fed upon the body of his father, and since it had "eaten the bearer up," other gold than that of the crown was to be more prized. At that moment, the prince continues, he had placed the crown on his head—not with any thought of pride or pleasure but as a kind of challenge to its tyrannical power. He concludes by saying that if selfishness had motivated his action, he deserved to become like the poorest slave who kneels before the crown in awe and terror.

Obviously affected by Prince Henry's words, the king replies that God had led his son so to comfort him. He bids his son listen to his last words. Sorrowfully, the elder Henry admits that he had come to the throne by bypaths and crooked ways, as God knows, and had experienced a troublesome reign. But young Henry, he is sure, will fare better, for his son will wear a crown by right of succession. Old animosities will have died. Nevertheless, the king fears that his son will not be firm enough. He points out that in order to forestall dissension among restive subjects, he had planned to lead a crusade to the Holy Land. The king then implores God to forgive him for deposing an anointed ruler (Richard II) and to grant that his son have a tranquil reign.

Prince Henry vows that since his father won the crown, wore it, and gave it to him, he will defend it against all the world.

Prince John of Lancaster enters and greets his father. The king praises him for bringing "happiness and peace" but says that Prince John sees him fatally ill. Prince Henry promptly calls for Warwick, who enters with the others. When the king asks the name of the chamber where he "first did swoon," he learns that it is called Jerusalem. He recalls that years earlier, it had been prophesied that he would die in Jerusalem, but he had assumed that the name referred to the Holy Land. Henry IV finally directs that he be carried to the chamber: "In that Jerusalem shall Harry die."

Commentary

In Scene 1, Richard Scroop, the archbishop, is fully established as the leading spirit among the insurgents. It is he who had drawn up the articles of grievances; it is he who, after listening to opposing points of view, makes the command decision. His address to Westmoreland, as well as his success in raising a large army, emphasizes his status as a formidable opponent.

Mowbray, the second Duke of Norfolk and Earl Marshal of England, remains the cautious, skeptical leader among the rebels. But if he is dubious as regards human motives and performance, he remains confident that the rebels can defeat the royal forces.

Lord Hastings, whose optimism regarding the possibility of a bloodless settlement of issues approaches wishful thinking, serves as a foil to Mowbray in the debate at Gaultree Forest.

The Earl of Westmoreland, second in command to Prince John, functions as the prince's emissary, just as Sir Walter Blunt had done for the king prior to the Battle of Shrewsbury. Like Sir Walter, he is the voice of political orthodoxy, summing up the royalist arguments against the rebel leaders.

Scene 1 advances the action in the main plot, bringing the major issues to a head and pointing to the possibility of an amicable settlement. The respective arguments of the insurgents and of the royalists are clarified. Also, the scene provides a review of antecedent action, going back to the quarrel between the first Duke of Norfolk and Henry Bolingbroke, the man who now rules England.

In Scene 2, Prince John of Lancaster, the third son of Henry IV and general of the royal forces, appears as a Machiavellian figure, one who will use any means to achieve his purpose. His apparent perfidy seems inexcusable to modern audiences. To them he emerges as a hypocrite. Certainly it would be more pleasing to see him manifest the chivalry and courage that marked his older brother's conduct at Shrewsbury. It may be argued that Shakespeare was restricted by his source or sources, that he could not take gross liberty with history known to all literate members of his audience. Or it may be argued that had John of Lancaster won a victory in honorable combat, he may well have emerged as the hero of the play. Finally, the historical approach must not be ignored in passing judgment on Prince John. According to orthodox Tudor political theory, which informs the chronicle-history plays by Shakespeare and which was to a large extent based upon the Scriptures, the king was indeed God's deputy on earth—God's "substitute," as the prince calls him (28). No subject for any reason had the right to oppose him actively. Just such promises as those made by the prince were made to the rebels against Henry VIII in 1536. When the insurgent leaders accepted the king's promises for a redress of grievances and dismissed their followers, Henry VIII's officers arrested them as traitors, and they went to their deaths. At that time, the question of perfidy was not even raised. Shakespeare's audiences, we may assume, were not offended by Prince John's action.

Scene 2 provides the resolution to the main action as regards the dominant theme of rebellion and fills in the outlines of Prince John's character, actually in contrast to that of the heir-apparent, Prince Hal. Prince John is depicted as a cold politician, a man who lacks the breadth and charm of his older brother. From a doctrinal point of view, the scene shows that "Thus ever did rebellion find rebuke."

Once more on the battlefield, Falstaff is presented in Scene 3, which balances the scene in *Henry IV, Part 1*, wherein he claimed to have slain Hotspur. So well individualized is the knight that it would be misleading to reduce him to a type character. Nevertheless, one aspect of his complex character is that of the Braggart Warrior, a favorite in comedy dating back to Roman comedy and taken over into popular drama of Western Europe during the Renaissance. Some among Falstaff's admirers will argue that he does not expect to be believed, so patently false are his claims, and from that point of view is not a liar at all. At least one thing is indisputable, however: Falstaff again proves that "a good wit will make use of anything." His soliloquy on the virtues of sack is a justly famous bravura piece, completely in character.

Sir John Coleville of the Dale is a representative of the upper class in northern England, many members of which answered the Archbishop of York's call to arms. His obvious good breeding and courage invite the sympathy of the audience.

However one may judge Prince John as a result of the ruse that led to the collapse of the revolt, it must be recognized that he is a firm, competent leader who moves relentlessly against enemies of the crown. Aware of Falstaff's tricks, he does not hesitate to reprove the knight, but he does not deign to engage in argument or raillery with him.

Scene 3 presents Falstaff at his calling now in the rebellious north, showing how he executed his commission as one of the king's officers, and thus enlarges the comic characterization of the knight. The scene also provides Falstaff with the opportunity to explain once more his philosophy of life and, in the process thereof, to illuminate not only his own character but the characters of Prince Hal and Prince John. Additionally, the scene forges the link between main plot and comic subplot of the play.

In Scene 4, after having heard several earlier references to the king's health, the audience now sees the ruler desperately ill in the Jerusalem Chamber. His concern about Prince Hal emphasizes one of the important conflicts in the play.

The purposes of Scene 4 include the following: to advance the important theme of the king's relations with his eldest son; to add details concerning the character and reputation of Prince Hal and thus to prepare for the resolution of the play; and to provide additional exposition regarding the present state of the realm and the king's aspirations.

In Scene 5, Henry IV, the titular hero of the play, emerges as a fully realized human being who wins the sympathy of all who behold and listen to him. He is above all the loving father, mourning because, now having reached the end of life, all the care he had bestowed upon his son and heir seems to have been wasted. Second, he is the conscience-stricken and penitent sinner, tormented by the knowledge that he had deposed an anointed ruler. He is sure that the civil dissension that characterized his reign and Prince Henry's waywardness are part of the punishment meted out by a just God. But his grief transcends the personal; he is deeply concerned for the safety and well-being of England.

Prince Henry, the heir-apparent, misunderstood by his royal father as in the earlier play, finally vindicates himself in his father's eyes. If there are any doubts about the sincerity of his avowals, one should recall earlier evidence in this play pointing unmistakably to young Henry's genuine affection and respect for his father. In this scene, Shakespeare takes special care to prepare the way for the prince's rejection of Falstaff.

ACT V

Summary

At his home in Gloucestershire, Master Robert Shallow insists that Sir John Falstaff remain his guest for the night and hospitably refuses to accept an excuse. He calls for Davy, one of his servants, and in his bumbling manner proceeds to give him instructions. Here the immediate source of the comic effect is incongruity and anticlimax. Orders and reports relating to preparations for dinner are mixed with those relating successively to planting wheat, a bill received from a blacksmith, the repairing of a chain for a well bucket, and fining the cook for losing sack at a local fair. Finally Davy is told that Falstaff ("the man of war") will stay all night. As the justice says, it is a good thing to have a friend at court. Davy is instructed to treat Sir John's men well, for they are "arrant knaves" and may "backbite." The term "backbite" gives Davy the chance to pun on the fact that all of Falstaff's men wear soiled linen infected with vermin.

Although dismissed, Davy remains to intercede on the behalf of one William Visor, who is to appear in a lawsuit before the Justice. He agrees that Visor is an arrant knave (one of Shallow's favorite expressions) but argues that in view of his eight years of service, he—Davy—should be allowed to gain special consideration for a knave who is an honest friend. Shallow says that Visor will not suffer and again dismisses Davy.

After greeting Bardolph and the page, the Justice invites Falstaff to follow him. Sir John gives orders to his servants and remains alone on the stage long enough to express his thoughts on the comic appearance of Shallow and to make some unflattering comments on the character of the Justice and of those who serve him. Shallow, it is clear, is as thin as his kinsman, Silent. If Sir John were cut into staffs, he would make no less than four dozen, each the size of Shallow. And if Falstaff had a case to be tried before the foolish Justice, he would go to work on the servants. He concludes with the moral reflection that all men should be careful of the company they keep if they are to avoid boorish behavior. Finally, plump Jack says that he will have enough fun at Shallow's expense to entertain Prince Hal continuously for a year. He then answers the Justice's call and leaves the stage.

In the palace at Westminster, Warwick greets the Lord Chief Justice of England. Learning that Henry IV has died, the latter expresses the wish that he had not outlived the king, in whose service he inevitably made some enemies. Warwick, aware of what the Justice has in mind, agrees that Henry V will be strongly prejudiced against him. The Chief Justice can add only sad words of resignation to fate.

The Princes Lancaster, Clarence, and Gloucester enter with Westmoreland. Observing them, Warwick expresses regret that the new king has not the temper of even the least favored of his three brothers. If young Henry were like any one of his brothers, nobles who flourished when Henry IV was alive would not have reason to expect the worst. "O God, I fear all will be overturned!" exclaims the Chief Justice.

After greetings are exchanged, Gloucester and Lancaster express sympathy for the Chief Justice. In the words of Lancaster, he stands "in coldest expectation." Clarence is sure that the Justice will now have to approve of Falstaff. The Chief Justice states that he had performed the duties of his high office honorably and impartially and that if the truth does not prevail, he will join the late king in death.

Henry V enters with his attendants and is greeted by the Chief Justice. He notes the evidence of fear as well as sorrow and reassures his brothers. None, he says, should expect cruelty in his court. His brothers properly grieve for their father as he does, but they have no other reason to be sad, for he will be both father and brother to them. Their replies are rather perfunctory ones, and Henry V is aware of their lack of confidence in him. Especially he knows that the Chief Justice expects to be castigated. To him young Henry now turns. When the Chief Justice insists that the king has no just cause to hate him, Henry reminds him of how he, the immediate heir of England, had been rebuked and imprisoned by the Chief Justice. Can this be forgotten?

With dignity and eloquence, the Chief Justice states his case. He had been the instrument of the king's justice; Prince Henry had dared to strike him in court, the "very seat of justice." If the new king wishes to reject the edicts of his father, let him have a son who will spurn the royal image in the same way. The Chief Justice concludes by inviting Henry V to bring his charges against him.

Now Henry speaks with no less eloquence and dignity. He has only praise for the amazed legal official. He approves of every word the latter had said and bids him to continue to serve—to wield the sword of justice boldly, justly, impartially. Moreover, Henry V welcomes the wise counsel of this man whom he addresses as the father of his youth.

Henry then assures his brothers that his wildness has died with his father—that is, as king he no longer would conduct himself in a manner that would invite censure. He points out that he had survived to prove how wrong were the doleful prophets who foresaw disorder and misrule when he came to the throne. He then gives the order for the assembly of the high court of Parliament and announces his intentions of selecting the best counselors. With them and the help of the Chief Justice, he will provide England with a government unsurpassed for order and effectiveness. Neither prince nor peer, he concludes, will ever have occasion to pray for a new ruler.

In Scene 3, a fine comic scene, Shallow flourishes as the always amusing yet gracious country squire conducting Silent, Falstaff, Bardolph, and the page to his apple orchard, where everyone enjoys the pleasures of merry old rural England. Despite Shallow's insistence that all is barren and beggarly, there is obviously plenty, and especially plenty of good wine, of which all partake. Justice Silent, the man who had hardly a word to say in the earlier scene, is irrepressible as he bursts forth with one drinking song after another and is completely unrestrained in his remarks. Falstaff, already well fortified with sack, commends Shallow on his hospitality and Silent on his unexpected conviviality. Davy, now the ubiquitous serving man, darts in and out, seeing to it that everyone is served. "Lack nothing; Be merry," are the words of Shallow. And indeed all have an abundance and all are merry.

Davy announces the arrival of Pistol, who has hurried from the court with momentous news. Falstaff, instantly alert, instructs Davy to admit him at once. Pistol indeed has important intelligence but takes his time in conveying it. Sir John, he announces, is now "one of the greatest men of the realm." Silent, now very deep in his cups, expresses the opinion that one Goodman Puff is greater. And this gives Pistol the cue to explode as he denounces the harmless Silent as a "most recreant coward base." Still ranting, he finally manages to inform Falstaff that he has "happy news of price." Sir John, adopting the bombastic style, urges him to report it. Silent revives to sing lines from a Robin Hood ballad, and Justice Shallow interrupts to adjudicate. He says that there are two courses to follow—either reveal the news or conceal it. And he adds that he has "some authority under the King." "Which King?" demands Pistol. "Speak, or die." And Falstaff at last learns that Hal, his "tender lambkin," now rules England.

Sir John has visions of grandeur. He orders Bardolph to saddle his horse and excitedly promises Shallow and Pistol high honors. At this climactic moment, Silent, having passed out, is carried to his bed. Then Falstaff, announcing that he is "Fortune's steward," commands Bardolph to take any available horse, for he, Sir John, "holds all the laws at his commandment." Blessed are his friends, he concludes, but woe to the Lord Chief Justice! Pistol, in his own extravagant style, adds his malediction on England's custodian of law and order as all leave the stage.

Two beadles draw the loudly protesting Hostess Quickly and Doll Tearsheet across the stage, not without difficulty. The hostess insists that the second beadle has dislocated her shoulder and says that she would die to see him hanged. From the words of the first beadle, it is learned that Doll is to receive the punishment of a convicted prostitute—a public whipping. Already established as the mistress of invective, she has a choice collection of scurrilous epithets for him and claims that as a result of his rough handling, she may lose her unborn child. The hostess fervently expresses the wish that Sir John Falstaff were present: "He would make this a bloody day to somebody." But she also hopes that Doll does miscarry. The first beadle scornfully remarks that if Doll did so, she would have a full dozen cushions. Doll adds more invective and, ordered to move along, demands to be brought to justice. The hostess has not remained silent by any means. She deplores the alleged fact that such righteous people should suffer. Her last words inevitably include a malapropism.

Near Westminster Abbey, two grooms strew rushes on the

streets, evidence that an important event impends. It is to be the coronation of Henry V, as one of the grooms states. Falstaff enters with Shallow, Pistol, Bardolph, and the page. He is all confidence as he assures the gullible Shallow that Henry will be overjoyed to see his old companion. He regrets that he had not had time to use part of the one thousand pounds he had gotten from Shallow: He and members of his group, stained by travel, need new liveries. But, he says, he had ridden hard day and night to prove his affection for the new king. At this point in the action, Shallow is the complete yes-man as far as Falstaff is concerned, for he expects at least to be knighted. When Pistol reports that Doll Tearsheet is in prison, the confident Sir John promises to arrange for her prompt release.

Shouts and the sound of trumpets announce the arrival of King Henry V. Prominent among his followers is the Lord Chief Justice. Falstaff and Pistol greet the king effusively. Seeing the knight, Henry instructs the Chief Justice to reprove him. Falstaff, incredulous, again addresses Henry: "My King! My Jove! I speak to thee, my heart!" And then Henry speaks the chilling words: "I know thee not, old man." He lectures his old companion of earlier, carefree days severely, making reference to Falstaff's buffoonery, so indecorous in a white-haired old man; to his gluttony; and to his neglect of his soul. Warning Sir John not to reply to him "with a fool-born jest," he pronounces sentence, instructing the Lord Chief Justice to see that it is carried out. Falstaff is banished. He is not to come within ten miles of the king on pain of death. But Henry informs Falstaff that he will provide a competence so that the knight will not resort to trickery to raise money. Further, he states, Falstaff will not lack advancement if he truly reforms.

After the king and others leave, Falstaff and Shallow converse. Sir John admits that so far at least, he has failed to earn the one thousand pounds his friend had given him. But he insists that he will arrange to see the new king privately and that Shallow will be given royal preferment. Shallow, however, is now completely disillusioned. Although Falstaff declares that the king was merely pretending to dismiss his old friend, Shallow remains unconvinced.

As the group are about to leave for dinner, Prince John and the Lord Chief Justice enter, accompanied by officers of the crown. On the orders of the Chief Justice, Falstaff and his companions are led away to prison. Pistol, in character to the last, revives a Latin tag he had used on an earlier, happier occasion: Fortune having deserted him, hope alone remains.

At the end of the play's last scene, Prince John and the Lord Chief Justice hold the stage. Both express their approval of the king's actions. Finally, the audience learns that Henry has called for the assembly of Parliament and, in all probability, will soon lead an invasion of France.

Commentary

In Scene 1, Robert Shallow, the country justice, once more provides excellent comedy of physical appearance and words. If some are inclined to feel that Falstaff is taking advantage of a well-meaning friend, it is well to note that Shallow's insistence that Sir John remain his guest is not motivated wholly by unselfishness and that the Justice's conduct on the bench is not exactly faultless.

Sir John Falstaff, the fat knight in contrast to Shallow, now appears as the urbane courtier and soldier. Content for a time to observe and listen, he is a keen judge of and commentator on what he sees and hears. His comic portrait of the emaciated Shallow, his shrewd remarks on the circumvention of justice, and his anticipation of the fun to be had at Shallow's expense—all are entirely in keeping with his own character.

The purposes of Scene 1 include developing the comic character of Justice Shallow, particularly as it is revealed in the dialogue with Davy and in Falstaff's soliloquy, and advancing the comic subplot, wherein Falstaff continues to be preeminent.

In Scene 2, Henry V, the now completely reformed Prince Hal of the earlier scenes, is the personification of magnanimity and dedication to duty. It is to be recalled that from the very beginning of the two-part chronicle history, Shakespeare prepared the way for this important scene in which the apparently wayward heir to the throne embraces order and justice.

The Lord Chief Justice, England's leading legal official, understandably expects to be severely reprimanded and removed from office. In his longest speech, he succeeds in emphasizing his absolute dedication to royal service and order within the realm.

Scene 2 presents the newly crowned Henry V as the youth who made good his promise to amaze the world by his reformation—or, better perhaps, show himself publicly in his true colors. In this sense, he does "falsify men's hopes," to use the words he had spoken in soliloquy at the end of Act I, Scene 2, of the earlier play. Also in this scene, the admirable Lord Chief Justice takes full opportunity to make the case for law and order in the State.

In Scene 3, Sir John Falstaff is completely at ease in a situation where he is afforded good food and an abundance of wine. He reaches the highest point in his career when he learns that Hal is King of England. Shallow, justice-of-the-peace and squire of Gloucestershire, now flourishes as the expansive, affable host, and Silent, kinsman of Shallow and himself a justice-of-the-peace, becomes the life of the party. Pistol, one of Falstaff's cronies, functions as the messenger in the comic subplot. He is given a fine chance to employ startling expressions culled from the more sensational plays of the era.

Scene 3 brings to a climax the action of the comic subplot and provides, at the comic level, significant elements of contrast in relation to the main plot, notably the action in the preceding scene.

In Scene 4, Hostess Quickly, owner of the disreputable Boar's-Head Tavern in Eastcheap and now in dire straits, continues to mix up words in a comic fashion. Doll Tearsheet is as voluble and scurrilous as ever.

The scene contributes to the resolution of the comic subplot and shows how order is being restored at all levels of society.

In Scene 5, Falstaff, the roistering companion of Henry's madcap days, is described by the new king as "The tutor and the feeder of my riots." The fat knight at last learns that his wit will not serve him. His basic lack of good judgment and, for that matter, his vanity are clearly set forth in this scene. Henry V is now completely reformed and a dignified ruler of England. Here he is presented as the public justice passing sentence on a leading representative of disorder in his kingdom. If he appears to some to be unduly cold and severe, it is to be recalled that he does not leave Falstaff destitute, nor does he close the door on the knight's possible restoration.

Scene 5 provides the resolution of the entire action, main plot and sub-plot, in a play the basic theme of which is disorder versus order. It completes the picture of a reformed young Henry, who now justifies himself by acts, not merely by promises, and prepares the way for *The Life of King Henry the Fifth*, the next English chronicle history written by Shakespeare.

1599

henRy v

HENRY V

LIST OF CHARACTERS

King Henry V

The ruling monarch, who is presented in the play as the ideal Christian king. The main purpose of the play is to convey the idea that Henry V represents in all aspects the model of the ideal ruler.

The Duke of Exeter

He is the uncle of Henry V and a trusted advisor; he functions as both a statesman and as a warrior. Even though he is left in charge of the city of Harfleur, where he is instructed to rule with leniency, he turns up at the Battle of Agincourt, and later he acts as the English ambassador and mediator of the treaty between Henry V and the King of France.

The Duke of Bedford

A brother to Henry, he is used to suggest the close familial bonds between the two brothers. (Historically, he was not present at the Battle of Agincourt since Henry had appointed him as Regent of England during his absence in France.)

The Duke of Gloucester

Henry's youngest brother. Although he is present in most of the scenes in which Henry appears, he has little function in the drama except to illustrate, as Bedford does, familial loyalty. He is placed in charge of some military operations, and he is gently chided by his brother Henry for hoping that the French will not attack while the army is tired. His remark allows Henry to speak on the necessity of relying on the Divine Providence of God: "We are in God's hand, brother, not in theirs."

The Duke of York

Henry's cousin, whom he is very fond of; upon learning of his death during the Battle of Agincourt, Henry is moved to tears when he hears of the duke's courage and his last words of loyalty to the king.

The Archbishop of Canterbury

He is a man of great learning and a master of the English language. He is one of the first persons who bring forth Henry's claim to the French lands, and by so doing, he protects the church's own property from being taken for royal expenditures. He is an extremely astute man, supporting Henry's army with heavy levies from the church; because of this, he is able to retain for the church the basic lands from which the levies are derived.

The Bishop of Ely

An assistant to the archbishop, he functions mainly as a sounding board for the archbishop's ideas.

The Earl of Cambridge, Lord Scroop, and Sir Thomas Grey

The conspirators who accept money from France to assassinate Henry V. They are discovered and immediately executed for treason. Their betrayal of Henry evokes from the king a bitter denunciation of their intentions and causes him to wonder whom he can trust. Lord Scroop and the Earl of Cambridge had been especially good friends and confidants of the king.

The Earl of Westmoreland

Another of Henry's administrators who, early in the play, urges him to press for his claims in France.

The Earl of Salisbury

His only function in the drama is to give a patriotic speech in Act IV, when it is discovered that the French armies far outnumber the English forces. He gives a six-line speech and is heard of no more.

The Earl of Warwick

Like the Earl of Salisbury, he plays no particular role in the drama. He appears in several scenes but speaks only one line in the entire play. He is sent along with Gloucester to make sure that Fluellen and Williams do not get into a real fight; otherwise, he has no function.

Captain Fluellen

An intensely loyal Welshman who provides much of the humor in the play by his eagerness to argue and to show off his knowledge of the classics, even though he gets most things mixed up. He is a very proud, opinionated, conceited, testy person who is willing to argue with anyone about anything.

Captain Gower

A friend of Fluellen's, he often serves merely to draw out Fluellen's eccentricities. He is a good soldier who is actually more perceptive about human nature than is Fluellen, and he realizes quickly that Pistol is a cowardly braggart.

Captain Jamy

A Scotsman who appears only briefly in Act III, Scene 2, and seems immensely to enjoy arguing.

Captain Macmorris

He appears only in Act III, Scene 2, when he gets into an argument with Fluellen concerning the Irish.

Bardolph

This character is retained from the earlier *Henry IV* plays, in which he was distinguished by having a bad complexion, a fiery red nose, and carbuncles on his cheeks. For some reason, he is now a lieutenant in this play, but he is still a coward and a thief. He is hanged during the course of the play for stealing a communion plate from a French church.

Pistol

Like Bardolph, Pistol also appears in the *Henry IV* plays and thus would be a character whom the audience would be familiar with. He is a ranting and raving coward, a "swaggering rascal," a "fustian rascal," and a "bottle-ale rascal." At the end of Act V, Scene 1, Pistol is finally dispensed with, thus bringing to a close a series of characters that began three plays earlier in *Henry IV, Part 1*.

Nym

A corporal who is as much of a coward as Bardolph and Pistol are, he is also an accomplice in their thefts. Like Bardolph, Nym ends up on the gallows.

The Boy

One of Shakespeare's magnificent minor characters, he is younger than the others, and yet he has the quick wit and intelligence to discern the cowardice of Bardolph, Nym, and Pistol. When they try to teach him how to pick pockets, he is outraged and threatens to leave their service. Unfortunately, he is killed when the French raid King Henry's supply area during the Battle of Agincourt.

Hostess Quickly

A simple, uneducated woman who is married to Pistol but has an unabashed admiration for Sir John Falstaff. She dies of the French malady (syphilis) just before Pistol is to return to England.

Michael Williams

One of the three soldiers whom King Henry, in disguise, meets the night before the Battle of Agincourt. He questions the king's rightness to wage this war, but he never questions his own obedience to the crown. He wonders if the king doesn't have a heavy moral obligation for the souls of those who die in battle. Williams even wonders if the king could not use himself for ransom so that the rest of them will not get killed. When Henry, in disguise, challenges Williams, Williams accepts and they promise to fight each other if they are both alive after the Battle of Agincourt. They exchange gloves so as to recognize each other. Afterwards, when it is discovered that he was arguing and challenging the king, Williams defends himself in such an honest and straightforward manner that the king rewards him with a glove filled with money.

John Bates and Alexander Court

Along with Williams, these two men represent the average or common English soldier. Court has only one line, but Bates has a slightly larger role; for example, he does not share Williams' concern as to whether or not the king's cause is a just one; it is sufficient enough for him to know his duty, and his duty is to fight for the king.

Charles VI

The quiet and dignified King of France, who is able to sense the impending danger caused by the approaching English forces, but whereas he grasps the significance, he cannot communicate his fears to the French nobility. He orders his son, the Dauphin, not to go to battle, but apparently this order is ignored since the Dauphin is at the Battle of Agincourt. In the final scene of the play, Charles delivers a gentle speech that is conciliatory as he looks forward to a time of peace and a prosperous union with England through the son whom he hopes his daughter Kate will provide King Henry.

The Dauphin

Next in line for the throne of France, the Dauphin is insolent, opinionated, and stubborn. He knows of Henry's wild, youthful escapades, but he is not perceptive enough to realize that Henry has changed. He still thinks of Henry as a mere wastrel, a young man to whom no attention should be paid. Therefore, he sends Henry a barrel of tennis balls, implying that Henry should content himself with playing ball and not waging war. At the Battle of Agincourt, the Dauphin is more concerned with singing the praises of his horse than he is with the serious business of war. After the defeat of the French, he bitterly feels the shame of it, and he does not appear again in the play.

The Constable of France

The official commander-in-chief of the French forces, he stands out as one of the most capable of the French forces. Yet ultimately, he too succumbs to the temptation of not taking the English seriously; as a result, he is soundly beaten by them.

The Duke of Burgundy

One of the powerful French noblemen and one of the officials of the court, he is responsible for drafting the treaty at the end of the play; he delivers a splendid speech on the virtues of peace.

The Duke of Orleans

Like the other French lords, he is boastful and contemptuous of the English forces, but he does defend the Dauphin when the Constable suggests that the Dauphin might not be as brave as he would like people to believe.

The Duke of Bourbon

One of the French lords who is terribly ashamed about the "ready losses" of the French to the English: "Shame and eternal shame, nothing but shame."

Montjoy

The French herald, or messenger, in charge of delivering the various ultimatums from the French to the English. After the defeat of the French, he comes humbly to ask for peace and request permission for the French to be allowed to collect their dead.

Rambures and Grandpré

Two French lords who appear only briefly.

The Duke of Bretagne and The Duke of Berri

Two noblemen who are onstage only briefly and receive orders from the King of France.

Queen Isabel

The French queen who joins in the negotiations for peace in the hope that her feminine voice will help soothe certain matters in the negotiations. She is pleased with the union between Henry and her daughter, Kate, and hopes for a strong union of the two kingdoms as a result of the marriage.

Katharine

A young girl of fourteen who accepts the fact that she will be given to Henry as his bride; consequently, she is beginning to learn English for that day when she will be Queen of England.

Alice

Katharine's lady-in-waiting; she is the well-mannered companion of the young princess.

SUMMARIES AND COMMENTARIES

ACT I

Summary

The Chorus (one person) enters and calls upon the "Muse" to help in presenting this play since it deals with such a lofty subject matter. The Chorus explains that the small Elizabethan stage can hardly transform itself into the fields of France, or into an English court, or into a battlefield upon which thousands of horses and soldiers fight; with imagination, however, when "we talk of horses . . . you [can] see them" moving across the landscape. Thus the greatness of the subject matter—a subject dealing with England's ideal king, Henry V—requires that the audience exert its greatest imagination to be able to see in their minds the vastness and the splendor that the play recalls. The audience must also be tolerant of the actors who attempt to portray personages of such high estate. And finally, the audience must be prepared for "jumping o'er times" back and forth, from England to France.

The opening scene is set in the antechamber of the king's palace in London. The Archbishop of Canterbury and the Bishop of Ely are discussing a bill that is still pending, one that was to be passed during King Henry IV's reign. The bill would have divested the church of more than half of its lands and wealth—in fact, it would "drink the cup and all." Because of civil strife at that time, the bill was forgotten, but now it is once again being discussed. Fortunately, King Henry V is a true lover of the church and, it is believed, can be dissuaded from supporting the bill.

Canterbury describes the changes that have overtaken Prince Hal since he became King Henry V: "Never was such a sudden scholar made; / Never came reformation in a flood / With such a heady currance, scouring faults" (32–34). While still a prince, Hal and his "unlettered, rude, and shallow" companions spent their time indulging in riotous living. The wildness of his youth seemed to have left him the moment his father died: "The breath no sooner left his father's body, / But that his wildness, mortified in him, / Seem'd to die too" (25–27). Henry V is now a sober, wise, and beloved king; in the same way that "The strawberry grows underneath the nettle / And wholesome berries thrive and ripen," so did Prince Hal conceal his real worth as a youth and then emerge fully ripened into a magnificent monarch.

Canterbury then discusses how he has been trying to sway the king against the bill. He has suggested to the king that instead of taking so much from the church's holdings, the king should regain some of France's domains, which would yield much more revenue. He maintains that Henry has a claim on the French crown derived from his great-grandfather, King Edward III. The Archbishop of Canterbury then explains that he and the king were earlier interrupted by the French ambassador and that he is to meet again with the king to further explain the matter to him. He has an appointment to see the king at four o'clock and must be on his way. Ely expresses his eagerness to know the outcome of the meeting.

Scene 2 takes place in the "presence chamber" of the palace. The king wants to hear from the bishops concerning the rightness of his claims in France before he sees the ambassadors from France. The Archbishop of Canterbury and the Bishop of Ely enter to explain to the king his rightful claim to the French throne. But before they begin, the king warns them to tell the truth. Henry understands that a legitimate claim would mean a war with France and would cost thousands of lives. He wants more information about the "Salic law" that France is using to disprove Henry's claim. Therefore, he urges Canterbury to begin and to speak with "your conscience wash'd / As pure as sin with baptism."

In a very long and involved speech, Canterbury explains that the king has a legitimate claim to the French crown. The Salique (Salic) laws were once applied to a small area in Germany (not even France) called Salique Land. There was, long ago, a decision made by the settlers of the area that decreed that the family's inheritance would not pass on to the women. This law "was not devised for the realm of France," for several of the kings of France obtained their right to the throne through their mothers' line. What is more, Canterbury explains, the French are simply using this law to keep Henry from the French throne.

King Henry asks if he can in good conscience make the claim. The Archbishop of Canterbury responds with a biblical quote from the Book of Numbers: "When the man dies, let the inheritance / Descend unto the daughter." He then urges the king to fight for his claim by remembering the great exploits of his great-grandfather, Edward III, whose mother was Isabella, the daughter of Phillip IV of France.

Here, the Bishop of Ely, Exeter, and Westmoreland all implore the king to remember his noble ancestry and his regal blood. They remind the king of his courageous heritage and the unswerving loyalty of his subjects. The Archbishop of Canterbury promises him that not only his subjects, but the clergy as well, will financially support him in his fight for the French throne:

> In aid whereof we of the spiritualty
> Will raise your Highness such a mighty sum
> As never did the clergy at one time
> Bring in to any of your ancestors.
>
> (132–35)

Henry expresses his fears for the Scottish defenses if he were to leave, recalling that every time that English kings have gone off to war, the Scots come pouring "like the tide into a breach." While Canterbury believes there is nothing to worry about, Ely and Exeter seem to agree with the king. Canterbury responds, then, using the metaphor of a bee colony in which he compares the working of a kingdom to that of a beehive: Every bee has an assigned task to perform, and they all work to accomplish a common goal for the total good. Therefore, he urges Henry to divide up his forces into quarters; with one quarter, he can conquer France and leave the other three-fourths to defend the homeland:

> If we, with thrice such powers left at home,
> Cannot defend our own doors from the dog,

Let us be worried and our nation lose
The name of hardiness and policy.

(217–20)

The king seems satisfied with this suggestion and pronounces that he and his forces are going to France. He then summons the ambassadors from France. They are sent by the Dauphin (the king's son) and not by the King of France. Henry assures the ambassadors that they can speak freely and safely because "We are no tyrant, but a Christian king," and he urges them to speak frankly about what is on the Dauphin's mind.

They say that the Dauphin is aware of Henry's claim upon the French throne, but the Dauphin believes Henry to be young and immature and worthy only of the gift that he sent with his ambassadors: tennis balls. King Henry, with dignity and clarity, responds that he will go to France to play a match that will "dazzle all the eyes of France." The tennis balls, he says, will be transformed into cannonballs, and many will "curse the Dauphin's scorn." Granting the ambassadors safe conduct, Henry bids them farewell. After their exit, he says that he hopes that he will make the "sender [the Dauphin] blush at it," and then he begins to prepare for war with France.

Commentary

Because of the ambitions of the playwright and the limitations of the Elizabethan stage, an introduction is in order and the Prologue serves as that introduction. Chronologically, this is only the second time in Shakespeare's career that he has used the device of a Chorus to introduce a drama (the first time he used a Chorus, it introduced *Romeo and Juliet*).

One of Shakespeare's purposes in using the Chorus is to be able to celebrate the greatness of Henry V directly; for that reason, he does not have to rely solely on the other characters to sing the king's praises. The Chorus also sets the time and place for the drama and excites the imagination of the audience. The audience, of course, must use its imagination in any type of drama, but now Shakespeare is demanding that they extend even further their imagination and create large battlefields and countries across the sea and hordes of horses charging up and down the landscape. This demand to the audience is partly an answer to the classicists who complained that Shakespeare took too many liberties with the Elizabethan stage and violated the classical sense of the unities of time and place. It is, nonetheless, effective.

Before each of the subsequent acts, Shakespeare will also use the Chorus as a device to compensate for the limitations of the stage and continually to remind the audience of a need for imaginative cooperation.

For a full understanding of King Henry in *Henry V*, it is essential that one knows something about him as Prince Hal, as Shakespeare conceived of him in the earlier plays, *Henry IV, Part 1*, and *Henry IV, Part 2*. This background information is necessary because Shakespeare probably conceived of the series as a related group of plays leading up to presenting Henry V as England's ideal king. Certainly, the traits and qualities attributed to Henry are a result, in part, of what he has learned from his past life and past experience.

Scene 1 opens with a discussion of Henry's qualities and his past escapades, emphasizing the differences between the wild youth he once was and the wise and prudent king that he has become. The discussion between the Archbishop of Canterbury and Bishop Ely reminds the audience of the tremendous changes that have taken place in Henry since his coronation. Upon the death of Henry IV, the wild behavior of Prince Hal's past was immediately rejected and replaced by the sober duties of kingship. Thus the opening scene begins the essential theme of the play—that is, the "miraculous" transformation of a wild, impetuous, and dissolute prince into an ideal, perfect Christian monarch, yet one who is also fully aware of various, earthly political intrigues.

After due praise of the new king, the churchmen bring into focus the political intrigue in terms of the bill that will deprive the church of a major portion ("the better half") of its wealth and revenues. The archbishop's interest lies first in the preservation of both the state and the church, and thus, he must be diplomatic when he ensures that neither church nor state be deprived; he is, of course, willing to make large levies on church revenues for the sake of the state, but he also must see to it that the church retains control of its revenues. As a result, with diplomatic cunning and political intrigue, the archbishop hopes to convince King Henry to seek additional revenues in France; to do this, he cleverly advances the theory that Henry is entitled to certain domains in France. If he is successful in this stratagem, the church will not be deprived of its

revenues. The archbishop's chances of success in persuading King
Henry are enhanced by the fact that King Henry is "full of grace and
fair regard," and he is also a "true lover of the holy church." Consequently, this ideal monarch, through his love of the church and
through his spiritual virtue, will be manipulated into a political conflict with France. Consequently, the theme of King Henry's moral
growth will be presented against a background of moral political
choices and political intrigues instigated by representatives of the
spiritual church.

In Scene 1, we only hear about King Henry V; in Scene 2, the
praise we heard is justified with Henry's appearance. Here is the
ideal Christian king who has rejected the depraved companions of
his youth. King Henry is seen as a prudent and conscientious ruler;
he has apparently already decided to wage war against France, and
now he seeks from the archbishop a public statement justifying
his actions. And furthermore, he is fully and conscientiously aware
of the loss of lives that this struggle will entail. To the archbishop, he
admonishes:

> Therefore take heed how you impawn our person,
> How you awake our sleeping sword of war:
> We charge you, in the name of God, take heed;
> For never two such kingdoms did contend
> Without much fall of blood.
>
> (21–25)

With this speech emerges the theme that will be carried forth to the
battlefield later in the play—the theme of the horrors of war and the
loss of many lives that this encounter will entail and, thereby, the
heavy responsibility that it places upon the *conscience* of the king
who decides to wage such a war.

Consequently, the king commands the archbishop to consult his
own conscience before speaking and justifying such an undertaking.
Here is the mature Christian king, concerned not with just matters
of state but with the conscience of the entire state (or nation) as well.
The archbishop explains the justification for Henry's actions in a
speech that has to be one of the most garbled, confused, and tedious
speeches in all of Shakespeare's works (in dramatic productions,
this speech is usually cut or altered severely). When the archbishop,
the head of the Church of England, pleads with Henry to let "the sin
[be] upon my head" if there be any wrongdoing, Henry resolves to

proceed; he has full assurance that he can go to war with a clear conscience.

When Henry expresses concern about an invasion from Scotland (it has happened before when the king and his army are absent from England), the archbishop answers with the now-famous beehive comparison. This elaborate comparison of the state or human society to a beehive is a familiar Renaissance idea: All classes (royalty, workers, drones, and fighters) are necessary for the welfare of the perfect state.

Another facet of Henry's character is revealed during his handling of the ambassadors from France. The Dauphin has apparently heard a great deal about the wildness and immaturity of the young Prince Hal and is openly insulting to the newly reformed king. (By the Dauphin's assumptions about Henry's past life, Shakespeare also assumed that his audience was familiar with his earlier plays about Prince Hal.) But Henry is not rankled by the Dauphin's insults; instead, he responds with an evenness of temper, amazing self-control, and complete courtesy: "We understand him well, / How he comes o'er us with our wilder days, / Not measuring what use we made of them" (266–68). Henry means, as was indicated in Scene 1 by the archbishop, that the "wilder days" were a part of the king's training and have been put to good use in his present knowledge of human nature.

In Scene 2, the archbishop is presented as a person of great learning and one who is a master at garbling the English language in a serious manner. He is completely dedicated to England, to the king, and, last but not least, to the church. He is an admirable diplomat in the manner in which he is able to inspire and convince the king of the rightness of the engagement against France. We, however, must always keep in mind that the archbishop's insistence upon the rightness of the claims against France is due, in part, to his desire to retain the church's revenues—with this in mind, he even promises more revenues for the war than any clergy has ever before provided.

With all the noblemen, kinsmen, and churchmen united behind the king, the first act ends with a perfect sense of unity of state and church and citizenry.

There is total and utter confusion concerning how *anyone* could make a strong, legitimate case for Henry's claim to the French throne. Henry's claim is based on a flimsy assertion that his great-great-grandmother, who was in line for the French throne, married his great-great-grandfather, Edward II of England. Yet there were many in the male line of descendants who are much more entitled to claiming a legitimacy to the French throne. And aside from all other matters, King Edward III renounced forever any claim by any of the sovereigns of England to the throne of France. In conclusion, King Henry V has absolutely no claim whatsoever, and the archbishop's speech simply obscures all these issues.

ACT II

Summary

The Chorus again appears onstage telling the audience that England has been preparing to go to war. Young men are leaving their farms and joining forces with the king; England is like a "little body with a mighty heart." The French are frightened upon hearing of England's plans to wage war. The Earl of Cambridge, Lord Scroop, and Sir Thomas Grey have been paid by France to kill the king; they plan to accomplish this when the king and his forces are in Southampton, ready to sail for France. Finally, the Chorus tells the audience again to use their imaginations and suppose that they are to be transported first to Southampton and "thence to France."

Scene 1 introduces several of Shakespeare's comic characters whom Elizabethan audiences were already familiar with from *Henry IV, Parts 1* and *2*. On a street in London, Corporal Nym and Lieutenant Bardolph meet. Bardolph tells of the marriage between Pistol and Hostess Nell Quickly, a woman who had apparently once promised to marry Corporal Nym.

No sooner do Pistol and Hostess Quickly enter than Nym and Pistol draw swords and launch into a verbal match. Efforts by Bardolph and Quickly do not calm them, but a boy enters and urges Hostess Quickly to come quickly to tend an ailing Falstaff. She exits, and Bardolph draws his sword and threatens to use it on both Nym and Pistol if they don't settle their feuding. They are hesitant, but after Bardolph threatens again, they agree to shake hands. Pistol agrees to pay Nym the eight shillings he owes him, and Pistol then says that he has a position in the army as a seller of provisions and the three of them can share in the profits.

Quickly reenters to tell the men that Falstaff is dying, and they all go off to see him, explaining on the way that the changes in the king's behavior brought about Falstaff's downfall.

Now in Southampton, Bedford (the king's brother), Exeter (the king's uncle), and Westmoreland are discussing the conspirators—Scroop, Cambridge, and Grey—who, for a price, are planning to kill the king. The king, however, is aware of the plot and those behind it.

Henry, Scroop, Cambridge, and Grey enter and begin to discuss the support and loyalty that the king has among his subjects. And as if to illustrate Henry's deserved loyalty to his goodness and wisdom, Shakespeare has Henry order a man who committed a minor offense the day before to be released from prison. Scroop, Cambridge, and Grey argue that the king must set an example and prosecute the offender to the full extent of the law, but the king argues for mercy and pardons the offender, explaining that if he punishes severely for petty crimes, how shall he punish major crimes? Henry then shows the three men some papers that prove that he knows about their plot. Cambridge, Scroop, and Grey each confess and ask him for mercy.

Henry, answering them in a moving and bitter speech, says first that these three who expressed no compassion for the minor lawbreaker deserve none now for themselves; he then speaks of the ideal of loyalty and the crime of betrayal. The treachery of Lord Scroop, who "knew'st the very bottom of my soul, / That almost mightst have coined me into gold" and who betrayed Henry for a price, is the most incredible. Henry cannot understand why these three so-called old friends have plotted against him for nothing more than French gold. He questions how he can trust *any* man if these three who he thought were most loyal could betray him. But compassionately he says: "I will weep for thee; / For this revolt of thine, methinks, is like / Another fall of man" (140–42). He then orders their arrest for high treason against the crown.

Exeter arrests the three, and they tell the king they are ready to die for their crimes; they ask him to forgive them, and each asserts that he is glad that their plan has been uncovered. Henry, in words that suggest his greatness as a magistrate, says that he holds no personal grudge ("Touching our person seek we no revenge"), but the safety of the nation is at hand. He therefore pronounces the sentence: death. Then, exhibiting further the qualities of mature kingship, he turns his attention immediately to matters of state and prepares for the embarkation to France.

In front of a tavern on a London street, Hostess Quickly tells her husband, Pistol, that she wants to accompany him to Staines on his way to Southampton. Pistol says no; they (Pistol, Bardolph, and Nym) are mourning Falstaff's death. Hostess Quickly describes for them the death of Sir John Falstaff, whom she attended until the end, and as they make ready to leave for Southampton, Pistol gives Hostess Quickly advice about running the inn. Then he kisses her, as does Bardolph, but Nym refuses. She bids them all adieu.

In the palace of the French king, the king expresses his fear of the approaching English forces. He tells the Dauphin to prepare for war "with men of courage and with means defendant." But the Dauphin maintains that the English will be easy to defeat and that Henry is a "vain, giddy, shallow, humorous youth."

The Constable of France believes the Dauphin is mistaken and has misjudged the character of the English king. The French king agrees and urges the Dauphin to remember that "King Harry" comes from the line of Edward, the Black Prince of Wales, a fierce warrior who won the Battle of Cressy: "This is a stem / Of that victorious stock; and let us fear / The native mightiness and fate of him."

Exeter enters, as the ambassador from King Henry, asking the French king to give up his crown and give it to King Henry, the rightful heir; if he refuses, bloodshed and war will follow. He warns the Dauphin that his gift of tennis balls was not appreciated and that he shall have to answer to King Henry for the insult.

The French king tells Exeter that he shall have to wait until the next day for his answer.

Commentary

The Prologue, or the Chorus, informs the audience of the length of time that has passed since Henry's decision to invade France and the present, actual time. All of the preparations for war have been made, and enough time has elapsed for the French to learn of the plans for war and, as a counter measure, to enter into a conspiracy to have Henry assassinated.

The Chorus also reminds the audience that they must continue to use their imaginations as the scene will soon shift from London to Southampton and then to France.

The characters introduced in Scene 1 have no real purpose in the play. Bardolph, Pistol, and Hostess Quickly are included only because they were in the earlier *Henry IV* plays, and Shakespeare's audience would expect to see them again. Furthermore, Shakespeare lets the audience know that Sir John Falstaff—one of Shakespeare's greatest comic creations—is not totally forgotten. Yet since the king has undergone a complete transformation, these comic characters, once his old drinking cronies, will never appear in scenes in which the king appears; they have very little or nothing to do with the main story. They simply provide the comic relief from the serious plot developments, and as noted, these characters were well known and well loved by the audience. However, this scene stresses that this is *not* the world of *Henry IV*, and the mere absence of Sir John Falstaff reinforces this idea. Even the humor has changed; the quarreling between these characters is more of the snarling type and thus loses much of the gusto of the earlier plays.

In *Henry IV, Part 1*, Bardolph was Falstaff's servant and held the rank of corporal. He is usually presented as having a large, flaming red nose, facial blemishes, and carbuncles on his cheeks, and, as was true earlier, he is often the butt of many jokes because of his physical appearance. In *Henry IV, Part 2*, he was still a corporal; Shakespeare never reveals how Bardolph received his present rank of lieutenant in this play, and critics who suggest that it could have been through Falstaff's influence miss the point that Henry's vow to be mature and responsible would not allow Falstaff to be in his presence, much less to have any influence over him. But even though Bardolph has been promoted, he is still just as much a coward as he was earlier; however, with his promotion, he has learned to conceal his cowardice better. His purpose of remaining in the army is that it provides him with a good opportunity to loot.

Pistol and Nym also provide comic relief through their worldly boasting, their blustering and swaggering, and their constant misuse of the English language. Many of their expressions are absurd, alliterative nonsense. Hostess Quickly is the same good-hearted, simple person that she was in the earlier plays. She has always had a great admiration for Sir John Falstaff, and presently she is deeply concerned over his serious illness.

The treason that the Chorus speaks of in the Prologue is now discovered in Scene 2 and resolved by King Henry in a very calm and reasoned manner. This scene emphasizes many of Henry's admirable qualities. In the first part of the scene, he shows great mercy in forgiving a person whose offense was unintentional. It is also ironic that the three traitors argue for exceedingly harsh punishment: "Let him be punished, sovereign, lest example / Breed, by his sufferance, more of such a kind." Ironically, King Henry allows the offenders to convict themselves.

The treasonable actions of Cambridge, Grey, and Scroop emphasize the many cases of duplicity which a true king must contend with, and Henry's treatment of the conspirators is firm, just, and decisive; yet in Henry's long speech of denunciation, there is also a note of deep personal tragedy. All of these conspirators have been the recipients of special favors from the king. The treachery of Lord Scroop is the most difficult for Henry to understand since Lord Scroop knew Henry's innermost person: Lord Scroop "knew'st the very bottom of my soul." Thus as Henry contemplates the contrast between appearance and reality, between the inner duplicity of the traitors and their outward show of loyalty, he is faced with not so much a political tragedy as he is with a *personal* tragedy. But however much the tragedy is personal, he must transcend it, and for the sake of England, he must send the traitors whom he has believed to be loyal friends to their deaths.

At the end of his speech of denunciation, he feels the betrayal so personally that he accounts for it in terms that would imply that man is sometimes simply born depraved and evil. At least, Lord Scroop's betrayal is, for Henry, deep-rooted enough to be compared with the original fall of man. But the mark of a great king is that he must rise above personal tragedy, and this Henry does as he tells the conspirators,

> Touching our person seek we no revenge;
> But we our kingdom's safety must so tender,
> Whose ruin you have sought, that to her laws
> We do deliver you. Get you therefore hence,
> Poor miserable wretches, to your death.
>
> (174–78)

Here, Henry sets aside his personal views and calmly sends the traitors to their deaths for the safety and welfare of the entire nation, a nation that could have been destroyed if the treachery had been successful. After dealing with the traitors, then, Henry turns his attention immediately to the duties at hand—the war with France.

Historically, both Cambridge and Lord Scroop wanted to replace Henry on the throne with Edmund Mortimer, who also had a claim to the throne, and who, in the earlier *Henry IV* plays, had support from Lord Scroop's father for the throne.

The main purpose of Scene 3 is to announce the death of Sir John Falstaff, and the manner of that announcement by Hostess Quickly contains as much humane feelings from these comic characters as we are to find from them in the entire play. We should remember from the earlier plays that Hostess Quickly did have a strong admiration for the marvelous fat knight. Her misused words and phrases are comically absurd, but they nevertheless possess a charm that is missing in the rest of the drama that concerns them.

Once Sir John's death is announced, Pistol expresses the common concern for greed and gain that the lower characters in this play have and their decision to join their king: "Yoke-fellows in arms, / Let us to France; like horse-leeches, my boys, / To suck, to suck, the very blood to suck!" (56–58). As noted earlier, the low characters will now function mainly as looters or bloodsuckers.

The basic purpose of Scene 4 is twofold: first, to show that the French court is not prepared for war, and second, to show the disunity that is prevalent in the court. The French king, Charles VI, is not characterized as an impressive king. Even though he is correct in his appraisal of King Henry, he does not possess a commanding presence.

The Dauphin, as was indicated by his insulting gift of the tennis balls in the first act, is characterized as a rather insolent, self-opinionated young man who will function as a direct contrast to the more noble Henry. The Dauphin believes that the French should have good defenses but not because of the approach of young King Henry; he is guided not by fear but only by the general principle that one should always have good defenses.

Of more direct concern in this scene are the words of Exeter, the English ambassador; he echoes the king's determination, and he anticipates the spirit of the scenes to come in his reference to the horrors of war, which can be avoided only by the French king's submission to the will of King Henry V. Exeter warns:

> . . . if you hide the crown
> Even in your hearts, there will he rake for it.

> Therefore in fierce tempest is he coming,
> In thunder and in earthquake, like a Jove,
> That, if requiring fail, he will compel.
>
> (97–101)

ACT III

Summary

The Chorus enters with a flourish and once more urges the audience to imagine the king and his troops setting sail for France and also to imagine an England emptied of all her stalwart soldiers, defended only by "grandsires, babies, and old women." The English ambassador has returned; the French king has offered his daughter, Katharine, and some minor dukedoms, but he has refused to give up his throne. Henry has rejected the offer, and he now sails to France to do battle.

Scene 1, consisting solely of a soliloquy by King Henry, contains many famous passages; in fact, this speech is probably the best-known speech in the entire play. The scene is Harfleur, where Henry, surrounded by his troops, urges them on to one more supreme effort. Henry's speech proves that he knows his men well; speaking plainly and to the point, he appeals to their manhood, their ancestry, and their love of England: "Follow your spirit, and upon this charge / Cry, 'God for Harry! England and Saint George!'" (33–34).

In another part of the Harfleur field, Bardolph, apparently inspired by Henry, calls, "On, on, on, on, on! To the breach, to the breach!" But Nym and Pistol remind him that they might be killed; they have no intention of dashing "to the breach." The Boy wishes that he were back in London. Fluellen, a Welsh officer in the English army, enters and commands them to fight. He drives them forward and leaves the Boy to reflect on the pickpocket schemes that Nym, Pistol, and Bardolph are involved in.

Fluellen reenters with another Welsh officer, Gower, who tells Fluellen to come with him, that the Duke of Gloucester wants to speak to him. Gloucester, along with the Irish Captain Macmorris, is "mining"—that is, digging tunnels under the city. Fluellen does not think highly of the captain.

Captain Macmorris and Captain Jamy, a Scotsman, enter then, and Fluellen compliments Captain Jamy on his military knowledge. Meantime, Captain Macmorris is angry that work on the mines has stopped and that he will not be able to blast the walls of Harfleur with his mines. Fluellen tries to goad Macmorris into an argument, but the captain is unwilling to waste words, so Fluellen makes a remark about the Irish, a remark that Macmorris immediately resents. A fight is about to ensue when Captain Gower steps in before swords are actually drawn. A trumpet announces that a parley has been called, and Fluellen promises to resume the argument when a break in the action occurs.

Scene 3 opens before the gates of Harfleur, where King Henry is warning the Governor and the local citizens of the dreadful things that will happen if the city does not surrender. The king and his men are prepared to show no mercy and will reduce the town to ashes if the Governor does not surrender. The Governor replies that the Dauphin, whom he entreated to come and defend the town, sends word that his forces are not yet ready "to raise so great a siege." He therefore surrenders Harfleur to King Henry and asks for mercy. The king responds by entrusting the town to Exeter and charging him to be merciful to all the people of the city and to fortify it. He will then lead the army to Calais.

In a room of the French palace at Rouen, Katharine, the king's daughter, and Alice, the old gentlewoman, have an English lesson. Alice knows only a little English, and Princess Katharine is trying to learn the language. All of the dialogue is in French except the few words—for example, hand, nails, arm, and elbow—that she learns from Alice during the lesson.

In another room of the Rouen palace, the King of France is worried about the presence of King Henry and his soldiers in France. The Dauphin is upset by the ladies of the court, who are, in turn, disgusted with the lack of manliness exhibited by the French officers of the army. According to the Dauphin, their wives think that "Our mettle is bred out, and they will give / Their bodies to the lust of English youth / To new-store France with bastard warriors" (28–30). The Duke of Bourbon and the Constable speak with disdain about England and its forces, and they note that Henry's army must be stopped quickly. The king calls on all of the French nobility to fight at once against Henry but commands the Dauphin to stay with him. The Constable remarks that such a battle between Henry's sick and hungry forces and all of the French nobility will be uneven enough to convince Henry to surrender.

The king then sends all of the French nobility to battle against Henry—with the exception of the Dauphin, whom he orders to remain with him.

In the English camp in Picardy, Fluellen meets Gower and tells him that they have saved the bridge which they were fighting for, and he extravagantly extols the Duke of Exeter's bravery and leadership. He also mentions that Pistol fought courageously. Pistol enters then and asks Fluellen to intercede for Bardolph, who is to be hanged for stealing a pax from the church. (A pax was a small plate, usually with an engraved picture of Christ or a saint, and it was used in the communion service to hold the wafers. In Holinshed's *History*, the object was a "pyx"—the vessel used to hold the consecrated communion host and, consequently, an object of much more value; from a mercenary viewpoint, the offense would be much greater. Thus again, Shakespeare alters history to lessen Bardolph's crime in order to allow Pistol to pun that Bardolph's death is "for a pax of little price." Actually, the intrinsic value of the object does not matter since theft from the church was punishable by death.) Fluellen refuses, saying discipline must be maintained and that he would not interfere—even for his brother. Angry, Pistol leaves, hurling insults at Fluellen. Gower tells Fluellen about Pistol's true character lest he be misled, and Fluellen pretends to understand; he promises to deal with him.

Henry and the Duke of Gloucester enter. Fluellen tells them how heroically the Duke of Exeter performed. When the king asks about the casualties, Fluellen tells him that there was only one—Bardolph is soon to be hanged for robbing a church. Henry reiterates his orders that the French populace is to be dealt with fairly; there is to be no plundering. He hopes in this way to win the people's loyalty and respect.

The French herald, Montjoy, enters and says that the French king demands that "Harry" pay for the damage that his troops have caused. Henry recognizes Montjoy's rank and admits that his English army is indeed small and tired; he would like to avoid a confrontation, but they will fight if harassed. Henry tells his brother Gloucester that God is on the side of the English army and then orders the march to the bridge.

It is the night before the battle in the French camp near Agincourt. The Constable, the Duke of Orleans, Lord Rambures, and the

Dauphin (who is present against his father's orders) are boasting about who has the best armor and the best horses. When the discussion turns from the wonders of the Dauphin's horse to the splendors of the others' mistresses, the Dauphin exits to ready himself for the battle. The Constable then has a discussion with the Duke of Orleans concerning the Dauphin's bravery. A messenger enters to announce that the English are camped only fifteen hundred yards away. The Constable and Orleans contend that the small English army cannot be very smart if they mean to fight them, but Rambures reminds them of the courageousness of the English. Nevertheless, the Constable and Orleans are certain that it will be an uneven battle and that by ten o'clock they each will have captured a hundred Englishmen.

Commentary

As with the previous prologues, this one serves to explain a lapsed time period, and again it reminds the audience that they must continue to use their imaginations—this time, however, the language of the Prologue is more elaborately descriptive. The king embarks on a "fleet majestical" that bears the English forces to France, and the entire "brave fleet" is adorned and lighted by dawn:

> . . . behold the threaden sails,
> Borne with the invisible and creeping wind,
> Draw the huge bottoms through the furrowed sea,
> Breasting the lofty surge.
>
> (10–13)

The king's speech in Scene 1 confirms for the audience the personal and inspiring leadership of King Henry V. Even though some critics have dissected the speech and found it lacking, it is nevertheless one of the most inspiring war speeches ever uttered, and apparently it is very successful in spurring the soldiers on to make one more supreme effort. Lines 6–17 seem to suggest that in terms of the various passions of man, his spiritual emotions are directly dependent upon his physical state. In times of peace, the manly virtues are quite proper and will suffice, but in times of war, man must put aside manly virtues and become a virtual beast. It is the duty of the soldier to become a beast, and his actions should be in imitation of a wild beast—the blood is to be "summoned" and the sinews "stiffened."

Scene 2, placed between Henry's charge to his armies and his confrontation with the Governor of Harfleur (and the surrender of the town), is Shakespeare's now familiar means of using a comic interlude to comment upon the serious scenes. In contrast to the nobility of Henry's inspired charge in the preceding scene ("Once more unto the breach, dear friends, once more . . . "), Bardolph repeats the charge in a bit of low, echo-like comedy, thus connecting the two scenes and also showing that not all of Henry's soldiers are inspired by his valiant and heroic leadership.

The behavior of Nym, Bardolph, and Pistol is a negative counterpoint to Henry's stress on the model Englishman's patriotic virtues. These low characters would prefer to be "in an alehouse in London . . . [and] would give all . . . for a pot of ale and safety." This comic scene, however, lacks the force of the scenes in the *Henry IV* plays, in which Sir John Falstaff imparted more pertinent observations about the situation. The Boy's earlier comments remind us of Falstaff, but they are, nonetheless, a poor substitute for the original.

Behind the comic aspects, however, even here Shakespeare seems to insert into these interludes something new, a deep concern about the serious waste of human lives. Nym doesn't have "a case of lives" to spare, and Pistol, in spite of his obvious cowardice and striking flamboyance, reflects, "knocks go and come; God's vassals drop and die."

When the Boy is left alone on the stage, we see another view of King Henry's inspired Englishman. In contrast to the young Boy, Bardolph is "white-livered and red-faced," Pistol has a vicious tongue but a "quiet sword," and Nym has never hurt anyone except himself—when he was drunk. Yet together, they will "steal anything, and call it purchase." For the Boy, their combined "villainy goes against my weak stomach." His inexperienced and untried manhood is admirable as he deserts the three and goes off to do "some better service."

The Welsh officer Fluellen, introduced in this scene, is one of the more interesting characters in the play. While he is eager to argue and quick to show off his knowledge on almost any subject, and while he is opinionated and conceited, he is also a good soldier who shows great courage and loyalty to Henry. Ultimately, in spite of all his flaws, he will become one of the more lovable characters in the play due to his quaint and amusing ways. His antagonist in this scene, Captain Macmorris, the Irishman, is seen no more, and the long argument presented in a heavy dialect is often severely cut or omitted from many productions since it does not move the plot forward.

In Scene 3, in the capitulation of Harfleur, we have the first significant surrender, and we see Henry as a victor for the first time. In this role, he is stern and undeviating in his demands that the Governor surrender the town peacefully. He depicts vividly the many horrors that could result if his demands are not met; yet, in contrast, he is willing to show great mercy if his demands are met. A new note, however, is introduced in Henry's closing speech. Winter is coming, and there is a growing sickness among the men. This problem will remain a constant concern throughout their encampment at Calais, when Henry's men will be seen as only tatters of their former selves.

In the Governor's surrender, we hear that the Dauphin refused to send help. We can assume that the Dauphin has still not taken Henry's threats seriously.

Katharine, the future Queen of England whom Henry will woo and become betrothed to in the final scene of the play, is introduced in Scene 4 as a girl of fourteen whose destiny has already been decided. The purpose of the scene is to give the audience some lighthearted relief from the battle scenes and also to show that Katharine, by her statement that "it is necessary" that she learn English, is already reconciled to the idea that she is to be Henry's queen.

In this scene, the French words and phrases that appeared in the early editions of the play were filled with errors and have been corrected by successive editors. Even though the content is trivial and hardly needs a translation, a loose translation follows:

Kath.:	Alice, you have been to England, and you speak the language well.
Alice:	A little, my lady.
Kath.:	I beg you to teach me because it will be necessary that I learn it. How does one say *la main* in English?
Alice:	*La main?* It is called de hand.
Kath.:	De hand. And *les doigts?*
Alice:	*Les doigts?* O my goodness, I have forgotten *les doigts*; but I shall soon

	remember it. *Les doigts?* I think that they are called de fingres; yes, de fingres.
Kath.:	*La main,* de hand; *les doigts,* de fingres. I think that I am a good student; I have quickly learned two English words. How does one say *les ongles?*
Alice:	*Les ongles?* They are called de nails.
Kath.:	De nails. Listen and tell me if I speak well: de hand, de fingres, and de nails.
Alice:	You have spoken well, my lady; it is very good English.
Kath.:	Tell me the English for *le bras.*
Alice:	De arm, my lady.
Kath.:	And *le coude.*
Alice:	De elbow.
Kath.:	De elbow. I will now repeat all of the words that you have taught me up to now.
Alice:	I think that it will be very difficult, my lady.
Kath.:	Excuse me, Alice; listen: de hand, de fingres, de nails, de arma, de bilbow.
Alice:	De elbow, my lady.
Kath.:	O my goodness, I forgot. De elbow. How does one say *le col?*
Alice:	De nick, my lady.
Kath.:	De nick. And *le menton?*
Alice:	De chin.
Kath.:	De sin. *Le col,* de nick; *le menton,* de sin.
Alice:	Yes. To your honor, in truth, you pronounce the words as though you were a native English lady.
Kath.:	I do not doubt it at all that I shall be able to learn it in a little more time.
Alice:	Have you yet forgotten what I have already taught you?
Kath.:	No, I shall recite to you promptly: de hand, de fingres, de mails,—

Alice:	De nails, my lady.
Kath.:	De nails, de arm, de ilbow.
Alice:	With your permission, de elbow.
Kath.:	That is what I said; de elbow, de nick, and de sin. Now how do you say *le pied* and *la robe*?
Alice:	De foot, my lady, and de coun.
Kath.:	De foot and de coun! O my Lord! These are very bad words—evil, vulgar and immodest, and not for ladies of honor to use. I would never pronounce these words before French gentlemen—not for the whole world. Foo! Le foot and le coun! Nevertheless, I am going to recite my entire lesson together one more time: de hand, de fingres, de nails, de arm, de elbow, de nick, de sin, de foot, de coun.
Alice:	Excellent, my lady!
Kath.:	It is enough for this time; let's go to dinner.

Since the English audience of Shakespeare's day would have known that the English were indeed victorious in their encounter with the French forces, Scene 5 is therefore filled with dramatic ironies. The French are so certain of victory that they are arrogant and overconfident. Rather than being apprehensive about Henry's forces, they hold his army in contempt: "His soldiers sick and famish'd in their march . . . when he [Henry] shall see our army, / He'll drop his heart into the sink of fear." Dramatically, the audience will take pleasure in seeing the insufferable pride of the French brought low by Henry's yeomen.

Dramatically, the Dauphin is presented as a worthy opponent of Henry even though his father, Charles VI, is still in charge. (Historically, Charles was actually insane at this time, and the Dauphin was in charge of the royal council; this is only one of many examples of the way in which Shakespeare alters history for dramatic purposes.) The Dauphin, even though he is ashamed of the French army's fighting record, is still shown here as being contemptuous of the English army; yet still, apparently, he does not take Henry seriously.

Historically, the events related by Fluellen in Scene 6 refer to the fact that King Henry had to march fifty miles out of his chosen path in order to find a bridge to cross the river. They discover a suitable bridge at a place called Teroune, but the French are on the verge of destroying it when the Duke of Exeter bravely drives them back. The additional fifty-mile march was an additional hazard on King Henry's men and further weakened them.

Fluellen, as a comic character, is further developed in this scene. Comically, he is totally mistaken about Pistol and is actually a terrible judge of character. In his speech about Fortune, we see once again his propensity for trying to show off his knowledge on any subject. But, as King Henry later points out, though Fluellen "appears a little out of fashion / There is . . . much valour in this Welshman"; particularly in his rejection of Pistol's pleas to intercede for Bardolph's life, Fluellen shows that he is a strong advocate for absolute discipline.

For students of Shakespeare, King Henry's actions are often puzzling. On the one hand, he is the exemplary, impeccable king who pronounces:

> We give express charge, that in our marches
> through the country, there be nothing compelled
> from the villages, nothing taken but paid for, [and]
> none of the French upbraided or abused in disdain-
> ful language; for when lenity and cruelty play for a
> kingdom, the gentler gamester is the soonest
> winner.
>
> (114–20)

In other words, he tells his soldiers to conduct themselves in the most respectable manner possible—even no abusive words are to be spoken. In contrast, when Fluellen casually announces that the only casualty from the encounter with the French is that Bardolph is to be executed for robbing a church, King Henry expresses no concern for, nor even recognition of, this old companion from his youthful days of tavern living. (In both of the *King Henry IV* plays, Bardolph, as noted earlier, was, along with Pistol and the late Sir John Falstaff, the drinking companion of King Henry when he was the "madcap Prince Hal.") It is difficult for some critics to understand how King Henry can so easily forget his past relationship with Bardolph that he can send him to his death with only the cursory comment, "We would have all such offenders so cut off." The contrast between Henry's order for lenity and mercy for the captured French and the strict enforcement of discipline among the English forces appears contradictory. Furthermore, Bardolph is to be put to death for stealing a small plate from the church, and yet King Henry himself has deprived the church of large sums in order to wage his wars with the idea of taking not a small plate but a large crown—the French crown. Thus the subplot here, involving Bardolph's theft, is also a comment on the main plot of Henry's war against France.

With the arrival of the French emissary, Montjoy, we see still another side of Henry—his concern for his men and the honesty with how he appraises his situation: "My people are with sickness much enfeebled, / My numbers lessen'd." Shakespeare is dramatically creating a situation in which the English will have to overcome tremendous odds to be victorious—all for the glory of "Harry, England, and Saint George."

In Scene 7, Shakespeare continues his satirical presentation of the French nobility by contrasting the seriousness and sobriety of the English with the superficiality and pretentiousness of the French. By doing so, Shakespeare continues to make the French appear rather ridiculous. On the night before a major battle, the French nobility join in an absurd banter concerning the value of their horses. The contrast between Henry, King of England, and the Dauphin, heir to the throne of France, is made obvious in the conversation of each man before the major battle. The Dauphin's main concern is with the beauty and perfection of his horse—a "beast for Perseus. He is pure air and fire; and the dull elements of earth and water never appear in him." When the Dauphin then goes on to remind his comrades that he once wrote a sonnet to his horse, which began with the words "Wonder of nature," the Duke of Orleans sarcastically says that he has "heard a sonnet begin so to one's mistress." The Dauphin, however, is not even aware of the subtle reversal of values. Furthermore, to continue the contrast between Henry and the Dauphin, Shakespeare introduces the subject of the Dauphin's bravery; the Constable wonders if the Dauphin will stand and fight, or if he will be like a hawk, which, when released, will take flight.

Throughout Scene 7, therefore, the French nobility reveal a rather fundamental moral carelessness that will be reflected in their resounding defeat at Agincourt. The Duke of Orleans and the other nobility speak of King Henry with utter contempt and of Henry's English soldiers as the king's "fat-brain'd followers" who, if they had any wits, must have left "their wits with their wives." In other words, Shakespeare is preparing his audience with reasons why the French nobility, outnumbering the English five to one and on horseback, are soon to be defeated by English yeoman, who are "with sickness much enfeebled." The French, believing in and relying on their inherent aristocratic superiority, will go to battle incompetently prepared and will meet their deaths at the hands of English soldiers, who are inspired by the noble spirit of their king and thus, by perseverance, discipline, and a belief in "Harry, England, and Saint George," will win the battle against overwhelming odds.

ACT IV

Summary

The Chorus gives us a picture of the two opposing camps on the night before the battle; there are the whispers of the sentinels, the firelight from each camp, the neighing of the horses, the sounds of armor, some roosters crowing, and clocks striking in two nearby villages. Inside the French camp, the confident soldiers play dice while waiting anxiously for dawn; meanwhile, the English, aware of their small number and of their weakened condition, contemplate the morning's danger. The Chorus describes King Henry's walking from tent to tent talking to his soldiers ("a little touch of Harry in the night"), calling them "brothers, friends, and countrymen." He looks strong and confident, and he is a comfort to his men.

The Chorus then apologizes once again for the inadequacies of the stage and urges his audience to be ready to imagine the Battle of Agincourt in their minds.

In the English camp on the night before the battle, the king tells his brother Gloucester that he is worried about the outcome of the battle. When Sir Thomas Erpingham enters, the king, on an impulse, borrows Erpingham's cloak and is thus no longer identifiable as the king. He sends the others out to "commend [him] to the princes in our camp," and since he wishes "no other company," he asks to be left alone to "debate" with himself.

Pistol enters and does not recognize Henry; he extols the king and asks the young man his name, and Henry tells him that his name is "Harry le Roy." When Pistol discovers that he is a Welshman and knows Fluellen, he tells him that he plans to fight Fluellen. "Harry" warns him he might be defeated, and Pistol becomes so incensed that he insults "Harry" with a vulgar gesture and leaves. As Henry steps aside, Fluellen and Gower enter, unaware of the king's presence. Fluellen is angry with Gower for speaking his name too loudly, afraid that the French might have overheard it. Gower maintains that "the enemy is loud" and cannot hear him; in order to end the argument, Gower promises to speak lower and they exit. The king remarks that Fluellen is odd but that he is a good soldier.

Next, three common soldiers, John Bates, Alexander Court, and Michael Williams, enter. Henry, unrecognized, tells them he serves under Sir Thomas Erpingham. Bates asks him if he thinks that the king should be told how bleak the situation really is. Henry says no, that the king is "but a man," as they are, and if he exhibited fear, he would discourage the army. Bates personally thinks that the king would prefer to be back in London, but Henry disagrees; he believes that the king is content to be where he is. Then Bates says that the king should be ransomed to save the lives of the men in the army. Henry responds by saying that he himself would not want to leave his king alone to fight the battle because of the king's "cause being just and his quarrel honourable."

Williams is unsure of the justness of the king's claim. Bates does not think it matters; if it is unjust, the guilt is upon the king's head and they will not have to share in the blame. When Williams suggests that those who die "unprovided" (unrepentant) will be a burden upon the king's conscience, Henry responds by saying that all who go to battle should be spiritually prepared but that the king is *not* responsible to God for their deaths.

When the discussion returns to the king's ransom, Henry says he overheard the king say it would never happen; Williams jokes that it could happen after they are all killed and they would not know the difference. After another exchange of quips, in which Henry intimates that if times were different, he might be angry at Williams, Williams takes up the idea and challenges "Harry" to a fight if they should both survive the battle. They agree to exchange gloves and wear them in their caps so they can find each other the next day. Bates calls them both fools and urges them to be friends, for there are plenty of Frenchmen for them to fight.

After the three soldiers leave, Henry is left alone with his thoughts. He talks about the custom of blaming everything upon the king and concludes that a slave has a better life than a king, for he can sleep soundly at night and not worry about affairs of state.

Sir Erpingham enters, finds the king, and tells him that his associates are waiting for him. He leaves, and alone once more, Henry prays to God, asking Him to fill his soldiers with courage. He also asks God not to recall the guilt of Henry's father concerning the death of Richard II because he has already made reparations and plans to do more.

Henry's brother Gloucester enters, and the king leaves with him.

The scene shifts to the French camp, where everyone is ready to go to battle. The sun has risen and it is time to begin. There follows a brief scene in French, loosely translated as follows:

Orl.:	The sun doth gild our armour; up, my lords!
Dau.:	Mount me on my horse; you, my valet, my lackey! ha!
Orl.:	Oh brave spirit!
Dau.:	Begone, water and earth.
Orl.:	Nothing more? only air and fire.
Dau.:	Heaven also, my cousin Orleans.

(This scene is a continuation or a conclusion of the last scene in Act III, when the Dauphin was discussing the merits of his horse, which, according to him, possesses only fire and air; he now adds to those qualities that of heaven also.) A messenger enters and says that the English forces are also ready, and the Constable gives the call to mount up. He and the others pity the small, beleaguered English forces and hope that they have said their prayers. He has so much confidence in his superior force that he is sure that the mere appearance of his army will cause the English to "crouch down in fear and yield." A French lord, Grandpré, enters and continues to ridicule the poor "bankrupt" and "beggar'd" condition of the Englishmen. Impatient for battle, the Constable grabs his banner and cries to his men to take the field.

In the English camp, Gloucester, Bedford, Exeter, Westmoreland, and Salisbury discuss the battle. There are five times as many French soldiers as there are Englishmen, and the French are fresh and rested. The Earl of Salisbury bids his friends goodbye, saying they may not meet again until they meet in heaven; he then exits to do battle.

The king enters and hears Westmoreland wish for ten thousand more English troops. In answer to Westmoreland, Henry says that if God plans for them to win, there will be greater glory with no more troops than these to share the honors with. He urges anyone who does not wish to fight to leave. Today is a day set aside for the celebration of the "Feast of Saint Crispian," and all of those English soldiers who survive the battle will be honored and remembered every Saint Crispian's Day. Henry promises that all of their names shall become household words and their deeds remembered "to the ending of the world." Every Englishman who fights with him shall be his brother, and all Englishmen who do not take part in the battle will hold their manhoods cheap on Saint Crispian's Day.

The Earl of Salisbury enters and warns the king that the French are ready to charge. Henry asks Westmoreland if he still wishes for more help. Westmoreland, inspired by the king's speech, is now willing to fight the French with only the king at his side.

The French herald, Montjoy, sent from the Constable, asks King Henry to surrender now, before the slaughter begins. The king is impatient and his speech is meant more for his troops than for the French herald: Henry and his troops will either defeat the French or die. Montjoy exits, taking the king's message back to the Constable. King Henry grants his cousin, the Duke of York, the privilege of leading the troops into battle.

On the battlefield, Pistol enters with a captured French soldier who mistakes Pistol for a gentleman of high quality. When Pistol asks for the Frenchman's name, he hears only *"O Seigneur Dieu!"* (O Lord God!). Pistol mistakes the French word "Dieu" for the Frenchman's name—"Dew." Pistol then rants and raves, causing the Frenchman to say: *"O, prenez miséricorde! ayez pitié de moi!"* (O, take mercy on me! Have pity for me.) Again, Pistol is confused; he thinks that the word "moi" means "moy," a coin of some denomination, and he asserts that he wants at least forty "moys" or else he will cut the Frenchman's throat. After further misunderstanding, Pistol calls for the Boy to come and translate. He then finds out that the man's name is Monsieur le Fer, and Pistol makes several puns on the English words "fer," "firk," and "ferret." Pistol then tells the Boy to tell the Frenchman that he is about to cut the Frenchman's throat immediately unless he is highly paid with English crowns. The Frenchman begs for mercy and his life, saying that he is from a good family who will pay well for his ransom—at least two hundred crowns. Pistol makes more threats and finally says that that amount will abate his passion. The Boy, however, translates Pistol's speech as follows: "[Pistol] says that it is against his oath to pardon any prisoner; however, for the sake of the two hundred crowns you have promised him, he is willing to allow you your freedom and your liberty." The French prisoner then responds: "I thank him on bended knees, a thousand thanks, and I consider myself lucky to have fallen into the hands of such a courtly gentleman—one who, I believe, must be the bravest, the most valiant, and the most distinguished nobleman in England." Pistol is satisfied and exits with his prisoner. Alone, the Boy comments upon the empty bravery and the hollow courage of Pistol, who roars like some devil from an old stage play. From the Boy, we also hear about the deaths of Nym and Bardolph and the prediction that his own fate is precarious since only boys like himself are left to guard the equipment.

In another part of the field, the Constable of France, the Dukes of Orleans and Bourbon, Lord Rambures, and the Dauphin realize that although they greatly outnumber the English forces, they are being defeated. There is much confusion on the battlefield, but they continue fighting, declaring their utter shame, realizing that in mere numbers, "We are [enough] yet living in the field / To smother up the English."

In another part of the battlefield, Henry notes that they seem to be winning ("Well have we done, thrice valiant countrymen"), and he asks about his kinsman, the Duke of York, whom he saw fighting and covered with blood. Exeter repeats York's last words and tells him in a moving speech how bravely York died. The Duke of York, wounded and dying, stumbled upon his noble cousin, the Earl of Suffolk, who lay dying. York took his cousin by the beard, kissed the gashes, and called upon Suffolk to tarry for a moment so they could die together. Then:

> So did he turn and over Suffolk's neck
> He threw his wounded arm and kiss'd his lips;

And so espoused to death, with blood he seal'd
A testament of noble-ending love.

(24–27)

Exeter tells how he wept like a woman at the sight, and King Henry is about to join "with mistful eyes" when, hearing an alarm, he realizes that the French have reinforced their armies, and he orders his men to kill all of the French prisoners.

In another part of the battlefield, Fluellen and Gower discuss Henry's order to kill all the French prisoners. Gower is delighted, and Fluellen compares the king to Alexander the Great.

The king and several associates enter, along with the French herald, Montjoy, who admits the French defeat and describes the carnage of the battlefield in great detail. The king declares that this victory will be remembered as the Battle of Agincourt. Fluellen expresses his love and loyalty to the king, and Williams enters and explains to the king that he is looking for his glove in someone else's cap; he is ready to fight the rascal if only he can find him. The king mischievously hands Fluellen his glove, telling him that he took it from the French Duke of Alençon. To make sure that there is no serious trouble, Henry sends Gloucester and Warwick to watch Fluellen and Williams; he will follow to observe the fun.

In another part of the field, Williams and Gower enter and then Fluellen enters and tells Gower of the king's order concerning him and suggests the possibility of a promotion. At the same time, Williams recognizes his glove in Fluellen's cap and strikes him. Examining the glove in Williams' hand, he recognizes it as the match to the glove of the French Duke of Alençon that King Henry has just given to him. He therefore assumes that Williams is some sort of traitor in league with Alençon, and they are about to fight when the Earl of Warwick and the Duke of Gloucester enter and stop the fight. The king and Exeter appear also, and Henry admits his part in the charade. Williams bravely confronts the king by saying it was the king's fault since the king was in disguise. Henry orders Williams' glove to be filled with coins.

An English herald enters with the casualty reports. Ten thousand French soldiers, including an exceptionally large number of French noblemen, have been slain. The English loss is miraculously light. Henry repeatedly gives all of the credit to God and orders a mass to be said. Afterward, he says, "To England then, / Where ne'er from France arriv'd more happy men."

Commentary

As before, the Chorus makes another apology for the limitations of the stage and the need for imagination on the part of the audience. In conformance with the Elizabethan tradition and Shakespeare's custom, there is no absurd effort to present a battle on the stage. Throughout Shakespeare's history plays, a few soldiers represent entire armies, but here, where England's ideal king is being presented, Shakespeare resorts to using the Chorus, urging and reminding the audience that they must imagine the two opposing camps at nighttime on the eve of the crucial Battle of Agincourt.

Shakespeare continues to depict the contrasting moods of the two camps. Again, as in the last act, the Chorus informs us that the French are overconfident and high spirited, whereas the English are so dejected that the king himself must wander through the camp, offering encouragement.

In the last scene of Act III, we saw how frivolous the French were with their light-hearted talk of horses, mistresses, and love poetry. Now, Act IV will open by contrasting the situation in the English camp.

Scene 1 serves, first, to emphasize the contrasting attitudes between the French camp—their joviality and overconfidence and superficiality—with the prevailing seriousness of the English camp. In contrast to the frivolity of the French, the entire scene in the English camp is essentially serious. Yet, there is an anticipation of great humor when the disguised king exchanges gloves with Williams and promises to meet him in a duel if they both survive today's battle; we anticipate Williams finding out that he was arguing with the very monarch for whom he is fighting.

The main purpose of Scene 1 is to further illuminate the character of King Henry on the night before the significant and decisive Battle of Agincourt. Any time that a king wraps himself in a cloak and goes among his men incognito, talking with the common soldiers, we have a very dramatic situation. Continuing a dramatic device of the earlier *Henry* plays, the rowdy and rebellious Prince Hal had to, at first, disguise himself to become a king; now as king, he disguises himself to become a common man. Now wrapped in the obscurity of a commoner's cloak and further obscured by the darkness of night, the king is able to learn the feelings of his common soldiers, represented not by the comic Pistol (who knew the king as Prince Hal) and not by the dedicated, if peculiar, Fluellen (and Gower) but as seen in the personages of John Bates, Alexander Court (even though this character speaks only eleven words in the entire play), and Michael Williams. Even the names "John Bates" and "Williams" suggest something of the basic nature of these good English soldiers—that is, this is the stuff of which an ideal Englishman is made and will help Henry win military glory for England.

Most critics value Scene 1 as proof of the greatness of Henry as a king—that is, it exhibits the simplicity and modesty, the democracy and the deep religious nature of the king. But Shakespeare no doubt hoped that his audience would be aware of some ambiguity in a situation in which the king is in darkness and is in disguise, suggesting that a man's actions by day are different from his words concealed by night. In the first act, the king was ready to place the responsibility for the war on the shoulders of the archbishop; here, when a common soldier suggests that the responsibility for the deaths of many Englishmen must rest on the conscience of the king, Henry vehemently denies this possibility. Williams maintains:

> But if the cause be not good, the King himself hath
> a heavy reckoning to make, when all those legs and
> arms and heads, chopped off in a battle, shall join
> together at the latter day and cry all, "We died at
> such a place."
>
> (140–44)

(Yet, at the same time that Williams makes this assertion, he also fully believes that it is the duty of the subject to obey: "To disobey were against all proportion of subjection.") To answer Williams, Henry eludes taking blame by this analogy: "So, if a son that is by his father sent about merchandise do sinfully miscarry upon the sea, the imputation of his wickedness, by your rule, should be imposed upon his father that sent him . . . " He further adds that "every subject's duty is the King's; but every subject's soul is his own." We see also that Henry believes that "the King is but a man, as I am. The violet smells to him as it doth to me. . . . His ceremonies laid by, in his nakedness he appears but a man; and though his affections are higher mounted than ours, yet, when they stoop, they stoop with the like wing." In other words, the king is like the common man except that he has more concerns, and when disaster or grief strikes, one man is the same as another.

In his soliloquy, Henry expresses the suffering he endures, and he pours forth his anguish and his sense of guilt for the crown that his father usurped; particularly, we sense his sorrow when he utters a final prayer, beginning "O God of battles." The sense of guilt that he feels for his father's crime against the preceding king (Richard II) is carefully scrutinized: "Not to-day, O Lord, / O, not to-day, think not upon the fault / My father made in compassing the crown!" (310–12). This passage alone, given in a soliloquy, ultimately attests to the deep religious nature of Henry V.

The remainder of Act IV reads, in part, like a pure chronicle—that is, Scene 2 is set in the French camp, and then we shift to the English camp in Scene 3, and then we have a comic interlude, and then we return to the French forces on the battlefield, and then to the English forces. As noted earlier, the frivolity of the French is contrasted with the seriousness of the English. The extended insults heaped upon the English by the arrogant French officers prepare the audience to relish even more the defeat of the French forces, which have shown such utter contempt for the English. The dramatic irony is that the audience knows what is going to happen, and the French forces are totally ignorant of their fate.

In the beginning of Scene 2, the Dauphin still speaks of his horse as being possessed of no such common elements as earth and water but of being made of pure air and fire, the same sentiments that he expressed in his last speech. In doing so, we now realize that the night has passed and, with the dawn, the battle is about to begin, and the French are still overconfident.

The opening of Scene 3 reestablishes for the audience the great odds against which the English are confronted. There are about sixty thousand French soldiers matched against somewhat less than twelve thousand Englishmen—five-to-one odds—and Westmoreland's wish for another ten thousand "of those men in England / That do no work to-day" (the battle was fought on a Sunday, and the majority of Englishmen would not be working on that day) allows Henry to enter and make his famous Saint Crispian's Day speech. (The battle was fought on the day set aside to honor two fourth-century saints—Saint Crispian and Saint Crispin—and both names are used by Henry during the course of his speech.) Henry's speech contrasts strongly in its dignity and manliness with the boastful frivolity of the French nobility.

In his speech, which is a superb rhetorical vehicle for theatrical declamation, Henry is able to rouse his soldiers to a high pitch of patriotism. He would not want to share the honor of this day with other men. The fewer men there are, the greater the honor will be to those who do fight. Furthermore, if any man does not want to fight, then

> Let him depart. . . .
> We would not die in that man's company . . .
> We few, we happy few, we band of brothers.
> For he to-day that sheds his blood with me
> Shall be my brother.
>
> (36, 38, 60–62)

Westmoreland then expresses this response to Henry's rousing speech: "Would you and I alone, / Without more help, could fight this royal battle!"

Henry is again given the opportunity to give a rousing speech when the French herald demands that Henry surrender himself for ransom. Henry reminds the envoy of the man who sold a lion's skin in advance but was subsequently killed while hunting the lion. Likewise, this very day might provide his English soldiers with new coats of lion skins:

> And my poor soldiers tell me, yet ere night
> They'll be in fresher robes, or they will pluck
> The gay new coats o'er the French soldiers' heads
> And turn them out of service.
>
> (116–19)

He assures the herald that the only ransom that the French will receive will be his bones ("joints"). On this note, the famous Battle of Agincourt begins.

Scene 4 is the first scene we have that deals directly with the battle that is taking place. Four more scenes dealing with the battle will follow. It is ironic, therefore, that our first knowledge of this key battle comes in the form of a comic interlude—that is, if some braggart so low, incompetent, cowardly, and as rascally as Pistol can capture a French soldier, then we must assume that the French are in total disarray and that the English are initially successful. It is further ironic that one of the greatest of cringing cowards is praised so highly by the French captive and is able to extort two hundred crowns; one wonders what the other soldiers, truly brave soldiers, are accomplishing. This scene, a comic interlude, is inserted here apparently because Shakespeare wanted to further emphasize the poetic irony of the French officers' having viewed the entire battle in such a frivolous manner and their looking upon the English so derisively.

The short Scene 5 is the second one dealing with the battle itself. It shows that the French are indeed being dispersed in spite of their great number. As is obvious, the main intent of the scene is to show the shame of the once boastful and arrogant French as they are being defeated by those "wretches that we played at dice for." The entire day, then, is nothing but "shame and eternal shame, nothing but shame!"

Scene 6 functions to announce the beginning of the English successes. Then it shifts its emphasis to narrate the death of the Duke of York, who has played only a small role in the drama, and the death of the Earl of Suffolk, who has not even appeared in the drama. This might seem confusing to the modern viewer, but from our knowledge of many of Shakespeare's history plays, some of the greatest moments are associated with a description of love and death; added to this is the bloody gore of the battlefield. Thus, in order to give a depth to the deaths of two who have played virtually no role in the development of the drama, this scene must be rendered within the context of a grim battle atmosphere.

Shakespeare's main purpose in Scene 6 is to show another aspect of Henry the King—one who can mourn and weep for his kinsmen and fellow soldiers fallen in battle and then, in the next moment, put aside all sense of personal loss and sternly command the deaths of all the French prisoners in order to ensure the safety of the English soldiers. This quality of decisiveness is the stuff which all great field commanders are made of (at least Shakespeare seems to be saying this). We see evidence of the complete presence of mind and control that Henry has in the midst of a raging battle and in the throes of passion because of the deaths of his kinsmen.

For many modern readers, Henry's command to kill all the French prisoners might seem extremely cruel and barbaric or savage, but unless Henry wants to be defeated and have all of his men put to death, he must execute the prisoners before they are freed or before they revolt. In terms of historical accuracy, Henry did not reportedly issue this order until he discovered that the French had massacred all of the young boys and lackeys left in charge of the English equipment in the camp.

Scene 7 is rather diverse and diffused in structure. The opening discussion by Fluellen and Gower over the senseless and unheard of slaying of the sick, the unarmed, the wounded, and, worst of all, innocent young boys by the French soldiers causes Henry's men to remark upon the king's sense of justice. Both Fluellen and Gower feel that such measures are absolutely justified, and in justifying them, Fluellen compares King Henry to Alexander the Great, one of the most bloody conquerors of the ancient world. Here, however, we should remember that whereas Henry is trying to establish an imperialism, Alexander was at a loss to know what to do when there were no more lands to conquer; for that reason, the analogy to Alexander is not necessarily a flattering one.

King Henry's appearance on the stage shows his incensed rage over the massacre of the young English boys: "I was not angry since I came to France / Until this instant" (58–59). His anger leads him to utter threats of harshness and inhumanity, and he threatens to kill those not yet captured if his orders are not obeyed. However, when he is assured of victory, his humility is restored in the moment when he gives full and complete credit for the victory to God: "Praised be God, and not our strength, for it!" At this point in the battle, Henry is still willing to carry on his private joke with Williams, the character he promised to do battle with if they were both alive after the day's battle. Instead, however, he gives the glove to Fluellen, a man whom he admires greatly, and then sends others to see that no real harm ensues.

Scene 8 concludes the comic incident involving King Henry's encounter with the common soldier Williams before the battle when they swapped gloves and promised to fight. Many prudish critics, forgetting what a penchant for a practical joke Prince Hal formerly possessed, criticize Henry for his handling of this situation. After all, there was a *promised* rendezvous between Henry and Williams; if they both were alive after the battle, they would fight, and Williams is willing to uphold his promise, but King Henry makes light of his own promise. Those who object to Henry not living up to his word of honor have no sense of comedy, or the Renaissance, or no sense of the concepts of honor as they were understood by the Elizabethan audience. It would be completely out of character for the king to enter into combat with one of his own soldiers; furthermore, it would be treasonous for a soldier to enter into combat with the king. When the king accuses Williams of abusing the person of the king, Williams boldly defends himself before the king:

> Your Majesty came not like yourself; you appeared
> to me but as a common man; witness the night,
> your garments, your lowliness; and what your
> Highness suffered under that shape, I beseech you
> take it for your own fault and not mine.
>
> (53-57)

For such an honest answer, Henry awards the soldier a glove filled with crowns. Fluellen, who has just been struck by Williams, now realizes that the soldier "has mettle enough in his belly" and offers some additional money, but his offer is refused by the good, honest Williams.

When the French and English dead are numbered and the tally is brought to King Henry, consistent with his character as Shakespeare has presented it, Henry once again takes no glory for himself but, instead, dedicates his miraculous victory to the will of God. Here, then, is the Christian king, proud of his human victory, but still humble before God as he, in a single speech, gives all credit to God, four times (111-25).

In Scene 8, we again see King Henry as a multi-dimensional man—a man among men enjoying a good jest, as a royal king receiving the miraculous news of his overwhelming victory, and as a model Christian ruler, placing his honors subservient before the might of God.

ACT V

Summary

As in the other four acts, the Chorus enters and asks the audience once again to imagine certain events. After the last act, Henry left France, crossed the English Channel, and set out for London. Many of his lords tried to convince him to let "his bruised helmet and his bended sword" go before him, as was the custom of the ancient Caesar upon returning victorious. Henry refused, believing that it might detract from the glory of God, to whom he attributes the victory. All of London poured out to acclaim him. The Holy Roman Emperor even came to England to try and arrange a peace, but he was unsuccessful, and now the audience must use its imagination once again and picture Henry now in France.

In the English camp, Gower asks Fluellen why he is wearing a leek when the Welsh national day to do so has passed. Fluellen explains that he is looking for that "rascally, scald, beggarly, lousy" Pistol, who made derogatory insinuations about the Welsh people's national custom of wearing leeks to commemorate "Davy," their patron saint. Pistol enters, and Fluellen immediately begins to berate him in fierce language; he orders him to eat the leek, and when Pistol refuses at first, he is roundly beaten by Fluellen until he agrees to eat it. When he falters, Fluellen spurs him on with more wallops until Pistol has eaten the entire leek. After Fluellen leaves, Pistol says of him: "All hell shall stir for this." Gower then verbally scathes him and leaves in disgust. Alone, Pistol is dejected because he has just heard that his wife, Hostess Quickly, has died of "the French malady" (syphilis), and Pistol has no place to go—he is finished, he says, and decides to turn to a life of stealing.

Scene 2 takes place in the French palace. King Henry and his court greet the King and Queen of France, Princess Katharine, and other French nobility. The queen urges that they talk of love and not of war. The Duke of Burgundy makes a long speech about the virtues of peace, to which Henry responds that only if all his demands are met is such a peace possible. Henry appoints a group to discuss his conditions with the King of France: Exeter, Clarence, Gloucester, Warwick, and Huntingdon. The queen volunteers to go along to help with the settlement, leaving King Henry alone with Katharine and her gentlewoman, Alice.

In this love scene in which Henry woos Katharine, the king's tone is gently mocking, and yet it is apparent that he is quite serious in his courting. He tells Katharine that he is an athlete and a soldier, but he is not a poet who can speak cleverly to win her love. Katharine seems hesitant, so Henry tells her that they will rule all of England and France and bear a son. When Katharine finally agrees, Henry tries to kiss her hand, which she claims is unworthy. He then tries to kiss her lips but is told that it is not the custom for maids to kiss before marriage. The king tells Katharine that they will *set* the customs—not *follow* them—and with that, he kisses her lips.

The French king and his advisors reenter. After some bantering exchanges between the Duke of Burgundy and Henry over Katharine's blushing, Henry asks if Kate shall be his wife. The acquiescence to this first demand must be met before any other aspects of the treaty can even be discussed. The French king agrees to the marriage, noting that Kate will bear sons to rule England and France. Henry seals the agreement by kissing Kate in front of all and orders preparations for the marriage to be made. Then there will be a gathering of all the other lords in order to work out the details of the treaty.

The Chorus enters and ends the play, explaining that the events on the stage were mightier than could be actually portrayed. Henry and Katharine did produce a son, Henry the Sixth, whose story is told in other plays.

Commentary

For many critics, Act V is not an integral part of the drama of *King Henry V.* Many see the real intent and the true action of the play as having ended with the victory of the Battle of Agincourt and find the entire last act to be superfluous, an anticlimax to the real intent of the play. However, Shakespeare was approaching the very height of his dramatic powers, and the act should be read for his intention and not for mere "plot."

For the critics who object to the final act, one can only quote the famous eighteenth-century critic Dr. Samuel Johnson, who says of this scene: "The comic scenes of the history of Henry the Fourth and Fifth are now at an end, and all the comic personages are now dismissed. Falstaff and Mrs. Quickly are dead; Nym and Bardolph are hanged; Gadshill was lost immediately after the robbery; Poins and Peto have vanished since, one knows not how; and Pistol is now beaten into obscurity. I believe every reader regrets their departure." Seemingly, Shakespeare knew that his audience would feel suspended if he did not give an account of the last of the group, bringing to a conclusion his story of a group of the most delightful and some of the most depraved low people in all of his dramas. The final picture of Pistol makes us not want to see this surly braggart any more, and yet we feel some compassion toward him because of the depths to which he has fallen. He is left empty of purse and devoid of friends, contemplating a career of masquerading as a wounded veteran in order to cheat and wheedle and steal.

Depending upon the mood of the reader or viewer, the love scene between Henry and Kate can either be the most charming reason for the existence of the fifth act or an absurd travesty on the theme of love. One possible objection to the scene is that the conditions for the treaty between France and England depend on Henry's insistence that Kate must first be his wife. No other terms are to be even considered until it is agreed that she will be his wife, and therefore, the wooing of Kate is an artificial pretense since it is a foregone conclusion before the wooing that Kate will be Henry's wife.

Yet, for most people, this is one of the most delightful love scenes that Shakespeare ever wrote. Theater conventions demand that we forget that all sorts of political intrigues and machinations are going on; Burgundy, the French king and queen, and the English counselors are tending to the political aspects, leaving Henry onstage to expose the audience to another side of his personality. We have seen Henry as a common man moving among men, as an administrator, as a judge both merciful and strict as the occasion demanded, and we have also seen him (or heard of him) as a superb warrior. Now, we see him in a new light—as the lover who woos and sues for the hand in marriage of the lovely young Katharine, Princess of France.

Even if Henry knows that all conclusions are foregone in regard to Katharine, yet the thrill is in the lovemaking itself. He will win her to him regardless of the political affiliations, and it is to this purpose that he begins his direct and simple wooing, filled with charm and wit and good-natured teasing. He pretends that he is not the person to speak fancifully of love, and yet he wins the lady's heart with his fanciful speaking.

Henry maintains that if Katharine's love depends on his performing some physical feat, then he would quickly win her, but he cannot muster up the proper words for doing so; yet his very words *do* win her over. Finally, he pretends to be plain spoken, and yet he uses language and ideas that dazzle the young lady. In conclusion, the final aspect of Henry that is presented to the audience is that of the successful lover. If the theater critics and drama analysts object to the fifth act, the audience leaves the theater wholly delighted with Henry's success in love.

The Chorus in the Epilogue simply reminds the audience once again that the stage has not been adequate for the subject matter, but then no stage could be large enough for an adequate presentation of the man who is the ideal king, the mirror of all Christian kings.

1613

henry viii

HENRY VIII

LIST OF CHARACTERS

Henry VIII

King of England; married to Katherine of Aragon, then to Anne Bullen (historically spelled "Boleyn"); father of Elizabeth I.

Duke of Buckingham

An opponent of Wolsey; he is accused of high treason against the king and is executed.

Cardinal Wolsey

An ambitious commoner who manipulates his way up the hierarchy of power and becomes the king's most powerful adviser; he dies before he can be brought to trial.

Queen Katherine

The daughter of King Ferdinand and Queen Isabella of Spain; wife of Henry VIII; a noble, elegant, dignified woman who is victimized in a foreign country by a system in search of a male heir for Henry VIII.

Earl of Surrey

The Duke of Buckingham's son-in-law; before the duke is executed, Surrey is sent off to Ireland by Wolsey so as not to present a threat; he returns to see Wolsey's downfall.

Gardiner

The Bishop of Winchester; a petty, ambitious man who attempts to drive Cranmer out of favor.

Cromwell

A servant to Wolsey; he is instructed by Wolsey to serve the king well; Henry makes him Master of the Jewel House and of the Privy Council; he becomes Henry's new secretary.

Cardinal Campeius

The pope's emissary from Rome; he arrives in London to assess Henry's proposed divorce from Katherine.

Anne Bullen (Boleyn)

A knight's daughter; lady-in-waiting to Queen Katherine; Henry falls in love with her and secretly marries her before his divorce from Katherine; Anne gives birth to the future Queen Elizabeth I.

Cranmer

The newly appointed Archbishop of Canterbury; he becomes Henry's closest adviser at the end of the play.

SUMMARIES AND COMMENTARIES

PROLOGUE

The playwright tells his audience that he no longer comes to make them laugh. His subject in this new production is "sad, high," and "full of state and woe." Nobility is what he intends to present, in a way that will command pity. Most assuredly, he stresses, this play is *not* a comedy or even an "entertaining" play; anyone who expects such a piece "will be deceived." Shakespeare urges his audience to be sad and to consider the people onstage as if they were real beings, not fictitious characters.

The Prologue is used to shape the audience's emotional frame of mind before the drama begins. Here, Shakespeare's primary point is: be prepared for a sad story in which noble people do unnoble things. *Henry VIII* is by no means a coherent drama; it is a succession of fine dramatic moments, but it lacks unity. An awareness of this fact will help readers move more easily through the various scenes.

ACT I

Summary

The Dukes of Buckingham and Norfolk discuss their last meeting in France. Buckingham was in his room, ill, but Norfolk witnessed the rendezvous between King Henry VIII and King Francis I of France. It was a stunning moment of earthly glory when the kings saluted one another on horseback and grew close in an embrace. Everyone was resplendent with sparkling gold, "like heathen gods"; even the dwarfish pages resembled gilt cherubs.

The kings were "equal in lustre" ("no discerner / Durst wag his tongue in censure"). Cardinal Wolsey arranged this royal meeting, and Buckingham expresses open disdain for the man: "No man's pie is freed / From his ambitious finger." He recalls that Wolsey is the son of a butcher, not a nobleman, and that he monopolizes the king at everyone else's expense.

The dukes analyze the much-hated Wolsey: He has no noble ancestry that might have given him such a position in society; he has accomplished nothing spectacular for the crown; and he has no connections with high-ranking officials. He is a self-made man ("Spider-like, out of his self-drawing web, he gives us note; the force of his own merit makes his way"). Foremost, he suffers from the excess of pride, a poison that seeps through every part of him. He even took it upon himself to appoint the officials who attended the king in his meeting with Francis I.

Buckingham knows of many people who ruined themselves by spending their estates on expensive clothing for the event. Norfolk believes that the trip cost more than the peace they sought. Moreover, the storm that followed their arrival in France foreboded a breach in the peace: "France hath flawed the league, and hath attached [seized] / Our merchants' goods at Bordeaux."

The fact that the peace was aborted by the French emphasizes the superfluousness of Wolsey's actions: At a very great expense, the English have ruined themselves in the plan and have nothing to show for it. But Wolsey is powerful and has the ministers in his control.

Wolsey enters, stays but a moment, and exchanges contemptuous glances with Buckingham. After Wolsey leaves, Buckingham becomes angry and starts to follow him, but Norfolk convinces him to be reasonable: "Heat not a furnace for your foe so hot / That it do singe yourself." Buckingham agrees but insists on exposing Wolsey to the king. He resents the fact that Wolsey "does buy and sell his honour as he pleases / And for his own advantage."

Brandon and a Sergeant-at-Arms arrive to arrest Buckingham for high treason. The duke knows that his days are numbered: Clearly Wolsey is behind all this and will scheme to bring harm to the duke. A word from Wolsey is enough to end anyone's life, and so Buckingham says to Brandon: "I am the shadow of poor Buckingham, / Whose figure even this instant cloud puts on / By darkening my clear sun" (I. i. 224–26).

The king enters, leaning on Wolsey's shoulder. He prepares to hear testimony concerning Buckingham's treason, but Queen Katherine enters with Norfolk and Suffolk. She is there to defend Buckingham. She explains that Henry's subjects are "in great grievance" over Wolsey's policies, that he has damaged the citizens' loyalty to the crown, and that rebellion is at hand. Wolsey is present as she presents her arguments, and she is careful to point out that the people are equally angered by their king—mostly because he gives such power to Wolsey.

Norfolk cries out that the taxations are intolerable and that tradesmen of all sorts are desperately poor. The king claims no knowledge of such taxes ("What taxation?") and requests an explanation from Wolsey. The latter suggests that he knows only about "a single part," one small aspect of the taxes. Katherine, however, argues that the taxes "are devised by you." One sixth of the common people's earnings is levied by the government, apparently to support the wars in France.

Henry is not pleased with what he hears. But Wolsey is shrewd to point out that he himself has only a single vote and that all such matters must pass through the hands of learned judges. His scorn for the people is clear: He insists that the government must not stint on quality or in its plans simply because a group of critics wishes to protest. Already it is obvious that Wolsey seeks to impose his own desires on the king, but Henry shows signs of independence. He does not want his subjects to be treated unfairly: "We must not rend our subjects from our laws / And stick them in our will." The idea of such taxation horrifies Henry. There is no precedent for such taxation, he says; thus, he orders that free pardons be given to every man who has denied the validity of Wolsey's taxation. The commissions shall be heeded. In an aside, Wolsey tells his secretary to word the letters so that the people will think that he, Wolsey, intervened on their behalf.

Katherine then returns to the subject of Buckingham's arrest. She regrets that such an event has occurred, and Henry agrees with her, but he says that he thinks that Buckingham's noble features have turned sour. He fears that the duke poses a threat to the monarchy:

> He, my lady,
> Hath into monstrous habits put the graces
> That once were his, and is become as black
> As if besmeared in hell.
>
> (I. ii. 121–24)

A surveyor who once worked for Buckingham is brought into the room and told to recount what he knows about Buckingham. The man begins, "It was usual with him, every day / It would infect his speech, that if the King / Should without issue die, he'll carry it so / To make the sceptre his." In other words, Buckingham is believed to want the throne. The surveyor adds that Buckingham has sworn to seek revenge on Wolsey.

Katherine sheds light on the surveyor's character: He was once hired by Buckingham and was fired because of his unpopularity with the tenants. But Henry wants to hear more; he is angered by the possibility that Buckingham may have uttered threatening or treasonous statements about himself or Wolsey. He has made up his mind. Buckingham is guilty of treason. Henry orders the duke to stand trial: "If he may / Find mercy in the law, 'tis his; if none, / Let him not seek it of us."

Scene 4 takes place in York Place, where there is a small table for Wolsey and a longer table for guests. Sir Henry Guildford announces that good fun—good company, good wine—is to be had by all. Lord Sandys jokes lightly that good fun is "as easy as a down-bed." Sir Thomas Lovell notes that Sandys ought to be their confessor—Sandys remarks that he would grant "easy penance." The Lord Chamberlain then begins to seat people at the table and places Sandys between two women.

Anne Bullen (Anne Boleyn's surname is spelled "Bullen" in this play) is seated beside Sandys. When she makes a comment concerning Sandys' father's "madness," he impulsively kisses her.

Wolsey enters then and decrees that pleasure will be the rule of the evening: "That noble lady / Or gentleman that is not freely merry / Is not my friend."

A drum and trumpet sound. Wolsey learns that, seemingly, a barge of French ambassadors has arrived, and so he sends the Lord Chamberlain (since he speaks French) to greet them. Within moments, the king enters with others, all disguised as shepherds, and salutes the cardinal, pretending not to speak English. They claim to have chosen this party since it is reputed to be an exciting event. The "ambassadors" select ladies to dance with, and, significantly, the king chooses Anne Bullen.

Wolsey guesses that the king is present, and so Henry unmasks for him and asks about Anne Bullen. He is told that she is one of Katherine's attendants. Henry is obviously taken with her: "By heaven, she is a dainty one." Thus, he takes full advantage of the epicurean theme of the evening—eat, drink, and be merry—dancing feverishly and enjoying his drink.

Commentary

Like many opening scenes, Scene 1 is an exposition in which Shakespeare quickly sets the stage for future action. We learn of King Henry VIII's trip to France to meet with Francis I and that a storm has augured badly, hovering above a breach of peace and suggesting that Wolsey is to be feared.

The pomp and glory associated with the king's entourage soon fade into the distance as Shakespeare punctures the facade and bears open the heart of his drama: the battle against the evils of power-hungry individuals. The expensive clothing has cost the English nobles dearly, and the cost may have ruined their meager fortunes. Shakespeare's message is this: External possessions are less significant than internal peace. All the money in England cannot purchase Henry's freedom or happiness; the latter will be obtained only by resolution of mind and determination. And, by the same token, the money spent by the spectators of Henry's encounter with Francis is ultimately meaningless. The meeting accomplishes little; their lavish expenditures serve no real and lasting purpose.

The contempt for Wolsey is clear from the very start. He has manipulated his way into the chambers of power through unscrupulous, self-centered means. No one is sacred to him, not even the king, and the people of England resent this deeply. Moreover, Wolsey is a commoner like them, and jealousy is no small factor in their emotions toward him. Now, Wolsey is seemingly responsible for Buckingham's arrest—before Buckingham can expose Wolsey's evil, ambitious designs toward Henry.

In Scene 1, we see Wolsey through the eyes of other people (Norfolk and Buckingham, for example). They find him despicable and vile. In Scene 2, we see Wolsey in person and discover that he is all that the others have described him as being. He manipulates and contorts reality to suit his own purposes, such as with the fraudulent letter to the citizens. He is low, common, and bereft of dignity. He has exerted himself in ways that the king does not fully realize the seriousness of (the taxation), and this is proof of Wolsey's evil interests: money and power.

Henry, on the other hand, is clearly to blame for not knowing more about his governmental affairs. His father, Henry VII, was notorious for his interest in the details of political events around him. Henry VIII, in contrast, is more of a renaissance man in that he finds excitement in a wide variety of pursuits unrelated to politics. But if Henry is somewhat misinformed about his government's policies, he is nonetheless a humanitarian: He stands up for the fair treatment of his people and orders an end to the outrageous taxation in effect at that time.

Katherine makes her first appearance in Scene 2. Her regal entrance is announced by a chorus chanting "Room for the Queen!" When she arrives, her composure and dignity fill the air. She is something to behold, a moving presence whose aristocratic demeanor offers a bold contrast to the lowly Cardinal Wolsey. Katherine is a noble. He is not. And since she represents justice and human rights, she immediately earns our respect and admiration.

The short Scene 3 serves only one purpose: It tells us that there is to be a large supper at Cardinal Wolsey's York Place that evening and that many lords and ladies will be in attendance.

In Scene 4, in the absence of the king, Wolsey plays his "pseudo-royal" role to the fullest. He commands total devotion and enters the room as if he were royalty. But there is an aura of viciousness about him, and one suspects that the guests nearby are no doubt intimidated. They refer to him as "my lord," yet when King Henry enters the room, this is, ironically, the very term that Wolsey uses with him. There is no question that Wolsey would like to be the most powerful man in the kingdom. But Wolsey has flaws and will make error after error in his attempt at ascension.

Henry is quick to notice Wolsey's ambitions: "You hold a fair assembly; you do well, lord. / You are a churchman, or, I'll tell you, Cardinal, / I should judge now unhappily." In other words, the king expresses an awareness of Wolsey's grand style, and there is a hint of warning against Wolsey's growing authority. Clearly, the king *alone* reigns victorious, and anyone attempting to supplant him should be aware of the consequences.

ACT II

Summary

Two gentlemen in a street in Westminster discuss the fate of Buckingham. One of them was present at the trial and announces that the duke was found guilty; Buckingham, he says, was condemned to execution after his surveyor, his chancellor (Sir Gilbert Peck), his confessor (John Car), and that "devil-monk," Hopkins, all "accused him strongly." Not surprisingly, his peers found him guilty of high treason.

But Buckingham held up well under the strain; he pleaded not guilty. It was not death that he feared but rather the idea of dying for such an injustice.

It is conjectured that Wolsey is behind Buckingham's indictment. Certainly he wasted no time in arresting the Earl of Kildare, Deputy of Ireland, for maladministration. In his place, he sent off the Earl of Surrey, Buckingham's son-in-law (lest he would help Buckingham); with the latter in Ireland, perhaps Wolsey will not be threatened by an attempt to reverse what he has done to Buckingham.

The second gentleman protests openly about Wolsey: "All the commons / Hate him perniciously, and, o' my conscience, / Wish him ten fathom deep." Moments before his death, Buckingham now appears before the people. He explains to them that he is innocent of the alleged crime. It is not the law, however, that he condemns since the process of law has been duly followed. On the contrary, it is those who manipulated the law whom Buckingham resents. Yet he departs in peace, asking his supporters to help elevate his soul to heaven. "I forgive all. . . . No black envy shall mark my grave."

Buckingham says that he has nothing but praise and love for the king. He wishes him many long years of successful rule. But he says that eventually truth will avenge this wrongdoing. His father, Henry of Buckingham, had revolted in protest against King Richard, the usurper. He was found guilty without the benefit of a trial, but Henry VII restored the Duke of Buckingham to his present position, thereby making his name noble again. Now Henry VIII, by "one stroke," has taken him "forever from the world."

Ironically, both Buckinghams have fallen by their servants, "by those men we loved most." The duke advises his listeners not to be too liberal with their love and trust in others. People tend to remain faithful only when the fortunes are vast.

When the duke is led off, the two unnamed gentlemen resume their conversation. The second one whispers the rumor that Henry and Katherine are about to separate; it seems, though, that when Henry heard the rumor, he sent a command to the Lord Mayor that it be stopped. The gentleman suspects that Wolsey has planted the desire for separation in the king's mind "out of malice." In order to confirm the rumor, Cardinal Campeius has arrived. The first gentleman concludes that it was indeed the plotting of Wolsey that is at stake here: He is angry with the emperor (Charles V of Spain, Emperor of the Holy Roman Empire) for not bestowing on him the archbishopric of Toledo.

The Lord Chamberlain meets with the Dukes of Norfolk and Suffolk to discuss Wolsey. Wolsey, they say, has ruined England's relationship with the emperor and has now succeeded in governing the king's thoughts. Norfolk refers sarcastically to Wolsey as "the king-cardinal." Only when the king gets Wolsey out of his life, says Suffolk, will he be able to think rationally.

The king is worried about his marriage, and Wolsey makes things worse by planting fears and suspicions. According to Norfolk, Wolsey "dives into the King's soul, and there scatters / Dangers, doubts, wringing of the conscience, / Fears, and despairs; and all these for his marriage."

Norfolk is supportive of Katherine; she has been a loving wife to Henry for twenty years and hardly merits this kind of treatment. He suggests that something must be done about Wolsey before the

latter reduces everyone "into what pitch he please." Suffolk is neither afraid nor enamored of Wolsey. He believes that eventually
Wolsey will be dealt with by the pope.

Norfolk and Suffolk then enter the king's chambers, hoping
to cheer him as he meditates. Henry, however, is disturbed—and
angry—that they have dared to come on business while he is trying
to relax and read. Just then, Wolsey arrives and is welcomed; hope-
fully he can soothe his (the king's) "wounded conscience"; Norfolk
and Suffolk are ordered away.

Cardinal Campeius has accompanied Wolsey, and Henry thanks
the cardinal for coming, and Campeius responds by saying that his
commission to investigate the divorce will provide an "unpartial
judging of this business." As for Katherine's defense in the trial,
Wolsey has "arranged" for scholars (that is, lawyers) to argue her
case; Henry agrees. He wants the best. When Gardiner, the king's
new secretary, is called into the room, Wolsey beckons him aside
and reminds him that he is "the king's now." Gardiner understands
but vows to remain faithful to Wolsey's wishes despite his new link
to the king.

In an ante-chamber of the queen's apartments, Anne Bullen and
a character simply designated as an old lady talk glowingly about
Katherine. They believe that it is a crime that anyone so flawless
should be tossed aside after twenty years of marriage. Anne thinks
it is better "to be lowly born" and happy than to be noble and miserable and "wear a golden sorrow." Says Anne, ironically: "By my troth
and maidenhead, / I would not be a queen." But the old lady snaps
back at her that she is being a hypocrite, that she would gladly
be a queen if given the opportunity, for she has a "woman's heart,"
which, by nature, sets great store for "eminence, wealth, [and]
sovereignty."

But Anne still claims that she would want nothing to do with
being a queen, "not for all the riches under heaven." The old lady
scoffs, and Anne repeats her vow.

The Lord Chamberlain passes by and relates to Anne that the
king is very much interested in her:

> . . . the King's Majesty
> Commends his good opinion of you, and
> Does purpose honour to you no less flowing
> Than Marchioness of Pembroke; to which title

A thousand pound a year, annual support,
Out of his grace he adds.

(II. iv. 60–65)

Anne is not sure that she is worthy of a king's favors ("More than my
all is nothing"), but she sends her "thanks" and "obedience" to
Henry. In an aside, Chamberlain confesses that he has examined
Anne closely and that she is both beautiful and honorable, one from
whom "may proceed a gem / To lighten all this isle"—that is, the
infant Elizabeth I.

Scene 4 takes place in a hall in Black-Friars. It is the courtroom
that will house the divorce hearings. Several people, including the
Archbishop of Canterbury, the two cardinals (Wolsey and
Campeius), some noblemen, bishops, and the royal couple, enter
the chamber.

When the proceedings begin, Katherine kneels at Henry's feet
and begs that he do her justice:

. . . bestow your pity on me; for
I am a most poor woman, and a stranger,
Born out of your dominions, having here
No judge indifferent, nor no more assurance
Of equal friendship and proceeding.

(II. iv. 14–18)

Quite clearly, Katherine does not understand how she has offended
Henry. She has been a true and humble wife, faithful at all times to
the king. Whenever Henry wanted to make love to her, she was willing. Her marriage to Henry has been deemed lawful by a wise council, so why should he now choose to abandon her?

Katherine pleads for time to consult with her friends in Spain.
Wolsey tells her that she doesn't need to; the lawyers present for her
defense are "reverend fathers" of her own choice. He is, of course,
lying since it was *he* who chose them. To this, she replies:

Sir,
I am about to weep; but, thinking that
We are a queen, or long have dream'd so, certain
The daughter of a king, my drops of tears
I'll turn to sparks of fire.

(II. iv. 69–73)

She reproaches Wolsey for being arrogant and asserts openly that he is her enemy. She condemns him for spreading this turmoil through the land and for bringing about the separation between Henry and herself:

> I utterly abhor, yea, from my soul
> Refuse you for my judge; whom, yet once more,
> I hold my most malicious foe, and think not
> At all a friend to truth.
>
> (II. iv. 81–84)

Wolsey tries to cheapen her by casting doubt on her character and by suggesting that she has lost touch with herself. He plays the solemn, pious man of God, but she rejects his words and retorts that his "heart / Is crammed with arrogancy, spleen, and pride." Wolsey's meek and humble behavior do not fool Katherine. She requests that her case be reviewed by the pope.

Katherine leaves then despite attempts to keep her there. Henry admits that she is a lovely wife and queen, "the queen of earthly queens." He confesses that she has carried herself nobly in this difficult task. He then turns to Wolsey and frees him from all responsibility for this divorce matter. To conclude the scene, he pronounces a lengthy explanation of his original reasons for considering a divorce: He was determined to have a male heir ("I weighed the danger which my realms stood in / By this my issue's fail") and realized the necessity for marrying another woman. The Bishops (Lords) of Lincoln and Canterbury give him their support.

In a final aside, Henry utters contempt for the entire process. He abhors the power of Rome and welcomes the return of Cranmer (who will eventually become Henry's chief adviser as Archbishop of Canterbury); Cranmer, he feels sure, will be able to bring him the right decision.

Commentary

Scene 1 is vital for two reasons: It depicts the Duke of Buckingham as an honest, righteous man whose death is unjust and whose destiny, it seems, will be revenged; but it also assumes as a fact that the cardinal will have his will and that Katherine "must fall." Her marriage to Henry is no small matter, however, and if Wolsey thinks himself powerful enough to manipulate the lives of royalty, then he must prepare for the worst: Destiny will deal its own blow; it is only a question of time before true justice reigns.

Wolsey has now scored two evil victories—he thinks—over potential adversaries. He has eliminated Buckingham (but not the Earl of Surrey, his son-in-law), and he has made plans for the removal of Katherine. Katherine's nephew is Emperor Charles V of the Holy Roman Empire, an immensely powerful figure of the day. When Wolsey was overlooked for an important archbishopric position, he used the occasion to get even with Charles. But since the act was initiated out of malice, not justice, only malice can result from it.

Early in Act II, the stage is set for a devastating blow to Wolsey. It graphically shows the fragility of English power and the deceptiveness that can grow out of deceit: Seemingly, Wolsey is extremely powerful; in fact, his days are numbered.

Note that Buckingham remains faithful to the king until his final moments. This is typical of the times: Royalty was at the very center of people's lives.

Katherine has already made an appearance, and we have seen her to be sympathetic, justly outraged, and noble. Let us now watch for her reactions to the idea of divorce, for herein lies the most moving thrust of the drama.

In Scene 2, notice the swift transition from Buckingham's death to the divorce trial. The death helps us see clearly the injustices attendant in Wolsey's "regime," and the upcoming process of divorce will serve to undo everything that Wolsey has contrived.

Wolsey ever more deeply immerses himself into trouble in this scene. We discover that he intends to further sabotage the trial of Katherine and Henry's divorce hearings by selecting lawyers who will not defend Katherine properly.

The scene also reveals Henry in a slightly new light. He is annoyed and irascible when the two dukes—Norfolk and Suffolk—approach his chambers; he is not the lighthearted, affable renaissance man of whom we often read. In particular, his dependence on Wolsey is a mystery. He shows no signs of intellectual awareness or objectivity about this relationship, and he seems completely vulnerable to Wolsey's wishes.

It is this vulnerability that Shakespeare seeks to highlight. Henry is still young, and he must learn to analyze personal and political intrigues for himself. Dependence on anyone—especially on a man (Wolsey) with misguided religious importance—can be fatal to a national leader. Quite obviously, self-respect and clarity of thought are necessary in order to establish a firm reign. Elizabeth I will show this to be true.

Scene 3 advances the plot by practically naming Anne Bullen as the chosen favorite of the king for his next queen. Of note here is the fact that Anne is genuinely uncomfortable with the idea of accepting the role of Henry's queen. But she is dutiful toward Henry, and she accepts with gratitude the praise that Chamberlain offers her. Anne is a sympathetic young woman whose devotion to Katherine is real. There is no sign of envy, malice, or social climbing; Anne is simple and beautiful—and about to become Henry's new queen.

In Scene 4, Katherine presents her own defense in a logical and moving fashion. Her arguments are neither maudlin nor unreasonable; she wishes, very simply, to know why she has been rejected after so many years of fidelity. She is a noble, beautiful woman with admirers throughout the land. There is no question that the theater audience is in full support of her and empathizes with her struggle for dignity. Significantly, Katherine's pride is a healthy, worthy pride unlike that of Wolsey's. Pride, for Wolsey, amounts to little more than unlimited ambition.

Henry is quite wrong about Wolsey. In a speech in which he excuses Wolsey from all involvement in the plan to divorce Katherine, he states,

> You ever
> Have wished the sleeping of this business; never
>   desired
> It to be stirred; but oft have hindred, oft,
> The passages made toward it.
>
> (II. iv. 162–65)

We know, however, that the opposite is true, that Wolsey has manipulated the divorce from the very beginning. So now we have both Henry and Katherine as victims of Wolsey's malice: Katherine is victimized by Wolsey's choice of lawyers, and Henry is duped by a sophisticated scheme of which he has no awareness. If Henry is not up-to-date on the country's taxation policies, it is not likely that he would know much about Wolsey's involvement in the divorce, a highly sensitive and secretive sort of negotiation.

Wolsey is a hypocrite par excellence. Katherine discerns his evil, but he cleverly parries with a woe-is-me approach. His appeal to those around him takes place on an emotionally subtle level: He seeks their sympathy and wants them to identify with him in this moment when he hopes that they will see an obviously disturbed woman making blind accusations about his hypocrisy. Yet, which person in the room is not also guilty of hypocrisy? It is not difficult for them to lend support to their "role model."

Scene 4 offers a vivid study in human trust, pitting Henry's faith in Katherine against his dependence on Wolsey. Both "competitors" for the king's favor appeal to his sense of equity and justice, yet this is done in two different ways: Katherine is clearly honest; Wolsey is very clearly dishonest. Katherine's arguments are based on truth, Wolsey's on desire and ambition. Since Henry is inclined to believe the arguments offered by a man, Wolsey, he is thus blinded by the man's lies. The more Wolsey distorts the truth, the more thoroughly Henry sides with him. Shakespeare's message is obvious: Even kings can be idiotic fools—and they have a responsibility to know what is going on in their kingdom and look out for the best interests of their people.

Henry seems still to be in love with Katherine, but he is desperate for a male heir and, thus, is attracted to Anne Bullen. But this does not prevent him from recalling the past and admitting to Katherine's virtues:

> That man in the world who shall report he has
> A better wife, let him in nought be trusted
> For speaking false in that. Thou art alone
> . . . .
> The queen of earthly queens.
>
> (II. iv. 134–41)

Ironically, Wolsey thinks he has selected a better wife for Henry—if we can believe Henry's words in the above passage, he ought not to trust Wolsey. Yet trust him he does.

Act II advances the plot, for the most part, emotionally; the audience feels protective of Katherine, bitter about Wolsey, and disapproving of Henry's actions. Act III will expand these feelings even further.

ACT III

Summary

In the queen's London apartments, Katherine asks a maiden to play a song on a lute for her because she is sad and needs cheering up. But no sooner has the maiden begun to sing than a messenger interrupts and says that two cardinals—Wolsey and Campeius—await her. Wolsey and Campeius enter, claiming to bring peace and counsel to her. Katherine, however, believes they have come to betray her ("Alas, I am a woman, friendless, hopeless!"). Campeius asks her to cooperate with Henry instead of forcing the divorce case further; he says that she should think of the king's protection—that is, Henry must protect the royal lineage by having a male heir. Katherine has little choice: If she balks at this idea, she will be banished in disgrace.

But Katherine sees through their ploys. She knows that these are the wishes of the two cardinals rather than what her husband desires: "Is this your Christian counsel? Out upon ye!" She scolds them for their unchristian behavior and says that they should mend their hearts. She is determined not to be debased by these creatures. She has spent most of her adult life dedicated to Henry's needs, having compromised, slaved, and remained obedient to him all these years. Now, she refuses to give up her royal title: "I dare not make myself so guilty / To give up willingly that noble title / Your master wed me to. Nothing but death / Shall e'er divorce my dignities."

Campeius warns her to act more nobly, to forget about her tears and remember her virtues; he says that the king still loves her but that she might lose Henry's love if she carries on like a fool. This warning jars Katherine into assuming a different pose: She becomes subservient to the two cardinals and begs them to counsel her.

In an ante-chamber to the king's apartment, the Dukes of Norfolk and Suffolk assemble, along with the Earl of Surrey and the Lord Chamberlain. Norfolk wants everyone to unite in their complaints about Cardinal Wolsey so that he will no longer be a threat. The Earl of Surrey is especially anxious to avenge his father-in-law's memory (the Duke of Buckingham). But Chamberlain cautions that nothing must be attempted against Wolsey unless they can bar the cardinal totally from the king because "he hath a witchcraft / Over the king."

Norfolk then relates a story of key importance: Henry has become aware of Wolsey's treacheries and is not likely to place too much credence in him anymore. The messy divorce affair, in retrospect, is seen by Henry as being wholly the doings of Wolsey. In the cardinal's attempts to communicate *privately* with the pope (trying to discourage Henry's marriage to Anne Bullen by citing the king's divorce from Katherine), Wolsey wrote a letter destined to the pope. But the letter was accidentally delivered to Henry, who was outraged to learn of his adviser's duplicity.

Chamberlain announces furthermore that Henry has *already* married Anne Bullen. What's more, Cardinal Campeius has returned to Rome, leaving the king's divorce case unresolved and vowing to support Wolsey's plot.

Meanwhile, not only does Cranmer support the king, but all the famous colleges of Christendom support the king's decision, and Cranmer will soon be made Archbishop of Canterbury. Katherine will no longer be called queen but rather Princess Dowager.

Wolsey enters with Cromwell, demanding to know whether the packet was given to Henry and whether he has read its contents. Cromwell replies positively to both questions. Obviously Wolsey does not yet know the extent of the damage done because, in an aside, he speaks of his desire for Henry to marry the Duchess of Alençon, the French king's sister. Wolsey wants nothing to do with Anne Bullen. She is a Lutheran and would not fit in with the scheme of things.

Moreover, Wolsey defines Cranmer as yet another threat ("one / Hath crawled into the favour of the King / And is his oracle"). Clearly he is jealous about this recent development.

Henry enters, studying a document that contains information about the amounts of money accumulated by Wolsey for his own use. Henry is livid with anger toward the cardinal and cannot imagine how such vast sums of money were accumulated by him. Wolsey has become too dangerously wealthy for safety, and the king realizes that religion seems to be the *last* thing on the cardinal's mind.

Henry summons Wolsey and confronts him with the truth. He gives him a packet of papers—including the incriminating letter to Rome—and an inventory of his wealth, and then he exits, disgusted. The cardinal, confused by the king's sudden anger, examines the materials and discovers two items: an account of Wolsey's wealth and the letter that he wrote to the pope. He realizes immediately that there is no way that he can extricate himself from this entanglement; he says to himself:

> Nay then, farewell!
> I have touched the highest point of all my
>   greatness;
> And, from that full meridian of my glory,
> I haste now to my setting. I shall fall
> Like a bright exhalation in the evening,
> And no man see me more.
>
> (III. ii. 222–27)

There is no pity or sympathy for Wolsey. He has destroyed himself and others in the process, and he seems worthy of no positive human emotion.

Norfolk and the others return and demand that Wolsey surrender the great seal. He has instructions to retire promptly to Asher House until hearing further from the king. Wolsey resists, accusing them of envy. The Earl of Surrey, however, succeeds in goading Wolsey with a series of pointed criticisms. He reminds the cardinal of various crimes committed in the name of loyalty to the crown.

Suffolk terminates the session by informing Wolsey that he must surrender and forfeit all his goods, lands, tenements, and chattels to the throne and that he is no longer under the king's protection. As they prepare to leave Wolsey, Norfolk says in contempt: "So fare you well, my little good Lord Cardinal."

Alone and left to his thoughts, Wolsey finally sees himself for what he is: "I have ventured . . . far beyond my depth. My high-blown pride / At length broke under me, and now has left me" (III. ii. 358–62). When Cromwell arrives on the scene, Wolsey tells him that he has never felt better—now he knows himself fully: "I feel within me / A peace above all earthly dignities, / A still and quiet conscience." Cromwell announces that Sir Thomas More has been chosen Lord Chancellor in Wolsey's place, that Cranmer has been installed Lord Archbishop of Canterbury, and that Anne Bullen has been officially recognized as Henry's wife and queen.

In a surprising reversal of mood, Wolsey makes a moving and truthful speech to Cromwell. This, seemingly, is the first time that his words have been absolutely genuine and when he actually utters a Christian message:

Cromwell, I charge thee, fling away ambition!
By that sin fell the angels; how can man, then,
The image of his Maker, hope to win by it?
Love thyself last. Cherish those hearts that hate
    thee;
Corruption wins not more than honesty.

. . . .

    Be just, and fear not.
Let all the ends thou aim'st at be thy country's,
Thy God's, and truth's; then if thou fall'st,
    O Cromwell,
Thou fall'st a blessed martyr! Serve the king!

                  (III. ii. 440–49)

Wolsey then resigns himself to death and asks Cromwell to lead
him away.

Commentary

Scene 1 portrays Katherine in full despair. She has fallen as low
as she can and fears the worst: She is friendless and without hope.
No one dares befriend her, for to do so would mean violating the
will of the king. When the cardinals arrive, they inundate her with
more hypocrisy and propaganda about their (fraudulent) good will.
Clearly, they seek to manipulate her—absolutely. When they tempt
her with a possible reconciliation with Henry ("The King still loves
you; / Beware you lose it not"), she finally complies with their wishes. Katherine is a broken woman and anxious to find peace—the
former peace of royal dignity alongside her husband.

The tragedy of this scene is twofold: On the one hand, we see a
proud, noble woman taken advantage of by two conniving men of
the church; on the other hand, we witness her unwilling surrender
to them on *their* terms, and thus we know that she has given up her
last strength—that is, her pride.

The message of Scene 2, an extremely long scene, is quite
simple: Truth conquers all. Wolsey's hypocrisy and lies have come
to a quick halt as soon as the king discovers the evil truth about his
once-trusted cardinal. It comes as no surprise, really, to learn that
Wolsey lies almost to the end. Yet when left to himself, Wolsey
realizes that only truth will rescue him. He despises himself for

what he has done and comprehends at last that heaven is his only hope.

This, then, is the key scene of crisis in this act. Henry realizes what Wolsey has done to him, and Wolsey discovers that his villainy is no longer secret. The denouement begins as we see Wolsey learn, point by point, that Henry has made several key changes in high-level positions. Wolsey has at last learned his lesson and can now prepare to die.

ACT IV

Summary

The mood of the play has changed to gaiety as two gentlemen discuss the forthcoming coronation of Anne Bullen. Pageants, shows, and "sights of honour," it is decided, will take place everywhere.

Katherine has now been moved to Kimbolton; the divorce has been completed. She is reported to be sick, however, possibly from the discovery that a reconciliation with Henry is impossible.

Henry and Anne's coronation procession passes across the stage, with two judges, the Lord Chancellor, choristers, the Mayor of London, and an assortment of nobles. When the new queen arrives, she is a picture of beauty in her stunning robe, her hair richly adorned and entwined with pearls. All of the gentlemen admire her beauty and compare her to an angel. They understand full well why Henry has chosen her as his new wife.

A third gentleman enters to relate the events of the wedding. The crowd was so enraptured of Anne, he says, that "such joy / I never saw before." Clearly, the entire kingdom has fallen in love with her. Already, however, trouble has begun, for the two bishops on either side of Anne are Stokesly and Gardiner (the latter being the Bishop of Winchester, who is anxious to become Henry's new secretary). Already the rumor is that Gardiner despises Cranmer, the newly appointed Archbishop of Canterbury. Plainly, trouble looms between these two.

An ailing Katherine asks her servant to relate the details of Wolsey's death. He was arrested by the Earl of Northumberland in York and was being transferred to London when he became too sick to travel. There, they arranged for a room in the abbey in Leicester, where Wolsey told the abbot, "An old man, broken with the storms of state, / Is come to lay his weary bones among ye; / Give him a little earth for charity!" (IV. ii. 21–23). Three nights later, about eight o'clock, he died "in peace." Katherine assesses his character, and her gentleman attendant, Griffith, speaks about Wolsey's virtues, particularly about his expertise in the area of education. Griffith's speech causes Katherine to readjust her opinion of Wolsey: Ironically, she now honors in death the man she hated when he was still alive. She sees the truth of Griffith's words: "Men's evil manners live in brass; their virtues / We write in water."

Sad music lulls Katherine to sleep, and she witnesses a vision wherein six personages clad in white robes exchange curtsies to one another and hold garlands above her head. Katherine awakens and cries out for "these spirits of peace," but no one else in the room has seen them. Griffith and the servant Patience suddenly notice that Katherine's face has grown pale and drawn. She appears to be near death.

Capucius, an ambassador from Katherine's nephew Charles V (Emperor of the Holy Roman Empire), arrives with the message that Charles sends his condolences. Katherine says that the emperor's condolences are "like a pardon after execution" and gives the messenger a letter for King Henry. In it, she requests that her servants be well looked after; she also tells Capucius to give Henry her best wishes and to tell him that she is about to die and that he will no longer have the burden of her presence to tolerate: "Tell him, in death I blessed him, / For so I will."

Katherine then outlines details of her funeral that she wishes done for her: the flowers, the embalming, and an honorable, queenly treatment.

Commentary

The purpose of Scene 1 is to emphasize the affection felt by the English people toward Queen Anne and also to set the stage for conflict between Cranmer and Gardiner. Political intrigue is omnipresent in every monarchy, and Henry's court is no exception, but curiously enough, Henry is the first monarch in more than a century whose claim to the throne is undisputed. Yet there is seemingly no peace in the orbit surrounding him. It is as if the tensions formerly associated with selecting the "correct" (legal, blood-line) monarch have now been shifted to the circle of the king's advisers. It would seem, however, that Henry pays little attention to detail—though indeed he should, especially after the Wolsey scandal. Wolsey's treachery should alert him to the possibility for more grappling for power in the ranks beneath him.

While it is not absolutely clear in Scene 2 whether Katherine is actually close to death or only imagining herself to be, we can nonetheless see her total despair about life. She is no longer a queen, though royalty is in her genes, and now she has shifted the focus of her thoughts from life to death. She amends her opinion of Wolsey and sees him as a man of honor.

She realizes that, on a symbolic level, Wolsey and she have led similar existences. They have both reached extraordinary heights of power, and each has been humiliated in a rapid procession of changes. The difference is that Wolsey's downfall was due entirely to his own actions; Katherine was wholly victimized by Henry's decisions.

Act IV functions primarily as a denouement: It provides two quite separate emotions as part of the unraveling of the drama. There is joy and ecstasy in Scene 1 when Anne becomes the new queen, yet there is also sadness and pity in Scene 2 for the dethroned Katherine. Since Shakespeare has structured the act so that sadness and pity follow the joy, it is possible that he meant to stress the tragedy of Katherine's debasement. Royalty, though exalted, is nonetheless human and subject to the same range of emotions as everyone else is. The psyche of a king or queen is no less fragile or vulnerable than that of a commoner. Love, self-esteem, and respect from others are important factors in monarchs' lives. Katherine is a tragic figure about whom one can only say: She did her best but was destroyed in the process.

ACT V

Summary

In one of the palace galleries, Gardiner meets with Sir Thomas Lovell, who is on his way to see the king before the latter goes to bed. Gardiner wonders why Lovell must see the king at such a late hour, and Lovell reveals his errand: Queen Anne is in labor and is likely to die before her baby is born. Gardiner cares nothing for Anne but hopes the baby will survive.

Lovell indicates a fondness for Anne, but Gardiner insists that all will not be well until Anne, Cranmer, and Cromwell are all dead. Gardiner continues by saying that he has incensed the lords of the council against Cranmer, claiming that the latter is "a most arch heretic." In fact, he is to appear before the council-board in the morning to answer for alleged "mischiefs."

The king discusses Anne's critical labor pains with Suffolk and Lovell, who then leave. Cranmer arrives, and Lovell lingers to listen to Cranmer and the king, but Henry notices Lovell and orders him away.

Henry tells Cranmer that he has heard many grievous things about him lately. He has arranged with the council to meet Cranmer in the morning. But Henry has no fears; he knows that Cranmer has integrity and will stand up well to the council. Henry also knows that Cranmer has many enemies who have a way of distorting truth: "You are potently opposed, and with a malice / Of as great size." Henry then gives Cranmer a signet ring which he must produce during the council if the members vote to condemn him. By this ring, he will demonstrate to them that the king is on his side.

In a lobby before the council chamber, Cranmer is abandoned to wait until the council has called for him. They had rushed him there, and now he worries about the reason for such haste. He confesses to himself that he never sought the council's malice, especially not in activities that were self-serving or ambitious.

Henry enters near a window above and sees Cranmer down below. He is appalled at the way in which the council members are treating the Archbishop of Canterbury, and he is glad "there's one above 'em yet. . . . By holy Mary, there's knavery."

Scene 3 takes place in the council chamber. The Lord Chancellor tells Cranmer that his teachings and opinions reflect heresy that, if uncorrected, may prove to be dangerously pernicious. At this point, Gardiner suddenly bursts forth in open protest about Cranmer and insists that he be ousted immediately from his position. Cranmer, however, defends himself well, claiming that *he* too despises those who agitate public peace. Not knowing that the king is listening above, Gardiner announces that it is Henry's will that Cranmer be sent to the Tower of London. Cranmer realizes that Gardiner is the real "voice" behind this nonsense, and so he thanks him for being "so merciful" and for being both judge and juror. He clearly sees that Gardiner wishes to ruin him, but as a man of the church, he is more interested in love and meekness than ambition.

Cromwell interrupts Gardiner and defends Cranmer by suggesting that the prosecutorial arguments are a bit too sharp. Despite an exchange of criticism between Cromwell and Gardiner, the members agree to send Cranmer to the Tower. In exasperation, Cranmer produces the king's ring and removes the discussion from merely the council level to that of the monarch.

Henry enters then, frowning on the members, and Gardiner realizes that he must do something quickly in order to save himself, so he lapses into a maudlin show of praise for the king: "Dread sovereign, how much are we bound to Heaven / In daily thanks, that gave us such a prince; / Not only good and wise but most religious" (V. iii. 114–16). His speech continues in this gushing vein, but Henry calls his bluff: "You were ever good at sudden commendations, / Bishop of Winchester. But know, I come not / To hear such flattery now." He declares that Gardiner has a cruel, bloody nature and that he is not interested in conversing with him. To Cranmer, Henry offers comfort and praise, daring the council members to object openly to the archbishop. His fury with the council mounts as he scolds them harshly for being incompetents.

Henry orders them to accept Cranmer as a worthy, respectable man, then he softens his tone somewhat and asks them to embrace Cranmer: "Be friends, for shame, my lords!" He then announces that his infant daughter requires a baptism and that he has chosen Cranmer as her godfather.

Scene 4 is a humorous scene of noise and tumult and includes a porter who orders his man to keep the merrymakers quiet. The christening is an important event, and the porter is not going to permit a bunch of lusty beer-drinking rascals to ruin things. People push from every direction to attend the event, and the porter finally shouts in despair, "This one christening will beget a thousand."

Cranmer blesses the newborn child and announces her name to Henry: She is to be called Elizabeth. Cranmer makes a very touching speech in which he expresses a premonition of Elizabeth's future talents: She will bring a thousand blessings to the kingdom; she will be a model to royalty everywhere and to future monarchs; and she will have wisdom and virtue, truth and respect from others: "She shall be loved and feared: her own shall bless her; / Her foes shake like a field of beaten corn / And hang their heads with sorrow"

(V. v. 31–33). Cranmer's speech moves Henry to great emotion. He has had no luck with siring children to this point, and now he has a strong heir: "This oracle of comfort has so pleased me / That when I am in heaven I shall desire / To see what this child does, and praise my Maker" (V. v. 67–69). He then thanks the mayor and everyone else for being present, and they leave to see Queen Anne.

Commentary

Henry has been wrong before about his advisers, but in Scene 1, he is convinced that Cranmer is a decent man. There is no evidence that Cranmer has done evil or that he has violated his duty to the crown, so Henry decides to give his full support to the man. The fact that Gardiner seeks to get rid of Cranmer is but one more incident of jealousy among the ranks. With Wolsey gone, Gardiner takes the fore and assumes this pretense to try and gain power. But Cranmer's ultimate victory will underscore Wolsey's warning to Cromwell: give up ambition and serve the king. Service to one's self amounts to nothing.

In Scene 2, it annoys and angers Henry that the council members have such little regard for his choice of archbishop and that their manners are so lacking. Justice will be done, however, since Henry holds the final trump.

Scene 3 is pleasant because justice comes to pass. We see the uselessness of flattery and dishonesty when truth prevails, and we witness the workings of a strong, just king whose love of equity for all is a major priority. He does not hold a grudge against the council members for being nasty with Cranmer. But there is no question that he understands their true motives and that he will monitor them closely in the future. Cranmer surfaces as a man of integrity and as an archbishop in whom everyone will place their trust.

Scene 4 is a robust scene, typical of many Shakespearean comedies. The beer-guzzling men are down-to-earth, bawdy, and unsophisticated, and they have no pretenses; very simply, they are what they are. And because of this, they offer a sharp contrast with the phony nobles who assume airs of importance well beyond their birth or position. Shakespeare was used to this kind of boisterous crowd at the Globe Theatre. Thus, he portrays them as ecstatic human beings, anxious to see an important event in the royal family. As always, the populace is exceedingly interested in their royal leaders.

The play ends on a positive, promising note: The newly christened baby, the future Queen Elizabeth, will be an heir of whom
Henry can be proud. Henry has now come full circle from the days
in Act I when he was anxious about his divorce, dependent on
Wolsey for advice, and uncertain of his country's future. Gardiner,
who is a vengeful, petty man, is of no importance now that Henry
has openly favored Cranmer, and it is Cranmer's final speeches
about Elizabeth that confirm in our mind the correctness of Henry's
thinking. As a king, Henry seems to hold true promise and can teach
his daughter many fine lessons about the monarchy that will be
hers one day.

EPILOGUE

At the play's end, there is a brief epilogue whose purpose is to tie
up loose ends, speak directly to the audience, and to offer Shakespeare's opinion of what spectators are likely to say about this
drama.

a chronology of
english monarchs

THE NORMAN CONQUEST

1066–87	William the Conqueror
1087–1100	William II
1100–35	Henry I
1135–54	Stephen

 **PLANTAGENETS**

1154–89	Henry II
1189–99	Richard I
1199–1216	John
1216–72	Henry III
1272–1307	Edward I
1307–27	Edward II
1327–77	Edward III
1377–99	Richard II (mother a Plantagenet; father a Lancastrian)

 **HOUSES OF LANCASTER AND YORK**

1399–1413	Henry IV (Lancaster)
1413–22	Henry V (Lancaster)
1422–61*	Henry VI (Lancaster) (1455–87 Wars of the Roses)
1461–70	Edward IV (York)
1470–71*	Henry VI (Lancaster)
1471–83	Edward IV (York)
1483–85	Richard III (York)

Henry VI had a split reign

THE TUDORS

1485–1509	Henry VII
1509–47	Henry VIII
1547–53	Edward VI (father Henry VIII; mother Jane Seymour)
1553–58	Mary I (father Henry VIII; mother Catherine of Aragon)
1558–1603	Elizabeth I (father Henry VIII; mother Anne Boleyn)

THE EARLY STUARTS

1603–25	James I
1625–49	Charles I
1649–60	The Civil Wars and Interregnum

 THE LATER STUARTS

1660–85	Charles II
1685–88	James II

 THE REVOLUTIONARY SETTLEMENT

1689–1702	William III
1689–94	Mary II
1702–14	Anne

 THE HANOVERIAN KINGS

1714–27	George I
1727–60	George II
1760–1820	George III
1820–30	George IV
1830–37	William IV
1837–1901	Victoria
1901–10	Edward VII

 THE HOUSE OF WINDSOR

1910–36	George V
1936	Edward VIII (abdicated)
1936–52	George VI
1952–	Elizabeth II

Think Quick

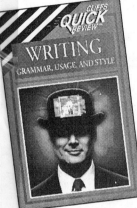

Now there are more Cliffs Quick Review® titles, providing help with more introductory level courses. Use Quick Reviews to increase your understanding of fundamental principles in a given subject, as well as to prepare for quizzes, midterms and finals.

Do better in the classroom, and on papers and tests with Cliffs Quick Reviews.

Legends In Their Own Time

Ancient civilization is rich with the acts of legendary figures and events. Here are three classic reference books that will help you understand the legends, myths and facts surrounding the dawn of civilization.

Cliffs Notes on Greek Classics and *Cliffs Notes on Roman Classics*— Guides to the idealogy, philosophy and literary influence of ancient civilization.

Cliffs Notes on Mythology—An introduction to the study of various civilizations as they are revealed in myths and legends.

Find these legendary books at your bookstore or order them using the form below.